BIG
ROAD
BLUES

BIG ROAD BLUES

TRADITION AND CREATIVITY IN THE FOLK BLUES

DAVID EVANS

UNIVERSITY OF CALIFORNIA PRESS · BERKELEY · LOS ANGELES · LONDON

University of California Press
Berkeley and Los Angeles, California
University of California Press, Ltd.
London, England
Copyright © 1982 by The Regents of the University of California
Printed in the United States of America
1 2 3 4 5 6 7 8 9

Evans, David, fl. 1971–
    Big road blues.

    Bibliography: p. 350
    Includes index.
    1. Blues (Songs, etc.)—United States—History and
criticism.   I. Title.
ML3521.E9   784.5′3   77-76177
ISBN 0–520–03484–8

To the memory of
my father

CONTENTS

ILLUSTRATIVE EXAMPLES

ACKNOWLEDGMENTS

It would be difficult to recall the names of all the people who have helped me with this project since 1964, so that I hope I shall be forgiven by anyone whose name I omit. Most important are those musicians and other informants whose names will be found scattered throughout this study. Others who helped in important ways, all of which are deeply appreciated, were my wife Cheryl Thurber Evans, my parents, Mr. and Mrs. David H. Evans, Marina Bokelman, Mr. and Mrs. Marinus Bokelman, George and Cathy Mitchell, Peter Welding, William and Josette Ferris, Barry Hansen, Bob Hite, Henry Vestine, Simon Napier, Bob Groom, Frank Scott, Laurie Forti, Steve LaVere, Richard Noblett, Don Kent, Paul Oliver, Tony Russell, Jeff Tarrer, Karl Gert zur Heide, Pete Whelan, Mike Rowe, Chris Strachwitz, Bill Givens, Nick Perls, Mike Stewart, Gayle Wardlow, Jeff Titon, Michael Taft, John Fahey, John H. Cowley, Dick Waterman, Marc Ryan, the late Alan Wilson, Rae Korson, Alan Jabbour, Joseph Hickerson, J. S. Hartin, Jimmie Smith, Joyce Oesterreich, Sandra Trego, D. K. Wilgus, Robert Georges, David Morton, Albert Lord, Wayland D. Hand, Donald J. Ward, Joesph Riddel, James Hill, Jaan Puhvel, Udo Strutynski, Alain Hénon, Richard Keeling, the Mississippi State Department of Archives and History, the John Edwards Memorial Foundation, the Archive of Folk Song at the Library of Congress, the Center for the Study of Comparative Folklore and Mythology at the University of California, Los Angeles, and the Department of Anthropology at California State University, Fullerton.

INTRODUCTION

THIS book is a study of the processes of folk blues tradition and composition, subjects which folklorists and blues researchers have largely neglected in favor of other aspects of blues research. In fact, these are subjects for which adequate data have not in the past been available, despite extensive documentation of folk blues throughout this century. Only through folkloristic fieldwork directed specifically at understanding these processes could the necessary data be obtained, data which could then be correlated with the documentary material already existing. It is through such fieldwork and correlation that the findings in this book have been reached.

It is not my purpose to discuss here the extensive literature which attempts to define terms such as *folklore, folksong,* and *folk music,* or to offer new definitions of them.[1] Suffice it to say that, as is the case with key concepts in many fields, there is no general agreement among folklorists as to their exact meaning. Nevertheless, most folklorists would agree that oral tradition is a central characteristic of folklore. The concern of most folklorists has been to describe and account for the products and processes of oral tradition. In almost all cases these processes produce change and variation in the items of folklore (songs, tales, proverbs, riddles, etc.), so that, in effect, folklorists must spend much of their effort in comparing and establishing the relationships between different versions of items. They also attempt to relate the items of folklore and their variations to historical, psychological, social, and cultural factors.

The term *folklore* carries the implication that it is concerned with a group of people, who are represented by the *folk-* half of this compound word. During the nineteenth century and well into the twentieth century folklorists spoke of "the folk" and generally equated them with the isolated and conservative rural peasantry. Their oral traditions were considered analogous to those of the primitive societies studied by anthropologists. In more recent years this concept of "the folk" has proven to be inadequate for the purposes of many folklorists, as has the concept of "primitive" for many modern anthropologists. Folklorists came to realize that many other groups besides the peasants had oral traditions. Now they use the term *folk group* to describe any group of people that shares oral traditions. The basis of a folk group can be a factor such as ethnic, cultural, national, regional, social, religious, occupational, or age-based identity, or some combination of these and other factors. Thus some folk groups can be comprised of millions of people. Yet the entire folk group seldom acts as one, and especially in cases of transmission of folklore we must deal with smaller segments of folk groups, such as single communities, groups of neighbors, families, and even individuals. Items of folklore are not normally transmitted to thousands of people at a single time or shared by all members of a folk group except when they are taken up by the mass media of popular culture. Yet the folklorist cannot afford to ignore these mass media, since they often serve as an extension of the oral tradition and have a powerful effect in spreading items of folklore and standardizing them so as to eliminate some of the variation that is normal in a purely oral tradition. The importance of mass media, particularly the phonograph record, should become abundantly clear in the present study.

The folk group that we are dealing with here consists of black Americans, yet for the purposes of this kind of study such a group is really much too large. Certainly not all black Americans perform folk blues, and many have little real knowledge of them. Many middle and upper class blacks are only vaguely aware of the existence of folk blues and might not enjoy them if they heard them. Many religious blacks attempt to shield themselves and their families from this kind of music, which they consider to be sinful. Others, who are neither religious nor middle or upper class, simply do not like the blues for one reason or another. Thus folk blues have achieved acceptance within and have been transmitted by only a segment of black Americans. This segment consists primarily of blacks who are southern or of southern origin, rural, lower class, and not devoutly religious. To a great extent this group also consists of people who are now middle-aged and older. Folk blues today are not performed or transmitted much among young blacks, who generally find various forms of popular music more appealing. Most of the performers mentioned in this study were born in the nineteenth century or the early years of the twentieth century. Even though many of the blues discussed here were recorded in the field in recent years, they represent a type of music that flourished in the 1920s and 1930s and has been gradually declining ever since. The original public functions of this folk music have largely been taken over by various forms of popular music, while folk blues have retreated to the level of home entertainment for small groups of friends and the personal gratification of the performers. Nevertheless, they are still an important and widespread form of folklore, worthy of study in their own right. Furthermore, a study of them as they are found today can reveal much about their more important status in earlier years.

Folk blues have existed also in southern white tradition, but they originated and have always been most prominent among blacks. Yet even the restricted group of blacks who have enjoyed and transmitted folk blues is too large a group for proper study of a subject so complex as the one treated here. Therefore, I have tended to concentrate on a single local manifestation of the overall folk blues tradition and on a relatively small group of performers, many of whom have long known and made music with each other. From the study of other such groups, I believe that this group is fairly typical of the overall tradition, but only further field research and analysis could confirm this conjecture.

There is also a -lore component to the compound word *folklore*. For this study the lore is the blues, though up to this point I have generally qualified blues with the word *folk*. A description of the blues will be given in the first chapter, but it is important to realize here that not all blues are purely folk blues, by which we mean traditional blues. Or rather, we should say that the "folk" element is stronger in some blues than in others. Perhaps all blues contain some traditional elements, such as "blue notes." Not all, however, are products of the folk groups mentioned above. Furthermore, many of the blues that are produced by members of a folk group draw little from the materials of oral tradition and, in turn, contribute little back to oral tradition. The main reasons for this are the mass media and commercialism. These factors have affected the blues almost since their beginning, so that now we must speak of both *folk* blues and *popular* blues. I do not mean to suggest that these are two opposite forms of blues or that all blues are of either one type or the other. The situation is much more complex than that. Instead, folk and popular blues should be viewed as two ends of the blues spectrum. The blues at one end are related to and affect those at the other end, and many blues would fall somewhere in between. This complex picture will be explained in greater detail in chapters 1 and 2, where it should become clear that it is possible to distinguish folk and popular aspects of the blues. Here we shall simply state that the folk blues are generally found in the southern countryside and small towns and that their music and lyrics tend to be traditional. Most of the blues studied here are folk blues or are close to the "folk" end of the blues spectrum. The popular blues, on the other hand, are generally found in cities and larger towns. They tend to be less traditional, more original, and more self-conscious, factors that make them better suited to mass media or stage presentation. Yet there are exceptions to these generalizations. Folk blues have often been composed and performed in cities and have been presented to a large popular audience through the mass media, while popular blues have frequently been composed and performed in the rural South and have entered oral tradition. In this process of transmission the popular blues have thus become folk blues. Popular blues, therefore, should not be viewed as lacking the characteristics of folk blues but simply as having them to a lesser degree in the sense that they are usually less traditional than folk blues.[2]

I want to make it clear that, unlike some writers, I am applying no value judgment to either folk or popular music.[3] There have been many good and many bad performances of each, and both forms must be judged by their own standards and on their own merits. From a sociological point of view both are important, popular music because it reaches many people in a short time and folk music because it lasts for a long time. Students of folk music must study popular music also because it draws material from folk music, transmits it back to folk groups, and contributes material to the oral tradition. It is for these same reasons that students of popular music should pay attention to folk music. The attitudes of blues writers on this point will be surveyed in chapter 1.

Another reason why folk and popular music should be considered together is that folk music in its original creation and often in its recreation by various performers displays some of the self-conscious originality so characteristic of popular music. I shall have more to say on this point in chapter 2, but here one might do well to follow the observation of Robert W. Gordon that "both the author element and the folk element are to be found in all folk-songs of civilized peoples today."[4] Gordon believed that these elements existed in different ratios in the various types of American folksong, a view that is somewhat similar to our view of the blues as constituting a spectrum from "folk" to "popular." I would not, however, share in Gordon's ultimate aim of separating the two elements or in his bias against the "author element." I believe that the two elements can be distinguished for purposes of analysis, but otherwise they exist together in songs and both are utilized by individual performers in varying degrees.

Earlier generations of American folksong scholars paid little attention to the role of the author in their material, preferring to concentrate on what was known to be traditional.[5] In recent years this state of affairs has experienced a dramatic reversal, and there are now a number of studies by American folksong scholars of "folk composers."[6] Richard Reuss has noted the importance to the folklorist of folk composer Woody Guthrie, who drew upon the traditions of his folk group but performed and composed largely for people in northern cities who were far removed from the traditions of his native Oklahoma.[7] Perhaps even more important was Andrew Jenkins, whom D. K. Wilgus has shown to be the composer of a large number of songs that entered the Anglo-American folksong tradition.[8] Jenkins composed over eight hundred songs, a good number of which were recorded by himself and others on phonograph records designed primarily for a southern white audience. He came from a folk group, knew and performed traditional folksongs, composed songs that utilized traditional elements and styles, and had some of his compositions pass into oral tradition in his own folk group. On these grounds he has every right to be called a "folk composer." But it must always be kept in mind that Jenkins's compositions entered the folk tradition almost exclusively through the mass media. They were popular songs just as much as they were folksongs, although they were aimed at members of his folk group. Many of his songs might never have entered the folk tradition if it had not been for the radio and phonograph record industry, and, of course, many of them never did enter the tradition despite their issuance on records. There are hundreds of blues singers, who, like Jenkins, have come from a folk background and have composed blues that were transmitted back to their folk group through phonograph records. Many folk composers of blues have also been studied, mostly by nonfolklorists, and the literature on a number of them will be discussed and utilized in this study. Any extensive folkloristic discussion of such persons must take into account the influence of the popular music industry and the mass media in shaping their performances and compositions. This influence will be discussed in chapter 1.

Let us, then, summarize the differences between folk and popular music, keeping in mind the important relationships between the two. As noted earlier, folk music is the product of a folk group within a larger society, though in some cases it can be shared by members of more than one such group. It is transmitted orally within that group or between folk groups. Yet at any one time folk music is usually shared by only a small segment of the folk group. By this I mean that a piece of folk music is performed for a community or other fairly small gathering of members of the folk group rather than for the entire folk group at large. Different versions of an item of folk music may exist in the same community or other communities, some versions may be performed more often than others, and different versions may be received with different degrees of appreciation by their audiences, but all of these versions coexist on approximately the same level.

In a large folk group a single version of an item of folk music does not reach the entire folk group or all communities within it unless it is transmitted through some form of the mass media. When such transmission does occur, then the item of folk music can also be considered popular music. The very nature of popular music is that it is designed to reach many communities, in fact, as large a segment of the society as possible. Popular music can occur within a folk group, as in the case of black American popular music or the "country and western" music of southern whites, but in such cases the popular music is aimed at the entire folk group or a large portion of it. The media of print, phonograph records, radio, television, and publicly promoted and advertised concerts by professional entertainers are the main means by which items of popular music are spread. When a person hears or reads in print an item of popular music, he is aware that thousands of other people from other communities have access to exactly the same item of music. Those who control the mass media consequently have a great deal of power to shape and control taste and opinion in music, though for monetary reasons they must also be responsive to taste and opinion. For reasons such as these, only certain items of popular music gain access to the mass media, not necessarily the items that would normally be most appreciated by the audience if given a choice between all those available. There is often competition for access to the media, and an ideology of survival of the fittest may set in among performers, composers, and those who control popular taste through the media. The spirit that lies behind popular music, then, is part of a larger democratic and competitive spirit prevalent in mass society, whereas the spirit that underlies folk music is of a more plebeian sort characteristic of smaller communities. It should be emphasized, however, that these are merely generalizations and that there can be gradations between the two.

As we have just noted, folk music tends to be traditional and to present to its folk audience what is already familiar. Yet I say "tends to," because no folk music is unchanging. In fact, the very nature of oral tradition is such as to produce variation. Although some of this variation may be the result of forgetfulness and other unconscious factors, much of it is due to deliberate recreative acts by folksingers and musicians designed to improve the folk music. These altered versions continue in oral tradition and undergo further alteration and recreation by others. In addition, folksingers and musicians can create wholly or largely new pieces. Some traditions, for example, the blues, encourage this tendency more than others, but the penchant to vary existing forms is found to some extent in all traditions. Without it these traditions would lose their vitality and eventually become moribund. Creation and recreation, then, are essential to some degree in folk music, yet they serve in part to produce material that will go on to become traditional. Many new creations and revisions, of course, never become traditional. Still, these items are important for the folklorist, for they come from people who participate in a folk music tradition, and they may help in an understanding of why other material does become traditional.

Composers of popular music tend to be creative and innovative to a much greater extent, though they can and sometimes do draw material from folk music. But when they do so, they present this material to their audience as a novelty or else recreate it in order to suit it for mass appeal. Popular music thrives basically on its novelty and on its capacity to provide people with something that they do not have and to convince them that they want it. When a folk musician performs traditional material via the mass media, he may perform it the same way as he does in his own community, yet many in his new audience will perceive his music as novel. The mass media, then, can document and present folk music, but at the same time they may greatly affect and alter the oral tradition.

Composers of popular music attempt to be up-to-date and pro- gressive and to improve upon previous offerings. In fact, there is an assumption on the part of its purveyors and audience that popular mu- sic is generally succeeding in these attempts. Popular music does have its "standards" or "oldies," which function somewhat as do the "clas- sics" in classical music in the sense that they are thought to have achieved a certain level of excellence, but in popular music these pieces are not invariably used as standards for judging new productions. Fur- thermore, they are at any time subject to rearrangement and revision so that their novelty value may again be exploited and appreciated. There is even some evidence that pieces of folk music can achieve a certain level of excellence and assume the role of classics for members of folk groups. One Anglo-American folksinger from Arkansas, Almeda Rid- dle, uses this very term for some of the pieces in her repertoire.[9]

The preceding distinctions between folk and popular music may seem overly simple, but they are made in order to give some structure to much of the material discussed later in this study. It will become quite clear shortly that the folk blues have been extensively utilized as popular music and that popular music in turn has had an effect on the folk tradition. It will also become clear that blues is a form of folk mu- sic that especially encourages creativity and that many blues singers strive for individuality of expression and try to be up-to-date in their music and tastes. These characteristics are similar to those of popular music. But it will also be shown that there is much that is the product of oral tradition in the folk blues.

This study will concentrate for the most part on the traditional side of blues. Much of the creativity to be discussed will actually be the recreation and reworking of traditional material in new ways or the combining of some traditional with some original material to make a product that is only partly traditional. I am concentrating on the tradi- tional component in the blues because so little work has been done in this area in the past, whereas the more innovative and original blues have been more fully discussed elsewhere. Yet I believe that, in the end, the entire blues tradition will be found to be exceptionally creative.

The folk processes that I shall discuss in this study are mainly those of transmission, learning, composition, recomposition, and han- dling of repertoire by blues singers. I shall examine in detail the blues repertoires of two folksingers. I shall also study one particular com- bination of traditional blues elements called "Big Road Blues" in order to see how different singers have treated it in their performances. In the final chapter I shall compare and contrast the folk blues tradition with the Anglo-American folksong tradition and discuss the place of the blues tradition with respect to the study of oral traditions in general.[10]

Essential to an understanding of the processes of folk blues com- position and tradition is the concept of the *local tradition*. The local tra- dition is the repertoire of song lyrics, melodies, and instrumental figures that a group of blues singers in a community synthesizes, shares, and draws from in composing songs. Each local tradition has its own peculiarities and idiosyncrasies developed by its participating musicians as well as many features in common with the traditions of neighboring communities and ones more remote. Taken as a whole, these traditions create the panorama of folk blues. The novice folk blues singer generally learns within a local tradition, and it is this local element and this local flavor that must be examined by the researcher of folk blues. In chapter 3 I shall examine the local tradition of Drew, Mississippi, and its extensions into other areas.

Naturally, a tradition cannot be studied apart from the people who participate in it, because it simply does not exist without these people and the recordings they have left to posterity. Therefore, part of this study details the life histories and complex network of relationships that prevailed among the musicians who participated in the blues tradition that was first synthesized around Drew near the beginning of this century, insofar as these facts are known. Much of the rest of the study is devoted to a discussion of their songs and how they were and still are composed.

If anyone should wonder why, in my attempt to explain the concept of local tradition, I chose the Drew tradition, which is hardly the most flourishing one in present-day blues, I can only answer that the concept was evolving in my mind while I was conducting research into the life and music of Tommy Johnson, who proved to be a participant in this particular local tradition. But the choice was a fortunate one, for the Drew tradition is very well documented. Tommy Johnson, Charley Patton, Willie Brown, and Kid Bailey had all made commercial recordings representative of this local tradition by 1930, and other representative artists, including Howlin' Wolf, have recorded commercially since then. There are also quite a few recordings by representatives of neighboring local traditions. Furthermore, almost all of the musicians discussed in connection with the Drew tradition played guitar, thus stabilizing the important variable factor of accompaniment. Through fieldwork I have been able to document many further aspects of this tradition and determine the relationships between its many songs and their singers. There is probably no other local blues tradition anywhere in the United States that has received such a thorough documentation on phonograph records and tape recordings over such a long period of time. In addition, many of the representatives of the Drew tradition, or other singers whom they have influenced, have won critical acclaim as some of the greatest folk blues singers of all time. It is only fitting, then, that this tradition should be the first to be studied in depth.

I hope that this study may provide a model for the investigation of other local blues traditions. The directions taken here may offer a new approach to the study of the blues by folklorists, who have thus far tended to avoid investigation of the traditional aspects of these lyric songs, beyond some collection and documentation and some comments about the blues tradition *as a whole*. This study may also make contributions to folklore and folksong theory in general. These contributions could be in such increasingly important areas of research as the investigation of the performers and creators of folk songs[11] and the investigation of the processes of creation within traditional genres.[12] This study of the folk blues may also prove to be of interest to record collectors and others, who have been trying in recent years to gather information about the blues artists who made records. Few of the researchers with this orientation have examined the totality of the blues tradition that consists largely of artists who never recorded commercially. Most recent writing on the blues has concentrated instead on the content of the song lyrics and their relationship to black American society, on the life histories and life-styles of blues singers, and on the history of the blues genre, with particular emphasis on the commercially issued blues designed for the black record buying public. This study will not attempt to duplicate these other valuable studies, but it will utilize some of them and will attempt to complement them. I hope that it will help to show how folkloristic methods and insights can best enhance blues scholarship.

My interest in blues began in the early 1960s through listening to LP records containing reissues of early commercially recorded folk blues, field recordings made for the Archive of Folk Song at the Library of Congress, and recently recorded blues performances.[13] After listening to a number of these records, it occurred to me that a system of traditional formulas existed that accounted for the texts, melodies, and instrumental accompaniments of many blues songs. This formulaic system reminded me of the formulaic manner of composition utilized by oral epic singers in Yugoslavia and elsewhere,[14] though it was equally obvious that there were major differences between blues and epics in respect to form and content. At this same time a number of folk blues singers who had made commercial recordings in the 1920s and 1930s were being "rediscovered" by blues enthusiasts and brought before predominantly white northern and urban audiences.[15] In November 1964 I was able to begin testing my hypothesis about the formulaic manner of blues composition by interviewing with Alan Wilson the newly rediscovered Son House. House had made commercial recordings in 1930 and had been recorded in 1941 and 1942 in Mississippi by Alan Lomax for the Archive of Folk Song.[16] Wilson and I questioned House intensively about the sources of his much admired early recordings. He stated that some of his textual and musical ideas came from an obscure blues singer from Lyon, Mississippi, named James McCoy, who never recorded. Other ideas, however, came from Willie Brown and Charley Patton, two deceased blues singers who had recorded with House in 1930. House's blues, then, were revealed to be links in a tradition and not simply products of his creative genius. In the spring of 1965 Marc Ryan introduced me to Babe Stovall, a blues singer from

Tylertown, Mississippi, who had recently moved to New Orleans and was currently on a tour of northern coffeehouses. Stovall seemed to compose several of his blues in a "formulaic" manner, and some of them displayed great variation from one performance to another. Stovall told me the sources of many of his pieces. One of them, "Big Road Blues," appeared to be derived from the late Tommy Johnson's 1928 recording of that title (Victor 21279), yet many of the verses in Stovall's performance of the song were not in Johnson's original recording, while many of Johnson's verses were not sung by Stovall. Stovall claimed that he had learned the song from Johnson in person in the 1930s and had not been influenced by the recording. This fact excited my curiosity. It seemed to indicate that Johnson might have performed the song differently from his recording on different occasions. It prompted me to wonder whether "Big Road Blues" could indeed be thought of as a "song" in the sense that I was familiar with.

It was apparent to me at this point that two major problems, both interrelated, needed to be solved. One was the relationship of a singer's blues to those of his sources—the other singers that he had learned from. The other was the problem of variation or stability from one performance of a blues to another by the same performer. It was clear to me that fieldwork was necessary in any attempt to solve these problems. They were the same two problems that Albert Lord and his colleagues faced in their work with the oral epic. They solved them by recording and interviewing epic singers in a number of Yugoslavian local traditions and then rerecording the same singers on different occasions.[17] It was obvious that I would have to do the same in order to understand the folk blues tradition.

My interview with Babe Stovall aroused an interest in Tommy Johnson and prompted me to make a series of field trips on which I was to record many blues singers who had known Johnson in Tylertown, Jackson, and Crystal Springs, Mississippi, three places where he had spent much of his life. Two short trips were made with Marc Ryan in August-September 1965 and in January-February 1966. During these we recorded mainly Stovall and his friends from Tylertown and laid the groundwork for more intensive field research later. One of the best and most important blues singers, whom I first recorded in 1965, was Stovall's friend Roosevelt Holts. Holts had also known Johnson, in Tylertown and in Jackson and Crystal Springs, and had learned a number of songs from him. During the 1966 trip we interviewed the Reverend Ishmon Bracey, a former blues singer and friend of Tommy Johnson in Jackson, Mississippi. Bracey stated that he and Johnson had played several times with Charlie Patton in the state's Delta region. This fact seemed to confirm a relationship between Patton and Johnson that was apparent in some of their early recordings as well as in the recordings of Patton's partner Willie Brown, though the precise nature of this relationship still remained unclear.

In August 1966 I returned to the South with Marina Bokelman

with the intention of investigating the life of Tommy Johnson and recording musicians who had been influenced by him, but also with the hope of establishing links between Johnson, Patton, and Brown, whose relationship the existing literature left unclear. This hope was realized when I found the Reverend LeDell Johnson, Tommy's older brother and a former blues singer himself, in Jackson. He told me that Tommy had learned to play blues from Patton, Brown, and others long before any of these men ever made records. Reverend Johnson's wife Maybelle was able to add some information on Brown and Patton. They traced the origin of the blues tradition in which these men participated to the Mississippi Delta town of Drew. They also mentioned other musicians there who participated in the local tradition. Unfortunately, I did not then have time to pursue the trail in Drew. I was, however, able to collect a great deal of information on Tommy Johnson on this trip and record many singers who had learned from him at various stages in his career. We interviewed Reverend Ishmon Bracey at greater length and rerecorded Babe Stovall and Roosevelt Holts. Other important singers recorded on this trip were Isaac Youngblood, Arzo Youngblood, and Boogie Bill Webb, all of whom learned much from Tommy Johnson. Most important of all was Tommy's younger brother Mager (pronounced "Major"), who had learned the blues in his hometown of Crystal Springs, Mississippi, from Tommy and LeDell not many years after they themselves had learned from Patton, Brown, and the others at Drew. Mager Johnson was a true representative of the Drew blues tradition transplanted by his brothers to Crystal Springs, one hundred and sixty miles to the south. Through a lead obtained on this trip I was able to locate another important associate of Tommy Johnson, John Henry "Bubba" Brown, in Los Angeles, where he had moved from Jackson. The previous trip had produced a lead which resulted in the "rediscovery" in Ridgecrest, California, of the Reverend Rubin Lacy, a former Mississippi folk blues singer who had recorded commercially in 1928 and had known Tommy Johnson and Charley Patton.

In August and September 1967 I returned to Mississippi with Marina Bokelman in the hope of finding blues singers around Drew who could still perform in the tradition of Patton, Brown, and Tommy Johnson. No such persons were located in a week of investigation there, but we did conduct several useful interviews with Patton's sister Viola Cannon, his nephew Tom Cannon, his former wife Millie Torry, and former blues singers Jake Martin and Robert Johnson. In Memphis we found Dick Bankston, a very important early blues singer from Drew and one of the influences on Tommy Johnson. Unfortunately, Bankston was in ill health and unable to perform blues, but he did answer a number of questions in an interview and confirm some of the information that others had given. A visit to Robinsonville, Mississippi, resulted in an interview with Fiddlin' Joe Martin, who had known Willie Brown there in the 1930s. Martin and his playing partner Woodrow Adams had also known Howlin' Wolf (Chester Burnett), another musician from the Drew area who had moved to Robinsonville, and Adams performed a couple of songs that showed Howlin' Wolf's influence. Returning to Jackson, we reinterviewed Reverend LeDell Johnson. In Crystal Springs we revisited Mager Johnson and recorded Houston Stackhouse, a blues singer who had played for many years with the Johnson brothers there and had later gone on to play with many of the most important blues singers in Mississippi and Arkansas. In nearby Terry, Mississippi, we found Mott Willis, a second cousin of the Johnson brothers who had made music with almost all of the important representatives of the Drew tradition and was still able to perform many songs. Willis proved to be a sort of missing link to my study.

On another field trip in March and April 1969 I revisited some of my old informants, but by this time I was investigating other local traditions more closely and finding that they displayed many of the same general characteristics as the Drew blues tradition. During a field trip in August and September 1970 I revisited Mott Willis and met his nephews Willis and Charlie Taylor and a friend of theirs, Floyd Patterson, all of whom performed some interesting blues and were able to enlighten me further on the Drew tradition. During July 1971 and August 1973 my wife Cheryl and I revisited Mott Willis, his nephews, and some of my other old informants and recorded additional blues and interview material, but most of our time was spent investigating other local traditions and other forms of folk music besides blues. In December 1978 I recorded a few fragmentary pieces by Reverend O. M. McGee of Merigold, Mississippi, a former blues singer in Drew. I feel now that I have enough information and recorded music to present a fairly thorough outline of the Drew tradition and its workings and to fill in other features of the overall folk blues tradition that this local tradition does not display.

In recording each musician I tried to gain some idea of the man's total repertoire, though this was not possible in all cases. Sometimes, too, it became obvious that the performer could contribute little to my particular interests. Such people were not recorded in depth. In dealing with those who performed traditional folk blues, however, I tried to go deeply into this aspect of their repertoires. It became quite clear to me that the blues tradition operated differently from that of other genres of folksong known by these men. Hence, I tried to record many of them on different occasions in order to understand how they handled their material over a period of time. I have visited several of them more than ten times.

In my interviews I tried to record a life history of each musician, though the length of these varies considerably. I especially concentrated on trying to learn the performers' musical influences, sources of pieces and ideas, and methods of composing blues and handling of repertoire. I interviewed a few nonmusicians, many of them wives and other relatives of musicians. From them I hoped to gain information about blues singers they had known. In one case I interviewed the

white talent scout responsible for the appearance on records of a number of the musicians discussed here about his activities, tastes, and standards. Some of my informants were much more articulate than others,
and this factor did not necessarily correlate with their importance as
musicians. Some of the best folk blues singers had little to say about
their songs. Others would claim authorship for almost all their blues,
even when it was obvious to me that they were drawing upon traditional sources or phonograph records. They were often right, of course,
in the sense that they had made their own arrangements of this material, but they lacked the concepts to describe objectively the processes
of their own tradition. The singers' subjective descriptions, however,
often proved extremely interesting and valuable in their own right.

In my fieldwork I tried to avoid as much as possible blues singers
who had performed in coffeehouses and concerts as part of the "folk
revival" of the 1960s. I do not mean to suggest that these artists can
provide no important information. Indeed, my own researches began
with such performers before I did fieldwork in the South. But folk revival artists have often been interviewed too many times, and this experience can color their answers and attitudes. In addition, regular
performance before audiences that are not of their own folk group or
community can affect their repertoires and styles. Fortunately, the folk
revival blues singers who contributed to this study were recorded early

The author taking a break from fieldwork.
Photo by Cheryl T. Evans.

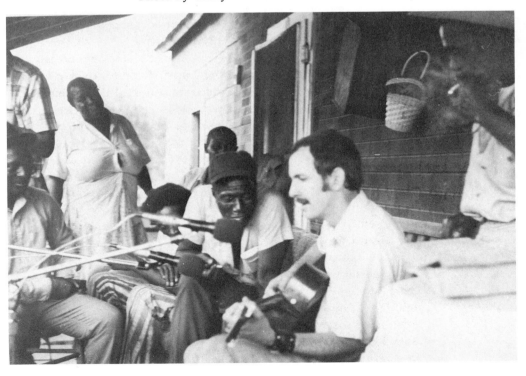

in this phase of their careers before these effects could possibly set in. But the great majority of my informants had never sat in front of a microphone before.

Because of my desire to interview my informants between songs, I tried to record most of them in quiet settings in their homes. Often family members and friends were present, but I did not usually try to induce the more normal blues context of an uninhibited house party, as the noise and crowded conditions of such an affair can make recording almost impossible. Nevertheless, a number of my sessions developed in this direction once the spirit of the music took hold of the performers and others present and the sound of the music and dancing drew additional participants. Modifying a term introduced by Kenneth S. Goldstein, I have called this kind of a recording session an "unintentionally induced natural context."[18]

The only consistent feature of my fieldwork experiences was the amazement that people frequently expressed at my interest in such a subject, usually followed by an expression of pleasure and approval. My genuine enthusiasm for the music, which many others consider out-of-date, was also a positive factor. Finally, my own ability to perform some blues from familiar traditions helped in the establishment of rapport and was an immense aid to my understanding of the music both as it was being performed and in later analysis. Most of this ability was, in fact, gained from the blues musicians themselves, as I observed their techniques of performance and composition. I was the student, and they, perhaps unknowingly, were the teachers. I consider this experience to be comparable to that of learning a language in the field. It was for me an important aid in communication. I should add, however, that I almost always performed only when asked. I rarely performed with other singers and players and never on my tapes except in a very few instances where other performers insisted that I accompany them. I tried as much as possible to avoid such situations. I have been able to find no instances where my own performances influenced those of my informants, unless they provided a sort of general stimulus to perform and recall old material. The people I recorded had all been playing for several decades and in almost all cases were not actively learning new material.

For this study it has been necessary to print transcriptions of the words and music of a number of blues. When set down in black and white, some of these songs may appear dull, trite, ungrammatical, or even absurd. This is because the songs were never meant to be written down or appreciated at such an intellectual distance. They are primarily performances to be heard and appreciated by a live audience. Their impact is meant to be felt by all of the senses, not merely by sight. Yet in order that the reader may fully understand this music, I feel it is necessary to use the medium of print for explaining its processes. I do, however, refer often to pieces that have been issued on phonograph records, and the reader is urged to listen to these whenever possible.

I want to emphasize the fact that this is not a collection, but an analytic study. I have not deemed it necessary to print or make mention of all the blues that I recorded. I have taped about seven hundred blues performances by more than eighty artists, mainly in five local traditions. Out of these I have chosen examples that illustrate most clearly the processes under study. In many cases I have dozens of potential examples to illustrate the same basic processes, but have not printed them lest the repetition become tedious. Not every text is printed with its tune or accompaniment, nor does every musical example contain a text. Only the portions that are pertinent to the discussion are printed.

Song texts have been printed in numbered stanzas with the place of instrumental choruses indicated, since the latter may function to separate sections of the text. I have not, however, felt the need to indicate the presence of instrumental responses after each line, since these are a standard feature of the blues form. Unclear portions of texts and unusual allusions are explained or annotated. All texts are printed exactly as sung, to the best of my abilities to transcribe them. Although the performances contain many repeated lines, I have considered it best to print them in full, because they often contain minor textual variations. For describing the vocal and instrumental lines I have found western musical notation satisfactory for my purposes. It is by no means completely accurate as a means of descriptive notation, but it is still quite useful for indicating note sequences and rhythms for simple comparative analysis. And besides, most readers, if they understand any notational system at all, understand this one.[19] Special symbols will be discussed when they are first used. Following Fahey,[20] I have transcribed the music in the key of the guitar position in which the accompaniment is played. This is done because of the importance of these positions and of guitar figures in general for this type of comparative analysis. Unless it is played with another instrument tuned to concert pitch, such as a piano or harmonica, the actual pitch of the guitar is arbitrary for the player. The fingering positions are most important. There can also be a great deal of slight variation in the tune or accompaniment from one stanza or chorus to another, though this is especially the case in more modern popular blues. When the performer sings entirely different tune contours or plays entirely different guitar figures at the same place in different stanzas or choruses, I have transcribed the alternate parts or discussed them in writing. Otherwise, only a representative stanza or chorus is transcribed. For purposes of comparison and reference, every fifth measure in the transcriptions is numbered.

FOLK AND POPULAR BLUES

Blues from the Performer's Point of View

ATTEMPTS to describe the blues have been made in almost every work of any length on the subject.[1] Various writers have tended to reiterate the same points about the blues, occasionally adding some new insight or stressing some characteristic that has particular appeal for them. They have described probably all the most important formal and stylistic features of the blues, yet there are so many exceptions to almost any statement about the blues that it is impossible to arrive at a concise definition of the genre. Many people can, however, recognize blues without difficulty when they hear them performed, because the term *blues* covers a broad range of formal, stylistic, and textual traits, and whenever enough of these occur together in a single performance, it is called a "blues." I will not offer a definition but rather a description that is a synthesis of earlier descriptions and a few of my own observations, with emphasis on the traits most pertinent to *folk* blues. Most blues will be found to have a great many of these characteristics, but the major exceptions will be noted. These characteristics will be exemplified later in this study.

In any attempt to describe blues, we should first see what blues singers themselves have to say on the subject. If we do this, we find that they rarely define what they regard as the blues' formal characteristics. Instead they concentrate on the blues as an emotional state. To a certain extent this emotional state is similar to that defined in standard English usage as a state of depression, melancholy, or sadness. Certainly a good number of blues songs describe such a state or produce it in listeners. This is not, however, the full meaning of the word.

A look at the epithets that singers most frequently attach to the word in their song lyrics and titles is a bit more revealing. Among the most common of these are "worried," "lonesome," "low down," "mean old," "bad luck," and "trouble." Blues are associated also with the night. One hears often of "late evening," "sundown," "midnight," "'fore day," and "early morning" blues. These epithets would suggest that blues are about having problems, being alone, and being "in the dark." To a great extent this is indeed what the blues are all about. The lyrics of blues, particularly folk blues, describe problems and sometimes offer possible solutions. Some of the problems are trivial or humorous, but most are not. Some of the more serious problems are noted in a number of traditional and widely used verses that begin with the words, "The blues ain't nothing but . . . ."[2] Among the phrases used to complete this thought are "a good man feeling bad," "an aching heart disease," "a low down hungry spell," "a good woman on your mind," "a woman loving a married man," and "a low down shaking chill."

Blues singers have also offered definitions of the blues and the things that can give one the blues. The blues are said to come from "trouble," "difficulty in your home," "a woman wanting to see her man and a man wanting to see his woman," "how you been mistreated and the things that happened to you in life," and "when my wife makes me mad."[3] The following are some additional definitions:

Well, your girl friend, yeah, and then you think about the way things is goin', so difficult. I mean, nothin' work right, when you work hard all day, always broke. And when you get off the tractor, nowhere to go, nothin' to do. Just sit up and think, and think about all that has happened how things goin'. That's real difficult. And so, why every time you feel lonely you gets that strange feelin' come up here from nowhere. . . . That's when the blues pops up! . . . The way I feel it's somethin' that is just as deep as it can go . . . Because the blues hurt you so bad. And you get hot and you find you workin' and ain't makin' nothin'. Half of the time hungry, and when you get the blues on top of that and you get to thinkin' about where can you go, or what can you do for to change. And there is no change. That's when the blues gets you. When there's nothin' else to do but what you doin' . . . and sing the blues. . . . It's a feeling that it's hard to do anything about: it's hard to know which way to go, what to do, the blues. (Robert Curtis Smith)[4]

What gives me the blues? . . . Unlucky in love for one, and hard to make a success is two; and when a man have a family and it's hard to survive for. (Little Eddie Kirkland)[5]

It's somewhere down the line that you have been hurt some place. . . . It's not only what happened to you—it's what happened to your foreparents and other people. (John Lee Hooker)[6]

Blues is a person who went in trouble and feeled depressed, something worrying him, been mistreated by someone in one way or another. And there's a happy feeling of the blues. Play the blues with a good feeling, it makes you feel good. Blues is an emotion,

*you see, of many different feelings. So it's called "individual
trouble." So you can't know how a man feel. Every individual has
an own feeling. He tries to bring it out in his songs, some happy or
some blue.* (Roosevelt Sykes)[7]

*I will say that the blues is an expression of the so-called negro in
America. Of his hard tribulations that he had. . . . See, this people
they had so much torment, lynched, burned, tarred and feathered,
and then they have sung sadder blues than we could ever imagine,
in this daytime, you see.* (Lonesome Jimmy Lee)[8]

*And the blues is sprung up from troubles and heartaches, being
bound and down, want a release. . . . Now that's what the blues is
originated from the blackman's headaches and his troubles. And he
have a lot of it.* (J. B. Lenoir)[9]

*What is the blues? Who has the blues? Sometimes the best
Christian in the world have the blues quicker than a sinner do,
'cause the average sinner ain't got nothing to worry about. He do
what he please, go where he please, use what he please. But a
Christian is obligated to certain things and obligated not to do
certain things. That sometimes cause a Christian to take the blues.
What is the blues, then? It's a worried mind. It boils down to
worry. Sometimes you worry so, it cause you to jump off the Frisco
bridge up here, worry so it cause you to stick a gun in you. . . .
That's all, it's worry. Some folks say, "Well, he went out of his
head." Well, if worry cause you to go out of your head, that's
what it is. But that's the blues.* (Reverend Rubin Lacy, former
blues singer)[10]

I have quoted this sampling of blues singers at some length because their opinions on the blues deserve more attention than they
often receive. It has become fashionable in some quarters to dismiss
these opinions because not all blues are sad or because such statements
do not describe the blues form.[11] Such criticisms, however, miss the
point of what the singers are saying. Problems of love, breakup, mistreatment, loneliness, depression, poverty, hunger, and racial oppression are causes of the blues as a feeling, and most of these problems are
frequent themes in blues lyrics. But, as Reverend Lacy says, "It boils
down to worry." For Lacy, this worry is expressed in religious terms as
a conflict between obligation and temptation. For others it is expressed
as uncertainty, indecision, frustration, and the inability to figure a way
out of a difficult situation: "hard to know which way to go or what to
do," "hard to make a success," and "being bound and down, want a
release." It is "an emotion of many different feelings." It is a feeling of
being drawn in two or more different directions. When we examine
their structural and stylistic features, we will see that a number of blues
reflect this feeling by means of various tensions and contrasts.

The blues feeling, then, is caused by a struggle to succeed combined with an awareness of overwhelming difficulties. The consequence is that in the long run "there is no change," so that "there's
nothin' else to do but what you doin' . . . and sing the blues." Blues

songs reflect both the struggles and the difficulties. In the former case they are apt to sound optimistic and happy, as they dwell on temporary successes. In the latter case they sound sad as they reflect the failures. For a sophisticated blues singer like Roosevelt Sykes, who has composed and recorded commercially hundreds of blues, these two aspects may be expressed in separate songs, "some happy or some blue." Sykes usually performs some of each on any given occasion. In the more traditional blues these two aspects are very often mixed in the same song, as a number of later examples will show. This makes the songs seem contradictory and inconsistent, but such is the very nature of the blues, as recognized by the performers themselves.

There are a number of traditional verses used by many folk blues singers that express these qualities of contradiction, conflict, and tension. Willie B. Thomas and many others have sung, "Got a mind to ramble, got a mind to settle down."[12] In 1930 Charley Patton sang:

> *Sometimes I say I need you; then again I don't.*
> *Sometimes I say I need you; then again I don't.*
> Spoken: *You know, it's the truth, baby.*
> *Sometimes I think I'll quit you; then again I won't.*[13]

And in 1971 Jack Owens sang:

> *I ain't going no higher, no lower down.*
> *Stay right here till they close . . .*
> *Stay right here till they close . . .*
> *Stay right here till they close me down.*[14]

The Blues Ideology

The blues form is especially well suited for expressing such universal facts of life as contradiction, conflict, and tension, and as a result this song-form has spread around the world and been enjoyed by most people who have come in contact with it. Some blues singers ascribe the blues to hunger, poverty, and oppression, and it is true that without these factors blacks might never have created blues songs. The blues contain much that is specific to black culture in the United States, yet basically the blues deal with universal themes. "Worry" is not the exclusive trait of any one culture. It is this universality that has been the basis of the blues' worldwide appeal and, I believe, its appeal for most black Americans as well.

I do not mean to suggest that blues singers are complete fatalists or that they see themselves simply as flotsam and jetsam on the sea of life, although these sentiments have at times found their way into the blues. Instead, blues simply reflect an attitude that, despite all of one's efforts, things are not likely to get much better in the long run. This is an attitude that many people have felt at times, but it has been, unfortunately, a predominant one for many blacks, particularly those who have performed and listened to the blues. Blues singers and their audiences tend to have little formal education and to be in the lower economic class. They may have struggled to improve their station in life, but their chances of actually doing so are slight. Lack of education and lack of economic opportunity are major causes of the other problems that are dealt with in the blues. As long as these conditions persist, the ingredients for the blues will be found. It is only when people believe that things can get or are getting better that the blues begin to lose their appeal.

Blues singers offer no solutions to life's problems but instead dramatize their existence and try to make the best of them by stating them on social occasions where their universality can be affirmed. This spirit is typified by Jack Owens, who sang "I ain't going no higher, no lower down." Owens was born in 1904 and has always lived in the country near Bentonia, Mississippi. He is illiterate, has only once been south of Jackson or north of Clarksdale, and has done farm work all his days. He has also sung blues and played the guitar since boyhood. When I first met him in 1966, he was living with his wife in a house with two rooms and a kitchen which had been given to him as a "lifetime house" by a white family that had "furnished" his father years before. Owens had cleared out one of the rooms for dancing on weekends. He would alternate his own blues with the latest popular hits from a jukebox which he had installed. His wife sold sandwiches and drinks from the kitchen. Owens also had a wage income from farm work, had money in the bank, owned a pickup truck, some chickens, two mules, and eight head of cattle, and kept a vegetable garden. By 1970 he had moved an old crib onto his lot and converted it into a juke house, adding on a small kitchen with a couple of tables. This gave him more room in his house. The following year there was a death in the family of his white patrons, and the new owner told him that he would have to vacate his house so that a tractor driver could move in. Owens used most of his savings in buying a small lot from a nearby black landowner and moving the juke house, which became his new home, onto it. He added another one-room building to it, and by 1973 had added two more rooms and had an enormous pile of old lumber ready for more building. He was trying to persuade his father in Chicago to sell his property and move back to Mississippi and was contemplating reopening his juke house. But later that same year Owens' wife fell and shattered her hip, and after almost a year spent in the hospital she has remained confined to a wheelchair. This turn of events prevented the reopening of the juke house, though Owens did add some more rooms to his house. His father did not move back to Mississippi and died in Chicago, leaving Jack three apartment houses there. Owens went north for the first time in his life and entrusted the property to a real estate agent who was recommended to him. After a year the agent had still not sold the property, and Owens, faced with property tax bills that he could not pay, assumed that the agent was collecting rent on the property himself and waiting for Owens to die. Throughout all of these changes of fortune Owens has continued to create and perform blues.

Jack Owens. Photo by Cheryl T. Evans.

Though most blues singers have probably seen more of the world, Owens's life is typical in the sense that, despite his own efforts, it is controlled to a great extent by forces larger than himself. He might appear to make some progress, but he cannot really believe in progress as an ideology because he is too much of a realist and is aware of the forces aligned against him. It is this realistic spirit that finds expression in his blues and those of most other singers.[15] The only other viable alternative to an ideology of progress and idealism is fundamentalist religion, which offers the hope of a better life in another world. Many blues singers and members of their audiences have turned to religion, but, in contrast, many children raised in religious families have become blues singers. Both ideologies stress human effort, but neither holds out much real prospect of general improvement of conditions in this world. Living the Christian life may lead to greater happiness, stability, and improvement of status, but for lower class blacks the church has been basically a refuge where they could prepare for heaven. Outside of the church one is said to be "in the world," which is full of temptations and troubles.[16]

The Blues Form

Although it is not necessarily the norm, most blues fall into one basic pattern, or an approximation of it—the twelve-bar AAB pattern. A blues in this pattern has several stanzas, each of which occupies twelve measures or "bars" of 4/4 time. These twelve bars are divided into three sections or "lines" of four bars each. The first line (A) is usually repeated as the second line (A), sometimes with a slight variation for emphasis, and the stanza ends with a different third line (B), which usually rhymes or is assonant with the first two. The entire twelve measures, however, are not devoted to the singing of these three lines. Instead, each line usually takes slightly more than two measures to sing. It is followed by an instrumental passage of slightly less than two measures as a "response" to the vocal line. The combination of three such vocal lines with their instrumental responses, each occupying four measures altogether, makes a complete twelve-bar stanza.

The AAB pattern of the vocal is set off against a more complex pattern in the instrumental accompaniment. The latter consists of musical phrases whose basis lies in a harmonic sequence of tonic (I), subdominant (IV), and dominant (V) chords. The typical sequence for a twelve-bar blues stanza is shown in Figure 1.

This is only the most common stanza pattern. Among the many others are AAA (12 bars), AAAB (16 bars), AB (8 bars), and AB with refrain (12 bars). Sometimes the first four measures are filled by a rhymed couplet, while the last eight contain a refrain. In some blues performances more than one of these patterns will be used. It also happens often that players will shorten or extend instrumental lines, producing stanzas of 11, 13½, 20 bars, and so forth. This occurs frequently

The sun's gonna shine in my back door some day . . . . (response)

/1. (I)   /2. (I)   /3. (I)   /4. (I)

The sun's gonna shine in my back door some day . . . . (response)

/5. (IV)   /6. (IV)   /7. (I)   /8. (I)

The wind's gonna rise and blow my blues away . . . . response)

/9. (V)   /10. (IV, V, or I)   /11. (I)   /12. (I)

Figure 1. The typical twelve-bar AAB blues pattern

in folk blues. Most of the examples in this study, however, conform to or approximate the twelve-bar AAB pattern.

Blues Singing and Blues Scales

Blues are almost always sung solo, though occasionally two singers will alternate stanzas or sing in harmony. The blues team of Brownie McGhee and Sonny Terry, for example, has sung in harmony on a number of records, and it was done earlier on records by Tampa Red with other singers. Blues have also been performed by vocal quartets, such as the Norfolk Jazz Quartet in the 1920s and groups such as the Midnighters in the 1950s. But blues sung by quartets in harmony are essentially adaptations of a solo performance style. Quartet singers will usually fill in the spaces left for the instrumental responses with internal vocal refrains or repetitions of the last few words of the line. A few examples of solo performances in this study show some of these characteristics, which may represent an influence from quartet blues singing back on solo singing. Finally, one should mention the "talking blues," which Harry Oster has described as "semi-rhythmic speaking or a mixture of speaking and singing, accompanied by rhythmic guitar."[17] Although talking blues are exemplified in this study, I have not encountered them often, and they may well be particularly distinctive of the regional tradition of Louisiana studied by Oster.

Blues singing uses a broad range of timbres and techniques. Growling, normal voice, and falsetto can all be used in the same song. Melisma (the singing of a single syllable over several notes) is common, as is vocal embellishment of all sorts. The main point is that the singing is supposed to be done with great feeling. Often blues singers accentuate this feeling in their voices by assuming a look of intense emotion, sometimes appearing to be in a state of trance. Another characteristic of blues singing is its extreme use of syncopation, the placement of a melodic accent on the offbeat. The syncopated rhythm of the singing is often offset by the more regular beat of the accompaniment. Syncopation is particularly common in blues just before bar lines, and many examples of it will be found in this study. In fact, it is so common in blues as to make any study of blues metrics virtually meaningless. If one were to look at the text only, one would note that the usual blues line in the twelve-bar AAB pattern is an iambic pentameter with frequent substitutions of anapests and other feet and with a caesura in the middle of the third foot. Yet when the line is sung, often the accent will fall on syllables not normally accented in speech, and the caesura may be displaced. This shifting of the accent is much more common in blues than in most other forms of black folksong, particularly earlier forms, and is one of the chief distinguishing features of the blues.

Most writers seem to think that in its full form the "blues scale" is like the Western diatonic major scale with two important exceptions, the third and the seventh degrees.[18] These two notes can be major, minor, or somewhere about midway between. The latter are usually referred to as neutral thirds and sevenths or simply "blue notes."[19] Often the major, minor, and neutral third or seventh are all used in the same performance. In fact, "neutral" probably would best represent an *area* between major and minor where notes can be sung, rather than any specific point between them. Blues singers often waver at the third or seventh or glide from a lower to a slightly higher pitch. The lower part of the third and seventh areas tends to serve as a leading tone respectively to the tonic and fifth below, the upper part as a leading tone to the fifth and tonic above. It may well be, however, that there are other "blue notes" besides the neutral third and seventh. A number of writers have pointed out the use of the flatted fifth, and I have heard several folk blues singers regularly use pitches between the major sixth and minor seventh and between the major second and minor third.[20] For the transcriptions in this study, neutral tones will be indicated by upward and downward pointing arrows (↑and↓). These will be printed above notes on the staff to indicate that such notes are sounded *approximately* a quarter tone above or below the pitch as written. In some cases these symbols will be printed above sharp, flat, and natural signs in the key signature to indicate that they affect such pitches throughout the piece. In other words, these arrows are to be treated the same as sharp, flat, or natural signs, except that they are printed above the staff rather than on it.

The blues scale, then, may contain more than seven tones, though if one counts the third and seventh degrees as "tonal areas," the scale would be heptatonic, or octatonic if one also included the flatted fifth. In any single performance, however, the scale might be only hexatonic or pentatonic. The latter is especially common, usually either as a scale lacking the second and sixth degrees or as one lacking the fourth and seventh degrees. Thus there is no single "blues scale" but many blues scales. A broad range of performances by different blues singers would have to be studied before further conclusions about such scales could be reached. Neutral tones, though, and the use of "tonal areas" within a single performance are definitely characteristic of the blues and are features that distinguish blues from many other forms of folk music.

The tonal range of a blues can vary from a fifth to over an octave. Some blues, like Robert Petway's 1941 "Catfish Blues" (Bluebird B 8838), can cover even two octaves. Blues lines tend to start on a high note or with a quick rise and descend gradually to the tonic note below. Sometimes the final note of a line will be the third (anywhere in its tonal area), fifth, or minor or neutral seventh. These are all notes within the tonic or tonic seventh chord, which was earlier noted as the chord of the instrumental accompaniment at the end of each line. Blues vocal lines almost never end on the second, fourth, sixth, or major seventh degrees of the scale. This fact is another one of the distinguishing characteristics of the blues.

Often, the second melodic line of a blues stanza is, like the text, the same as the first, although the underlying harmony of the accompaniment changes from tonic to subdominant. In a few cases, all three lines of the stanza have the same tune, or some vocal lines might parallel each other by a fourth or a fifth in accord with the harmonic changes in the accompaniment. But many blues have stanzas in which each line has a different melody. Furthermore, there is usually a great deal of slight improvisational variation in a line from one stanza to another, so that no two stanzas are exactly the same melodically. Sometimes the singer employs two or more different strains in a single blues. Charley Patton, for example, sang three different strains in his "Pony Blues" (Paramount 12792, Example 24).

Blues Accompaniments

Blues instrumental accompaniments display many of the same characteristics as the vocal melodies, such as syncopation, blue notes, improvisational variations from one stanza to another, and the use of several strains or "parts" in the same piece. Often only one instrument is used to accompany a blues, especially a folk blues. The most important instruments are the guitar, the piano, and the harmonica. The mandolin and the violin were once used in string band accompaniments but are not often heard now. The banjo has rarely been used for blues. In popular blues it is not uncommon to hear reed and brass instruments, and a good many blues have been recorded with large mixed ensembles. In contrast, children often learn to play blues on such simple homemade instruments as a single strand of broom wire attached to the wall of a house.[21]

In most cases the blues singer plays his own accompaniment, sometimes with the help of other instrumentalists. The playing is never simply a harmonic and rhythmic background to the singing; it interacts with and answers the voice. Spaces between the vocal lines and phrases are filled by notes played on instruments. The instrumental part really acts as a second voice, and often as a third or fourth. The highest praise that can be given to an instrumentalist's skill, in fact, is to say that he can make his instrument "talk." Even a single guitar player may be able to keep several voices and rhythms going by creating different lines simultaneously on his instrument while maintaining the basic beat by tapping his foot. Except in some quartet singing, accompaniment is deemed essential to blues performance. A singer who cannot play an instrument will almost always try to find someone who can. I have even observed singers imitating an instrumental sound with their voices when no instrument was available. Quartet singers, too, recreate an instrumental effect by filling in the spaces following their lines with nonsense words or "answering" their lines by repeating the final phrases. Although blues can be sung without an instrument, they are not considered the norm by the singers.

Blues instrumentalists use a variety of special effects and techniques not often employed in playing classical music. They may, for example, modify their instruments. Pianists often don't use the pedals, or they may stuff newspapers behind the wires to achieve a "damped" effect. Harmonica players will cup the instrument in their hands or tap on it to give it a fluttering sound. Guitarists may add extra strings or tap on the body or "hammer" on the strings with their fingers. In general, playing tends to be percussive, and a "dirty" tone is heard along with a clear one. Guitarists often use unorthodox or open tunings, and with the latter they may slide a knife or a bottleneck or piece of metal tubing worn over a finger of the left hand on the strings to create a whining effect.[22] This slide technique makes it easy to play blue notes. They can also be played by "choking" or bending the strings, and, on the harmonica, by "bending" notes.[23] The pianist must play the major and minor notes simultaneously or in rapid succession to achieve the effect of blue notes.

Often a blues accompaniment does not consist of full chords played behind the singing but only the suggestion of chords. The subdominant harmony in the fifth and sixth measures of a twelve-bar blues might be suggested by the inclusion of the fourth or sixth degree in a chord that is otherwise based on the tonic, and similarly for the dominant harmony. Sometimes there is no suggestion of chord changes and the harmony remains in the tonic chord throughout, or in some tunes a drone or ostinato is set up over which a single line is played. Many blues accompaniments, particularly those produced by only a single instrument, are not really "harmonic" at all. Instead, only one note may be played at a time, and the harmonic feeling is created by arpeggios and other sequences or by occasional chords.

There are, of course, instrumental blues. These are often simply blues accompaniments minus the usual singing. Usually in such cases one instrumental line will fulfill the role of the voice. However, since the standard twelve-bar AAB form with its typical harmonic sequences has proliferated, various composers have created a number of blues designed as instrumental pieces. Players may not know any words to sing to these blues. Musicians will also perform instrumental choruses or "breaks" between stanzas of vocal blues. The frequency of this practice varies greatly among blues singers and is not entirely correlated with their degree of instrumental skill. Some very good players almost never perform instrumental choruses, and the only time one can hear their playing unimpeded by the vocal is at the ends of lines. It is possible that an important function of the instrumental chorus, besides that of demonstrating skill, is to set off distinct thoughts or thought groups in the text.[24] Instrumental choruses may consist of a restatement of the normal accompaniment part behind the vocal, one or more alternate parts, something improvised at the time of performance, or a combination of features of all three.

There are some songs performed without instrumental accompaniment that various writers, as well as singers themselves, have called "field blues," "field hollers," "field cries," "arwhoolies," and so forth. They are a sort of worksong sung in the fields and levee camps or while walking or riding. They tend to be very loosely structured, highly embellished, and rhythmically free, often consisting of falsetto whooping or hollering with no words or a very minimal text. Some, of course, do have more complex texts. Vocally they are very much like blues, and they were an important ingredient in the original creation of the blues, but without an accompaniment they have quite a different function from blues. In this study we shall consider field hollers to be a separate genre, related to blues in content, form, and style, but distinct in function, just as, conversely, there are other folksongs that can fulfill the same functions as blues but are distinct in content, form, and style.

Blues Lyricism

Textually speaking, blues can best be characterized as *lyric* songs, as distinct from *narrative* songs. Their message is delivered from a first person point of view, stressing the emotional dimension. Blues do not normally tell stories in the sense of a series of events, although they may portray an event or situation in such a way that its underlying story can be reconstructed by the listener. The real emphasis of the blues is on feelings and perceptions. The question naturally arises whether these feelings and perceptions are products of the actual experiences of the singer or composer or simply products of his imagination. Much misunderstanding has arisen over the question of whether or not blues texts are "autobiographical."[25] Obviously they are not, if by "autobiography" one means an actual life history (or even episodes in a life history) told by the singer. Blues rarely give any kind of lengthy descriptive detail or balanced account of events. Yet there is much evidence that many blues are composed as the result of personal experiences and do reflect the feelings of the singer or composer about these experiences. There is evidence too that blues can be an expression of the singer's feelings at the actual time of performance. Blues singers have claimed to have composed songs inspired by the experiences of others as well. There is also much obvious exaggeration and imaginative expression in the blues. Often the singer will create a dramatic *persona* who speaks in the first person. The important thing is that the lyrics appeal emotionally to the singer and to his audience, not that they reflect an actual event. The blues singer takes realistic, though not necessarily real, situations and treats them imaginatively. Although he appears to sing for himself, most of his lyrics are meant just as much for those around him.[26] We shall examine these subjects later in greater detail.

There have been many surveys of the subject matter of blues texts.[27] Two primary facts emerge from these: the blues are distinctly secular in outlook and they deal mainly with man/woman situations. They are secular in the sense that they do not hold out hope for escape from one's problems through organized religion. Yet, although blues singers may make fun of preachers and churchgoers in their songs, they are not necessarily opposed to religion as such. They are simply uncommitted to it as a way of life for themselves.[28] This secular outlook is turned in the blues toward the opposite sex. For the most part, blues celebrate the joys and frustrations of love. Often this is done in a very frank manner, and the blues have developed a rich sexual imagery. The problems of love, such as desertion and infidelity, receive a great deal of attention, and these often lead to another very important theme in the blues, wanderlust and travel. Other common subjects are farming and its problems, industrial work, poverty, alcohol and drugs, sickness and death, gambling, voodoo and magic, crime and prison, the color hierarchy within the black community,[29] natural disasters, and important national and local events as they affect the singer and his community. On a more general level, Stanley Edgar Hyman has detected five major themes that pervade blues lyrics.[30] One of these is leaving/travel/journey, or perhaps we should call it "escape."[31] Blues singers often express an intention of leaving or bemoan the fact that they have been left. This theme may also be expressed conversely as a desire to return home or to resume a former relationship, or the blues singer may present himself as a stranger who has just arrived in town and is seeking to establish a new relationship. A second theme is dramatic self-pity.[32] Blues singers are often telling about their troubles, though, in contrast, there is Hyman's third theme, compensatory grandiose fantasy.[33] Boasting about oneself, particularly as a lover, is common in the blues. A fourth theme is abuse and bawdry.[34] Blues singers frequently "put down" their partners or others of the same sex. Yet, just as frequently, they are effusive in their praise of someone else. We might notice that up to this point the major themes can be grouped into contrasting pairs: leaving and returning or arriving; self-pity and boasting or grandiose fantasy; abuse and praise. Hyman's fifth and last theme is "cynicism," which I think would be better stated as a noncommittal attitude toward life. Although the other themes are often expressed in the most extreme and exaggerated manner possible, the blues singer does not commit himself to any one of them exclusively. He will have a repertoire of songs that includes them all, or he may even juxtapose the opposite themes in the same song. This noncommittal attitude is at the heart of the blues ideology and is closely related to the factors of contradiction, conflict, and tension discussed earlier.

It should be obvious that the subject matter of the blues is related to the main problem areas of life within the black lower-class secular community. The man/woman relationship is the most prominent topic for two reasons. It is the area most subject to daily change and fluctuation in people's lives, and it is closely related to the dancing and partying context in which blues are most often performed. Other topics are found less frequently in blues verse simply because they are problems that have to be dealt with less often, though as problems they may be much more serious. Some topics are not treated at all. For example, although blues use imagery and similes drawn from nature, they do not describe the beauties of a sunset or a landscape. These present no problems to the blues singer. Nature is the subject when the blues deal with floods, dry spells, and hurricanes.

It is notable that blues do not devote a great deal of attention to perhaps the biggest problem area of all, racial discrimination. There are some blues on this subject, but in most cases this problem seems to lie in the background of other subjects and is not confronted directly. Some might take this as an indication that blues singers are resigned to an inferior status. Possibly this is true for a few of them. One could also speculate that blues singers channel the problem of discrimination into less controversial subject areas.[35] If they do so, they do so unconsciously. Basically, the problem of discrimination was until recently so overwhelming and so institutionalized that it had become a fact of life for the average blues singer. There was no point in singing about segregated facilities because the singer knew nothing else. Blues instead have dealt with the *results* of discrimination, such as broken homes, poverty, crime, and prison. In these areas there are at least some fluctuations. For blues to attack the institution of discrimination itself, they would need to express an ideology of progess and a belief in ultimate success in overcoming the problem. As noted earlier, this kind of ideology is alien to the spirit of the blues, which instead allows only for temporary successes. This does not mean that blues singers have been uninvolved in efforts to change the pattern of discrimination but simply that they don't usually express these efforts in their blues. John Henry "Bubba" Brown, for example, is a blues singer who also, in the face of great difficulties, organized the first black labor union in Mississippi in the 1940s within a completely segregated social system. Even so, his blues dealt with the typical themes of love, loneliness, and so forth. He even composed a nonblues song and a poem in praise of the companies that he worked for. His songs, then, clearly served other purposes than protest against discrimination.[36] Within black folklore there are other outlets for protest, such as folktales and legends.[37] I have recorded a number of these myself from blues singers in contexts in which I have recorded blues but have found that this subject matter does not carry over into their songs. The genre of folksong in which overt protest is most prevalent is the worksong. This is because these songs are so often performed in a context that is closely tied to oppressive conditions of sharecropping or other hard manual labor for low pay. Many of the published examples of worksongs have been collected from prisoners and chain gang workers.[38] The most dramatic incidents, such as lynchings, beatings, and Ku Klux Klan raids, are not treated in blues simply because they are subjects more suited to narrative genres. Finally, most blues have been collected and published by whites or have been issued by record companies owned by whites. It is conceivable that some expression of protest has been censored by these people or by the blues singers themselves.[39] In any case, there can be no doubt that the general failure of blues to take a firm and forthright stand against discrimination is a factor in their decreasing appeal to younger and more militant blacks.[40]

Blues are full of striking imagery and highly expressive language.[41] Stephen Calt has noted that some sources for this are the Bible, white ballads, popular Tin Pan Alley and sentimental songs, nursery rhymes, spirituals, and everyday colloquial conversation.[42] However, most of the imagery and language used is unique to the blues. It is not simply a case of setting everyday speech to song. Metaphor, simile, irony, and exaggeration abound, and many of the traditional verses have the sententious quality of proverbs. Traditional and widely used verses and phrases are not clichés, as Calt would have it,[43] but instead have for their singers and audiences "a shorthand significance with a wealth of unstated associated meanings permitting a maximum of content with a strict economy of means."[44] At times, blues can even be surrealistic.[45] Images are often not "logically" connected from one stanza to another and sometimes not even within the same stanza. Often the singer will make his lines seem more immediate and personal by preceding them with words such as "says," "crying," "well," and "now." He will address his verses to some anonymous "baby" or use apostrophes like "Lord" or "Lordy" for emphasis. Many examples will be given later in this study, but here we might note a few typical images from the vast repertoire of traditional verses. A beautiful woman might be a "long tall woman," a "sweet mama," or she might be "lightning when she smiles" and have a "mouth all crowned with gold." Or she might be a "big fat mama with the meat shaking on her bones" or "low and squatty, right down on the ground." A cruel partner might be a "dirty mistreater" or have "a heart like railroad steel." A singer may say that he is "going down South where the weather suits my clothes" or "going up North to get my hambone boiled," or perhaps his "mind got to rambling like the wild geese in the West." Some of the most remarkable images are not completely clear, yet they are somehow strangely effective when sung. William Harris asks, for example, "Did you ever wake up with bullfrogs on your mind?"[46] And Howlin' Wolf sings about a "smokestack lightning, shining just like gold."[47] There can be no doubt that the blues contain some of the finest folk poetry produced anywhere.

Part of the effectiveness of blues imagery and language can be attributed to the structure of the blues stanza. In all cases, each line is a complete sentence or clause. Enjambment is unknown in the blues. In a typical AAB stanza, the A and B lines have a relationship to each other in which the B line "answers" the A line in a "statement and response" fashion. Janheinz Jahn has called this process "blues logic," stating that it can be achieved in two ways. "Either the response part expands, illuminates, justifies, explains, or gives grounds for the statement; or it offers an antithesis to them [*sic*], so that the statement and response form a confrontation."[48] "Justifying" and "confronting" blues logic can even occur together in the same stanza. Any of the examples printed in this study will illustrate this process.

The Blues Form and the Blues Ideology

It should be clear by now that a great many of these features of form, style, and content serve to create contrasts, tension and release of tension, and a sense of ambiguity and uncertainty, and that they do this within an extremely compact form.[49] Ambiguity and compactness are undoubtedly responsible for much of the appeal of the blues to performers and listeners alike. The call and response principle provides several forms of tension and contrast in the blues. There is the "blues logic" of the B line "answering" the A line. The accompaniment also "answers" the singing at the end of each line and "comments" on individual notes and phrases within the line. The repetition of the A line in an AAB stanza builds up tension, which is further increased by the change to a subdominant harmony behind the second A line. Then the tension is released by the B line. Thus there is tension and release in the call and response pattern of each line and in the stanza pattern as a whole. The tension is extended from one stanza to another or even from one song to another by the juxtaposition of inconsistent images and topics and by the balancing of themes of leaving and returning, self-pity and fantasy, abuse and praise. This tension is often intensified by the contrasting rhythms of the voice and accompaniment. For example, one might use a duple rhythm and the other a triple rhythm, or both might alternate between duple and triple rhythms over the course of a performance. In some cases the accompaniment keeps both rhythms going simultaneously. Often it is impossible to determine whether one is hearing an essentially duple or triple rhythm. Instead, the rhythmic pattern is based on a figure that is somewhere between a pair of eighth notes (♫) and a triplet quarter and eighth note (♩♪). In this study I have had to transcribe such rhythmic figures in what seem to be their closest approximations. Rhythmic tension and uncertainty are created also through offbeat phrasing or syncopation and through improvisational variation. In addition, many blues have a gradually accelerating tempo, which gives a rushing sensation and builds excitement. Melodic tension and release are created by the practice of beginning many vocal lines on a high note and gradually descending to the tonic note below, only to start high again in the next line. Blue notes, particularly when played on instruments not constructed to produce them, create an additional sense of ambiguity between the major and minor. Further contrast, between what is said and what is meant, is found in the use of double meaning, metaphor, and irony. Blues lyrics deal with the problem areas of life with no final resolution or commitment to an overall plan of action. Temporary solutions and escapes may be offered, but new problems are always raised. The lyrics also frequently create contrasts between the first and second person (I-You) or first and third person (I-She/He). There is, as well, a contextual contrast between singer and audience, emphasized by frequent verbal comments and responses by members of the audience to the singer and sometimes by the singer explicitly addressing his audience.

These contrasts, ambiguities, and tensions are not found only in the blues, nor are all of them found in every blues performance. Certainly many forms of folksong and music in general display a contrast between performer and audience or deal with problem areas of life. Duple-triple rhythms and blue notes are characteristic of other forms of black music as well as music of other cultures, and metaphor and double meaning are probably universal. But it would be difficult to find another song-form in which so many of these contrastive, ambiguous, and tension-building and tension-relieving elements are found.

Early Reports of Blues

The blues are a fairly recent development in American folk music, a product almost entirely of the twentieth century. There are no accounts of blues singing before the 1890s. Until this time black folk music in America consisted mainly of spirituals and hymns, songs for various kinds of group and individual work, lighthearted social songs, banjo and fiddle music, a few blues ballads, and various survivals of African music.[50] In 1876 journalist Lafcadio Hearn spent many evenings in Cincinnati waterfront dance halls frequented by black longshoremen and roustabouts and observed the music and dancing there. It would have been a likely social context for blues, but not one of the twelve song texts Hearn prints resembles a blues. Instead they are all typical nineteenth-century social, minstrel, and riverboat songs with banjo and fiddle accompaniment.[51] Music critic Henry Edward Krehbiel, in a study of black American folksongs first published in 1913 but based on his researches of more than a decade before and on the earlier work of others, also cites no examples of blues.[52]

The year 1890 marks the first emergence of folk blues from their previous underground status. In the last decade of the nineteenth century and especially in the first fifteen years of the twentieth century there are increasingly frequent reports of their appearance. Although a number of these reports are recollections of this early period published many years later, there is enough general consistency among them to give us a fairly reliable picture of the early folk blues.

From South Texas in 1890 Gates Thomas recalled a song called "Nobody There," with the following single stanza:

> *That you, Nigger man, knockin' at my door?*
> *Hear me tell you, Nigger man, "Nobody there no more."*[53]

Thomas does not indicate whether the singing was accompanied by an instrument, but he prints a pentatonic tune containing the tonic, minor third, fourth, fifth, and minor seventh, which is strikingly like a typical blues tune.

W. C. Handy prints a blues that was sung around 1890 by a black quartet in Florence, Alabama.[54] It is said to be a guitar song in spirit, but it was used when the quartet was hard up for material. Handy later played the song with mandolin and guitar trios as far north as Evansville, Indiana.[55] It is a twelve-bar blues with the line, "Got no mo' home dan a dog," repeated three times. Instead of an instrumental response, the quartet extended the word "dog" and added the exclamation "Lawd" at the end of the first and second line. Handy also states that in 1892 in St. Louis he "heard shabby guitarists picking out a tune called *East St. Louis*. It had numerous one-line verses and they would sing it all night.

> *I walked all the way from old East St. Louis,*
> *And I didn't have but one po' measly dime.*

That one line was an entire stanza."[56] The tune that Handy prints is a typical eight-bar blues tune,[57] and variants of the lyrics are common in other traditional blues.[58]

Ernest Borneman has gathered many recollections from boogie-woogie piano players about early uses of that style, which is essentially a blues style.[59] Some of these recollections go back to the 1890s. The style was played in the barrelhouses of New Orleans, Shreveport, and other southern and northern cities, and on the riverboats. The great New Orleans jazz pianist, Ferdinand "Jelly Roll" Morton, recalled a number of piano blues from the 1890s and shortly after the turn of the century that were played in the brothels and dance halls of his native city.[60] These pieces contain typical traditional blues verses in AAB, AB, and other stanza patterns. One of them, recalled from 1901 or 1902, contains the words, "I got the blues so bad I cannot remember the day," as the last line of an AAB stanza, indicating that this stanzaic form was already beginning to be associated with the word *blues*. [61] Also from the 1890s, John Jacob Niles has recalled "Black Alfalfa's Jail-House Shouting Blues," composed in Kentucky in 1898 by Ophelia Simpson, in jail at that time for killing her husband.[62] This song was later performed in Dr. Parker's Medicine Show, for which Ms. Simpson sang when she was not preparing tapeworm eradicator. Niles does not say whether it was one of the songs with instrumental accompaniment in the show, but the eleven stanzas he prints show that it was a typical AAB blues. Textually, however, it is the most complex and coherent blues from this early period, perhaps a consequence of Ms. Simpson's status as a professional entertainer.

After the turn of the century, reports of blues singing are more frequent and are often based on contemporary accounts rather than recollections. In 1901 and 1902 archaeologist Charles Peabody, while excavating an Indian mound near Stovall, Mississippi, heard and wrote down some of the songs of his black laborers.[63] Some of these pieces had guitar accompaniment, but Peabody did not indicate which ones. In an article on this music he prints the tunes of some wordless field hollers and the words to some worksongs and discusses "ragtime" playing on the guitar. He also prints some one-line tunes that are strikingly like parts of blues tunes and mentions

> *distichs and improvisations in rhythm more or less phrased sung to an intoning more or less approaching melody. These ditties and distichs were either of a general application referring to manners, customs, and events of Negro life or of special appositeness improvised on the spur of the moment on a topic then interesting. Improvising sometimes occurred in the general class, but it was more likely to be merely a variation of some one sentiment. The burden of the songs of the former class were [sic] "hard luck" tales (very often), love themes, suggestions anticipative and reminiscent of favorite occupations and amusements.[64]*

As an example of one of these compositions Peabody prints a verse that has been used by many blues singers:[65]

> *They had me arrested for murder*
> *And I never harmed a man.*

Peabody's description of the subject matter of these songs and of improvisation could easily be a description of blues or of worksongs well on their way to becoming blues. Stovall is in the heart of Mississippi's Delta, a region that has produced probably more blues singers than any other.

In 1902 a woman in a small town in Missouri sang a blues for Gertrude "Ma" Rainey, a singer whose traveling show was passing through. Rainey liked the song and incorporated it into her act, calling it simply "the blues."[66] Later she went on to become one of the most famous of all popular blues singers and a prolific recording artist in the 1920s.

One year later band leader and composer W. C. Handy encountered the blues again at a railroad station in the Delta town of Tutwiler, Mississippi. There a man pressed a knife on the strings of a guitar and sang the line, "Goin' where the Southern cross the Dog," three times in succession. This line referred to the Southern and Yazoo Delta ("Yellow Dog") railroads. Handy described the performance as "the weirdest music I had ever heard."[67] Not long afterward Handy's own sophisticated orchestra was upstaged at a dance in nearby Cleveland, Mississippi, by three local men playing guitar, mandolin, and string bass. They played "one of those over-and-over strains that seem to have no very clear beginning and certainly no ending at all," an "agonizing strain," "haunting," with "a disturbing monotony." Quite possibly it was a blues. When Handy saw the enthusiastic reception and shower of money this music received, he resolved to become a composer and arranger of blues and other folksongs. "Then I saw the beauty of primitive music," he wrote, remarking on the money to be made from it. Shortly thereafter Handy began writing arrangements for the folk blues that were all around him.[68]

Gates Thomas heard more blues in south Texas in the early years of the twentieth century.[69] The songs he prints are especially interesting because they contain some of the same verses noted by others at this time, an indication of the development of an oral tradition. "Baby, Take a Look at Me," a song whose lyrics mention drug and alcohol addiction, reproduces a line heard by Charles Peabody in Mississippi. "Alabama Boun' " and "C. C. Rider" are versions of blues that Jelly Roll Morton reported from New Orleans. In Texas the latter song used ABB and ABA stanza patterns, but in New Orleans it used an AB pattern. Another song from Texas, "Alice Brown," used an AB pattern with a two-line refrain.

By far the most important early account of blues is sociologist and folklorist Howard W. Odum's lengthy article based on field collecting done mainly in Lafayette County, Mississippi, and Newton County, Georgia, between 1905 and 1908.[70] Odum prints 115 song texts, about half of them blues or field blues, which, he felt, reflected the secular life and mental imagery of "the Negro." He was not familiar with the term "blues" as designating a type of song, but two of his texts use this word. In number 11 the singer repeats the line, "I got the blues, but too damn mean to cry," and in number 75 a man sings, "I got de blues an' can't be satisfied." Both of these lines, and many of the others Odum prints, are traditional and have been used in other folk blues. Like Handy, Odum noted that many of the songs he collected were accompanied by stringed instruments, mainly the guitar. He described bottleneck and knife style guitar playing and train imitations on the guitar and pointed out the important roles of the semiprofessional "songsters," "musicianers," and "music physicianers." Among the stanza patterns he printed, the most common were AAAA, AAAB, AAA, AB, AA, and AB with a one- or two-line refrain. Sometimes there were slight textual variations in repetitions of the A line. Other patterns were AABC, ABCA, and ABB. Strangely, the AAB pattern was used only occasionally in songs that also used other patterns (numbers 8, 32, 72, and 75). Odum also noted a phenomenon that the singers themselves called the "one-verse song," a single line repeated several times, constituting the entire song. He believed that such songs evolved into more complex ones as singers became tired of repeating one line and so found a rhyming line for it and then added others. Odum stated that such singing was "simply a musical 'thinking out loud'," and he gave the following hypothetical example of the evolution of a one-verse song into something more complex:

> A negro is driving a delivery-wagon; the weather is cold, and the wind is blowing with a drizzling rain. He pulls his coat around him, and says, "The wind sho' do blow." Not having any special song which he wishes to sing at the moment, he sings these words

and others: "Sho' God is cold dis mornin'," "Ain't goin' to rain no mo'," "Goin' where chilly win' don't blow." In the same way he sings whatever happens to be foremost in his mind. Perhaps it is, "I bin workin' so long—hungry as I kin be;" "Where in de worl' you bin?" "I'm goin' 'way some day;" "Jus' keep a knockin' at yo' do';" "Had a mighty good time las' night;" or as many others as there are common scenes in the negro's life.[71]

Odum stated that the secular songs of the blacks fell into three general classes: the current popular songs, such songs greatly modified and adapted, and the folk songs proper that were the original creations of blacks. The blues would have fallen into the third class. Odum noted, however, that individual performers sang a mixture of songs from all three classes. The wandering "musicianers" and "music physi-

Howard W. Odum. Photo courtesy of Mrs. Mary Odum Schinhan.

cianers" would take these songs with them from town to town, spreading them among the locally based performers. Most of the instrumentally accompanied songs were performed in the evenings after work. Typical occasions for this music were

> when large or small groups are gathered for gayety; when a lonely
> negro sits on his doorstep or by the fireside, playing and singing;
> when couples stay late at night with their love-songs and jollity;
> when groups gather after church to sing the lighter melodies; when
> the "musicianers," "music physicianers," and "songsters" gather to
> render music for special occasions, such as church and private
> "socials," dances, and other forms of social gatherings. Special
> instances in which a few negroes play and sing for the whites
> serve to bring out the combined features of restrained song and the
> music of the instrument.[72]

None of the other early reports of blues is as extensive and detailed as Odum's, but, taken together, they help to fill out the picture of the development of the song-form. E.C. Perrow, in a large collection of folk songs gathered from whites and blacks in various southern states mainly before 1910, prints only one blues.[73] This blues was collected in Mississippi in 1909 and contains the line, "I've got the blues; I'm too damn mean to talk," a line very similar to one reported by Odum from Georgia. While Perrow reported only one blues, Henry C. Davis reported none at all in a 1914 collection of fifteen black secular songs from South Carolina.[74] John Jacob Niles, however, gives a very interesting description of Jack Spicer, an itinerant white guitarist encountered in 1908 in a saloon near Pikeville, Kentucky.[75] Spicer sang traditional southern white mountain lyric songs, like "I Wish I Was a Mole in the Ground," "Careless Love," and "Who'll Rock the Cradle," but he recast them into twelve-bar AAB and ABB stanzas. Spicer would have been an interesting person to interview further about possible black-white musical interchange, but unfortunately he was killed four years later.

In 1912 Will H. Thomas printed a few more blues texts from Texas, including one titled "The Railroad Blues," which also contained the line, "I got the blues, but I am too damn'd mean to cry."[76] The latter song had an AAB stanza structure. In 1914 Anna Kranz Odum, the wife of Howard Odum, printed the texts of two blues or field blues collected in Sumner County, Tennessee.[77] She noted that both were sung in a high pitch, apparently unlike the other songs she collected.

One of the most intriguing and frustrating of the early reports of blues comes from W. Prescott Webb.[78] He tells of meeting a young singer named Floyd Canada in a Beeville, Texas, pool hall, in 1915, who performed blues to the accompaniment of guitar, banjo, and harmonica. Canada sang a song to the tune of "The Dallas Blues" which ran to a length of eighty stanzas of four lines each, rhyming in couplets. It is likely that Webb simply combined two AB stanzas to make the quatrains. Whatever the case, if Webb's account is correct, this song would be the longest blues ever recorded. It is possible that Canada sang several blues to the same or a similar tune, a common enough practice in the folk blues, and that Webb simply ran them together. We are unlikely to find out what Webb did, however, because he printed only thirty-three of the eighty quatrains and rearranged them into five sections of reasonably coherent subject matter: the singer's wandering, the mother and home he has left, his sweetheart, domestic troubles and quarrels, and trouble with the law. Webb called this song variously "The Railroad Blues" and "The African Iliad," the latter because he believed it told the full story of the modern Negro, "what the negro held to be of highest importance, . . . his desires and aims, his love and hate, his ethical and chivalrous ideas, his philosophy of life, code of morals, and idea of the future."[79] Although Webb was stereotyping all blacks on the basis of one song, the piece nevertheless does show the broad range of subjects covered by the blues. Because of Webb's tampering with the text, it is mainly useful as an inventory of traditional blues verses.

In 1917 John A. Lomax published an article containing a number of blues lyrics from his earlier fieldwork in Texas.[80] Most of his texts, however, are actually composites from his own collectanea and those of Odum and Perrow. Lomax's article is the first after Odum's to attempt any significant analysis of the songs, if we exclude the rather amateurish attempts by Webb and Will Thomas. All four of these men were white southerners, and all saw the lyrics of the songs they printed as reflections of the secular life of "the Negro." It did not occur to any of them that the songs dealt only with certain problem areas of black life, that they might be imaginative or even humorous exaggerations of certain facets of black life and thought, or that they might represent the lives and thoughts of only certain individuals within the larger black society. The result of their assessment was a stereotyped view of black secular society. Lomax carried this approach to its greatest extreme. While the others noted that the songs covered a broad range of experience and feeling, Lomax felt that the predominant feeling was self-pity, apparently unaware that this was balanced by grandiose fantasy and boasting. Yet Lomax was still a bit puzzled by the predominance of this feeling, for he stated that

> there surely exists no merrier-hearted race than the negro,
> especially in his natural home, the warm climate of the South. The
> negro's loud laugh may sometimes speak the empty mind, but at
> the same time it reveals a nature upon which trouble and want sit
> but lightly. . . . It is credible, at least, that the negro's self-pity is
> based on his feeling of race inferiority—a feeling of which he may
> well be only sub-consciously aware. . . . And it seems further
> credible that he has come to lump the troubles for which he himself
> is largely to blame along with the inevitable hardships of his
> situation until he has grown to regard himself as the victim of
> hard luck, generally abused by everybody; and, at least in many
> instances, he seems not averse to nursing his gloom a little.[81]

This grossly stereotyped view was related to another view held by Lomax, that "the singing of the negro . . . is largely unaffected by convention" and that "the words of his songs have usually no rigid poetic form in view and thus can become more readily a medium for spontaneous lyric expression." To Lomax, the Negro was "a na'chul bo'n singer." He stated that "the bulk of the negro's songs are not dead tradition of slavery days, are by no means past history, but are living, growing organisms mirroring his mind as it is to-day."[82] It is true that the blues Lomax printed did represent a relatively new folksong genre and that black folksong style does allow a great deal of improvisation and spontaneous expression, but by 1917 he should have been aware that he was dealing with largely traditional material, even if the tradition was a recent one. He was familiar with Odum's large collection, yet he says nothing about the processes of tradition. Lomax's belief that the Negro singer was a spontaneous improviser is probably responsible in part for his own readiness to conflate his texts with those of other collectors.

Additional important evidence of early blues was published by Mary Wheeler in 1944.[83] She had done extensive fieldwork along the Ohio and Mississippi rivers, deliberately seeking out older informants in an attempt to recover the folksongs associated with the steamboats and the various river industries of an earlier era. Although many of her texts are worksongs and ballads, or otherwise predate the blues in their origin, she does manage to give a good number of blues texts and tunes, some of which evidently had instrumental accompaniment. They almost certainly represent the kind of blues sung at the turn of the century. There is a great variety of stanza patterns, and most of the verses are traditional. Wheeler sometimes prints variant texts and shows an awareness that she is dealing with traditional material in such statements as the following: "'I'm goin' up the rivuh' or 'down the rivuh' are favorite beginnings for songs in various moods—usually plaints containing familiar lines that mirror the hardships of the life of the deck hand."[84] Wheeler's collection sets a standard of reporting we might have wished for the other early collections.

Despite the gaps of information and stereotyped interpretations of many of these early reports, in the aggregate they give a fairly good picture of blues around the turn of the century and shortly thereafter, a picture that is confirmed by our knowledge of later folk blues. The early blues were definitely folksongs and used many traditional verses. Field blues and quartet blues were reported, but a great number of the blues were accompanied by musical instruments. Unfortunately, it is this aspect of these songs that the reports leave the least clear. The textual orientation of the early writers led them to give few details about the vocal melodies and almost none about the instrumental parts. However, several of them do mention instruments being played, and the general pattern of the information points to the prevalence of stringed instruments in the country and small towns, and of pianos in the cities. Most of the singers were male, particularly those who played instruments. Two female singers, however, Ophelia Simpson and Ma Rainey, are mentioned as performing in traveling shows, and others sang locally or for themselves. The performance contexts of the early blues were quite varied. Blues were sung on the streets, on riverboats, at railroad stations, poolhalls, bars, barrelhouses, brothels, house parties, dances, medicine shows, in jailhouses, for courting, for general socializing, occasionally for whites, and when alone. In these various contexts the blues could function both as group entertainment and as personal expression.

Social Origins of the Blues

Why did the blues originate among black people in the 1890s rather than at some earlier time? The answer is probably related to social factors affecting black people at that time. It is important to realize that the 1890s coincided with the coming to maturity of the first generation of blacks born out of slavery. It was almost certainly this generation that created the blues. Jelly Roll Morton told Alan Lomax of the young pimps and gamblers of New Orleans who played and enjoyed the blues. John A. Lomax pointedly contrasts the younger blues singers with the older singers of traditional slave songs. Howard W. Odum also contrasts the younger singers from whom he collected with "the old-time negro."[85] Finally, W. Prescott Webb noted that Floyd Canada was a young man of about twenty-seven, and he contrasted Canada's songs with others of "the ante-bellum darky" that he had collected.[86]

This was certainly an appropriate time for young blacks to create the blues, those songs of uncertainty and tension, for they had been brought up in a world of problems and enormous difficulties without the experience of an older generation to fall back on. The attitudes of older blacks were a response to slavery, and their songs reflected this in large part. Slavery was brutal and oppressive, but it offered the black a well-defined role as an anonymous member of a slave society whose basic physical needs would be taken care of by his master. Post-Reconstruction "freedom," in contrast, offered black people economic independence, individualism, industrial life, and the chance for a greater expression of love and family responsibility. It also, however, left blacks educationally and economically unprepared to cope with this new responsibility and sense of individualism and with the economic competiton of industrial life. It offered, as well, racial discrimination, Jim Crow laws, the Ku Klux Klan, jail, the chain gang, sharecropping, and the life of the itinerant worker. If economic failure, breakup of the family, and a desire to escape through travel resulted from these conditions, it is no wonder. And it is no wonder that the blues arose at this time.[87]

This period was, in fact, a time of great musical ferment in general in the black community, as older forms were abandoned or greatly modified and new forms were invented. Besides the blues, the period around the turn of the century saw the creation and flowering of the cakewalk, ragtime, jazz, the blues ballad, barbershop quartet singing, black gospel music, and pentecostal music. It also saw the first flowering of black classical music, poetry, and fine arts.[88] It was a period of unprecedented opportunity for those blacks who were equipped to take advantage of it, but for many others it was a period of terrible hardship and frustration. Of course, blacks were not the only people who had problems at this time. Many poor whites suffered from some of the same problems, though they did not have to face the added burden of racial discrimination. Whites even participated in and shared in the creation of some of these musical forms at a very early period, particularly the blues ballad, ragtime, and barbershop quartet singing. Yet there can be no doubt that blacks as a whole felt the problems of this age more acutely and were generally the leaders in these new musical developments. Whites, in fact, perhaps in response to this great musical creativity among blacks, created a new popular song form that parodied the life-style and self-expression of young blacks, the "coon song."[89] Some blacks even learned to perform and compose these parodies, a further sign of the confusion of the times.

The blues, then, arose in a time of both opportunity and confusion, a time particularly of problems for young black people who had grown up in a "freedom" they did not fully understand. Many of these problems were not faced exclusively by black people, but they were more acute for blacks. To the extent that whites faced or understood such problems, the blues may have appealed to them also. Perhaps the awareness on the part of black people of the universality of many of these problems helped them to feel more a part of the world, even if their position was a tenuous one at the bottom of the social ladder. Whenever an awareness of such problems and the great difficulty of overcoming them has persisted, the blues have had an appeal.

Origins of the Blues Form

In the preceding discussion of early blues, the field blues or field holler has often been mentioned. Many of the early writers did not distinguish between these songs and instrumentally accompanied blues. It is obvious that the two are closely related. The relationship would seem to be that the hollers have served as a major source for the creation of the blues. Most blues writers are agreed on this point.[90] Though many hollers are wordless or textually very simple and repetitious, their melodic and thematic characteristics are generally in accord with those of the blues. The main difference is that the field hollers are much freer and more embellished melodically and rhythmically, probably because their form is not restricted by an instrumental accompaniment.

Many of the texts and tunes printed by Charles Peabody, Gates Thomas, John Lomax, and Mary Wheeler were actually hollers or unaccompanied field blues. There is considerable evidence that the holler was sung by blacks during slavery.[91] One of its earliest appearances in print was in a journal kept by Frances Anne Kemble on a coastal Georgia plantation in 1839. She wrote the following about a slave song that she overheard:

> To one, an extremely pretty, plaintive, and original air, there was but one line, which was repeated with a sort of wailing chorus—
>
> "Oh! my massa told me, there's no grass in Georgia."
>
> Upon inquiring the meaning of which, I was told it was supposed to be the lamentation of a slave from one of the more northerly states, Virginia or Carolina, where the labor of hoeing the weeds, or grass as they call it, is not nearly so severe as here, in the rice and cotton lands of Georgia.[92]

Kemble could easily have been describing an unaccompanied version of one of Odum's "one-verse songs."

The singing of hollers did not end with Abolition but lingered on wherever blacks continued in agricultural work and other heavy labor, such as among the river roustabouts. Johann Tonsor, writing on black singing from Louisville, Kentucky, in 1892, mentioned hearing "a distant chorus, rising and falling in unearthly, plaintive cadences, like the moaning of the wind or the cry of a lost spirit."[93] Tonsor observed the singing of a note that was "neither A nor yet A flat, but between the two," [94] in other words, a blue note. Tonsor stated that this was probably an African trait. He noted also, as did John Lomax some years later, that women would sing while working. He stated, "It is quite a common thing for the negro women to improvise words and music while they are at work, a sort of Wagnerian 'melos,' or endless melody, as it were. I have often heard them drone softly thus all through the livelong, bright summer day."[95] Tonsor must have been hearing the kind of singing which, within a few years, would be transformed into the blues.

Hollers have continued over the years to provide words, melodies, and much of its general vocal freedom to blues singing. They have even entered the southern white folksinging tradition as part of a general pattern of borrowing from black music over the years.[96] Hollers are not encountered so often today simply because much agricultural and other heavy work has become mechanized. A black tractor driver could not hear himself holler over the noise of the motor, nor would a man driving home from work in an automobile, rather than riding a mule, be likely to feel the urge to holler. Levees are no longer built by hand labor. One has to go deep into the country or to some of the archaic southern prison farms to hear hollering today.

Folk blues singers themselves tend to attribute the origin of blues singing to the field hollers. Eddie "Son" House, a Mississippi blues singer, says:

> People wonder a lot about where the blues came from. Well, when I was coming up, people did more singing in the fields than they

*did anywhere else. Time they got to the field, they'd start singing
some kind of old song. Tell his ol' mule, "Giddup there!," and he'd
go off behind the mule, start plowing and start a song. Sang to the
mule or anybody. Didn't make any difference. We'd call them old
corn songs, old long meter songs. They'd make it sound good, too.
You could hear them half-a-mile off, they'd be singing so loud.
Especially just before sundown. They sure would go a long ways.
Then they called themselves, "got the blues." That's what they
called the blues. Them old long meter songs. You'd hear them
talking and one would say, "You know ol' so-and-so really can
sing the blues!" They didn't use any instruments. Just natural
voice. They could make them rhyme, though, just like the blues do
now, but it would just be longer meter. Holler longer before they
say the word. They'd sing about their girl friend or about almost
anything—mule—anything. They'd make a song out of it just to
be hollering.[97]*

By "long meter," House means that words were drawn out and highly
ornamented, as in the singing of "long meter" hymns in black Baptist
and Methodist churches, songs which are also unaccompanied by any
instrument.

Booker White, also from Mississippi, attributed the origin of the
blues to men in the country relaxing after a hard day's work:

*That's where the blues start from, back across them fields, you
know, under them old trees, under them old log houses, you know.
Guys will sit there at night—the moon was shining—and drink,
you know. . . . It didn't start in no city, now. Don't never get that
wrong. It started right behind one of them mules or one of them
log houses, one of them log camps or the levee camp. That's where
the blues sprung from. I know what I'm talking about.[98]*

Jack Owens, a farmer and a blues singer, described how he still
composes blues in the original manner:

*See, you just be out in the fields. Sometimes you strike a little tune,
something like that, and it come to you. Something like that. Then
you come back and strike your box [i.e., guitar] and start to hum
it on your box. When you know anything, you got a little tune.
That's the way I do all the time. . . . And when I get the tune with
my voice and the box, I got it. . . . It's kind of hard to do, I'll tell
you, but I does it.[99]*

This very process of transition from field holler to accompanied
blues is demonstrated by Othar Turner, also a Mississippi farmer, in a
song that he calls "just the old cornfield blues."[100] Turner's text is
highly repetitive, and in both an unaccompanied version of the song
and one accompanied by the guitar he sings the same kind of long,
strident, highly ornamented, descending lines. The only important
musical difference between the two versions is that when he accom-
panies himself, he leaves spaces between the sung lines for his simple,
highly percussive, guitar playing. His song must be close to the sound
of the first accompanied blues.

The more rhythmic group labor songs, also a very old form with African antecedents, have had some influence on the blues. Samuel Charters, for example, shows how the first line of Ishmon Bracey's "Saturday Blues" (Victor 21349) is like that of a typical group work-song.[101] In addition, most of these worksongs make use of blue notes. The common twelve-bar AAB blues pattern, however, is not normally performed by a work group, and in any case the blues are normally sung by only a single voice. The influence of group worksongs on the blues, therefore, could be of only secondary importance, compared to that of the solo field holler.

Some writers have also tried to make a case for the influence of spirituals on the blues.[102] Indeed, as we have just noted, blues singer Son House compared his "corn songs" to "long meter" hymns. There is a similar degree of emotional depth in the best blues and spiritual singing, but the actual influence of the spirituals on blues could have been of only the most general sort. Many blacks have their first singing experiences in church, and in this sense the singing of spirituals could have stylistically affected some blues singing. But such stylistic features would be those that characterize black vocal music in general. There is very little actual similarity between the blues and church songs in respect to stanza patterns, melodies, or lyrics. Almost all of the spirituals are in couplet or quatrain form, and the older ones were normally sung by groups rather than solo.

Alan Lomax has proposed that four-line southern white mountain songs, like "Careless Love," provided the mold into which the hollers were poured in order to form the blues.[103] This suggestion might explain the origins of four-line AAAA and AAAB blues through a tailoring of the loose field hollers to the fixed eight-bar and sixteen-bar patterns of white folksong. The particular song "Careless Love," however, was not likely to have been a model for the blues, since its second line usually ends on the major second of the scale, a characteristic rarely found in blues melodies. Furthermore, we cannot be certain whether "Careless Love" is of white or black origin, as it is known in both traditions.

In our search for immediate antecedents of the blues form, we should essentially be seeking an accompaniment pattern for the blues vocal. Most four-line white mountain songs were probably sung unaccompanied around the turn of the century. Furthermore, most blues approximate the three-line, twelve-bar AAB pattern. The loose field hollers by themselves do not provide a form or pattern for most blues but instead serve more as raw material for the blues. Therefore, I find Paul Oliver's suggestion the most plausible, that the field holler vocal was combined with one of the common harmonic accompaniment patterns of the blues ballad.[104] Blues ballads are narrative folksongs that tell a story in a very loose, subjective manner and tend to "celebrate" events rather than relate them chronologically and objectively in the manner of other American folk ballads. Most of the blues ballads whose subjects can be dated would appear to have been composed between 1890 and 1910, although some, like "John Henry," refer to earlier events.[105] They have been sung, quite often with instrumental accompaniment, by both black and white singers, and the original composers of most are unknown. A great many of them have twelve-bar stanza patterns with three vocal lines and the standard chord progression of blues accompaniment. The vocal lines consist of a rhymed couplet and a one-line refrain. The same refrain is repeated in each stanza. Typical blues ballads that often fit this pattern are "Frankie and Albert," "Delia," "Railroad Bill," "Stagolee," "The Boll Weevil," and "McKinley's Gone" ("White House Blues"). Mississippi John Hurt's recording of "Frankie" could be taken as an example of this pattern. The melody of the first stanza is transcribed below with the chords suggested by the picked guitar accompaniment printed above each measure.[106] Hurt was born in Teoc, Mississippi, in 1892 and spent most of his life in nearby Avalon as a farm worker.[107] His 1928 recording of this piece is probably typical of the way it was performed around 1910 and earlier. (The symbol → indicates an acceleration of the tempo over the course of the performance.)

Example 1. "Frankie." Mississippi John Hurt, vocal and guitar in open G tuning (DBGDGD). Memphis, Feb. 14, 1928. Okeh 8560, reissued on *American Folk Music, Volume One, Ballads,* Folkways FA 2951, 12" double LP.

The harmonic pattern of the accompaniment to this piece can be seen to be basically the same as that of a typical twelve-bar blues (Fig. 1, p. 23). Hurt extends the IV chord into the seventh measure and in some stanzas cuts short the twelfth measure to begin a new stanza or instrumental chorus, but these are typical of the variation one finds in twelve-bar patterns and should cause no concern. There are, however, some major differences from the typical blues stanza pattern that we discussed earlier. One difference is the extremely fast tempo of the piece. Hurt begins at ♩ = 208 and by the end has accelerated to ♩ = 230. This is about twice as fast as an average blues tempo, though it is fairly typical of accompaniments to blues ballads using this pattern. Another difference is that Hurt's piece has very short breaks of only a quarter rest after the first and second vocal lines, while most blues have over a measure of rest. In Hurt's song, as in most other blues ballads using this pattern, these two lines are each slightly over three measures in length. Blues vocal lines, however, are usually only slightly over two measures in length. In fact, Hurt's first two lines use a different meter from that of the blues. They are simply a very loose form of the meter typical of Anglo-American balladry, a quatrain that alternates lines of four and three iambic feet. If we were to write Hurt's two lines in this ballad meter, they would look like this:

$$(\smile) - | \smile\ - | \smile\ - | (\smile) - |$$
Frankie was a good girl,

$$(\smile) | \smile\ - | \smile\ - |$$
Ev'rybody know.

$$\smile\ \ - | \smile\ - | \smile\ - | (\smile) - |$$
She paid a hundred dollars

$$\smile\ - | \smile\ \ \ \smile\ - | \smile\ - |$$
For Albert's one suit of clothes.

Hurt's third line is the refrain, which is repeated in every stanza with only slight variation. It is in a typical blues metrical pattern with a caesura in the middle, something not found in the first two lines.

Hurt's pattern, as noted earlier, is typical of a number of well-known blues ballads. It must have been adapted to the nonnarrative blues in the following way. First, the tempo was slowed down considerably. This was done because new types of couple and individual dances, which required slower tempos, were replacing the older square dances and others with called figures. Quite likely the twelve-bar AB-refrain' pattern of the blues ballad was played at the slower tempo by string bands and guitarists as an instrumental piece for dancing. Then people began adding singing derived from the field hollers. With the slower tempo it became possible to take longer breaks after the first two vocal lines and let the instruments respond to the singing. The result was the blues.

If such was the case, we should expect to find transitional pieces exemplifying this process, and we do. Howard W. Odum, for instance, prints a number of texts of lyric songs, evidently blues, with an AB-refrain pattern.[108] These demonstrate the change from narrative to lyric, still using the blues ballad stanza pattern. There are, as well, a few narrative ballads that have been cast into an AAA or AAB blues stanza pattern with instrumental breaks after each line. Probably the best known of these is "Joe Turner," a song about a penal officer, actually named Joe Turney, who transported convicts in Tennessee between 1892 and 1896.[109] Many musicians call the song a "blues," even though it has a narrative thread. From the standpoint of its stanza structure it is, of course, a blues, yet its narrative text makes it a blues ballad. Some of the early singers of this piece may have been uncomfortable with the longer breaks at the ends of the first and second lines, for there is a tendency in some performances to fill these in with a vocal phrase such as "Oh, Lordy." Handy prints a version, set to a typical twelve-bar blues chord progression, containing the following stanza:

> *He come wid fo'ty links of chain, Oh Lawdy.*
> *Come wid fo'ty links of chain, Oh Lawdy.*
> *Got my man and gone.*[110]

Several early blues texts also display this trait at the ends of lines.[111]

Lucius Smith, a Mississippi banjo player born in 1885, who began playing around 1902, describes "Joe Turner" as the origin of all blues. Smith uses a twelve-bar pattern with stanzas that are sometimes AAB and sometimes AAA. After the first line he usually sings, "Oh Lord," thus filling out the space at the end. Smith says that Joe Turner was a handcuffed prisoner who escaped from a moving train. Of the song's beginning, around 1900, he says:

> *That's old "Joe Turner" when it first came in, maybe seventy years*
> *ago. . . . All these blues come from "Joe Turner" more or less. . . .*
> *"Tell me Joe Turner done come" [a line from the song]. . . . See,*
> *when "Joe Turner" first come in, it wasn't in the blues way. And*
> *they changed it to the blues, all, you see.*[112]

Lucius Smith played for many years in Sid Hemphill's string band, a group that performed mainly older reels and blues ballads for set dancing. He vividly recalls the slowing of the tempo in the music when the blues arrived on the scene and the accompanying change in the dancing and audience behavior. Here he describes the difference between the two forms of music:

> *Blues is, I'd say, a whole lots of difference. It's owing to the*
> *dances, new dancing. Now the blues is swinging dancing, like*
> *double together, you know. . . . That done ruined the country. The*
> *blues done ruined the country. . . . It just make 'em go off at*
> *random, I'd say, frolicing, random, you see. More folks have got*
> *killed since they start playing the blues than ever been. It's just a,*
> *you know, just a out of order piece. Now such as "Walking in the*
> *Parlor" and all them other old pieces, that's dancing on a set, . . .*
> *calling figures, promenade, swing your right partner, all that, you*
> *know, object partner, you see. But the "Memphis Blues" and all*
> *that, it done brought about a whole lots of it, you know, I'd say,*
> *trouble. They started that "Memphis." That's these young folks.*
> *Started that "Memphis." Hear 'em say, "Oh, do it once for me!"*
> *Done started a mess then. You see it. You see it. I done told you.*
> *Makes a racket, you know, with young folks, you see. But that*
> *other dancing, it didn't have time to make no racket, 'cause you*
> *got to pick up your foots and go. I'll tell you. But all that old stuff*
> *is but eternity, the blues, you know. Yonder got all in the church*
> *houses and everything. It's just something kind of out of order like,*
> *you know. Oh, it done got everywhere, the blues. It done got*
> *everywhere. . . . It's just kind of, you know, old drunkards, you*
> *know, frolicing. . . . Now we have been in places, you know, and*
> *somebody would ask Sid Hemphill maybe to play a waltz. And*
> *they in there playing, hollering and singing the blues across him.*

You see, well, this brings about eternity, that blues does. Sometimes
he had to close down. "I can't play. They singing something else,
you know." See, I just call it a racket. The blues ain't nothing but
a racket. A whole lot of drunk folks, you know, don't care for
nothing, and they just bring eternity, the blues do. Heap of folks
love to hear it, but it just brings eternity. A lot of trouble while
that stuff going on, you know. Oh, I don't care. Don't none of it
bother me, 'cause I ain't no racket man. It don't bother me, but it's
just a racket thing. It get all in your home, tear up the church
house, everything. The blues do. You hear 'em hollering, "Play the
'Memphis Blues'." They gonna start something. You can't do
nothing with 'em. Get a little drink in 'em, and that's just trouble.
It's just a racket, you know.[113]

Smith is a conservative, and his views are representative of the
preblues generation. His is the complaint of every older generation in
America against the music of the young. The blues have not proven as
socially disruptive as Smith claims, but they can be considered as representative of a new social outlook. Certainly the lyrics of the blues display, in general, a greater seriousness and awareness of the world than
did the older secular dance songs of the nineteenth century with their
emphasis on humor, animal activities, and slave life. The blues also
represented a greater spirit of individualism in the black community.
They were often performed by self-accompanied individuals, in contrast to the older music performed by aggregations like Sid Hemphill's
four-piece string band. The individual and couple dancing done "at
random" to the blues could also be considered a model of greater individualism among blacks, in contrast to the square dance, a model of a
more cohesive, cooperative community. Finally, the blues were sung in
the first person, while much of the older music was sung in the third
person about animals or folk heroes of the black community.

Characteristics of Early Folk Blues

The blues are not, however, totally individualistic, for while in their
first person delivery they purport to express the sentiments and feelings of the singer, many of their verses are, in fact, traditional and
known to thousands of blues singers and members of their audiences.
If these verses were ever original and unique, they did not remain so
for long. They entered the oral tradition and spread throughout black
communities across the country. Out of 108 blues texts in the early
sources surveyed above, I can find only eight that do not use variants
of recognizably traditional lines and stanzas. The most individualistic
blues of them all is the one reported by John Jacob Niles as sung by
Ophelia Simpson. In eleven three-line AAB stanzas Ms. Simpson tells
how she killed her husband and has been sent to prison, how she is
afraid of hanging, and how she wishes that her other man from New
Orleans would do something to help her.[114] The song is rooted in a
particular experience, one that can easily be reconstructed from the lyrics. Significantly this song is the composition of a professional travel-

Lucius Smith. Photo by Cheryl T. Evans.

ing singer, one of the early popularizers of the blues, a person whom we might expect to be more individualistic in her songs.

The vast majority of early blues texts, however, employ traditional verses, and most of them do not maintain a single coherent theme throughout the song. If we omit from our survey the various single-stanza blues, the conflations of John Lomax, and Webb's "African Iliad," we find that only thirty-eight texts maintain a single coherent theme, while fifty-eight do not. Many of the more thematic blues are on such topics as jailhouse experiences, railroads and hoboing, and work. A typical example of this type is a blues collected by Odum in Lafayette County, Mississippi.[115]

Example 2. "K. C." Unknown artist. Lafayette Co., Miss., 1905–08.

1. *Well, I thought I heard that K. C. whistle blow,*
   Blow lak' she never blow befo'.

2. *I believe my woman's on that train,*
   Oh babe! I b'lieve my woman's on that train.

3. *She comin' back from sweet ole Alabam',*
   She comin' to see her lovin' man.

4. *Fireman, put in a little mo' coal,*
   Run dat train in some lonesome hole.

Most of these lines are traditional and appear in different combinations with other lines in other blues. There is no way of knowing what personal meaning, if any, this song might have had to the anonymous singer, but the scene which the singer creates is obvious. The singer hears the whistle of a train on which his woman is probably riding, returning to him from Alabama. He wishes that the train would go faster, even if it means speeding at a reckless pace.

Contrast the preceding with another blues from the same county in Mississippi.[116]

Example 3. "Baby, You Sho' Lookin' Warm." Unknown artist. Lafayette Co., Miss., 1905–08.

1. *Baby, you sho' lookin' warm,: [three times]*
   O my babe! you sho' lookin' warm.

2. *Baby, I'm feelin' so tired,: [three times]*
   O my babe! I'm feelin' so tired.

3. *Got no whar' to lay my weary head,: [three times]*
   O my babe! got no whar' to lay my weary head.

4. *Sometimes I'm fallin' to my face,: [three times]*
   O my babe! sometimes I'm fallin' to my face.

5. *I'm goin' whar' de water drinks like wine. [as before]*

6. *Gwine whar' I never been befo'. [as before]*

7. *Baby, I love the clothes you wear. [as before]*

8. *War' in de worl' my baby gone? [as before]*

9. *Gone away never come back no more. [as before]*

Again, most, if not all, of the verses are traditional. But in this piece there appear to be four distinct themes. Stanzas 1 and 7 are compliments addressed to a woman. Stanzas 2, 3, and 4 are an admission of weariness by the singer with, perhaps, connotations of failure in life and of desperation. In stanzas 5 and 6 a more confident mood is apparent, as the singer asserts his independence and readiness to strike out for parts unknown. In stanzas 8 and 9 the singer's woman has left him, apparently for good. The only unifying element in these themes is the phrase, "O my babe!," in the last line of each stanza, but this phrase hardly makes the song thematically coherent.

Odum was quite aware of this lack of coherence in many of the texts that he printed. He offered the following explanation for it:

> The negro song often begins with one conception of a theme, and ends with another entirely foreign to the first, after passing through various other themes. This may be explained by the fact that when the negro begins to sing, he loves to continue, and often passes from one song to another without pausing. In time he mingles the two or more songs. Most of the groups and "socials," and especially the dance, require continuous music for a longer period of time than the average song will last. It thus happens that the negro could sing the great majority of his songs to a single tune, if the necessity called for it; although it is likely that the last part of his melody would scarcely be recognizable as that with which he began. In words, as in music, variation seems unlimited.[117]

Odum felt that these songs were unclassifiable and that the best he could do would be to arrange them by subject, although even here he recognized problems. He stated: "Themes are freely mingled; verses, disjointed and inconsequential, are sung to many tunes and variations. Repetition of words and thought is thus most common. Each song may consist of a number of themes, which in turn are sung to other songs of other subject-matter."[118]

From these statements Odum would appear to have believed that each verse was properly part of a thematically coherent song. Yet for some peculiar reason, as Odum believed, black singers never made the texts of these songs long enough to last out the dancing. Hence they had to draw verses at random from other songs and add them onto the pieces they were performing. This was a good attempt at explanation, certainly more tenable than John Lomax's later explanation that these songs were products of spontaneous creation; nevertheless Odum was only partially correct. As shall be demonstrated, folk blues singers often do add verses to their blues in order to lengthen them, but they do not necessarily draw them from other songs to which they more properly belong, nor do they concatenate songs in such a random fashion as Odum suggested. Odum's mistake was not looking at individual performers to see how they handled their repertoires. Instead, he treated his informants as anonymous representatives of the black secular community, who apparently all thought and acted alike. He constantly referred to "the negro" and never suggested that different performers might treat their song material differently. Of course, in all fairness, such was not the main concern of this pioneer American sociologist and folklorist, and we must be thankful to him for a report that surpasses all the other early ones combined in length, insight, and quality.

When Odum wrote in 1911, the blues were perhaps too new a phenomenon for him to grasp fully their nature and characteristics. Certainly many of the texts that he collected do appear incoherent, yet if Odum had understood that ambiguity and contrast were basic to the nature of folk blues, he might have viewed this incoherence as normal and even appropriate. If we look at Example 3 with these criteria in mind, we find that it is, in fact, a rather well constructed blues. The four themes can be grouped into two contrasting pairs: the praise of the woman's appearance (1 and 7) contrasted with the bedraggled condition of the singer (2, 3, and 4), and the singer's intention of leaving (5 and 6) contrasted with the fact that the woman has already left (8 and 9). Both of these contrasts are extremely common in the folk blues and could be considered basic structural patterns. These four themes are held together by the phrase, "O my babe," addressed to some anonymous woman. The song is, in actuality, addressed to the entire audience, but by maintaining the convention of addressing the words to a woman, the singer makes this blues take on the appearance of a courtship monologue, in which the singer uses four tried and true methods of winning a woman's affection. He praises her, appeals for her sympathy (the abject lover ploy!), asserts his own independence, and expresses his desperation when she leaves or threatens to leave. This blues, then, is not as incoherent as it first seems, for the structural configuration provides meanings which the words in themselves do not convey.

From this early period up to about 1915, we have over a hundred blues texts of varying length, giving us a fair understanding of early blues lyricism. Unfortunately, outside of the few descriptions by Odum and other early observers, and a handful of tune transcriptions (the best ones being by Wheeler), we have little direct knowledge of the musical side of the early folk blues. We can, however, reconstruct the music with some assurance from the performances of artists who were active at that time but who did not record until after 1920. If such artists are like the majority of later folk blues artists, their styles of performance were shaped by the kinds of blues that they first heard and tried to play. Some of the folk blues singers who were active performers in the early twentieth century and who made commercial recordings beginning in the 1920s were Charley Patton (born between 1881 and 1890), Willie Brown (born between 1890 and 1895), Joshua "Peg Leg" Howell (born in 1888), and Gus Cannon (born in 1883). The picture provided by artists like these is supplemented by recent field recordings of blues veterans such as Elijah Brown (born in 1895), Herb Quinn (born in 1896), and Myrt Holmes (born in 1890).[119] All of these artists use mainly traditional lyrics, usually not arranged in a coherent fashion to develop a single theme. In the tonal and rhythmic characteristics of both singing and instrumental accompaniment, the blues of these men are fairly typical of blues in general. Syncopation and blue notes are found throughout their performances. The recordings also reveal a great variety of distinctive melodies and instrumental techniques, such as bottleneck or "slide" guitar style and various percussive effects. But perhaps the most distinctive musical feature of these blues is their metrical variety. While the standard twelve-bar pattern can be found, it is only one pattern of many. Not only are eight- and sixteen-bar blues also found, but such patterns as 13½ and 14½ bars appear frequently. Out of twenty-two blues stanza patterns of Charley Patton transcribed by John Fahey, only six conformed to the twelve-bar model, and even some of these were not maintained throughout the song or were otherwise anomalous. Besides a standard two-line eight-bar blues, the remainder of Patton's blues display such three-line patterns as 11½, 12¼, 12½, 13, 13½, 14, and 14½ bars, and there is even one four-line blues with a 15¼-bar pattern.[120] Furthermore, many performers vary the number of bars in each stanza in a single piece, usually by repeating an instrumental figure or "riff" as many times as they wish at the end of a vocal line. Patton does this in several of his blues. Herb Quinn varies every stanza of his "Casey, You Can't Ride This Train," a blues played in knife style and a textual variant of some blues printed by Odum.[121] Quinn's five three-line stanzas contain the following number of measures: 11 (3½ + 3½ + 4); 11 (4 + 3½ + 3½); 12½ (3½ + 4½ + 4½); 12 (3½ + 3½ + 5); and 12½ (3½ + 4 + 5). We would find even further variation if we were to include his guitar choruses. It should be obvious, then, that if the twelve-bar AAB pattern served as a mold for early blues, it did not remain a very firm one. The overall impression one gets from these early blues is one of great freedom and variety in the use, arrangement, and combination of traditional lyrics, melodic ideas, and accompaniment patterns and techniques.

The Folk Blues Aesthetic

The fact that early blues lacked a standardized form might be taken as an indication that the blues singers and their folk audiences lacked agreement on an aesthetic standard. But, in fact, there is one overriding standard for all of the early blues and for later folk blues as well. This standard becomes obvious when one talks to any older blues singer. Rubin Lacy, a blues singer born in Mississippi in 1901 who later became a preacher,[122] stated it simply:

> Sometimes I preach now, and I get up and tell the people now that I used to be a famous blues singer, and I told more truth in my blues than the average person tells in his church songs. . . . If you're playing the blues, you say, "I never missed my water 'til my well went dry." That's the truth. If you got a well where you get your water, when it go dry, you miss it. You got to go somewhere else and hunt a well, ain't you? You got a wife and she quit you, you may not miss her 'til she quit you. She quit you and you want her back or some other one, don't you? Well, that's the truth.[123]

Here we see the essence of the folk blues. It is telling the truth. The example that Lacy offers is drawn from one of the oldest traditional blues stanzas, one used by many other singers:[124]

> *I never missed my water 'til my well went dry.*
> *I never missed my rider 'til she said good-bye.*

This truth, then, is not necessarily drawn from the singer's personal experience or his thoughts at the time of singing. It may be instead a generalized kind of truth. Lacy explains:

> *Sometimes I'd propose as it happened to me in order to hit*
> *somebody else, 'cause everything that happened to one person has*
> *at some time or other happened to another one. If not, it will. You*
> *make the blues maybe hitting after someone else, and all the same*
> *time it's hitting you too. Some place it's gonna hit you.*[125]

One of Lacy's own blues makes his point clear. In 1928 he recorded "Mississippi Jail House Groan," a blues he had learned before 1920 from an older musician in his hometown of Pelahatchie. It is in the twelve-bar form, but, as with many early folk blues, the guitar ac-

Reverend and Mrs. Rubin Lacy. Photo by David Evans.

companiment remains based in the tonic chord with only faint suggestions of the subdominant harmony in the ninth and tenth measures achieved by the inclusion of the fourth (G) in a sequence otherwise based in the tonic chord. In the fourth measure Lacy plays a leading minor seventh but does not resolve it in the fifth measure to the subdominant harmony. He also alludes to a dominant harmony by emphasizing the fifth (A) in the first two beats of the ninth measure. Lacy helps himself to stay within the single chord by using an open D minor tuning, played in the key of D. His third string (G string) is actually tuned slightly flat, so that when he stops it at the first fret, he obtains a neutral third, which lends a very "blue" effect when played as part of the full chord. This, combined with the moaning in the first and fourth stanzas, the singing of the sharp fourth (or flatted fifth), and the brooding singing style in general, makes the piece one of the "deepest" blues ever recorded. The guitar playing is extremely percussive and uses a slow, insistent, basically duple beat, but with a slight triplet feeling. The guitar part contains a repeated descending bass figure as the "response" in measures 3, 7, and 11, and a treble ostinato pattern particularly prominent on the D note of the open first string. Lacy seems to muffle the strings much of the time with the heel of his right hand. The piece begins with a short guitar introduction. Except for the fact that the similar melodies of the first and second lines are interchangeable in some stanzas, there is little variation in the singing or guitar part from one stanza to another.[126]

Example 4. "Mississippi Jail House Groan." Rube Lacy, vocal and guitar in open D minor tuning (DAFDAD) with the third string slightly flat, key of D. Chicago, Mar., 1928. Paramount 12629, reissued on *Country Blues Encores*, Origin Jazz Library 8, 12" LP.

1. *Eeeeeh, heeeey.*
   Mmmmmm, hmmmmm.
   I promised not to holler now; now, mama, hmmmmm, hey, hey.

2. *Mmmm, laying in jail, Lord, my back turned to the wall.*
   And I laid in jail, my back turned, hmmm, to the wall.
   And I laid in jail now with my back turned to the wall.

3. *And she brought me coffee, and she brought me tea.*
   And she brought me coffee, Lord, and she brought me tea.
   She brought everything now but that lowdown jailhouse key.

4. *Hmmmmm, hmmmmm.*
   Hmmmmm, hmmmmm.
   I promised not to holler now; now, mama, now, hey, hey, hey.

5. *And my mama told me; my papa told me too.*
   And my mama told me; my papa stood and cried.
   "You got too many women now, now, for any boy your size."

6. *I looked at my mama, and I hung my head and cried.*
   I looked at my mama, and I hung my head and cried.
   "If my woman kill me now, Lord, I'm ready to die."

All of the lines and stanzas of this blues are traditional. As in many folk blues, the lyrics are not thematically coherent. The "mama" of stanzas 1 and 4 is probably a girl friend, while the "mama" of stanzas 5 and 6 is definitely the singer's mother. Only the second and third stanzas are clearly related to the title's jailhouse theme. The first and fourth stanzas simply mean that the singer is unable to restrain himself from hollering. They might mean that he is hollering because he is in jail, but probably they are meant to refer to the actual performance context of the piece. The fifth and sixth stanzas could represent a flashback to a time when the singer, as a precocious youth, was warned by his parents against having too many girl friends. Such an interpretation might imply that the singer is in jail on account of his involvement with one or more women. But if the song is thematically coherent in this manner, it is ambiguously so, and alternative interpretations such as we have noted are possible. We need not, however, seek coherence for this blues on such a superficial level, for at a deeper level the piece can be seen to be well constructed. The text is obviously divided into two equal sections, each introduced by a stanza probably related to the context of performance (1 and 4). The two sections are otherwise linked by the similarity in imagery of the singer having his

Advertisement for Rubin Lacy's "Mississippi Jail House Groan."
Reproduced from *Chicago Defender*, June 2, 1928.

back to the wall in stanza 2 and being ready to die in stanza 6. Furthermore, the statement about hollering in stanzas 1 and 4 can be compared to the crying references in stanzas 5 and 6. Finally, there is the contrast between the first section, where a faithful woman tries to help the singer but is unable to give him what he needs, and the second section, where his parents give him what he needs (good advice), but he fails to accept it and plays the field, refusing to be faithful to one woman and thereby risking his life. This piece provides a typical example of the use of the techniques of *contrast* and *association* in constructing folk blues. We shall discuss these techniques further in this study.

Lacy states that this song told the truth, although it was not an autobiographical truth:

> *You see, that didn't hit me, but it hit somebody in Mississippi. But I was in Chicago when I was making that record. I never have been no jailbird, if you want to know the truth of it. I never have been arrested for nothing but getting drunk, and I was soon out for that. I never stayed in jail no time.*[127]

Despite the fact that Lacy was a law-abiding person, he sang the song with great conviction and sincerity, and there can be no doubt that it did "hit" somebody in Mississippi. Lacy was a very well-known blues singer in Mississippi until he joined the church and became a preacher in the 1930s. He is well remembered by other blues singers from that state.

Lacy's statements about truth in blues and trying to "hit" some-one with the lyrics are paralleled by the statements of many other older blues singers. Henry Townsend feels that the heart of the blues is "the true feeling." Furry Lewis says, "All the blues, you can say, is true," and J. D. Short says, "There's so many true words in the blues, of things that have happened to so many people, and that's why it makes the feeling in the blues." Memphis Willie Borum states, "A blues is about something that's real."[128] The Reverend Robert Wilkins, also a former blues singer, says:

> *It's some kind of sorrowful feeling that you have of your own self. It's something that happened to you and cause you to become sorry or something, maybe grievous about it. Then you would compose the song to that feeling that you have. And then you would sing it and after you begin to sing it, then you become accustomed to it through psychology that 'most anybody could have that same feeling as you did. It's universal, but it don't bring joy in the spirit. The blues are true words of existence among human nature. . . . Singing blues helps to relieve your natural soul—from your natural soul—but not from a spiritual soul. The only thing you can get relief from in the spiritual soul is by praising God and giving Him thanks for ALL things, because He knows what to do, when, where, and how. . . . In blues, I'm just rhyming it for myself, but I'm thinking I'm rhyming in a way that somebody will be happy and enjoy it as I sing it.*[129]

Wilkins goes on to describe how he once composed a blues in the first person based on the experience of a friend, a bootlegger who was sent to the penitentiary.

The main aesthetic standard, then, for early folk blues was truth. But it was a truth based in universal human experience or at least a kind of experience that was known to the singer and audience. Unlike

other major forms of black folklore, the blues did not deal with the
imaginary animal world of Br'er Rabbit or the deeds of legendary heroes like John Henry and Stacker Lee. As a result of following this
standard, with its emphasis on universality, a vast body of traditional
verse material was built up, upon which blues singers were free to
draw. Along with this went traditional melodies and instrumental patterns and techniques. These too had to be delivered by the performers
with conviction and "truth." Familiarity was the rule in folk blues. Except to himself, it mattered little whether a blues was strictly a product
of the singer's own personal experience. Julius Lester states this point
well when he says, "The roots of the blues . . . are social. The rural
blues men were intent on telling their listeners what the listener already knew, but could not articulate. . . . Even the most personal blues
of the rural blues singers never said, 'Look at me!' Invariably, it said,
'Look at you!' "[130]

Early Popular Blues: Sheet Music

The blues did not long remain purely a folk product, passed orally
from one performer to another, sung mainly to small local groups, and
drawn largely from traditional material. Commercialization and popu-
larization were soon to have an effect on them. As was discussed previously, Niles noted a blues composed as early as 1898 by a professional
singer in a traveling medicine show, Ophelia Simpson. This blues on a
jailhouse theme is by far the most coherent and developed text of all
the early blues that have been reported. Later, in 1902, Gertrude "Ma"
Rainey, another traveling professional entertainer, added blues singing
to her stage act. We don't know what kinds of blues she sang at this
early period, but the dozens of blues she recorded in the 1920s are
mostly thematic in the manner of Ms. Simpson's piece. Odum too
noted the presence of semiprofessional traveling "songsters," who
went from town to town, living in part from their music. These early
trends toward professionalism, however, were simply normal popular
outgrowths of a kind of folk music with an entertainment function.
They were still basically within the folk tradition and probably did not
have a major effect on it at the time. The songs were still transmitted in
person, and it is likely that most of the traveling singers covered only a
local or regional circuit.

In 1912 a new type of blues began to compete seriously with the
older folk blues, introducing also a new aesthetic standard. In that year
four blues songs were copyrighted and subsequently published in
sheet music form.[131] Hundreds more appeared in the following years
by black composers like W. C. Handy and Perry Bradford and by some
whites as well.[132] These blues were written mostly for female singers,
who performed them, accompanied by a pianist or a jazz band, in cabarets and theaters in the metropolitan centers of the North and South
and in traveling shows in the southern towns.

The folk blues had been sung mostly by men and were composed and accompanied by the singers themselves. The blues of sheet music had none of these characteristics. There were other major differences as well in the lyrical and musical structures of the two kinds of blues. Despite the fact that the blues of sheet music drew upon the folk blues for general inspiration and for their basic tonal and rhythmic characteristics, they were very sophisticated compositions. Their lyrics almost always told a story or developed a single theme and rarely contained verses that did not pertain to this story or theme. Even though these compositions, particularly those of Handy, did often contain some lines or stanzas drawn from the traditional folk blues, such lyrics were integrated into the overall theme or story. The composers normally did not simply string various traditional stanzas together, as did the folk blues singers. Indeed, the composers considered this practice dull and primitive. For them, the folk blues' value was their potential as material to be reworked by their own talents. As W. C. Handy said of the performance of folk blues singers, "Their music wanted polishing, but it contained the essence."[133] Handy and the others used this "essence" to create something new, something that in most cases was far removed from the early folk blues. Of the inspiration that these older folk blues provided, Handy stated, "It should be clear by now that my blues are built around or suggested by, rather than constructed of, the snatches, phrases, cries and idioms such as I have illustrated."[134] Handy could take, for example, the traditional folk blues verse, "Going where the Southern cross the Dog," and construct from it a thematically coherent "Yellow Dog Blues" (copyright 1914) about a woman whose man had deserted her to go "where the Southern cross the Yellow Dog."[135]

Obviously the songwriters did not value tradition and familiarity to nearly the same extent as did the folk blues singers and their audiences. This is not surprising, for any composer who copyrights his material is going to strive for originality of expression. Since the process of songwriting gave the composer the opportunity to plan and revise his song, and since the reader of the sheet music could contemplate it at leisure, it was almost inevitable that the lyrics of the sheet music blues would be thematic or would tell a story. From a musical point of view there was also a necessity for the composers to write well structured pieces that could serve as guides to performance by the singer and accompanist. The improvisation characteristic of folk blues could not be indicated on sheet music, nor could the folk practice of sometimes varying slightly the length of stanzas. Eight-, twelve-, and sixteen-bar patterns became the norms for these composers. When they felt the need for variety, they simply followed the practice of contemporary white composers of popular songs and constructed their pieces out of two or three different musical strains. Handy, in discussing his 1914 composition, "St. Louis Blues," noted this practice, saying, "Here, as in most of my other blues, three distinct musical strains are carried as a means of avoiding the monotony that always resulted in the three-line folk blues."[136] Some of the composed pieces did not even use the three-line form or one of the other traditional stanza patterns as one of their strains. Such songs were much like other popular Tin Pan Alley pieces of the period except for the word "blues" in their titles and their use of syncopation and blue notes. They might more accurately be called "ragtime songs."

Either the subtleties of folk blues escaped the trained musical ears of Handy and his fellow composers, or, more likely, their aesthetic standards did not permit them to accept folk blues except as raw material for recreation at their own hands. The composers were sophisticated city-dwellers, often sharp businessmen whose life-styles were remote from those of the people who had first created the folk blues. The folk blues aesthetic emphasized truth in the lyrics, and musical and structural freedom within the context of the traditional and familiar, while the aesthetic of the blues songwriters emphasized storytelling, lyrical originality, and novelty within fixed musical structures.

It is difficult to judge the influence of sheet music blues of this period on the folk blues singers. Few of them could read music, and it is doubtful that they could learn much new material from a passing show. However, some of the composed blues probably did reach the folksingers at this time. One such piece was Handy's "The Hesitating Blues," which he composed in 1915 based on a traditional blues.[137] Within a year after its publication Newman White recorded three versions of the song in Auburn, Alabama.[138] All contain the song's characteristic refrain, but only one version contains stanzas from Handy's composition, and even this one contains two additional stanzas not printed by Handy. Two later versions of the song recorded by White in 1918 and 1919 contain only the refrain but no stanzas from Handy's composition.[139] It is possible that White's field-collected versions of this song are simply products of the same folk tradition that Handy drew from, but the fact that so many of them were collected so soon after the publication of Handy's song suggests some degree of influence upon them by the commercial product.

Such evidence seems to indicate that folk blues singers were simply reversing the process of the composers of blues sheet music. The composers had drawn inspiration and some textual and musical material from the folk blues. Now the folk blues singers were taking these compositions and breaking them up into smaller elements (lines, stanzas, and tune strains), which they then combined with other traditional elements to form new blues in the typical folk manner. This indicates the strength and resilience of the folk blues aesthetic. Yet by incorporating elements of the more sophisticated compositions into their songs, the folk blues singers could not help being at least partly influenced by the aesthetic of the composers. The result of this influence was that the folk blues singers themselves began composing blues in the style of the more sophisticated composers of blues sheet music. John Jacob Niles prints several examples of such compositions collected from black soldiers in France during World War I.[140] Niles also noted that the same singer could perform a blues of his own composition in the older folk manner as well as a piece from sheet music that "can be bought in every music-store in the land."[141] It would appear, then, that some folk blues singers at this time were developing a dual aesthetic for the blues.

Blues on Phonograph Records: Women Singers

In 1914 instrumental blues performed by white bands were issued on phonograph records, and the first blues vocal, a rendition of W. C. Handy's "Memphis Blues" by Morton Harvey (Victor 17657), was issued the following year.[142] Blues increased in popularity during World War I, both in America and France, and by 1919 a white vaudeville singer, Gilda Gray, was performing them in a Broadway review called "Gaieties of 1919."[143] In 1920 blues were first recorded commercially by black vocalists. In that year songwriter Perry Bradford, after encountering initial opposition, persuaded the Okeh Record Company to record some of his compositions sung by Mamie Smith, a cabaret performer, accompanied by a small orchestra.[144] The records were a success, and hundreds more followed by Mamie Smith and other female vocalists.

Before 1920 all of the record companies were uninterested in recording blues by black singers. We can assume, then, that these companies had no values or standards in regard to such blues. Their initial motivation in 1920 for recording this music at all was purely monetary. It is not surprising, then, that the sophisticated blues of the composers were recorded before the folk blues, even though both kinds were available, for the composed blues were by far the more commercialized type and had been selling successfully in sheet music and on records by white vocalists. The black singers of this type of blues attracted paying crowds at northern theaters and cabarets, and to the record companies this attraction could be translated into money from the sale of their records. Probably most of the company executives had never heard of the folk blues being played at house parties and southern juke joints.

The composed blues of the songwriters proved to be commercially successful, and until 1926 they were the main type of blues recorded by black vocalists. In the early and middle 1920s a regular craze for blues swept across America. White Tin Pan Alley songwriters began turning out many pieces called blues, though these had little relationship to folk blues except for syncopation and blue notes. Some of these pieces were recorded by the black vocalists, and many white vaudeville singers performed them as well. In 1924 George Gershwin wrote "Rhapsody in Blue," and in 1926 the black poet Langston Hughes published original poems in the blues idiom and created a minor literary stir.

By 1923 the musical trade papers had taken special notice of the blues. An unsigned article in *The Metronome*, which reads like an unpaid advertisement for the E. B. Marks Music Company ("The House of Hits"), stated,

> *The craze for "blues" is now at its height. The end is not yet. Mechanical companies are tumbling over each other in their eagerness to discover "real blues." There are bushels of inferior compositions on the market labeled "blues," but the genuine article by born writers of "blues" is as scarce as the proverbial "hen's teeth." A "real blues" has a certain "struttin' " rhythm that is irresistible. It sways the hearer almost with every note, and underneath it all there is the wail of the aborigine.[145]*

The "real blues" were said to be the compositions of blacks, and the Marks Company arranged a special tour of the South in order to obtain these blues. But the song purchasers seem to have gone only to the cities and visited only established songwriters. In Memphis and other cities they became aware of the "African Opera Series" of nine blues, and they accepted two of them. These were quickly given to a number of female recording artists. Ironically, the composer of this series of blues was a Memphis white man, Bob Miller.

Most of the "blues" of the whites could hardly be called blues at all, although the general public was content to accept such a designation for them. Many of the compositions by blacks were quite similar in style to those by white composers, but others tended to be intermediate between them and folk blues, perhaps using an occasional traditional line or tune and keeping to the three-line twelve-bar format. A. Glander, publicity representative for the General Phonograph Company in New York, which produced Okeh Records and recorded the first vocal blues by a black singer, also noted this difference between the blues of white and black composers. He said in 1923,

> *There are two distinct kinds of "blues" numbers—"white blues" and "low down blues." The former are popular numbers with a ballad strain and jazz tempo, while the "low down blues" are the typical numbers of the Southern colored folks. No white man can write "low down blues"—nor can a colored man, for that matter, unless he was born and brought up in the South. For this reason, "blues" numbers are frequently purchased from uneducated, untrained colored writers down South.[146]*

Yet these "uneducated, untrained" writers were still much more sophisticated than the folk blues singers, many of whom could write little more than their names. Charles Handy, the brother and business partner of W. C. Handy, one of the first southern black composers of blues, said,

> *There is as much thought and care given to the writing of "blues" numbers as to any other kind of music. In the lyric an attempt is always made to actually tell a story or convey a message, while harmony and the various other musical attributes are invariably taken into consideration by the high class "blues" composer. It*

might interest you to know that a good blues number could very easily be arranged for a symphony orchestra. As a matter of fact, my brother is right now making symphonic arrangements of some of his most popular blues numbers.[147]

Here is a situation where black composers who considered themselves "high class" were writing what the white music publishers and record companies considered "low down blues"! If the record companies thought they had acquired "the wail of the aborigine," they were kidding themselves.

Although the traditional content of most of these compositions ranged from moderate to minimal, many of them were quite good as popular songs. Ultimately, their effectiveness rested, as with all blues, on the degree of feeling and sincerity that the singer and her accompanists were able to convey. Many songs with poor lyrics were transformed into good blues records by enthusiastic vocals and hot jazz accompaniments. Others had good original lyrics to begin with. A small percentage of the blues sung by female singers did use traditional verses. These blues usually proved to be the compositions of the singers themselves, indicating that the singers were somewhat closer to the folk blues than were the songwriters. But the singers got the majority of their blues from others. Probably their traditional blues were songs they had learned early in their careers before becoming professional entertainers. We might take as an example of such a blues Alberta Hunter's "Down Hearted Blues." It is credited as the joint composition of the singer and Lovie Austin. Ms. Austin was a jazz pianist and arranger and was most likely responsible for the piece's musical arrangement, while Ms. Hunter probably contributed the lyrics.

Example 5. "Down Hearted Blues." Alberta Hunter, vocal; possibly accompanied by Eubie Blake's Orchestra: unknown trumpet, trombone, two clarinets, alto saxophone, piano, and tuba. New York, early July, 1922. Paramount 12005.

1. *Gee, but it's hard to love someone, when that someone don't love you.*
   I'm so disgusted, heartbroken too. I've got the downhearted blues.
   Once I was crazy about a man. He mistreated me all the time.
   The next man I get, he's got to promise to be mine, all mine.

2. *'Cause you mistreated me, and you drove me from your door.*
   You mistreated me, and you drove me from your door.
   But the Good Book says, "You've got to reap just what you sow."

3. *Trouble, trouble, seems like I've had it all my days.*
   Trouble, trouble, seems like I've had it all my days.
   Sometime I think trouble is gonna follow me to my grave.

4. *I ain't never loved but three men in my life.*
   Lord, I ain't never loved but three men in my life.
   One's my father, and my brother, and the man that wrecked my life.

5. *Now it may be a week, and it may be a month or two.*
   I said, it may be a week, and it may be a month or two.
   All the dirt you're doing to me is, honey, coming back home to you.

6. *I've got the world in a jug and the stopper in my hand.*
   I've got the world in a jug and the stopper in my hand.
   And if you want me, pretty papa, you've got to come under my command.

© 1923 by Mills Music, Inc. Copyright renewed MCA Music, Inc.
Used with permission. All rights reserved.

The first stanza of this piece is a typical sixteen-bar introduction to set the theme. Openings like this are found in many blues of the period, and the use of one in this piece would seem to be a bow to the conventions of the composers. After this original introduction, however, the piece becomes a typical twelve-bar blues with entirely traditional stanzas. The stanzas are all related to a theme of mistreatment, but this theme is expressed only in a generalized way. The singer's man mistreats her all the time, does her dirt, and wrecks her life, but we are never told specifically what he has done to her. This generalized form of expression is typical of folk blues. Much is left to the imagination of the listeners, who can think of times when they themselves have been mistreated and apply these thoughts to the song they are hearing. In the more original compositions a much greater part of the imagination is exercised by the composer, and the text is usually much more specific in its treatment of a theme. The audience, consequently, must make a greater effort to find the message relevant to their own lives.

Most of the female singers recorded only a few of their own compositions and instead got their material from composers, who were often also their pianists, or else they "covered" the hits of other singers. Consequently, little of the material that they sang was traditional. We can document this fact by surveying the composer credits on the records of these singers. This can be done conveniently with two companies, Paramount and Columbia, that were very active in making "race records," as records designed for the Negro market were then called. Discographies are in print for the Paramount 12000 and 13000 and Columbia 13000-D and 14000-D series on which most of their race records were issued.[148] Although a few of the Paramounts have not been traced, most were available for the listing. The majority of records by the female singers have a composer listed. When none is given, it is usually an indication that the piece was composed by the singer but was never written down or copyrighted, a procedure which incidentally resulted in the singer not receiving royalties if the piece was a hit. In a few cases the singer is listed as a co-composer with someone else. I have included such pieces among the compositions of the singers, since the other co-composers were probably responsible for only the musical arrangement or perhaps for "touching up" the lyrics a little.

Paramount seems to have given its singers a greater degree of freedom in recording their own material, perhaps because J. Mayo Williams, a black man, was until 1927 the recording manager of the company's "Race Artist Series." Williams must have been somewhat more sensitive to the creative potential of the singers and not content to rely on old formulas. In fact, he even asked the public for advice. A 1924 Paramount catalog, which bore his picture, asked,

> *What does the public want? What will you have? If your preferences are not listed in our catalog, we will make them for you, as Paramount must please the buying public. There is always room for more good material and more talented artists. Any suggestions or recommendations that you may have to offer will be greatly appreciated by J. Mayo Williams, Manager of the Race Artists Series.*[149]

It is not surprising that two years later Paramount was to be the pioneer in recording authentic folk blues.

Ma Rainey was the female singer recorded most extensively by Paramount. Between 1923 and 1928 she recorded ninety-four blues, her entire output, for this company. Forty-seven of these are listed as her own compositions, while twenty-six are the compositions of other songwriters. Nineteen have no composer listed, and two are untraced.[150] Most of those with no composer listed should probably be credited to Rainey. It is likely that the extraordinarily high percentage of self-composed pieces in her total output resulted from her having sung blues professionally in the South for more than twenty years before she recorded them. She even increased the percentage of self-composed blues in her last two years of recording. Ida Cox was another Paramount artist, who sang thirty-one self-composed pieces (and fifteen with no listing) out of her total of eighty-seven recorded between 1923 and 1929. She made one recording on another label in 1923 and continued recording for other companies after 1929, but information on the composers of these songs is unavailable. Elzadie Robinson was a third Paramount artist with twelve self-composed pieces (and fourteen with no listing) out of the thirty-two that she recorded between 1926 and 1929. The remaining Paramount female artists, however, were apparently more inclined to sing the compositions of others. Of Trixie Smith's thirty-six blues recorded between 1921 and 1926, only three were self-composed, twenty-seven were by others, two were not listed, and four are not traced. Priscilla Stewart recorded twenty-four blues between 1924 and 1928, but only five are credited to her, while seventeen are by others, and two are not listed. Alberta Hunter recorded thirty-nine blues for Paramount between 1921 and 1924 before she moved on to a series of other labels. She recorded two pieces for Columbia in 1929, bringing the total in our sample to forty-one. Only five of these are credited to her, while thirty-two were composed by others, three were not listed, and one is untraced. The five original compositions she recorded, however, were closer to the folk blues and were among her biggest hits. Besides "Down Hearted Blues" (Example 5), they were "Chirping the Blues," "Mistreated Blues," "Down South Blues," and "Experience Blues." It would appear that black record buyers were more willing to purchase traditional blues than the companies were to provide them.

Columbia Records had much lower percentages of self-composed blues by their female artists. Consequently there was less likelihood that these singers would be performing traditional blues. Figures are given for five of the six most extensively recorded female blues vocalists on their 13000-D and 14000-D race series in Figure 2. Twenty-nine pieces by Ethel Waters and four by Maggie Jones, recorded earlier on Paramount, are also included in these figures for Columbia, but they do not significantly alter the percentages. All the recordings were made between 1921 and 1931.

ARTIST	SELF-COMPOSED	COMPOSED BY OTHERS	NOT LISTED
Ethel Waters	6	50	7 (10 not traced)
Maggie Jones	4	32	0
Clara Smith	5	99	6
Martha Copeland	1	25	0
Lillian Glinn	0	7	15

Figure 2. The composer credits on records by five female artists on Columbia

It is quite likely that many of Lillian Glinn's blues without any listed composer were her own material. If so, she would be the exception among Columbia's female blues singers.

Bessie Smith was Columbia's best selling female blues singer and certainly one of the greatest blues vocalists of all time.[151] Although she composed more of her own songs than the other female singers on Columbia, these songs still comprise slightly less than one-quarter of her total output of 160 songs. I have included in the total of her thirty-eight compositions three songs credited to her husband Jack Gee, which are almost certainly by her. Her husband acted as her business manager and probably took credit as a matter of convenience.[152] One piece has no composer listed. The remaining 121 were composed by other songwriters.

Bessie Smith's career is especially well documented. She is considered by most critics and collectors to have been one of the most forceful and "down home" of the female stage and cabaret singers of the 1920s.[153] She certainly was "down home" in the sense that she was born in the South, in Chattanooga, Tennessee, in 1894. But she was not a country girl when she came to record in 1923. By that time she had been a professional stage entertainer for eleven years. Her style was then given further refinement by Columbia's artist and repertoire manager, Frank Walker. W. G. Monroe, manager of the record department of the Columbia Phonograph Company, said in 1923, her first year of recording,

> One of our most popular "blues" singers is Bessie Smith, who was unknown and practically broke when our Mr. Walker discovered her. She was brought up north and given a tryout. Her first few recordings were terrible, for her voice was absolutely uncultured. However, she had a deep, powerful voice, particularly suitable for "blues" songs, and Mr. Walker, realizing that she possessed latent

talent, put her through a course of training. She finally came through in splendid style and her rendition of "Gulf Coast Blues," "Downhearted Blues" and several other numbers helped to make them big sellers on the Columbia records.[154]

Walker himself has stated that most of her blues were thematic in their lyrics. He says:

Almost all of the blues she sang told sort of a story, and they were written especially for her. I don't want to give you the idea that Bessie Smith was incapable of writing her own blues, not at all. She probably could have. She would get an idea, then we would discuss it. But once she started to sing, nobody told her what to do. Nobody interfered.[155]

It would appear, then, that after her initial "course of training" she was allowed to deliver her songs in her own manner, but her choice of material was carefully supervised.

Many of the pieces that she did not compose herself could hardly be called blues at all if it were not for the "bluesy" delivery given them by Ms. Smith and her accompanists. Her other recordings are mostly twelve-bar blues, almost all of which develop a single theme in their lyrics, as is typical of popular composed blues. Her own compositions fall mainly in this category. Out of the thirty-eight pieces that she composed herself, twenty-three use a twelve-bar blues pattern, and most of the rest use a sixteen-bar pattern typical of the more sophisticated compositions. All but four of her compositions develop a single theme, and three of these four were recorded during the first two years of her recording career. Only seven of her compositions use more than one recognizably traditional verse, and five of these came from her first two years of recording. Since she recorded only six self-composed pieces during these two years, it would appear that, when she was given an opportunity during this period to record her own compositions, she tended to rely on traditional material. However, as time went on and she became more conscious of herself as a popular recording artist, she developed a talent for original composition within the blues form and created thematic blues on specific subjects.

A comparison of the lyrics of two of Bessie Smith's blues will make clear the transition in her compositions. In 1924 she recorded "Sorrowful Blues" with only guitar and violin accompaniment, her only blues without a piano or jazz band. The lyrics are traditional and do not develop a single theme. This is only the second of her own compositions to be recorded, but it is her thirty-fourth issued piece.

Example 6. "Sorrowful Blues." Bessie Smith, vocal; John Griffin, guitar; Robert Robbins, violin. New York, Apr. 4, 1924. Columbia 14020-D, reissued on *Empty Bed Blues*, Columbia G 30450, 12" double LP.

1. *Twee twah twah, twee twah twah twah, twee twah twah twah twah twee.*

2. *If you catch me stealing, I don't mean no harm.
   If you catch me stealing, I don't mean no harm.
   It's a mark in my family, and it must be carried on.*

3. *I got nineteen men, and I want one more.*
   I got nineteen men, and I want one more.
   If I get that one more, I'll let that nineteen go.

4. *I'm gonna tell you, daddy, like the Chinaman told the Jew,*
   I'm gonna tell you, daddy, like the Chinaman told the Jew,
   "If you don't likee me, me sure don't likee you."

5. *It's hard to love another woman's man.*
   It's hard to love another woman's man.
   You can't get him when you want him; you've got to catch him when you
       can.

6. *Have you ever seen peaches grow on sweet potato vines?*
   Have you ever seen peaches grow on sweet potato vines?
   Just step in my back yard and take a peep at mine.

The simulated bird chirping in the introductory stanza enjoyed a slight vogue among blues singers at the time. Probably it is a code for "sweet twat," as evidenced by an unissued piece recorded in 1937 by The Za Zu Girl (Elton Spivey Harris) with a more blatant title, "My Tweet Twaat Twaat." If Bessie Smith's chirping is a code, it should be viewed in conjunction with the closing stanza, which seems to be a general invitation to sample her wares, although the metaphor is more appropriate for a male singer. The other stanzas all deal with various facets of the problem of unfaithfulness but do not treat a single theme exclusively. In stanza 2 she says that she must be unfaithful ("stealing") because of heredity. Then she says that she will be faithful if she can only get the man she wants. In the fourth stanza there is a picture of incompatibility. Then in the fifth stanza we have another reference to "stealing," but here the man must cheat on his wife in order to visit the singer. Considering that this blues does not develop a single theme, we would have to grant that it has a remarkably cohesive and symmetrical structure.[156]

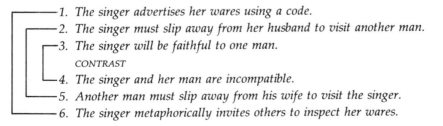

1. *The singer advertises her wares using a code.*
2. *The singer must slip away from her husband to visit another man.*
3. *The singer will be faithful to one man.*
   CONTRAST
4. *The singer and her man are incompatible.*
5. *Another man must slip away from his wife to visit the singer.*
6. *The singer metaphorically invites others to inspect her wares.*

Certainly not all traditional blues are as symmetrical as "Sorrowful Blues," but the kinds of contrasts found here are typical of folk blues. Quite a different picture is provided by one of Bessie Smith's later, more thematic compositions, "Please Help Me Get Him off My Mind," recorded in 1928. It is supposed to be autobiographical, at least in a general sense if not in specific details, and is concerned with the singer's troubles with her husband, with whom she broke up a few months later after a very stormy marriage of six years' duration.[157] The piece is in the typical twelve-bar pattern.

Example 7. "Please Help Me Get Him Off My Mind." Bessie Smith, vocal; Porter Grainger, piano; Joe Williams, trombone. New York, Aug. 25, 1928. Columbia 14375-D, reissued on *Empty Bed Blues*, Columbia G 30450, 12" double LP.

1. *I've cried and worried; all night I laid and groaned.*
   I've cried and worried; all night I laid and groaned.
   I used to weigh two hundred; now I'm down to skin and bone.

2. *It's all about a man, who always kicked and dogged me 'round.*
   It's all about a man, who always kicked and dogged me 'round.
   And when I try to kill him, that's when my love for him come down.

3. *I've come to see you, gypsy, begging on my bended knee.*
   I've come to see you, gypsy, begging on my bended knee.
   That man put something on me; oh, take it off me, please.

4. *It starts at my forehead and goes clean down to my toes.*
   It starts at my forehead and goes clean down to my toes.
   Oh, how I'm suffering, gypsy, nobody but the Good Lord knows.

5. *Gypsy, don't hurt him. Fix him for me one more time.*
   Oh, don't hurt him, gypsy. Fix him for me one more time.
   Yes, make him love me, but, please ma'am, take him off my mind.

© 1928, 1974 Frank Music Corp. © Renewed 1956 Frank Music Corp. International Copyright Secured. All Rights Reserved. By Permission.

The story behind the song, whether true or not, is easily reconstructable. The singer, believing that her man has conjured her and has her in his power, visits a conjurer herself in order to take counteraction. In stanzas 1 and 4 she describes the symptoms, in 2 and 3 she names the suspected perpetrator, and in 5 she describes the kind of remedy she would like. This is a much more straightforward style of composition than "Sorrowful Blues" and is typical of nontraditional popular blues.

Folk Blues on Phonograph Records

In 1926 the Paramount Record Company began releasing records by Blind Lemon Jefferson, a Texas street singer of blues who accompanied himself on guitar. His records sold phenomenally well, and he continued to record extensively until his death in 1930. He was recorded at the instigation of a Dallas furniture and record store proprietor, who must have been closer to the folk blues than the record company executives in the songwriting centers of New York and Chicago. Jefferson was a real folk blues singer, who put his own songs together out of traditional lyric and musical elements. He had been performing blues and other folk songs for a living for about fifteen years before he recorded.[158]

Jefferson's commercial success led the record companies to seek other self-accompanied male singers. Often they made field trips into the South for recording. The years between 1926 and 1931 saw an un-paralleled amount of commercial recording of real folk blues. Blues were even recorded by "hillbilly" folksingers for the southern white market.[159] All of this activity was prompted by a number of events that combined with Jefferson's fortuitous success. For one thing, the record companies were facing stiff competition from radio, which was under-going major expansion in the mid-1920s. Record sales declined, and the companies began to seek new markets for new kinds of music. Further-more, by 1926 the major record companies had adopted the new electri-cal recording process. This eliminated much of the extraneous noise on records and enabled voices to be heard much more clearly. This was especially important for folk blues singers, many of whom sang in ac-cents that would have made their songs virtually incomprehensible under the old acoustic recording process. The electrical process was also much more favorable for recording the guitar. Formerly, the only kind of guitar music to be recorded extensively was Hawaiian guitar playing, which used a special technique for achieving a penetrating tone that could be picked up clearly by the recording horn. Finally, the electrical process enabled the companies to use multiple microphones and portable equipment that could be easily transported to temporary studios in the South, the heartland of folk blues.[160]

Obviously the record company executives were operating largely in the dark with this new type of blues, trying to produce the big hit record. But they had at least developed some basic standards and values by this time for choosing blues singers and songs to be recorded. Most of our information on these standards applies in particular to hillbilly records and artists, but these artists were scouted, chosen, and recorded mostly by the same people who worked with blues in this period. Un-doubtedly they applied the same standards to both kinds of music.

Art Satherly, who recorded both white and black singers for sev-eral companies beginning in the 1920s, was aware of the fact that much of the material he dealt with was folk music, yet he said that he would travel long distances to record a hillbilly artist "who has a very original ballad."[161] Presumably, such "original" songs could include traditional ones that had never been recorded commercially before. Satherly told Maurice Zolotow that the qualities he sought in hillbilly music were "simplicity of language, an emotional depth in the music, sincerity in the rendition, and an indigenous genuineness of dialect and twang. . . . But, above all, sincerity, even if it's awkward unpolished sincerity, is the criterion used to judge the performer."[162] These standards are cer-tainly in accord with the blues aesthetic developed by the early folk blues singers themselves. Yet Satherly had a second criterion in addi-tion to sincerity, one which was not consistent with the aesthetic stan-dards of all types of folksongs, particularly of many folk blues. He said of hillbilly music, though it undoubtedly applied equally to blues, "The person who listens to mountain music wants to hear a story. . . . My singers must get the picture of the words. I've got to instill into them a picture of what they are singing about."[163] Certainly many folk blues do not tell a "story" or paint a "picture" but deal instead in contrasts and move from one theme to another. It is quite likely that Satherly rejected many such folk blues, although he probably accepted some on the basis of his prime criterion, sincerity. That Satherly could be highly selective, however, is shown by the fact that from one southwestern group led by Al Dexter he accepted only twelve of thirty-five offered songs.[164]

Frank Walker of Columbia Records, the man who produced Bessie Smith's records, told of the limitations of the black and white folksingers he recorded and the need for selectivity.

> *Their repertoire would consist of eight or ten things that they did well and that was all they knew. So, when you picked out the three or four that were best in a man's so-called repertoire you were through with that man as an artist. It was all. He was finished. It was a culling job, taking the best that they had. You might come out with two selections or you might come out with six or eight, but you did it at that time. You said goodbye. They went back home. They had made a phonograph record, and that was the next thing to being President of the United States in their mind. Then, out of it, there were a very few who could learn or could adopt something that somebody else might be able to do but not record. So you put those two together, so that one might be able to teach the other and you came up with a saleable or recordable article.[165]*

What Walker said is indeed true of many folksingers; they are capable of performing, at the most, eight or ten good songs. Even so, apparently it was profitable enough to record such singers, though it seems clear that the company preferred those few who "could learn or could adopt something that somebody else might be able to do but not record."[166]

Ralph Peer of Victor Records wanted each performer to sing original compositions, "songs of his own."[167] Yet he did not distinguish between totally original material and traditional material that had not previously been recorded, probably because he was not very familiar with the traditions. H. C. Speir, a white Mississippian who was the proprietor of a music store in Jackson and an independent talent scout for several record companies in the late 1920s and 1930s, was familiar with a similar set of standards. Speir was responsible for getting a large number of folk blues, as well as some hillbilly music, on record during this period.[168] When I interviewed him in 1966, he said that he himself was not motivated by commercial standards. He simply chose artists whose music appealed to him personally. Since he grew up in Mississippi hearing and enjoying folk blues, we can assume that his taste and aesthetic standards in blues differed little from those of most black people in that state. Certainly the large number of folk blues singers that he got on records would support this view. But Speir claimed that the record companies did have standards of their own for the singers that he scouted. The main requirement was that each artist had to have at least four different original songs. By *original* it was meant that none of the singer's four songs could show the influence of anything recorded or published previously. This is basically in agreement with the standards of Satherly and Peer. Probably the chief reason for this requirement was the fact that the record companies often owned subsidi-

H. C. Speir. Photo by Marina Bokelman.

ary publishing houses and therefore could publish their artists' "original" songs without having to pay publisher's royalties to someone else. In Peer's case, he himself owned a publishing company that handled the songs he recorded. Also, the record companies had a desire to produce new popular hits rather than copies of older songs, for the latter rarely sold as well as the original versions. By the term *different* the companies simply meant that the singer could not duplicate any lyrics or musical figures in his songs.

In view of the folk standards of tradition and familiarity, these seemingly simple requirements must have become major hurdles for folk blues singers. These performers regularly use a limited supply of lyrics, melodies, and instrumental figures in various combinations for many of their songs. Therefore, not all of their blues are completely different from each other. In addition, since 1920 thousands of blues had been issued on phonograph records. Folk blues singers eagerly learned many of these blues or added portions of them to their repertoires. Furthermore, as already noted, there was some traditional material in the blues already recorded by female singers. Thus, an auditioning male folk blues singer could sing a stanza or melody that had already been used by a female singer on a record, and he might be considered unoriginal, even though he had not learned it from the record. Many good folk blues singers must have been rejected by the talent scouts and companies for just such reasons. From my own field experience, I would estimate that the average folk blues singer would have to sing about twenty blues before he could meet the record companies' requirement of "four different original songs." How many talent scouts were willing to listen to twenty blues by one singer when there was a wealth of other talent waiting to be auditioned? A man like Frank Walker must have been extremely patient to get his few usable pieces from each performer. When it is considered also that many folk blues do not tell a story or paint a picture, it is a remarkable fact that any were recorded at all.

Much of the credit for getting so many traditional folk blues on records at this time rests with persistent men like H. C. Speir, who genuinely loved this kind of music and knew there was a market for it. Speir told of the problems he faced when he tried to get blues singer Tommy Johnson on record for Victor. Johnson was probably the best liked blues singer in Jackson when Speir met him in 1928, yet Speir claimed that he was able to perform only two different original songs at his first audition. Speir said that he worked with Johnson until he was able to add some others. But Johnson seems not to have learned his lesson very well. Of the eleven extant songs that he recorded, three use the same melody, and melodic and guitar phrases from one blues often occur in his other blues. He sings the same stanza in three different songs and another in two different ones, while three single lines occur in two songs each.[169]

A similar practice is in evidence on the records of many other folk blues singers who recorded during this period, such as Furry

Lewis and Charley Patton.[170] Many later, somewhat more sophisticated performers like Kokomo Arnold and Peetie Wheatstraw used the same melody or instrumental accompaniment in many of their blues. Others would use different verses or musical lines in a blues on different occasions of performance. Such practices caused a great deal of difficulty for Lester Melrose, a man who recorded many popular blues singers for several different companies beginning in the 1920s. He said,

> Some of the artists who could not read or write made it very difficult to record them. Every time they would record a number they could never repeat the same verses. The result would be to record the number about four times and select the one with the best verses. I have rehearsed some of them at least six times on four selections and when we reached the studios, they would sing two or three different verses for each song. Of course, this was only a small percentage of the artists.[171]

It was a small percentage probably because such artists were usually rejected before they ever reached the recording studio.

Many fine traditional blues singers were recorded between 1926 and 1931. Often they had only a single session, probably of the sort described by Frank Walker, where the company representative culled out the few pieces he considered to be the best in the performer's repertoire. If a record made at the first session sold moderately well, the performer might be invited to one or two more recording sessions. Only a few performers recorded regularly, and they were forced to conform to the standards of the companies by the continual pressure to produce new material. Most folk blues artists who recorded regularly soon ran out of traditional material that was "original and different" and had to compose blues that were thematic or else use the compositions of other songwriters, which were also thematic. In addition, it is likely that these singers became gradually more conscious of themselves as popular recording artists and composers. They must have felt a need to be more creative and original than the folk blues aesthetic dictated. This increasing individualism and use of thematic lyrics can be observed in the careers of many commercially recorded blues singers, such as Blind Lemon Jefferson, Barbecue Bob (Robert Hicks), Little Brother Montgomery, and Sleepy John Estes. Interestingly, this greater commercialization did not always result in greater sales for these artists. Many, in fact, enjoyed better sales with their earliest records, which tended to be more traditional in content.

The recording career of Blind Lemon Jefferson can serve as an example of this trend toward commercialism. Between 1926 and 1929 he recorded seventy-five blues with alternate takes of several of them. His brilliant career was cut short when he froze to death in a Chicago snowstorm in the winter of 1929–1930. Jefferson's first issued blues was advertised by Paramount Records as "a real old-fashioned blues by a real old-fashioned blues singer."[172] This would indicate that the company had some awareness of Jefferson's status as a folksinger using traditional material, but it is also a sign that he and his music were considered a novelty, even if they were an anachronistic novelty! In 1927 a change began to take place in the type of blues that he recorded. His lyrics grew more and more thematic, and most of his songs became more deliberately conceived. In the last two years of his career almost all of his blues were thematic, and finally he began recording the songs of a composer named Lamoore. In some of these later sessions he would even have someone whisper the words of the blues into his ear before he sang them.[173] Even earlier in 1927 he recorded five blues credited to George Perkins, a man who accompanied him on piano on three of them. Two of these pieces, "Right of Way Blues" and "Teddy Bear Blues," are almost certainly Jefferson's compositions, however, as they have all the characteristics of his style. It is probable that they were credited to Perkins by mistake. The only other song not his own was "How Long How Long" from 1928, a "cover" of a hit by Leroy Carr recorded that same year. It would thus appear that Jefferson gradually accepted the values and standards of the songwriters and record company executives.

Figure 3 represents a summary of all of Jefferson's seventy-five issued blues. All were recorded for Paramount except his first two recordings of 1927, which were made for Okeh. Jefferson also recorded four religious titles and two versions of "See That My Grave's Kept Clean." One of these versions was coupled on a record with a religious song and the other with a blues. In any case, the song is not really a blues, nor are the folksongs "Beggin' Back," "Jack O' Diamond Blues" [sic], and "Hot Dogs." In the listing of composer credits for each year BLJ stands for Blind Lemon Jefferson and GP for George Perkins. A question mark means that the information is unavailable, and a dash means that no composer was listed. In most of the latter cases we are almost certainly dealing with Jefferson's own compositions. I have classified each text as thematic (developing a single theme), nonthematic, or partly thematic. The latter have at least three stanzas, but not all, on a single theme. In addition, I have classified each text as original, traditional, or partly traditional. In traditional texts all, or almost all, of the stanzas are found in different combinations in other folk blues, excluding, of course, ones which were obviously learned later from Jefferson's own records. Partly traditional texts have about half original verses and the rest traditional. I have listed "How Long How Long" as nontraditional because it is obviously a "cover" of another record.[174]

The trends in Jefferson's recording career should be clear from Figure 3. In 1926 he relied almost wholly on traditional verses and never fully developed a single theme in a blues. He continued in this vein for most of his 1927 recordings, but in that year he also recorded three original thematic blues by another composer. His own "Chinch Bug Blues" was composed entirely of original verses, but it is not wholly on a single theme. At the same session, his last in 1927, he recorded two of his compositions that were both original and thematic, "Sunshine Special" and "Gone Dead on You Blues."

	1926	1927	1928	1929
Number of blues per year	16	17	20	22
Composer credits	16 BLJ	4 BLJ	2 BLJ	9 BLJ
		5 GP		6 BLJ-Lamoore
		2 ?		7 Lamoore
		6 —	18 —	
Thematic	0	5	15	22
Partly thematic	5	4	5	0
Nonthematic	11	8	0	0
Original	0	6	15	21
Partly traditional	3	3	4	1
Traditional	13	8	1	0

Figure 3. The composers, styles, and traditional status of Blind Lemon Jefferson's blues

The year 1928 marked an almost complete reversal of his original style. Perhaps after recording thirty-three mostly traditional blues, he had run out of traditional verses and had been forced to produce original material. In fact, he had already repeated verses on several of his recordings in the manner typical of folk blues singers. In his last two years Jefferson did not record a single nonthematic blues. Only five of his blues in these years were even partly thematic, and these were all from 1928. He recorded only one blues during this period with mostly traditional verses, "Prison Cell Blues." In 1928 he sang only four other blues that were even partly traditional, and only one such blues in 1929. In this last year he used the services of another composer in thirteen of his twenty-two blues.

A look at some of Jefferson's blues texts will illustrate this increasing commercialization, thematicism, and self-consciousness. His first recorded blues was "Got the Blues," a piece that is especially notable for the startling imagery of the opening line. The performance is brilliant throughout, as Jefferson extends each line with extra guitar phrases played at a rapid tempo and featuring many subtle rhythmic shifts. He did this on most of his recordings, but it is more pronounced on his earlier ones. The "fatmouth" in stanza 6 is a man who follows a woman around, obsequiously complimenting her in an effort to win her affections. "Raising sand" in stanza 7 means simply "carrying on, creating a commotion."

Example 8. "Got the Blues." Blind Lemon Jefferson, vocal and guitar in open G tuning (DBGDGD). Chicago, ca. Mar., 1926. Paramount 12354, reissued on *Blind Lemon Jefferson 1926–29*, Biograph 12000, 12″ LP. (Note: This piece is reversed with "Long Lonesome Blues" on the reissue LP.)

> 1. *Well, the blues come to Texas loping like a mule.*
> *Well, the blues come to Texas loping like a mule.*
> *You take a high brown woman; man, she's hard to fool.*

2. *You can't ever tell what a woman's got on her mind.*
   Yes, you can't tell what a woman's got on her mind.
   You might think she's crazy about you; she's leaving you all the time.

3. *She ain't so good looking, and her teeth don't shine like pearls,*
   She ain't so good looking, teeth don't shine like pearls,
   But that nice disposition carry the woman all through the world.

4. *I'm going to the river, gonna carry my rocker chair.*
   Well, I'm going to the river, carry my rocker chair.
   Gonna ask that transfer boat, "Have the worried blues reached here?"

5. *I think I heard my good gal calling my name.*
   Hey, hey, good gal calling my name.
   She don't call so loud, but she call so nice and plain.

6. *I was raised in Texas, schooled in Tennessee.*
   I was raised in Texas, schooled in Tennessee.
   Now, sugar, you can't make no fatmouth out of me.

7. *Can't a woman act funny, quit you for another man?*
   Can't a woman act funny, quit you for another man?
   She ain't gonna look at you straight, but she's always raising sand.

This blues obviously does not develop a single theme, but there are a number of interesting associative linkages and contrasts between individual stanzas. The opening line introduces the subject of the blues in a most dramatic fashion. It has no logical connection with the line that rhymes with it, a fairly common feature of Jefferson's blues, but perhaps any attempt at using a related line would detract from the effect of the first line. In any case, the final line of the first stanza leads into the next stanza, as a woman who is hard to fool becomes one who fools men. In the third stanza we are presented with a contrast, a woman with a "nice disposition" but poor appearance instead of the beautiful but tricky "high brown woman." The pivotal fourth stanza employs a startling image of attempted escape from the blues and contrasts with the imagery of the blues' arrival in the first stanza. Then in the fifth stanza we have another picture of a "good gal." In the next stanza the singer states that he will not be fooled, in contrast to the situation in the first two stanzas. Finally, we see again the unfaithful woman, as in stanza 2. "Got the Blues," then, is a song that deals with the problem of one partner trying to "fool" the other. The singer explores the complexity of this problem by noting that beauty and a "nice disposition" are usually not found in the same person. All of this is discussed in two sections, each introduced by a surrealistic image of the blues' arrival "loping like a mule" or the singer's attempt to escape from the blues by crossing the river carrying his "rocker chair."

All or nearly all of the lines in this blues are traditional and occur in variant form in many other folk blues. It is quite possible that Jefferson created this combination of verses in the very act of performing. Other evidence, at least, strongly suggests that he was capable of doing so. In 1927 he recorded three versions of "Match Box Blues" on different dates, one for Okeh and two for Paramount.[175] Fortunately, all of them were issued, affording us an unusual opportunity to compare the ways in which an early commercially recorded folk blues singer handled a song in his repertoire. The three versions are all basically similar musically, although with Jefferson such a statement would have to be applied with caution, since he was a master of improvisation both melodically and on guitar. In any case, he uses many of the same musical ideas in each version of the song. The texts, however, are quite different. There are only two stanzas that are used in all three versions, whereas each of these versions has six or seven stanzas altogether. One other stanza is used in two of the three versions, but otherwise all of the other eleven stanzas he sings are different. It would appear, then, that only two stanzas and the melody and guitar part formed a stable unit in Jefferson's repertoire, while the rest of the stanzas were added at the time of performance. We shall see later that this is, in fact, a common practice among folk blues singers. Jefferson's alternate takes of some of his other blues are, however, nearly identical. This could mean either that these blues were stable units in his repertoire and never varied or that the company forced him to reproduce exactly his earlier versions.

Jefferson also recorded a number of blues that were partly traditional and partly thematic. These tend to appear in the middle of his recording career and serve in a transitional role between his traditional nonthematic blues and his nontraditional thematic blues. An example of one of these transitional pieces, recorded late in 1926, is "Rabbit Foot Blues," whose title has little to do with the song's content beyond the mention of a rabbit in the first stanza. Again there is a great deal of improvisation in the guitar playing.

Example 9. "Rabbit Foot Blues." Blind Lemon Jefferson, vocal and guitar in open G tuning (DBGDGD). Chicago, ca. Oct., 1926. Paramount 12454, reissued on *The Immortal Blind Lemon Jefferson*, Milestone 2004, 12″ LP.

GUITAR CHORUS.

1. *Blues jumped a rabbit, run him one solid mile.*
   Blues jumped a rabbit, run him one solid mile.
   That rabbit sat down, cried like a natural child.

2. *Well, it seem like you hungry. Honey, come and lunch with me.*
   Seem like you hungry. Honey, come and lunch with me.
   I'm gonna stop these nice looking women from worrying me.

3. *I have Uneeda biscuits, gal, and a half a pint of gin.*
   Uneeda biscuits, gal, and a half a pint of gin.
   The gin is mighty fine, but them biscuits is a little too thin.

4. *Baby, tell me something about the meatless and wheatless days.*
   I want to know about those meatless and wheatless days.
   This not being my home, I don't think that I could stay.

GUITAR CHORUS.

5. *I cried for flour, and meat, I declare, it was strong.*
   Well, I cried for flour, and meat, I declare, it was strong.
   Keep a feeding me cornbread, I just can't stick around long.

6. *Got an airplane, baby, now we're gonna get a submarine.*
An airplane, now we're gonna get a submarine.
Gonna get that Kaiser, and we'll be seldom seen.

7. *Mmmm, hitch me to your buggy, mama; drive me like a mule.*
Hitch me to your buggy; drive me like a mule.
Reason I'm going home with you, sugar, I ain't much hard to be fooled.

The first and last stanzas are traditional, and probably the sixth, with its reference to the First World War, is also. The rest of the stanzas deal with the theme of hunger, often ironically, although their continuity is not always clear. The last stanza, in which the singer expresses his willingness to be driven like a mule by his woman, contrasts with the preceding stanzas, in which he states his readiness to leave.

Jefferson's wholly thematic blues are all carefully constructed and are among some of the finest ever composed. "Peach Orchard Mama," a blues from 1929 with an elaborate sexual metaphor, is one such composition. It is much slower paced than his pieces using traditional verses, perhaps so that the novel lyrics can be better comprehended by listeners.

Example 10. "Peach Orchard Mama." Blind Lemon Jefferson, vocal and guitar in open G tuning (DBGDGD). Chicago, ca. Mar., 1929. Paramount 12801.

1. *Peach orchard mama, you swore nobody picked your fruit but me.*
Peach orchard mama, you swore that no one picked your fruit but me.
I found three kid men shaking down your peaches tree.

2. *One man bought your groceries, another joker paid your rent,*
One man bought your groceries, another joker paid your rent,
While I work in your orchard and giving you every cent.

3. *Went to the police station, begged the police to put me in jail.*
Went to the police station, begged him to put me in jail.
I didn't want to kill you, mama, but I hate to see your peaches tree fail.

4. *Peach orchard mama, don't treat your papa so mean.*
Peach orchard mama, don't treat your papa so mean.
Kick out all those kid men, and let me keep your orchard clean.

GUITAR CHORUS.

5. *Peach orchard mama, don't turn your papa down,*
Peach orchard mama, don't turn your papa down,
Because when I gets mad, I acts just like a clown.

Another thematic composition, descriptive rather than metaphorical, is "Saturday Night Spender Blues," also recorded in 1929. It is a typical twelve-bar blues, unlike his more improvisatory traditional blues. The surprise ending of this song is a typical device of popular commercial blues.

Example 11. "Saturday Night Spender Blues." Blind Lemon Jefferson, vocal and guitar in standard tuning, key of E. Chicago, ca. Mar., 1929. Paramount 12771.

1. *Every Saturday, works and I draws my pay.*
   Every Saturday, mama, go to work and I draw my pay.
   But when night come, I goes out 'cross town and play.

2. *I have five, six, and seven women, and I sure do love their corn.*
   Five, six, and seven women, and I sure loves their corn.
   Then we go out and break 'em down, honey, till early morn.

3. *I don't mind no men friends, but I'm scared they might cramp my style.*
   I don't mind no mens, but I'm scared they might cramp my style.
   I don't like me plenty of women, but, man, I likes them wild.

4. *All through the week I works hard, and I'm regularly paid,*
   All through the week I works hard, and I'm regularly paid,
   So on a Saturday night I can get all the loving I crave.

5. *Now I can't have the good times like I once have had.*
   And now I can't have good times like I once have had.
   My regular found out I'm a Saturday night spender, and it sure did make
   *   her mad.*

The Influence of Records on the Folk Tradition

The records of Blind Lemon Jefferson and other recording artists of the 1920s, both male and female, were extremely influential on singers who did not record. Today it is possible to make field recordings of blues from older singers that are derived almost word for word from some record. Even some of the early recorded singers themselves showed the influence of the earlier records of others in their songs, although the companies generally tried to keep from recording such blues in their efforts to obtain original material. In 1932 King Solomon Hill recorded three blues that show a heavy influence from earlier records by Lonnie Johnson, Memphis Minnie, and Jack Ranger. These three records comprise 75 percent of Hill's extant recordings! Hill had simply memorized the lyrics and melodies and adapted them to his bottleneck guitar style, escaping the notice of his record company probably because his sources were not well-known big hits. Charley Patton was able to integrate blues from phonograph records more fully into his own creative processes. Nine of the thirty-two extant blues that Patton recorded between 1929 and 1934 show a discernible influence from previous records, and two more nonblues pieces were learned from Tin Pan Alley songs, probably via records. But in all cases Patton used only a portion of his source, a tune and usually one or two stanzas, and added material of his own, either traditional or original.

Blues recording virtually ceased during 1932 and 1933 on account of the Depression, as many of the companies went out of business. When recording resumed, far fewer traditional blues were put on records. By this time many of the traditional lyrics and musical elements had already been recorded, and over the years folk blues performers had continued to incorporate songs learned from records into their repertoires. It must have become increasingly difficult for a folk blues performer to satisfy the companies' requirements. If a singer wanted to be recorded, it became imperative for him to compose original songs. Such songs generally dealt with some novel theme or extended and elaborated an unusual metaphor, usually a sexual one. This trend toward novelty in blues records has continued to the present time.[176] Some blues singers, like Big Bill Broonzy and Washboard Sam and more recently Willie Dixon, have even become composers of blues for other performers. There has also been an increasingly rapid series of musical innovations and trends in the recorded blues, such as guitar-piano duets, boogie-woogie, the so-called "Bluebird beat" popularized by Chicago-based ensembles during the late 1930s and early 1940s, blues shouting, the "Chicago sound" with amplified guitar and harmonica, and the modern urban blues.[177] Altogether, according to the estimate of Robert M. W. Dixon, about ten thousand blues titles were recorded commercially between 1920 and 1942, and it seems likely that at least that many have been recorded since 1942.[178] The only period since 1931 that saw much commercial recording of highly traditional blues was the period between 1947 and 1955 when many independent record companies sprang up, headed by men who were largely ignorant of previous blues recording or else were not averse to having their artists duplicate older material. It is probable that many traditional blues were thought by these men to be original. But in even these companies the same commercial values gradually developed, as in earlier decades. Meanwhile, the larger, more established companies dropped out of blues recording almost entirely.

The American record industry has never really been very interested in presenting traditional music unless it was profitable, and the "hit" system of popular music production assures that in most cases it will not be profitable. A statement by Eddie Shuler, a man who since 1952 has produced records of blues, country and western, rock and roll, rhythm and blues, and Cajun music in Louisiana, gives a good idea of the values of the owner of a small company. He says,

> *The music business never stands still and today ninety days is a long life for any record. Folk musics like Cajun do live longer than this, but only in the areas where they bring a nostalgic and psychological reaction to the people. To my knowledge, no music has repeated itself on record in its original form and I don't expect it ever will, in spite of many people's hopes.[179]*

Shuler deliberately recorded artists for his Goldband Record Company who already had an orientation toward popular commercial styles rather than toward traditional music. He says, "I have recorded several great artists for Goldband and many were completely original in their approach to their own music."[180] In fact, Shuler did not search for musicians to record but waited for them to approach him. He justified this practice, saying,

> *It may sound stupid saying sit around and wait, but it isn't, for there is a never ending stream of talent around, and if you wait long enough they are bound to show up asking to audition. An excellent example of this is Juke Boy Bonner, one of the finest blues artists I recorded, who came to find me after he saw one of*

*my records on a Jukebox! Another is Big Chenier, who I had
known for many years. I had often thought about recording
Chenier, but never got round to it, until the man himself came
round one day and asked if he could make a record.*[181]

J. D. Miller, another Louisiana producer of blues records for various small, independent companies, expresses a similar view, saying,

*I never do go out, not for the blues type of singer. And the reason
is this: I want them to be sold on the idea—wanting to do
something. Because this is a very, very hard field. Some singers
don't turn out to be good blues singers and as far as this is
concerned it's like this. If they don't feel the material they're
singin'—that's it. People can distinguish whether they're authentic
or not or whether it's just a synthetic singer and that's all. But I've
had boys come in here and sing and actually they had the blues so
bad they were cryin' when they got through. They really had their
heart and soul in it. And to my way of thinking, that's a good
blues man.*[182]

Miller is right, of course, that such a singer is likely to be "a good blues man," but he is not likely to be one who performs much traditional material. Highly traditional blues singers rarely see much point in putting their music on records and are often aware of the fact that it is somewhat different from the popular blues. They are usually content to perform before local audiences and have little or no thought of establishing careers as popular blues singers. Unless they are deliberately sought out, there is little chance that their music will appear on records. With a few exceptions, most of the recording of highly traditional blues in recent years has been done by folklorists and dedicated amateur blues researchers, and their efforts have not been aimed at exploiting the music commercially in the black record buying market.

Inevitably, a singer's status as a blues recording artist has an effect on the kind of music he produces. We have observed this in the careers of early recorded blues singers like Bessie Smith and Blind Lemon Jefferson, and many more examples could have been given. Lowell Fulson serves as a more recent example. Fulson grew up in Oklahoma and learned to perform folk blues there. After service in World War II, he moved to Oakland, California, where he made his first recordings in 1946. He had not intended to make records but had simply walked into a radio repair shop where he heard some music and asked to play some pieces on a guitar. The owner happened to be starting a record company and asked Fulson to attend a recording session, offering him cash. Fulson accepted and launched a successful recording career that continues today. Very soon after his first recordings for the SwingTime label, he made a change in his style of music, as he revealed in an interview to Don Lindeneau. "While with SwingTime, Lowell decided that his style of blues, the brooding, moaning type, with only acoustic guitar accompaniment, would get him nowhere. He felt that people in the clubs would respond more readily to a more 'modern' sound—music they could dance to: rather than archaic folk-blues."[183]

John Lee Hooker, another extensively recorded blues singer with an early background in traditional folk blues, also states that he has modernized his style. He says,

> *Oh, I brush it up a little bit, put a little more modern in, 'cause you got a lot of kids in the modern days like the upbeat stuff and things like that, so I just have to do those things to stay in the field. My type of music, I got a variety—for the young folks and the older folks, and the folksingers. Now that's a field I'm getting more into. I have created about three different fields; a folk field, a blues field, and a jump field for the kids. If it was necessary I could do hillbilly stuff but I don't do it. I can do it. The big market today is folksongs and blues and jump.*[184]

The "folksingers" that Hooker refers to are the predominantly young and white participants in the folk revival of the 1960s. For them he deliberately revived an archaic style that he had largely abandoned for his black audiences.

One of the most sophisticated and commercially successful modern blues singers is B. B. King. He has always been in the forefront of modernizing trends in the blues and was a pioneer in the single-string style that most modern blues guitarists now use. He has also worked for many years with large backup groups with horns and in his most recent recordings has used strings and girl choruses, typical traits of mainstream popular music. King has been very conscious of the need for improving the public's image of blues and blues singers and likes to stress the fact that he listens to other forms of music, such as jazz, popular, and light classical, and that he is learning musical notation. Although King grew up in rural Mississippi, he has constantly striven to break away from the limitations of his background, and part of his continuing popularity with blacks is due to his having come so far. In the last few years, however, most of his audiences have been white, simply because that is where the most money is. He and his black fans now justify this position by noting that for many years King "paid his dues" working one-night stands in sleazy clubs.[185]

Over the years the record companies have taken an increasingly active and participative role in producing the blues.[186] With the improvement in recording technology in recent years, overdubbing, splicing, and many special effects have become common. Even earlier the producers were tampering with arrangements and rewriting lyrics. Jimmy Rogers, a Mississippi-born blues singer who recorded a number of traditional folk blues for Chess Records in Chicago in the early 1950s, bitterly complained recently about the increasing interference of Leonard Chess in his later recording sessions. Rogers said,

> *Only time it'd be a rerun would be somethin' Chess would want to change, and that would be the end of a good record. When he changed it, he'd take all the soul and everything from it. And that happened quite a few times. . . . When we'd start takin' a lot of time, you know, sometimes it'll take you two or three days to*

record, you'd come up there owin' the studio $4000 and the record would sell about 100 copies. So I figure the best way to do a blues tune, catch it as you play 'em as you feel it.[187]

Rogers eventually became disillusioned with the popular blues scene and dropped out in 1961. In 1969 he was "rediscovered" by blues researchers and has been performing occasionally for whites since then.

The producers justified their interference with their artists' songs on the grounds that they produced a more saleable product. Ted Berkowitz reported of Bob Shad's Sittin' In With label, which operated in Houston in 1950 and 1951, that "few of the performers knew very many blues and often their songs were only a minute long; because of this, Shad wrote a lot of lyrics for them and beefed up songs by others. Most lyrics were adapted from those of Arthur Crudup and other similar artists popular at the time."[188] This is very reminiscent of the attitudes of the blues talent scouts and producers of the late 1920s. Mike Leadbitter has reported of J. D. Miller that "the songs were left to the artists to create, but Jay would often rewrite or add to them."[189] Of Eddie Shuler he has reported, "Often he will rewrite the lyrics if he doesn't like them, and then make the vocalist and musicians do the number over and over until he feels it is right."[190] Shuler himself has said, "I very seldom get a chance to handle an artist that has established himself, but have to take the 'raw material' and develop it, while trying to decide what songs would suit which individual style."[191] Even after all this personal effort at remolding their "raw material," the blues record producers sometimes have little confidence in the artistic integrity of their product. As Eddie Shuler puts it, "The record business is nearly always 90% hype and 10% record!"[192]

Since the early 1960s the rate of commercial blues releases designed for black record buyers has declined rapidly. Many companies have now gotten out of the blues field altogether. Eddie Shuler wrote in 1963, "Down Home style blues is a thing of the past in this Country. It still has a limited market, but that is very limited to say the least. Now they still record blues songs, but each year you see less and less issued."[193] Despite the efforts of the producers, blacks were simply no longer buying blues records. In part the blues had splintered off into rock and roll, and what remained entered what Paul Oliver has called "a late stage of flamboyant embellishment" similar to the rococo phase of many other declining art styles.[194] About the only factor that has kept the popular blues recording industry alive in recent years is the resurgent white interest in the music, generated by the folk music revival of the 1960s and stimulated even further by the use made of blues by British rock music groups and subsequently by American white blues bands and "acid rock" groups. Enough whites are interested in hearing the "real thing" to keep a good stream of blues records by black performers appearing. Very few blues records are now oriented toward black buyers, and these few rarely enjoy large sales. Outside of the South the popular blues scene at clubs for blacks has largely dried up, except in a few places like Chicago and the San Francisco Bay Area, where blues attract mainly blacks with strong southern roots. Popular blues are by no means dead, but they have been on the decline, and there are few signs of an upturn yet. The white interest is not enough to sustain a viable type of blues. No art style can long remain creative without the support of the society from which its artists come. Whether the present trend means that the blues will revert to being strictly a folk music among blacks, or whether the blues will disappear completely as a song form, is not possible to predict. Only time will tell.

There are two interrelated reasons for the decline of the popular blues among blacks. One reason is the continuing movement of the black population during the twentieth century from the rural South to America's urban centers. Blues have always thrived best in the country and small towns or among recently arrived rural migrants in the cities. The majority of blacks now live outside the rural South, and many of those who have remained are quite familiar with city ways through radio, television, and modern transportation. Thus, blues have simply lost much of their population base.[195] The second reason for the decline of popular blues is that they no longer express the values of most modern blacks. For better or worse blues have become a reminder of the old South and earlier times of hardship and suffering. It is true that blues deal mainly with love problems and other universal subjects, but they tend to offer no solutions to problems and say instead that the world will probably always be as it is and has been. Such a point of view, if translated into political, economic, and racial terms, is anathema to modern blacks. Consequently they have tended to turn to "soul music," which also deals mainly with love problems but more often conveys the message that "we can make it if we try!" Certainly such a viewpoint is more compatible with the aspirations of younger blacks, who tend to buy most of the records. Neither point of view is necessarily better than the other as a philosophy of life, but the soul ideology appears to young blacks to offer the best hope for personal success.[196]

To summarize, then, the commercial record companies have always valued originality of lyric expression and regularity of musical structure in the blues. The great majority of commercially recorded popular blues intended for the black buying public have thematic texts and conform to the standard twelve-bar pattern or one of the other typical structures. In this respect they resemble the blues of songwriters from 1912 through the 1920s, many of which were, in fact, later recorded. These values have persisted in the record industry at all times, but from 1926 to 1931 and from 1947 to 1955 a significant number of folk blues were commercially recorded that used traditional lyrical and musical elements and techniques.

The approach and aesthetic of the older folk blues have also persisted to the present day. The folk audience has not rejected what is familiar and traditional in blues lyrics and music, even though this is rarely heard through the popular media outlets. Recent fieldwork has shown that highly traditional blues are still appreciated by black performers and audiences. The tradition has even been enriched over the years by many commercially recorded blues, which may once have been original compositions but have since been incorporated in whole or in part into the repertoires of many singers and through their resultant familiarity have passed into the realm of traditional blues.[197]

Sixty years of commercial recording have definitely had an effect on the older folk blues aesthetic. Field recordings reveal that many blues singers, particularly ones who are living outside of a rural environment, in cities or southern towns, have composed original blues that are lyrically thematic and usually in the standard twelve-bar form.[198] Since blues of this sort rarely appeared in early field collections made before the advent of blues sheet music and commercial recording, it can be assumed that these recently recorded singers have been influenced by the values of commercial blues artists and producers. A double folk aesthetic has thus gradually developed among blues performers and audiences, with the older values of tradition and familiarity on the one side and the more recent commercially influenced values of lyric originality, thematic coherence, and standardization of musical structure on the other. Both sides share the values of truth and sincerity. It is important to note, however, that both types of blues can be performed by the same singer and that a number of blues performances display some characteristics of each type. Therefore, we ought to view this double folk aesthetic as a spectrum rather than as a set of polar values. Blues performers and audiences have had much less difficulty in accepting and enjoying all kinds of blues than have the songwriters and record company executives who were responsible in large part for broadening the folk aesthetic spectrum.

The Folkloristic Aesthetic

The only early writers on blues who applied much analysis to their material were folklorists Howard W. Odum and John A. Lomax. Both wrote at a time before the effects of commercialism on the blues could be accurately gauged. It was not until 1919 that analysis of commercialized blues appeared in the form of an unsigned article in *Current Opinion* on "Enigmatic Folksongs of the Southern Underworld."[199] The focus of this article is on Gilda Gray, a white vaudeville singer who had starred in a recent Broadway revue. A list of several of her songs indicates that she used both traditional material and the works of various composers. Texts are given for the traditional "The Dirty Dozen" and W. C. Handy's "Beale Street Blues," to which Ms. Gray added several traditional verses. The article makes no mention of oral tradition, but it does call the blues "folksongs" and stresses their southern origin, while calling for a serious study of their "archaeology" similar to that which Cecil Sharp gave to Appalachian ballads. The article quotes the opinions of two New York journalists on the origins of the blues and reviews the blues' subject matter, constantly stressing their "illegitimate" and "underworld" associations and their expression of the "outlaw emotions." Unfortunately this kind of journalistic "slumming" was to affect much of the later analysis of the blues by white writers and result in the presentation of a distorted view of their origins and subject matter.

In the 1920s articles on the blues began to appear fairly often in popular publications. A 1923 article in the trade magazine *Sheet Music News* attempted to define the blues and discuss their origin and current status.[200] In 1925 and 1926 Carl Van Vechten wrote a series of articles in *Vanity Fair*, which brought the popular blues of the black female singers in New York to the attention of sophisticated white readers. In "The Black Blues" Van Vechten gave a fairly good general description of the blues and quoted his friends, poet Langston Hughes and composer W. C. Handy, at some length on the blues' origin and meaning.[201] He considered the blues to be folksongs and concluded with a call for their study "as they are sung under primitive conditions." In "Prescription for the Negro Theatre" he suggested that the female cabaret singers of blues would be successful in black musical reviews and would inject some much needed vitality into these stage presentations.[202] He recommended several of the current blues recording artists to theatergoers. In "Negro 'Blues' Singers" Van Vechten contrasted the performances of Bessie Smith, the "elemental conjure woman," the more refined Ethel Waters, and the crude but still artistic Clara Smith.[203] This article is very significant for its description of black audience reaction and the distinctions it draws between the styles of different singers.

In the latter half of the 1920s several amateur and academic folklorists published works on or related to the blues. Carl Sandburg printed in *The American Songbag* several traditional blues texts and tunes collected by others, but he offered no significant commentary.[204] In 1927 John Jacob Niles published *Singing Soldiers*, a book which contained songs collected from black soldiers in France during World War I. Niles noted that many singers could perform the popular songs of the day, such as "St. Louis Blues," but he was not interested in these and did not collect them. Instead he sought and collected "something original—a kind of folk music."[205] The songs he prints do appear to have been the original compositions of the soldiers, but many of them nevertheless show the influence of the style of the blues songwriters of the period. Niles appears not to have noticed this influence, for he did not investigate it further or comment on it.

In 1925 Dorothy Scarborough, a Texas folklorist at Columbia University, published *On the Trail of Negro Folk-Songs*. She confessed that she was originally uncertain whether blues, which were so popular at the time in sheet music and vaudeville, were really folksongs.[206] Therefore, she consulted W. C. Handy on the question. Her choice of an informant was a good one, and she came away from her interview with several enlightening observations. Handy stated that his own compositions were indeed folksongs, both because they were "racial expressions of Negro life" and because they were all based on traditional folksongs that he had known or overheard. He illustrated his point with several examples of how he had written thematically coherent blues songs based on folk blues.[207] Handy may have been stretching a point in calling his own compositions "folksongs," but he did make their sources clear enough to the folklorist and her readers. Scarborough printed the texts and tunes of several folk blues sent to her by friends and noted the common practice of stringing together thematically unrelated stanzas, but unfortunately she attributed this practice to the fact that "the colored mind is not essentially logical, and the folk-song [i.e., blues] shows considerable lack of coherence in thought."[208] She also observed that folk blues singers often adopted and altered blues from sheet music.[209] She did not follow up this observation, however, and in fact seems to have viewed it in negative terms. Toward the close of her book she stated, "I hope that I may some time spend a sabbatical year loitering down through the South on the trail of more Negro folk-songs, before the material vanishes forever, killed by the Victrola, the radio, the lure of cheap printed music."[210]

In 1926 W. C. Handy edited a collection of his own blues compositions and those of others, with an introduction and notes to the songs by Abbe Niles.[211] The songs ranged from folk blues and earlier types of folksongs recalled by Handy, through adaptations of folk blues with added original material, to completely original compositions. Niles contributed a good discussion of the characteristics of folk blues and the history of the blues genre. He viewed the early folk blues as an amorphous mass of traditional elements which were not given stable form until Handy and other composers began to write them down. About the tune of "Joe Turner," which he considered to be the prototype of the twelve-bar blues, he wrote,

> A singer might fit his impromptu lines to such a tune; the melody itself might help in framing the words, or there might already be associated with the tune other verses—plaintive, smart, or obscene—which the singer might tack on after the lines he had invented. If his verse had merit, his listeners might adopt it, and it would be added to the common storehouse of blues lyrics. Or, if his tune had a melodic or rhythmic twist of its own, it might be accepted eventually as a standard vehicle for old and new blues expressions. However, few blues tunes in their entirety seem to have had wide acceptance in the early days.[212]

This statement is an oversimplification, but it does illustrate many of the difficulties in studying the folk blues tradition. It was the kind of general statement that would be made by many later writers on the blues.

Niles went on in 1928 and 1929 to document current commercial releases of race and hillbilly records in a series of reviews in *Bookman* magazine.[213] These reviews show a remarkably broad range of taste and contain many discerning comments on folk blues and other types of folk music that were being commercially recorded at the time. Niles regularly lavished praise before his sophisticated readership on the performances of such authentic folk blues singers as Peg Leg Howell, Jim Jackson, Rabbit Brown, Tom Dickson, Cannon's Jug Stompers, and the Memphis Jug Band. It seems unlikely, however, that Niles's reviews actually caused many whites to buy race records. Probably more influential was the opinion of music critic Henry Osgood, who in reviewing Handy's book wrote, "The blues are indeed folk songs, but most of them, to speak frankly, are pretty poor stuff. As a rule they are improvisations out of the mouths of musical illiterates—and they sound like it."[214]

In 1925 Howard W. Odum and Guy B. Johnson combined Odum's 1911 article with an earlier one by him on black religious songs to form *The Negro and His Songs*. The book contained little that was new. The authors expanded Odum's earlier discussion of the importance of improvisation in the creation of the songs and noted the great difficulty of classifying the secular material.[215] The main additions were a discussion of the subject matter of the songs and a good chapter on "Imagery, Style, and Poetic Effort."[216] The authors made no attempt to discuss the relationship of their material to later folk or popular blues.

Much more significant was a book that Odum and Johnson published the following year, *Negro Workaday Songs*, which contained the most important and extensive examination during this period of the relationship between folk and popular blues.[217] The authors distinguished between "folk" or "native" blues and the "formal" blues of the phonograph records and popular composers, recognizing the importance of both types.[218] They wrote,

> The folk blues will also undergo modification, but they will always reflect Negro life in its lower strata much more accurately than the formal blues can. For it must be remembered that these folk blues were the Negro's melancholy song long before the phonograph record was invented. Yet the formal songs are important. In their own way they are vastly superior to the cruder folk productions, since they have all the advantages of the artificial over the natural. They may replace some of the simpler songs and thus dull the creative impulse of the common Negro folk to some extent, but there is every reason to suppose that there will be real folk blues as long as there are Negro toilers and adventurers whose naïveté has not been worn off by what the white man calls culture.[219]

Recent fieldwork has borne out this prophetic statement.

Odum and Johnson listened to the current blues records and noted their considerable influence on the folk blues they had recently collected in North Carolina. In fact, they stated that "it is no longer possible to speak with certainty of the folk blues, so entangled are the relations between them and the formal compositions. This inter-relation is itself of such interest and importance that it demands the careful attention of students of folk song."[220] They urged folklorists to pay more attention to the phonograph records as folkloric documents and stated that the history of the blues needed to be written.[221] They wrote, "One thing is certain, however, and that is that the student of Negro song tomorrow will have to know what was on the phonograph records of today before he may dare to speak of origins."[222] This prophecy was accompanied by numerous examples throughout the book of the influence of formal blues on the folk product.

Negro Workaday Songs was published in the same year that Blind Lemon Jefferson recorded his first blues. If it had been written a few years later, Odum and Johnson would have found the interrelationship between folk and formal blues even more complex, as hundreds of commercially recorded folk blues would have been on the market by that time. But unfortunately the authors were not primarily interested in this aspect of the blues. Instead they continued in the vein of Odum's 1911 article, trying to show that the lyrics of folk blues were a reflection of the life-style of the "common Negro folk." Odum took this approach in three novels based on the life of a typical wandering blues singer called Black Ulysses.[223] Johnson contributed an article on double meaning in blues texts, using phonograph records as his source material.[224]

Unfortunately, any inspiration that Odum and Johnson might have given other folklorists to study contemporary blues was dampened in 1928 by the publication of Newman I. White's *American Negro Folk-Songs*.[225] Although his standards for editing and annotating his texts were higher than those of Odum and Johnson, White clearly had a distaste for the blues, particularly the formal composed kind. He considered blues to have been originally the product of "the Negro underworld,"[226] a view which was supported by Odum's collaborator Guy B. Johnson.[227] While White recognized that blues arose as a form of folksong, he stated that "the value of the blues as an expression of the folk-Negro's mind is somewhat impaired by the fact that the folk blues and the factory product are today almost inextricably mixed" and added that the blues "do not speak for the groups, but only for the singer."[228] He claimed that "most blues sung by Negroes today have only a secondary folk origin; their primary source is the phonograph record."[229] But he concluded optimistically by stating that "the vogue of the blues is already on the wane."[230] In an article the following year (1929) White sharply distinguished folk blues from the popular blues of the cabaret singers, sheet music, and phonograph records, saying, "The folk themselves had no part of this factory product, other than a few genuine folk-phrases which remained in some of the songs."[231]

Almost all of these statements by White were a distortion of reality or were completely wrong. Actually he was in no position to comment on contemporary blues. He had obviously not listened to many phonograph records, particularly those of the self-accompanied male singers. Even most of his own printed texts were collected by other contributors, and White probably had little firsthand knowledge of the songs. Almost all of his blues were collected before 1920, when the influence of the commercial products was still slight, but as a folklorist White was a purist who felt that folksongs were of reduced value once they had been tainted by contact with any commercial products. Perhaps for this reason he disguised the identity of many of the blues texts in his book under such headings as "Songs about Women" and "The Seamier Side" and placed the remainder of his examples at the end of a chapter entitled "Blues and Miscellaneous Songs."

In contrast to Odum and Johnson, White believed that there was nothing important left to be said about the blues.[232] Unfortunately, this opinion seems to have been adopted by most other folklorists for the next three decades. While the record companies continued to record blues by the thousands, including a fair number of traditional folk blues, folklorists gave blues only the most superficial treatment in their writings and devoted less attention to them than they deserved in their fieldwork.

John A. Lomax and his son Alan were the most important folkloristic field-workers during the 1930s and 1940s. They were attempting to document the entire range of American folksong, and as part of this effort they recorded a fair number of blues. Most of their recordings were deposited in the Archive of Folk Song at the Library of Congress. In their writings they tended to view blues simply as part of the vast panorama of American folksong. Thus, there are sections on blues in several of their folksong anthologies with brief general introductions and a few examples drawn from their own fieldwork, the work of other collectors, and phonograph records.[233] Their great folk biographies continue this same trend. Leadbelly (Huddie Ledbetter) is presented as a black folksinger whose vast repertoire included some blues,[234] and Jelly Roll Morton, of course, is presented primarily as a jazz composer and musician, although his biography contains some valuable data on early blues.[235]

The Lomaxes appear to have been drawn to performers who displayed a breadth of repertoire in several genres of folksong rather than a depth in a single genre such as blues. But unlike Newman White, they did exhibit a positive attitude toward blues on phonograph records and considered these to be folksongs. In fact, they did not make clear distinctions at all between folk and "formal" blues. In their writings they continually emphasized the factor of creativity within the folk tradition, and naturally the requirements of commercial recording tended to encourage such creativity. John Lomax even helped Leadbelly to obtain some commercial recording sessions in 1935, and a few years later Alan Lomax published a list of commercially issued folksongs.[236] In their fieldwork they were drawn to a remarkably large number of blues singers who had already made commercial records, such as Son House, Willie Brown, Henry Sims, Willie Blackwell, Bukka

**John A. Lomax with Uncle Rich Brown near Sumterville, Alabama, 1940.
Photo courtesy of The Library of Congress.**

White, Oscar Woods, Sonny Terry, Blind Willie McTell, Jaybird Jones, and Forest City Joe. Many of these men were still highly traditional performers. The Lomaxes also recorded several blues singers who would later go on to make somewhat less traditional records, such as Gabriel Brown, Ivory Joe White (Ivory Joe Hunter), McKinley Morganfield (Muddy Waters), David Edwards, and Calvin Frazier. Although it would be inappropriate to criticize their efforts in the field, it must be considered unfortunate that the Lomaxes never found the opportunity to offer the public biographical portraits of some of these blues artists comparable to those of Jelly Roll Morton and Leadbelly or a historical discussion of the blues such as Odum and Johnson had earlier proposed. Even more unfortunate is the fact that almost all of these field recordings lay in the vaults of the Library of Congress, unknown to or ignored by other researchers, until blues enthusiasts began to issue them on documentary LP records within the last few years. Before this Alan Lomax had published only two highly personal articles about his field experiences with blues singers and a phonograph album containing a few blues and hollers.[237]

A few folklorists collected blues as a by-product of other folksong research during this period. Mary Wheeler's *Steamboatin' Days*, a book of songs associated with the Mississippi and Ohio River steamboat industries, contains some important texts and tunes of folk blues whose origins date back to the turn of the century, though most of the book consists of worksongs associated with an even earlier era. Lawrence Gellert printed a few blues from his researches into black protest songs, but most of his material, like Wheeler's, came from worksongs.[238] Saxon, Tallant, and Dreyer printed a few blues texts from New Orleans in a collection of folklore from that city,[239] and Carmer, Hurston, and Cohn printed useful descriptions of the contexts of southern blues performances.[240]

Other folklorists like Herbert Halpert, John W. Work, and Willis Lawrence James contributed additional blues field recordings to the Archive of Folk Song during the 1930s and 1940s, but with the exception of a few pages by Work they wrote nothing about the results of their fieldwork in this genre.[241] This pattern of folklorists documenting the blues for archival purposes but remaining silent about them in print is difficult to understand. These researchers may have agreed with Newman White that there was nothing important left to be said about the blues, or perhaps they felt that the Lomaxes were covering the subject satisfactorily. It is also possible that they felt overwhelmed by the complexity of the relationship between folk blues and the commercial products and therefore consciously avoided writing on the subject. Without discographies and extensive record libraries available to them, one can understand why they may have hesitated to plunge into this thicket of folk and commercial cross-influences. The ignorance of most folklorists of this period about these relationships is exemplified by a 1939 article by Muriel Davis Longini in which the author prints many blues from her fieldwork in Chicago. She called them "folk songs" and showed only the vaguest awareness of their relationship to current commercial blues records.[242] Even the Lomaxes printed "I Been a Bad, Bad Girl" collected from Ozella Jones, whom they described as "an unspoiled singer in the South," contrasting her with Bessie Smith, but they were unaware of the fact that Ms. Jones's blues was an almost exact reproduction, except for the change of sex, of Barefoot Bill's singing on his 1930 record of "Bad Boy" (Columbia 14526-D).[243]

Some of the most enlightening folkloristic commentary on the blues from this period came from Russell Ames, who had not done fieldwork himself. In a 1943 article he vigorously defended the style and artistic qualities of traditional black folksongs, including blues, and insisted that they be judged on their own merits.[244] In a later article

Ames compared the blues favorably with modern English poetry and stated that blues contained important social meaning.[245]As examples for analysis he chose two commercially recorded blues by Ida Cox and Roosevelt Sykes. The latter in particular had little traditional content, but Ames's analysis does exhibit the willingness of a folklorist to deal with such material.

Several major black literary figures during this period had important things to say about the blues. James Weldon Johnson in 1930 recognized the blues as "essentially folk-songs" and saw in them a great repository of folk poetry.[246] This repository was gleaned that same year for some of its best verses in an article by the poet Sterling Brown.[247] Brown did not give specific sources for his many examples, but he did list many popular blues recording artists and urged his readers to listen to the records that were available. He noted that many authentic folk blues were being issued on commercial records and cited the names of performers like Blind Lemon Jefferson, Blind Blake, Ramblin' Thomas, Barbecue Bob, and Henry Thomas. Brown showed a tremendously wide range of taste and listening experience equaled by no other writer at the time except Abbe Niles. He also showed good judgment in introducing his survey of blues subject matter, saying, "Stoicism is here as well as self-pity, for instance; rich humor as well as melancholy. There are so many Blues that any preconception might be proved about Negro folk life, as well as its opposite. As documentary proof of dogma about the Negro peasant, then, the Blues are satisfactory and unsatisfactory. As documents about humanity they are invaluable."[248] Brown published a similar article in 1952, in which he stressed traditional folk elements in the popular blues.[249] He gave many examples from more recent records and also noted the blues of white folksingers.

In 1936 Alain Locke, with the advice of Sterling Brown, wrote a brief description of the blues, noting quite correctly that folklorists in the past had neglected the study of the music in favor of the lyrics.[250] Locke made a naive but historically important attempt to distinguish regional styles of blues and other secular folk music. He recommended a good number of blues phonograph records, including ones by highly traditional singers like Henry Thomas, Jim Jackson, and Peg Leg Howell, and called for the scientific study of blues on records.[251] He also defended the morality of blues and jazz as "healthy paganism" rather than "morbid eroticism."[252]

In 1941 W. C. Handy published his autobiography with the editorial assistance of Arna Bontemps.[253] In it is contained much valuable information on the early blues and later commercial developments, in which Handy played a major role. Bontemps went on in 1958 to edit *The Book of Negro Folklore* with Langston Hughes, but their section on blues simply reprints Sterling Brown's 1930 article and several blues texts from other printed sources along with a few items of original collectanea without commentary.[254]

While folklorists made field recordings of blues and deposited them in archives, and while literary figures produced occasional works of commentary, the groundwork for modern blues scholarship was being laid by a group of jazz writers starting in the late 1930s. Ramsey and Smith's *Jazzmen*, published in 1939, represents a milestone in jazz and blues writing. Although E. Simms Campbell's contribution on "Blues" is a disappointing, impressionistic description of the genre, William Russell's fine article on "Boogie Woogie" represents the first important historical study of blues on commercial phonograph records.[255] Russell described this blues piano style and told what facts were then known about its main recorded exponents.

Early jazz was undergoing a revival of interest at this time, mainly among whites, and a number of collector and fan magazines began to appear in America, England, and Europe. These not only documented current musical events but contained biographical and discographical articles on various jazz musicians. This interest overflowed into the field of blues, and a number of blues artists were interviewed, "rediscovered," and rerecorded. Most of these were the female singers of the 1920s, who had used hot jazz accompaniment, and the male boogie-woogie pianists. But inevitably the record collectors began to notice the records of folk blues singers which had been made since 1926. In New York they could also attend live performances by Leadbelly, Josh White, Brownie McGhee and Sonny Terry, all of whom performed many traditional folk blues.

Most books on jazz have contained a section on blues, but only a few have had anything original to say. The year 1946 marked the appearance of two of these original works, one in England and one in America. The English contribution was Max Jones's article, "On Blues," in a jazz yearbook.[256] Jones showed a familiarity both with previous literature on the subject and with a broad range of blues records. He considered blues to be essentially folk music and did not distinguish between folk and popular blues. He did, however, recognize the importance of tradition and made some interesting observations on blues composition. He noted that many blues singers had a "floating repertory of song lines and ideas." He stated, "It must be realised that the enterprising singer can, and does, make a blues out of odds and ends of song from the store, adding, changing, taking away as he thinks fit, according to the impulse of the moment and the needs of the song."[257] He added, "Blues is part-created *in the performance* from scraps of verse and melody known to the community as a whole. For that reason the music has special appeal for the community. But it is usually respected by them as the momentary invention of the song-maker whose job it is (at that particular time, anyway) to give back to the people their own songs in acceptable form and with new, and often topical, flavouring."[258] In the rest of this essay Jones discussed the characteristics of the blues form and surveyed the blues' origins, history, and current status. He also mentioned their most common themes and stressed the fact that, in general, blues express a feeling of dissatisfaction. Many of the points made by Jones would be developed further by later writers.

Jones recognized a rural-urban continuum in blues styles. In the same year an American jazz writer, Rudi Blesh, took the two ends of this continuum and made them into distinct styles of blues. Blesh, who had made active attempts to rediscover early jazz and blues artists and to reissue early records, was a member of the "moldy fig" school of jazz criticism, which saw a progressive degeneration in jazz after 1926. His *Shining Trumpets: A History of Jazz* had a generous section devoted to blues, in which he set forth his views with a great deal of purple prose and many extreme value judgments.[259] For example, he castigated W. C. Handy for calling himself the "father of the blues" and boosted instead Jelly Roll Morton as a true jazz and blues performer. Despite their extreme nature, Blesh's views were very influential on later American blues scholarship.

Blesh abandoned the folklorists' distinctions between folk and popular blues and instead set up a tripartite classification system of archaic, classic, and postclassic blues, mainly on the basis of performance styles. Drawing all of his examples and transcriptions from commercial and "jazz revival" records, he rarely mentioned the words "folk" or "traditional" and instead concentrated on creativity and intensity in performance. His emphasis was on the singer rather than the song.

The archaic blues (also called "preclassic") were described as "country blues" and characterized as "free" and "natural." Boogie-woogie and other blues piano styles were viewed as outgrowths of the archaic blues. Most of the performers who exemplified the archaic style were self-accompanied guitarists and pianists. Most of the classic blues singers were women, accompanied by a jazz band or pianist. Classic blues were city blues with artistic and dramatic qualities, which combined the spiritual simplicity, greatness, and natural poetry of the archaic blues with the clarity and power of the greater singers. Blues by female singers which did not meet these criteria or which had the flavor of popular songs were dismissed as "pseudo-blues." The postclassic blues, which Blesh disliked, fell into three subcategories: contemporary, decadent, and eclectic. Contemporary blues had been extensively recorded since 1930, mostly by male singers like Roosevelt Sykes and Lonnie Johnson. They were described as smooth but without sophistication, using clichés and set patterns, and lacking a deep committed feeling. Decadent blues featured sophisticated singing but were cheap, slick, trivial, and frequently pornographic. Eclectic blues were artful and intellectualistic, giving the impression of a sophisticated revival.

Most of Blesh's categories have continued in use by blues writers, though their names have been changed. Archaic blues have become "country" blues.[260] Almost all singers of country blues are male and are either self-accompanied on guitar or harmonica or are accompanied by a string band or jug band. Solo boogie-woogie and barrelhouse pianists are often grouped with country blues singers, though they may also be treated separately. Ideally the performance style of country blues is free and intense. The female blues singers of the 1920s are still called "classic," though sometimes the less intense performers are known as "vaudeville" blues singers. Blesh's postclassic blues have now become "city" blues, but within this category a distinction is usually made between prewar and postwar city blues. In both categories the singers are usually male, but before World War II they used acoustic instruments in various combinations with a less intense style of singing, while after World War II the blues became amplified and more intense.

While Max Jones and Rudi Blesh set the stage for modern blues scholarship by writers who were oriented toward commercial records, folklorists continued through the 1950s and even into the early 1960s to have only a vague awareness of the recorded history of the blues. Frederic Ramsey, who began as a pioneer jazz writer in the 1930s, made folkloristic field trips to the South in the 1950s with the purpose of documenting a broad range of black folk music. He made some very important recordings of other genres of folksong, but his work with blues is less satisfying from both a folkloristic and an aesthetic viewpoint. Ramsey devoted much attention to and issued three whole albums of the music of Horace Sprott, a performer of little importance, whose repertoire was derived largely from records, while he gave only scant details on the more significant performances of the Mississippi String Band, Scott Dunbar, and Cat Iron, failing in the latter case even to obtain the artist's correct name, William Carradine.[261] Folklorist Harold Courlander also did fieldwork in Alabama in the 1950s in an attempt to document a full range of black folk music, but he encountered very little blues activity there.[262] In 1959 Alan Lomax made his first major southern field trip since the early 1940s and recorded some outstanding blues, which he issued on a series of record albums.[263] Although Lomax concentrated on more traditional types of blues, a number of commercial influences can be detected in the pieces he recorded. He did not always show an awareness of these influences in his commentary.

This ignorance on the part of folklorists about commercial developments in the blues actually served to pave the way for a broadened folkloristic outlook in this genre. Gone were the strictures of Newman White, and instead blues of both folk and commercial origin could be collected and published, as long as they were recorded from people who gave the impression of being true "folksingers," i.e., older southern blacks living mainly in isolated rural areas. Folklorist Kenneth Goldstein helped to broaden even further this concept of the folksinger by including blues by urban and commercial performers in a series of documentary records which he supervised for the Prestige/ Bluesville label in the early 1960s. These records presented blues that ranged from the most purely traditional to the most highly commercialized.

By the end of the 1950s commercial record companies had issued thousands of blues of all kinds, though they were now turning largely to other forms of black popular music. Folklorists had shown themselves to be unable to keep abreast of commercial developments in the blues and their effect on the blues as a whole. Those folklorists who were working with blues tended to consider all blues that they recorded to be folksongs, although they were often aware of the further distinctions between country and city blues made by jazz writers on stylistic grounds. However, even these folklorists were few in number, and none of them made blues a major research specialty.

By this time there had grown up a corps of avid blues record collectors and enthusiasts who were eager to blaze trails where folklorists feared to tread. Although commercial blues recordings had been treated to some extent by earlier jazz writers, it was the publication in 1959 of Samuel B. Charters's *The Country Blues* that really began the flood of publications, documentary phonograph records, and intensive research that has come to be known as "the blues revival."[264] In Charters's study, which was based on a combination of his fieldwork and record research, he borrowed the rhetorical style and much of the terminology of Rudi Blesh. Charters showed little awareness of the traditional elements in many of the blues he was dealing with. Consistently he overemphasized or misunderstood the "originality" and "creativity" of folk blues. When he recognized familiar elements, he labeled the performers who used them "thinly derivative." Despite advances in blues research by other writers, Charters has continued this line of criticism in his more recent publications, calling traditional elements "undistinguished," "overly familiar," "conventional," and "derivative."[265] He appears to believe that the country blues singers who recorded earliest were individual creative geniuses and that most of those who recorded later were imitators. He writes,

> Before the period of recording began the styles grew like weeds along the road, a few men on a plantation, two or three singers in one of the small towns sitting in a crowded room with a bottle of corn whisky, their shirts soaked with perspiration, following each others' fingers on the neck of the guitar. Even in the delta counties, with their scattering of farms on the back roads, the styles were often highly individual, but there was a tendency for a few men to cluster around a strong creative personality.[266]

In this environment of creators and imitators Charters saw little evidence of any real tradition. At one point he even wrote, "The country blues is a highly individual style, rather than communal folk music."[267] Although Charters's research has been concentrated on the highly traditional "country" blues, he has adopted an extreme version of the commercial aesthetic standard in his critical discussions.

Some of the best recent blues writing has been produced by non-Americans, who are often removed from much firsthand contact with the blues but who can thus perhaps gain greater objectivity. British writers in particular have devoted much attention to the blues, even more than have American writers. Of these, the most prolific has been Paul Oliver. He followed Max Jones's earlier article with a survey article of his own in 1959[268] and in 1960 published *Blues Fell This Morning*, titled in America *The Meaning of the Blues*. This book is a study of blues lyrics as reflections of black American society. Oliver's 350 textual examples, most of them only parts of songs, are drawn almost exclusively from commercially issued blues records. Little attention is paid to traditional blues lyric expression, nor are the commercial pressures that prodded singers and composers toward novelty, originality, and topicality as fully assessed as they should have been. Nevertheless, this book remains an important work of blues sociology and a worthy successor to the writings of Odum and Johnson.

A field trip to the United States in 1960 and careful attention to the work of other researchers have led Oliver to an increasing awareness of the traditional aspects of the blues. *Conversation with the Blues*, published in 1965, presents the results of his fieldwork in the form of interviews with folk and commercial blues singers. Oliver's next book, *Screening the Blues* (1968), is aptly subtitled "Aspects of the Blues Tradition." Most of the essays in this book continue in a sociological vein, treating such "traditional" themes in the blues as sex, attitudes toward religion, gambling, the black sports hero, and obscenity. Throughout the book Oliver deals with folk as well as commercial blues. Although his claim that all blues are folksongs sounds like an oversimplification, in actual practice he shows a healthy awareness of the interaction of folk and popular forces.[269] Oliver prints variant texts of several obscene blues and uses a historical and comparative methodology typical of folklore studies. Particularly noteworthy is his chapter on "The Forty-Fours," the first major study of the tradition of a single blues song. Yet even though Oliver deals with many traditional elements in this study, he exhibits at times a curiously ambivalent attitude toward them. He criticizes John Lee Hooker for his pentatonic guitar playing, a typical folk practice, saying that Hooker lacks musical knowledge and the ability to form a chord. Of the traditional verses he writes, "For the minor singer with small creative talent they are an indispensable substitute for original thought; for the more inventive bluesman they are sometimes too easy a solution for the verse problems posed by his own song."[270] This is too facile a dismissal of a complex subject.

Oliver's *The Story of the Blues* (1969) is the best available historical survey of the blues. Although it concentrates on commercially recorded blues, considerable attention is paid also to the traditional folk blues, many of which were themselves recorded commercially. At one point, however, Oliver makes a statement reminiscent of Charters's division of blues singers into "intensely personal" creators and imitators. Oliver writes,

> One of the characteristics of the blues is that it is highly personalized—blues singers nearly always sing about themselves—but there are also groups of singers who show certain common features in song or instrumental technique, in choice of melody, idiom or verse. Small "schools" of blues singers emerge, often dominated by a major personality with a markedly individual or original turn of phrase or manner of delivery, who has his immediate disciples.[271]

Oliver is not wrong, of course, in distinguishing between major and minor performers or in noting that some performers tend to copy others, but each such case must be studied individually and at first hand, something that is usually difficult to do when phonograph records constitute the main evidence.

In his most recent work, *Savannah Syncopators* (1970), Oliver deals exclusively with traditional elements in trying to trace African retentions in the blues. Oliver's main thesis is that the music of the Savannah culture area of West Africa, with its professionalism and emphasis on stringed instruments, had an especially heavy influence in shaping the blues. Much of Oliver's evidence pertains to black folk music in general, and his findings are controversial and in need of further detailed investigation,[272] but even so this book represents a pioneering folkloristic, anthropological, and ethnomusicological effort. Earlier researchers had sought Africanisms mainly in the less promising areas of jazz and the spirituals and had largely ignored the rich source material in the blues.

Blues scholarship and documentation have also been furthered through the medium of the phonograph record. Hundreds of albums of studio and field recordings and of reissues of older commercial recordings, all designed for the blues revival audience, have appeared in recent years, while a small number of blues records continues to be issued mainly with black buyers in mind. Some record companies specialize in blues or general folk music records.[273] The task of working with the records as documents has been made immeasurably easier by two recent discographies. Godrich and Dixon's listing of blues records through 1942 is outstanding for its accuracy and comprehensiveness.[274] The compilers have written a separate study detailing the activities of the record companies during this period.[275] Leadbitter and Slaven's discography of blues records between 1943 and 1966 is less comprehensive, omitting artists who perform mainly in a jazz or "rhythm & blues" style.[276] Additional discographies are available for the important early race record series on the Columbia, Paramount, and Victor/Bluebird labels.[277]

A large number of specialist blues magazines have appeared in several languages with articles of discographical, biographical, and historical interest, as well as record reviews and news of current happenings in the blues. The most important of these have been the British *Blues Unlimited* and *Blues World* (now defunct) and the American *Living Blues*. *Blues Unlimited* has published two anthologies of articles that have appeared in various issues of the magazine.[278] Additional important articles on blues have appeared in folksong magazines like *Sing Out!* and jazz magazines like *Down Beat* and *Jazz & Blues*. The level of scholarship of the predominantly amateur writers in these magazines has improved steadily, and the magazines are now essential reading matter for any informed researcher into the blues. Their orientation is largely toward blues on records and their performers, but they often contain analytical articles as well.

Many of the regular contributors to the blues magazines have written book-length studies on particular regional or historical styles and trends in the blues. Though they tend to deal almost exclusively with recorded blues singers and their records, in discussing particular performers they are often careful to place them in the context of a larger blues scene. In older styles, Tony Russell has examined the interaction between black and white musicians, Derrick Stewart-Baxter has discussed the careers of the female "classic" blues singers, and Bengt Olsson and Bruce Bastin have written respectively the histories of the blues in Memphis and the Carolina Piedmont country.[279] More modern styles have been examined by Mike Leadbitter, Mike Rowe, and John Broven for the Mississippi Delta, Chicago, and New Orleans respectively.[280]

The historical books and the articles in the specialist magazines have presented numerous short life histories of individual performers.[281] Many of these are based on interviews and contain valuable comments by singers about their songs and their sources. Longer studies of individual artists include three autobiographies. Besides W. C. Handy's earlier effort, these autobiographies are by Big Bill Broonzy, a very influential performer whose career spanned the folk, commercial, and folk revival scenes, and Perry Bradford, an important blues songwriter and a force in the "classic" and vaudeville blues scene.[282] Books on Bessie Smith, Charley Patton, Tommy Johnson, Eurreal "Little Brother" Montgomery, Muddy Waters (McKinley Morganfield), Peetie Wheatstraw (William Bunch), and Robert Johnson describe the careers and commercial recordings of a variety of folk and popular blues singers, often in considerable depth.[283] Writers in recent years have also devoted a great deal of attention to literary and artistic values in the blues, surveys of their lyric content, discussions of their social context, and musicological analysis.[284]

Several recent writers have had folkloristic training and have applied it to their research. Not all of the work done by folklorists, however, is concerned with purely oral traditions. Perhaps the most ambitious folkloristic study has been Harry Oster's *Living Country Blues,* based on his extensive fieldwork in Louisiana between 1955 and 1961. Oster's 221 examples represent both purely traditional and commercially influenced blues. He took care to trace the sources of the latter by consulting record collectors and other authorities. In his study Oster revealed some hitherto little known forms of blues, the "talking blues" and a kind of "stream of consciousness" blues that owed little either to the stock of traditional verse formulae or to commercial recordings. The latter are best exemplified by the performances of Robert Pete Williams. Oster's book is a study of "country blues," which he distinguishes from "city blues" in the manner of Rudi Blesh and Samuel Charters. The former are said to exhibit "spontaneous expression of thought and mood" and "fluid use of form," while the latter have "planned, arranged texts and music" and "precise classical form, predictable twelve-bar structure."[285] Oster recognizes the two types as two ends of a continuum, but nowhere in his descriptions is there mention of traditional elements or the lack of them.

Oster does, however, mention tradition in making distinctions between different types of country blues singers. He contrasts the imitative "synthesizers," who rely largely on traditional elements, with the creative "innovators," who compose their own blues. Oster writes,

> The true blues singer improvises as easily as he speaks, sometimes more easily. The musical and poetic structure of the blues, its heavy reliance on standard verses and phrases, and the singer's possession of a mental reservoir of blues verses which flow into consciousness with the fluidity and often disorder of thought, in combination make improvisation a natural and simple act for the singer who has absorbed the tradition since childhood. The result may be simply a mélange of traditional verses, inconsistent in combination, or it may be an effective synthesis held together by an emotional logic of association. Most blues singers are essentially imitators; the end product of the improvisation is original primarily in the particular combination of standard parts the singer has hit upon—a patchwork quilt made of already fabricated pieces the maker has put together in a pattern which suits his impulses. Such singers, as for example Butch Cage and Willie Thomas, are not sufficiently creative to express their own lives directly in images and events fashioned from their own personal experiences, but they voice their feelings obliquely, reflecting the basic elements and attitudes of the folk Negro environment rather than specific events in their own lives. The gifted and imaginative blues singers, on the other hand, often put into words and music their own experiences and feelings; they are directly autobiographical; although they draw on standard verses and phrases, they use their raw materials cleverly, coming forth with songs which have traditional elements and at the same time original and poetically exciting turns of phrase and thought—artistic creations which have the impact and vividness of deep personal involvement. Such are the best songs of Robert Pete Williams, Otis Webster, Roosevelt Charles, and Herman E. Johnson.[286]

While Oster's distinction is made on the basis of real stylistic differences, and while he does not feel, like some of his predecessors, that the "imitators" are imitating the creative artists around them, his terminology is still unfortunate. If the "imitative" singers "reflect the basic elements and attitudes of the folk Negro environment," then surely their songs deserve special attention. In fact, such "imitative" singers as Cage and Thomas have for years been mainstays of the Baton Rouge blues scene, while singers like Williams, Webster, Charles, and Johnson, all men of undeniably great talent, have performed most of their lives only for their own benefit and enjoyment. (Williams, since his discovery by Oster, has made many concert appearances outside of his local community, but his audiences have been predominantly white.) Oster is a folklorist, who is certainly aware of the traditional elements in blues, yet his values appear closer to those of a literary critic or to the commercial aesthetic standard rather than to the older folk aesthetic standard. In any case, he straightforwardly presents a generous sample of his findings, and the reader can make his own judgments on the artistic and folkloristic value and importance of various singers and their songs.

Over the years the interests of folklorists in the blues have undergone several changes. Throughout the twentieth century folklorists have continued to document the blues through fieldwork. The earliest analytic discussions of Howard W. Odum and John A. Lomax were concerned mainly with blues lyrics as personal or group expression of feelings and social conditions. In the 1920s Scarborough and especially Odum and Johnson showed an interest in the interplay of folk and commercial influences, but the negative assessment of blues by Newman White seems to have carried more weight. For the next three decades folklorists were content mainly to document the blues through fieldwork. Investigations into folk and commercial interaction were either not made or not reported. This attitude was not confined to blues research, for a similar neglect of commercial factors was exhibited by folklorists in the study of Anglo-American folk music.[287] The main counter to White's opinion was the tendency by folklorists of this period to consider all blues they recorded in fieldwork to be folksongs, though this tendency was mainly the result of ignorance of contemporary commercial developments.

Meanwhile, a "blues revival" was growing out of an earlier "jazz revival" among nonfolklorist record collectors and enthusiasts, who were not terribly concerned with distinctions between folk and popular blues. Instead they made distinctions between country and city blues on the basis of musical style and intensity of performance, often recognizing various phases within each form. At first the orientation of most of these nonfolklorist writers was mainly toward commercially issued blues. They emphasized originality and creativity, despite the fact that many of the most highly acclaimed blues contained much that was traditional and were pure folk blues. Gradually there has developed an increasing awareness of the blues as a tradition, thanks in part to the work of more recent folklorists. At the same time, American folklorists have gained a much needed awareness of commercial influences on the folk tradition through the often outstanding research of the amateur enthusiasts. The prospects for future cooperation between folklorists and blues enthusiasts look very good, as fieldwork continues to be done, articles and books published, university courses, concerts, and festivals presented, and blues records issued and reissued.

Blues scholarship is in good shape today, although there are still many areas in need of further investigation. One of these areas where folklorists especially can contribute is the study of the operations of the oral tradition in the blues. It is indeed surprising that folklorists, whose field encompasses the study of the products and processes of oral tradition, have in the past devoted so little attention to this aspect of the blues. Instead, they have simply tended to consider all blues to be folk-songs and have adopted the country/city distinctions of the record collectors. There would now appear to be a need to reconcile the earlier folk/popular distinction with this more recent country/city distinction. This should not be impossible, since, in general, folk blues are characteristic of the country and popular blues of the city. But we must recognize that these two forms are really two ends of a continuum. Blues singers may move between country and city. Rural singers listen to the phonograph records of city singers. Highly traditional performers can compose original songs in a manner typical of popular blues. We can make generalizations about the blues, but we must first study individual singers and individual songs. A knowledge of the life history, personality, and world view of performers is important and should be correlated with their songs. We should also seek to learn the stylistic influences on their music and the background of the elements in their repertoires. Because of their training folklorists should be well equipped to investigate these subjects.

THE BLUES SINGER

The Black Folksinger's Repertoire

WHEN we refer to certain performers categorically as "blues singers" or "bluesmen," we risk describing them in a distorted manner. In fact, most such artists are black folksingers or popular singers, part of whose repertoire consists of blues. The exact percentage of blues in the repertoires of most of these singers would be impossible to determine. Among such singers a repertoire is rarely a collection of distinct songs that a person has stored in his head and can recall upon request at any time. Instead, his real repertoire is the body of songs that he performs at any one occasion or period of time. The nature of this repertoire and how it is performed are determined by the type of audience that is present, the occasion, and the preferences and orientations of the singer himself.

One of the important factors affecting repertoire is the strong distinction made by most black folk musicians and their audiences between religious and secular songs. Not only are they obviously different in content and structure and performed usually on different social occasions, they are also frequently thought to symbolize two different and mutually exclusive life-styles. The preacher or gospel singer may be a former blues singer, and the church organist or pianist may once have played in barrelhouses, but if a musician has joined the church, he is expected to perform only church songs. He may well forget his earlier blues repertoire. For instance, Robert Johnson, whom I recorded in Skene, Mississippi, in 1967, was quite willing to discuss his former blues repertoire and even demonstrate songs in it for the purposes of my research. The only problem was that he simply couldn't remember much of it, even though he was once so notorious for playing blues and keeping late hours that he was nicknamed Robert Nighthawk. In 1967 his mind was no longer on the blues, and he had become completely devoted to his family and church and had taken up performing religious songs.[1] The Reverend Rubin Lacy was similarly willing to show me how he used to play blues, but by 1966 he had not played guitar in almost thirty years and remembered little. There are, of course, some church members who are willing to risk possible censure by continuing to perform blues. Those who do so usually perform only in their own homes or else far away from their communities, although there are a few exceptions like the late Thomas Shaw, a Texas blues singer who moved to San Diego in the 1930s. Shaw had continued to play blues publicly in recent years while serving at the same time as pastor of a church.

Conversely, a nonchurchgoer may be reluctant to perform church songs, feeling that he could not sing them with the requisite degree of sincerity. Not wishing to be considered a hypocrite, he sticks to secular music until such a time as he might join the church. I have met a number of blues singers with this attitude. Others do perform church songs but not at parties where there is drinking and dancing, while some singers don't care where they perform them. In any case, most secular singers can and do perform some church songs. Charley Patton, for example, was known mainly as a blues singer, but at one point in his life he was a preacher, and among his extant commercial recordings are ten religious songs and a short portion of a sermon. Some of his relatives, whom I interviewed in 1967, remembered him particularly for his church songs. Tommy Johnson recorded only secular songs, but he too knew a few church songs, which he played mainly for members of his family. His brother recalled that "he'd near about make you cry playing church songs."[2]

It is plain that whether a singer performs church songs, and to what extent, is determined largely by his disposition and factors of audience and occasion. He may not perform these songs unless he is a church member, in which case he may perform them exclusively. Or he may perform them only for his family, only on Sundays, or only in answer to requests for specific songs. He may have learned many religious songs in his youth at church or from members of his family, but as a worldly adult he might cease to perform them for a while and then later take them up again after joining the church. To speak abstractly of his "repertoire" would be difficult.

Similar factors affect the repertoire of a man who performs mainly secular songs. Blind Lemon Jefferson, for example, once refused an offer of twenty dollars to play a blues because his mother had told him never to play on a Sunday. His friend Rubin Lacy, who was later to become a preacher, played the requested piece and took the money.[3] Other singers might perform different kinds of songs for different audiences. Charley Patton, for instance, recorded fifty extant songs, among which are thirty-two blues, three blues ballads, ten religious songs, three nonblues lyric folksongs, and two versions of popular Tin Pan Alley songs. Everyone remembers him primarily as a blues singer, a fact which his recorded output reflects, but in their recollections of the rest of his material his surviving relatives emphasized his church songs, while fellow musicians Jake Martin and Mott Willis pointed out to me that Patton often played nonblues lyric songs such as "Ain't Gonna Rain No More." Martin and Willis themselves both preferred the latter type of song and therefore remember it well from Patton's repertoire. Martin and Patton, in fact, both began their musical careers near Bolton and Edwards, Mississippi, under the influence of the Chatman family, who played mainly dance pieces and ragtime songs for white audiences. Both Martin and Patton moved to Dockery's plantation in the Delta, but, whereas Patton began to orient himself mainly toward black audiences who wanted to hear blues, Martin found it more profitable to continue to play for white audiences who appreciated blues much less. Nevertheless, Martin claims that he could play blues like Patton and the other local musicians, while Patton is known to have played on occasion for white audiences and with white harmonica and fiddle players. It is probable that both men knew many of the same songs and, in a sense, had similar repertoires. Yet in actual performance Patton was likely to play one type of music and Martin another. Mott Willis, in contrast, spent part of his career playing popular and ragtime songs in minstrel shows for white or mixed audiences and part playing blues at house parties for black audiences, meeting equal success in both.[4]

Almost all writers on blues have made a distinction between the "songster" and the "bluesman." The former is generally described as someone who performs a broad variety of song types, such as ragtime pieces, popular songs, blues, and church songs, while the latter is someone who performs blues almost exclusively. Although these terms admittedly can be useful for some purposes, in this study I try for several reasons to avoid using them. One of the main reasons is that "songster" is used by other writers in a different sense than black folksingers themselves use the word. Howard W. Odum reported the correct meaning in 1911 as "any negro who regularly sings or makes songs."[5] This is how I have always heard the term used by black folksingers and audiences. Thus, those who perform blues exclusively are called "songsters," as are all other people who have a reputation for being good singers, no matter what kinds of songs they sing. "Bluesman," on the other hand, often carries with it the implication of a greater commitment to the blues and a more intense performance style than others with wider repertoires have. In one sense, of course, this implication is true, since whatever commitment to music the "bluesman" has is channeled into the blues. Yet there are some so-called "bluesmen" who consistently give bland, unemotional performances, while a "songster" like Charley Patton is considered by many to have been the greatest country blues singer ever to have recorded. The term "bluesman" is also sometimes attached to performers on the basis of recorded evidence only. Eleven of the twelve extant recordings of Tommy Johnson, for instance, are blues, so that he has generally been described as a "bluesman," but actually his repertoire was much broader and included church songs, dance pieces, ragtime pieces, and various songs for whites.[6] Johnny Temple, another singer originally from Mississippi, recorded sixty-two issued blues between 1935 and 1949, yet in his live appearances in Chicago he could usually be heard playing polkas and Italian music for underworld kingpins.[7] Because of such problems I prefer in this study to use the term "blues singer" for anyone who sings blues, regardless of what other songs he might sing.

Exactly why musicians choose particular types of music and particular directions in their careers would have to be related in part to their personalities. Yet such relationships are difficult to establish other than impressionistically, and when we ask these questions, we are often at a loss for answers. Why did a fine performer like Mississippi John Hurt spend almost all of his life in one small town and never travel about except to make a handful of commercial recordings?[8] Why did an inventive blues composer like Sam Chatmon, whose blues often display an urban sophistication, spend most of his life in rural Mississippi?[9] And why did Charley Patton play mostly for blacks and Jake Martin mostly for whites? The difficulty of establishing the relationship between personality and role among professional urban blues singers has been noted by Charles Keil.[10] Among rural performers, for whom music is only a part-time activity and who often perform other types of songs besides blues, this difficulty is greatly increased. For such persons it is possible that music is not so much a direct expression of their personalities and lives as it is an activity which complements or serves as an escape from other activities and feelings. In any case, it is much easier to speculate about and describe these problems than to provide hard answers.[11]

It is clear, then, that many black folksingers have the ability to perform different kinds of songs, but they often tend to specialize in one particular kind, depending upon the audience, the occasion, and their own personal and musical orientations. These factors can present serious problems to the field researcher, particularly if he is not aware of their existence. This can be illustrated by one of my own field experiences in Crystal Springs, Mississippi, in 1970. I was recording the musicians Floyd Patterson, Mott Willis, and the latter's nephews, Willis and Charlie Taylor. All four men knew each other well and had played together often. All were likewise capable of performing a wide variety of songs. Since my own time was very limited, I was trying to record mainly their blues and was deliberately neglecting spirituals, rags, and popular songs. They, on the other hand, thought of me as an audience and persistently tried to determine my likes and dislikes. Since I am white, they assumed that I would want to hear mainly nonblues songs, and I don't believe that they ever did fully comprehend my interest in blues. The following portion of an interview will illustrate our problems of communication. I was interviewing Patterson about his life as a musician when Willis Taylor interrupted.

> W. Taylor: *Do they care too much about swing music now? Rock 'n' roll or blues? You know what I mean. I always like to get to the root of a thing myself.*
> Evans: *Do you play all these different kinds of things too?*
> W. Taylor: *I'm asking a question.*
> Evans: *I'll record the other stuff too, but I like the blues.*
> C. Taylor: *I likes 'em too. I do.*
> Patterson: *Well, I've always liked the popular songs. You know, when I was playing, I played more for house parties. I never did care much for the blues on account of the way I learned.*
> W. Taylor: *Mostly everything I do, I try to do to satisfy. What little I do, I try to do . . .*
> Evans: *You can play all the different kinds?*
> W. Taylor: *That's what I was talking about. You know what I mean. I think that's the way to do. I don't know. Might do wrong.*[12]

Patterson then went on to tell me how he had led a twenty-four-piece orchestra in Europe shortly after World War II, which played sentimental popular songs. In his earlier years he had played blues in the Delta with Charley Patton and others, but when he returned home to Crystal Springs, he played waltzes, fox-trots, and sentimental songs for white house parties.[13] Patterson wanted to play mainly sentimental songs for me; the Taylor brothers, since they were unsure of my taste, tried to give me a representative sampling of their repertoire; and Mott Willis, their uncle, constantly tried to play church songs and ragtime pieces. To add to the problem, a young woman dropped in on the session and tried to persuade the men to play soul music and rock 'n' roll. When it was plain that they were not going to do so, she left. Only by making persistent requests was I able to record a significant number of blues. Otherwise, I am certain that I would have been entertained with more songs like "Stardust," "Shanty Town," and "Just Because." In this situation there was no correct or "scientific" way for me to proceed, because my presence in itself had a major effect in determining what songs would be performed. But I feel that the way I handled it made the situation no more artificial than it would have been if I had simply let the musicians play what they felt like playing. In either case they would have taken me into consideration as their audience, just as they would with any other audience.[14]

The Blues Repertoire

The preceding discussion of repertoires has been presented mainly in order to place blues in a wider context and to make the reader aware of how limited the concept of "repertoire" is in the study of black folksong. In the study of blues specifically the concept is even more

limited. Theoretically one could visit a folksinger with a wide repertoire, like Tommy Johnson or Charley Patton, and record his performances on many different occasions and before different types of
audiences. Ultimately the researcher would collect the singer's "repertoire" of church songs, ballads, and ragtime and popular songs. He
would collect some of the songs many times, but eventually he would
meet the point of diminishing returns for new material. But there
would probably be no end to the performer's blues. This is because
many folk blues are composed in a manner quite different from the
other types of folksong. Indeed, it is sometimes difficult to speak of folk
blues as "songs" in the usual sense. Instead of repertoires of blues
songs, we must often deal with *outputs of blues performances*. Many folk
blues singers do not learn or compose blues at some particular point in
time and then repeat them the same way in all subsequent performances. Instead, each blues performance often produces a new song,
one that may never again be performed by the singer. In such cases,
composition and performance are identical and inseparable. The singer
does not have a blues repertoire of distinct songs but a collection of
lyric, melodic, and instrumental elements that he uses in various combinations to produce these blues performances. This collection of elements is the real repertoire of such a folk blues singer.

Many of these elements are traditional and are shared by hundreds of folk blues singers. Those singers who perform together over a
long period of time in the same community naturally tend to share a
large number of these traditional elements. Yet no two singers in a
community may ever perform the same "song," even though they may
have made music together on many occasions or learned blues from
each other. The sum total of the elements shared by the blues singers
in a community is what I call a *local tradition*. The blues produced by
one local tradition will be discussed in the next chapter.

Some folk blues singers, in contrast, learn or compose songs
which they may perform the same way every time. These may be built
out of elements in their own local traditions, they may be learned from
other singers or from phonograph records, or they may be quite original and distinctive compositions. Most singers, in fact, use several of
these approaches to learning and composing, showing greater or lesser
preference for certain ones.

In studying the processes of learning, composition, and handling
of repertoire, we must be wary of accepting at face value the claims of
blues singers to originality. Almost every field-worker has encountered
singers who claim to have composed blues which were actually learned
from other singers or from records.[15] A blues singer usually is not deliberately trying to deceive when he claims as his own a song whose
source lies elsewhere. Instead, he may simply mean that he has produced an "original" combination of traditional elements, that he has
given a piece a new tune, accompaniment, or arrangement, or simply
that he has personalized a song through some meaningful association

with its lyrics. Unless the field-worker can get the singer to explain precisely what he means by his claim of original composition, or unless he is familiar with the singer's local tradition and other possible sources, particularly phonograph records, he is apt to print misinformation when writing about the singer and his songs. Since few local blues traditions have been carefully documented, and since research tools for dealing easily with the traditional aspects of blues on phonograph records are not available, we are often forced to accept the statements of blues singers about their songs and hope that they are accurate.

Performers' Attitudes Toward Composing Blues

Blues singers themselves have differing opinions on the proper state of mind needed for composing or performing blues. Since blues generally deal with problems, most singers agree that one has to have experienced worry in order to sing or compose them. Yet it is not necessary to be worried at the actual time of performance or composition. Leonard "Baby Doo" Caston says, "You don't always have to have the blues to write a blues."[16] The Reverend Rubin Lacy recalled that he usually felt good when he was singing or composing blues. He said,

> *I've sung 'em on many a day and never thought I had 'em. What did I want to have the blues for, when I had everything I wanted, all the liquor, all the money I needed, and more gals than I needed? What did I need with the blues? I was playin' 'em because everybody loved to hear me play 'em and I loved to play 'em. I could play 'em, yeah. I was having fun. Sometimes I'd be kind of bothered and worried as any other man would be. I wasn't lively all the time. Plenty times I would feel lonely as other people did. But as a whole I had more blues since I been preaching than I ever had when I was playing the blues. . . . I had to sacrifice, I had to put down something to go to preaching. Ain't many men put down what I put down, but I had to put down a whole lot just for preaching. And I've had a heap of blues since I been preaching. . . . When I was in the world, I got as much of the world as I needed. . . . I'd play sometimes better, sing better and everything when I was feeling good. . . . Sometimes I'd lay down at night, wake up the next morning and get my old guitar and just tune it up and go to playing something I never played before.[17]*

Others, however, believe that blues come from a sad and depressed feeling and that composing or performing them makes one happier. Boogie Woogie Red states, "Blues is something that relax your nerves. . . . But there's so much good feeling in the blues, that's the main thing about the blues."[18] J. D. Short adds, "It's a lot of times we can get very worried and dissatisfied, and we can get to singing the blues and if we can play music and play the blues we play the blues for a while until we get kind of pacified. That cuts off a lot of worry."[19] Perhaps the therapeutic functions of blues singing have been stated best by Hogman Maxey, a prisoner at the Louisiana State Penitentiary in Angola: "Whenever you sing the blues jest right, why you feels like a million, when you may not have a dime. . . . That's the best part of my life is blues."[20]

Probably most blues singers would admit that both happy and sad feelings can cause one to sing or compose blues, though some singers would emphasize one over the other. Roosevelt Sykes, who has composed and recorded hundreds of blues since 1929, many of them ebullient or humorous, emphasizes the good feeling, saying,

> *If you go into the feeling, slow blues give you one feeling, fast blues give you a jolly feeling. The more depressed you are and lonesome and sad, seems like the more you get out of it if you play it slow and sing and concentrate better. Looks like it's unravelling your troubles and discord and everything. Then when you plays fast, you jumps and you dances and you feels good. Usually that's the way I feel when I approach a bandstand.*[21]

Henry Townsend recognizes that both happy and depressed feelings can inspire him to sing and compose blues, but he adds,

> *In most cases the way I feel, the song will come to you when you are really depressed you know. I mean, words'll come to you and you feel them and you decide you'll do something about it, so the thing that you do about it is more or less to put it in rhymes and words and make them come out. It gives you relief—it kinda helps somehow.*[22]

Booker White, another prolific composer of blues, claimed that the best state of mind for blues is somewhere between worry and satisfaction. He said,

> *Go into it with all your soul. Have a little something on the outside to kind of contain your mind while you're making them good blues. . . . You don't want to be too worried, and you don't want to be too satisfied either, but you want to have your mind a little mixed up just enough to keep from being too bothered or too happy. . . . You got to be into music and have it in your soul. Sometimes I don't have it.*[23]

White's statement is in perfect accord with the basic blues ideology of contrast and tension. He added that a person with a "strong mind" would not sing the blues, because he would not know the feeling of uncertainty and indecision. He said,

> *You don't have to be in trouble a lot of times to have a worried mind. You can just get to sitting down there thinking about things, just your girlfriend, something. You don't know where she is. You can't get her over the telephone. You can't write her no letter. You don't know her address. And your mind is shouting in there. . . . Just most anything can pass along and upset you if you ain't got a mighty strong mind.*[24]

Many blues singers feel that their music and words "just come to them" and refer to their songs as "air music," because they are in the air and ready to be made manifest at any time by a blues singer who has the proper talent. Such a concept makes our study of blues composition difficult, for it includes what we would call tradition, inspiration, and improvisation. The blues singer sees all of these abstractions as one process or force. He does not isolate something called a tradition, and therefore, even when being traditional, he does not feel restricted. Likewise, he does not feel obliged always to improvise. "Air music" can encompass both improvisation and the use of traditional material. A song may, in fact, be completely traditional with respect to its component elements yet also be totally improvised and never performed again the same way. Tommy Johnson improvised many such blues out of traditional elements and called his pieces "air music."[25] Booker White applied the term "sky songs" to improvised blues with a much greater degree of originality.[26] Roosevelt Sykes uses a similar expression to describe his original blues, although these tend to be more deliberate and less improvised in composition. He says, "I always try to get mine right out of the blue sky. I always were a pioneer, always tried to do something that's never been done before, and I don't find it hard because most of it just comes to me. New things always comin' up."[27] Robert Pete Williams, another blues singer who, like Booker White, improvises many of his pieces at the time of performance, says that he literally hears the blues in the air. He claims that a change in the air around 1942, after he had been playing blues for about ten years, caused his performance style to become more experimental. He says,

> *The sound of the atmosphere, the weather changed my style. But I could hear, since me being an air-music man. The air came in different, with a different sound of music. Well, the atmosphere, when the wind blowing carries music along. I don't know if it affect you or not, but it's a sounding that's in the air, you see? And I don't know where it comes from—it could come from the airplanes, or the moaning of automobiles, but anyhow it leaves an air current in the air, you see. That gets in the wind, makes a sounding, you know? And that sounding works up to be a blues.[28]*

It is possible that by "air music" some singers simply mean "ear music," as contrasted with music that is read from a printed score, but the above statements by blues singers would indicate that most view it as a process of composition and performance. For a performer like Robert Pete Williams, the blues seem to exist as an almost spiritual force that enters and possesses the singer. In fact, many singers do personify the blues as a sort of supernatural being, and some address songs to "Mr. Blues." [29] Son House, for example, sang the following stanza in his "Preachin' the Blues—Part 2" (Paramount 13013), recorded in 1930:

> *Well, I met the blues this morning walking just like a man.*
> *Ooooh, walking just like a man.*
> *I said, "Good morning, Blues; now give me your right hand."*

When blues are personified, the representation is generally as a malevolent being or trickster. Their character is quite like that of the devil, and, in fact, the blues were once known as the "blue devils."[30]

Tommy Johnson, who claimed that his blues were "air music," also
claimed that he learned his music from the devil. His older brother, the
Reverend LeDell Johnson, said,

> *He could just sit down and just think up a song, which is blues,*
> *and make 'em hisself without anybody learning him. I remember*
> *since I been here in Jackson. Me and him would play for some*
> *white folks here, and he'd just set up and just set there and follow*
> *with his box, and he could make a song in ten minutes. Now if*
> *Tom was living, he'd tell you. He said the reason he knowed so*
> *much, said he sold hisself to the Devil. I asked him how. He said,*
> *"If you want to learn how to play anything you want to play and*
> *learn how to make songs yourself, you take your guitar and you*
> *go where a road crosses that way, where a crossroad is. Get there,*
> *be sure to get there just a little 'fore twelve o'clock that night so*
> *you'll know you'll be there. You have your guitar and be playing a*
> *piece sitting there by yourself. You have to go by yourself and be*
> *sitting there playing a piece. A big black man will walk up there*
> *and take your guitar, and he'll tune it. And then he'll play a piece*
> *and hand it back to you. That's the way I learned to play anything*
> *I want." And he could. He used to play anything, don't care what*
> *it was. Church song. You could sing any kind of tangled up song*
> *you want to, and I'll bet you he would play it.*[31]

Motifs about learning from the devil to play a stringed instrument are
quite common in both black and white American folklore and have
both European and African antecedents,[32] but perhaps they are particularly appropriate to a kind of music like the blues. This may partly
explain why blues are so vigorously opposed by some churchgoers.
Some blues singers, however, like the late Babe Stovall, consider their
ability to perform or compose to be a God-given talent, while others
attribute it to inheritance.[33]

The Influence of Phonograph Records and the Handling of Recorded Sources

Despite some singers' claims to supernatural help or to hearing blues in
the air, many of them have very down-to-earth sources for much of
their material. One of the most important of these sources is phonograph records, which have been appearing by the thousands since
1920. Blues singers hear these records and try to reproduce them for
local audiences. In many cases they try to reproduce the songs exactly
as they sound on the record in order to satisfy the requests of members
of their audiences. I have recorded a good number of these more or less
accurate imitations and have even observed blues singers criticizing
each other and arguing over the faithfulness of their performance to
the original version on the record. Houston Stackhouse and Boogie Bill
Webb, for instance, can give extraordinarily accurate imitations of their
recorded sources, including reproductions of the guitar parts note for
note and mimicry of the vocal delivery. In other pieces they may offer
only minor variations from their original sources. One such variation is

shortening a song by omitting verses or instrumental breaks. This may be done either because of forgetfulness or because these portions of the piece do not appeal to the singer who learns it from the record. Conversely, some performers repeat verses or instrumental breaks in order to make the blues longer than the limit of approximately three minutes imposed by the 78 or 45 rpm record.

The reasons for this imitation of records are obvious. They are the same reasons that cause high school dance bands to imitate the current rock hits on the top forty charts. The popular records simply carry with them a great deal of prestige. Furthermore, they have all of the value of novelty and currency, of being the "latest thing," and in years to come they acquire great value as items of nostalgia. The artists who make the records have their music enshrined in a permanent form, which can reach a potentially unlimited number of people. Those who hear the records may imagine that the artists have acquired wealth and fame. In short, the artists become popular heroes, a status which is reinforced when people consider that the artists began in the same condition as themselves. When a blues singer recreates a currently popular record for an audience, everyone present shares vicariously in the real or imagined success of the recorded artist. The performer is praised for being able to sound "just like" the record. For a brief time all participate in a massive popular cultural experience which takes them out of their small community and unites them with other singers and audiences everywhere that the record can reach. This feeling persists even when performers recreate older established popular records. Many blues singers now refer to their songs as "records," whether they were actually learned from records or not. I have also heard blues singers quote proverbs and attribute them to blues singers who used them in the lyrics of records.[34]

Boogie Bill Webb serves as a good example of a blues singer whose music is based largely on records. He was born in 1926 and has spent most of his life in New Orleans, where he works as a longshoreman. In the 1940s he was active in the blues scene of Jackson, Mississippi, and learned much from his association with performers like Tommy Johnson and Bubba Brown. Since then he has constantly tried to update his music by keeping abreast of the latest trends. He recorded four songs for Imperial Records in 1953, two of which were issued on a record that did not sell very well. All of these recordings showed the influence of recent popular blues records. Since then, Webb has modernized his style and repertoire even further. Although he still performs some songs learned from the Jackson blues singers and has a few original or partly original compositions, most of his songs are imitations of popular blues records of the last three decades, even down to the guitar parts. Webb is quite proud of his ability to answer requests for a wide variety of blues, and if he doesn't know a requested piece, he will attempt to learn it. To this end, he keeps a large record and tape collection at his home. His definition of a good musician, in fact, is a person who can answer any request. He also likes to meet and associate with other more successful blues musicians. He once drove all the way to Shreveport to meet a musician he had heard about. Webb is proud of the fact that he sat in on guitar with Fats Domino a few times, but his greatest thrill was meeting several of the most popular blues singers in Chicago in the 1950s. He says,

> The only group I was with in Chicago was Muddy Waters'.
> Actually I wasn't in the band, but I was with them—Muddy
> Waters, John Lee Hooker, Jimmy Reed, all of them. We was at
> 62nd and Cottage Grove. And also Chuck Berry. Yes indeed. They
> thought I was good. . . . That must have been about the best time
> of my life, when I was among all those real good guitar players,
> and all of them was famous but me. I think that was the best time
> of my life, right then.[35]

So great is the prestige of records that in some cases blues singers who have been unable or unwilling to keep up with the latest songs and styles have lost their audiences. I have heard many performers complain about this situation. Perhaps their greatest complaint is against the jukebox. Many of the owners of clubs, bars, and "juke joints" have installed jukeboxes and no longer hire blues musicians to play for dancing. Their reasoning is difficult to counter. Instead of having to pay musicians, they can be paid themselves for music by their patrons. Furthermore, they can be sure that they are providing the latest hits performed by excellent musicians. Some owners might hire live musicians occasionally as a novelty, or (in the larger places) they might be able to hire a popular recording artist, but most blues performers today who have not made records are forced to play mainly at house parties and picnics or for their own amusement. Even at the house parties and picnics one occasionally encounters the amateur disc jockey with his collection of records and portable sound system, spinning his discs and "talking some shit" between selections. Even as early as the 1920s it was common for people to bring their portable record players to parties.[36] Live performers probably began to notice this competition not long after the first blues record was issued.

At this point we shall examine some of the processes that blues singers use when converting records into something that is their own. All of these processes can be applied equally well to songs that are learned in person from other performers. The reader should also keep in mind that these processes usually occur in combination rather than individually. (Further examples of the handling of recorded sources will be presented in chapter 4.)

The processes we have mentioned so far of outright imitation, shortening, and repetition of elements do not produce any really significant alterations of the original records, because the end products are still based entirely on what is on the records. A more important change made by performers is the alteration of the instrumental accompaniment. The player might use a different instrument from that on the record, he might use only one instrument where the record had several, or he might play a different part on the same instrument. This part might come from another record, from another blues in the performer's repertoire, or from his local tradition, or it might be deliberately invented for this particular piece. In any case, this process of changing the accompaniment is extremely common and constitutes an important step in the conversion of a popular record back into a folk blues. Almost all blues singers make use of it to some extent.

Alteration of a record's instrumental part can lead to a further process, concatenation of portions of two or more blues records so that a medley is produced. A performer can accomplish this as long as he plays all of the pieces in the same key. For instance, when Babe Stovall played guitar in the key of A, he would often combine stanzas from Kokomo Arnold's 1934 record of "Milk Cow Blues" (Decca 7026) and Arthur "Big Boy" Crudup's 1941 record of "Black Pony Blues" (Bluebird B8896). At other times he would perform these pieces separately. He would retain the melodies of each of the original records, but his guitar part was unlike Arnold's or Crudup's and was adapted instead from traditional sources. King Solomon Hill's 1932 recording of "Whoopee Blues" (Paramount 13116) is simply a combination of stanzas from both sides of a Lonnie Johnson record from 1930, "She's Making Whoopee in Hell Tonight"/"Death Valley Is Just Half Way to My Home" (Okeh 8768), set to a new guitar accompaniment by Hill. Concatenation is not a particularly common process, but some performers favor it as a means of extending their pieces when they, or members of their audience, feel in the mood for something longer.

Another way to make a song from a record into one's own piece is to personalize the lyrics. Since most blues lyrics are set in the first person, this process undoubtedly takes place many times unconsciously without any change in the words. But sometimes a singer inserts his own name or that of someone in his audience or community into a blues learned from a record. For example, Boogie Bill Webb performs an instrumental blues with a short spoken part that he calls "Bill's Boogie Woogie." The first line of his spoken part is, "I want all of you to know this is 'Bill's Boogie Woogie'." The piece, in reality, is simply a guitar arrangement of a very popular piano blues record called "Pine Top's Boogie Woogie" (Vocalion 1245) made in 1928 by Pine Top Smith. Webb's spoken part is similar to Smith's except for the substitution of his own first name. To one who did not know the source, the piece would seem to belong thoroughly to Webb, and, in fact, it is this very piece from which he earned his nickname. Webb also sings a version of "Red Cross Store," a blues about the government relief program for the poor during the Depression and World War II, which is derived ultimately from a commercial blues recorded by Walter Roland in 1933, "Red Cross Blues" (Banner 32822). Webb sings only three stanzas from his recorded source but repeats each of these, thus doubling the song's length. He has changed the accompaniment from piano to guitar, but the vocal melody is basically unchanged. Except for the instrumental part, the main significant alteration by Webb is a personalization of the text produced by the insertion of his name and that of his wife, Carol, into the lyrics and by a spoken introduction as follows: "I'm gonna tell you about it, people, just like it is. I think this was in 1945, on the ninth of September." By these simple changes Webb again appears to have thoroughly personalized someone else's song.

Boogie Bill Webb also uses the process of localization to alter a recorded blues. This consists of setting the scene of a blues in or near the singer's own community. The process is best documented by the text of Webb's "Seven Sisters Blues," which is derived from Johnnie Temple's 1937 recording of "Hoodoo Women." Temple's original text is as follows:

Example 12. "Hoodoo Women." Johnnie Temple, vocal; Odell Rand, clarinet; Horace Malcolm, piano; Joe McCoy, guitar; Charlie McCoy, guitar; unknown artist, string bass; Fred Flynn, drums. New York, Oct. 6, 1937. Decca 7385.

1. *Yes, I've been out on the mountain, looked over in Jerusalem.*
   Well, I went out on the mountain, looked over in Jerusalem.
   Well, I seed them hoodoo women, ooh Lord, making up their lowdown
       plan.

2. *Well, I'm going to Newport just to see Aunt Caroline Dye.*
   Well, I'm going to Newport just to see Aunt Caroline Dye.
   She's a fortune teller. Ooh Lord, she sure don't tell no lie.

3. *And she told my fortune as I walked through her door.*
   And she told my fortune as I walked through her door.
   Said, "I'm sorry for you, buddy. Ooh Lord, your woman don't want you
       no more."

4. *Well, I turned around, said, "I believe I'll go downtown."*
   Well, I turned around, said, "I believe I'll go downtown,
   To Chicago River, ooh Lord, and jump overboard and drown."

5. *The hoodoo said, "Son, please don't act no clown."*
   The hoodoo said, "Son, please don't act no clown,
   Because it's a many more women, ooh Lord, laying around in this no good
       town."

6. *The hoodoo is all right. It's a lowdown plan.*
   The hoodoo is all right. It's a lowdown plan.
   But they will take your woman, ooh Lord, and put her with another man.

Temple's text is typical of commercially recorded blues in being thematic, although the continuity is not perfect. Temple is credited as the song's composer, and most of the lyrics appear to be original with him, except for the second stanza, which is traditional. The song expresses the ambivalent feelings of many lower-class blacks about practitioners of voodoo or hoodoo. Aunt Caroline Dye was one of the most famous of these and was the subject of a number of blues. She died in 1918 in her home town of Newport, Arkansas, allegedly at the age of 108.[37]

Johnnie Temple. Photo by Marina Bokelman.

Webb reduces Temple's text to four stanzas, gives it a new instrumental accompaniment, personalizes it by inserting his nickname, and localizes it to the city of Algiers, which is across the Mississippi River from his home in New Orleans. He drops Aunt Caroline Dye and makes the hoodoo instead the Seven Sisters. These were probably one woman, a "seventh sister," whose name was suggested by the widespread belief that a seventh son or daughter in a family will have supernatural or psychic powers. This woman in Algiers had a house on the waterfront with seven rooms and would send her clients into each in succession while appearing to them in seven different guises. Her fame inspired imitation Seven Sisters in Alabama, Virginia, and South Carolina, as well as "Seven Brothers" in New York.[38] Webb's text is as follows:

Example 13. "Seven Sisters Blues." Boogie Bill Webb, vocal and guitar in standard tuning, key of A. New Orleans, Apr. 1, 1969. Recorded by David Evans. Issued on *High Water Blues*, Flyright LP 512, 12" LP.

1. *I'm gonna swim the river to Algiers, Louisiana, just to see have the Seven*
        Sisters died.
    I'm gonna swim the river to Algiers, Louisiana, just to see have the Seven
        Sisters died.
    They is a noble fortune teller, ooh well, and they sure don't tell no lie.

2. *Well, they told my fortune as I walked into their door.*
    They told my fortune as I walked into their door.
    She said, I'm sorry for you, Boogie; ooh well, that little woman don't want
        you no more.

GUITAR CHORUS.

3. *The hoodoo said, "Boogie, please don't act no clown."*
    The hoodoo said, "Boogie, please don't act no clown.
    They got many more of them little women, ooh well, laying 'round this no
        good town."

4. *The hoodoo girl's all right. It is a lowdown plan.*
    The hoodoo girl's all right, but it is one lowdown plan.
    They will take your good gal from you, ooh well, and put her with another
        man.

Another way of changing recorded blues is to modernize them. A performer might simply play an updated instrumental accompaniment for the newer dances.[39] For example, Dr. Ross's 1954 recording of "Going to the River" (issued on *Dr. Ross, His First Recordings*, Arhoolie 1065, 12" LP), with its strong danceable boogie-woogie guitar accompaniment, is an updated version of Blind Lemon Jefferson's 1926 record of "Wartime Blues" (Paramount 12425). The process of modernization can affect the text also. In 1936 Robert Johnson recorded "Terraplane Blues" (ARC 7-03-56), with his own guitar for accompaniment, using imagery based on an automobile then being produced by the Hudson company. The record was a minor hit. In 1965 it was updated by Johnny Shines as "Dynaflow Blues" (issued on *Chicago/The Blues/Today!*, Vol. 3, Vanguard VSD 79218, 12" LP). The main changes were in the name of the automobile model and the more modern amplified ensemble accompaniment.

Many blues singers make more extensive changes in their sources by using the records merely as jumping-off points for creating their own personal versions of songs. Some singers perform these versions the same way each time, while others improvise and recreate at each performance. The process consists of beginning a song more or less as an imitation of a record and then departing from the source by adding new material. For example, Son House's "Shetland Pony Blues" uses Charley Patton's 1929 recording of "Pony Blues" (Paramount 12792, Example 24) as a jumping-off point.[40] House knew Patton personally but had heard Patton's record before their first meeting. House sings a melody similar to one of the three strains used by Patton and plays a bottleneck part based on Patton's original nonbottleneck accompaniment. Patton's original text contained only two stanzas that mentioned a pony before it moved on to other themes. House, however, goes on to describe the attributes of his pony throughout his version.

Another example of this process is found in Esau Weary's version of Jimmy Reed's big hit of 1953, "You Don't Have to Go" (Vee Jay 119). Reed's song was largely responsible for popularizing the "walking bass" style of guitar playing, and it has continued to be one of the most imitated of all blues records. The record has a three-stanza text and accompaniment by Reed's harmonica and guitar (the latter almost inaudible), second guitar by Eddie Taylor in the walking bass style, and drums played by Morris Wilkerson. Esau Weary's version, also with just three stanzas but having only his own guitar for accompaniment, starts out like Reed's but gradually departs from the sound of the record. Weary's text is as follows:

Example 14. "You Don't Have to Go." Esau Weary, vocal and guitar in standard tuning, key of E. Bogalusa, La., Aug. 26, 1970. Recorded by David Evans. Issued on *South Mississippi Blues*, Rounder 2009, 12" LP.

Boogie Bill Webb. Photo by David Evans.

1. *Oh baby, darling, you don't have to go.*
   Oh baby, darling, you don't have to go.
   Yeah, I'm gonna pack up my suitcase; down the road I go.

2. *Said, I give you all of my money, trying to treat you right.*
   You leave home early in the morning; you don't even come back till late at
       night.
   Oh baby, darling, you don't have to go.
   Yeah, I'm gonna pack up, woman; down the road I go.

3. *Said, my mama told me; my daddy sat and cried.*
   Said, my mama told me, and you know my daddy sat and cried.
   "Son, you got more women than any little bitty man your size."

GUITAR CHORUS.

Weary's guitar accompaniment is in a boogie-woogie style, close enough to suggest the walking bass of Reed's record but still distinctive. As Weary begins singing, the piece sounds like it is going to be an imitation of Reed's record with only the accompaniment changed. He sings the same melody as Reed, and his first stanza is the same as Reed's. He starts the second stanza like Reed with a couplet substitution for the first line of the AAB pattern, but soon he begins to depart from

Esau Weary. Photo by David Evans.

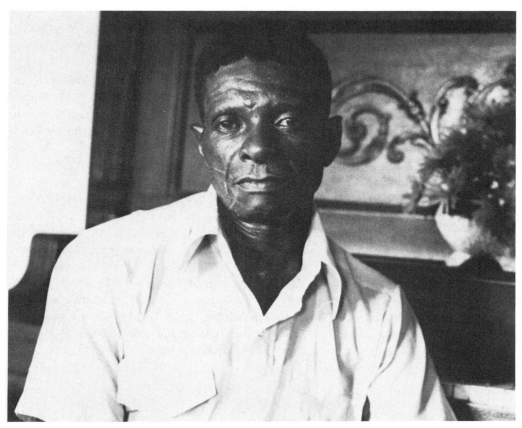

the record. Reed had sung, "Well, I give you all my money, and you go downtown; and you get back in the evening, call me all kinds of clown." Reed's couplet ended in an almost unintelligible mumble, a common characteristic of his records, which nevertheless does not seem to have detracted from his popularity. Weary, however, was faced with the problem of whether to repeat Reed's apparent nonsense or to transform the stanza into something meaningful. He chose the latter course while still sticking as closely as possible to Reed's stanza. But Weary's third stanza is a traditional one (cf. Example 4) and completely different from Reed's final stanza. Reed's third stanza continued the theme of mistreatment by his woman, whereas Weary's offers a contrast with his second stanza. He goes from complaining about being the victim of an unfaithful woman to being accused himself of having too many women.

A further technique of blues singers is to use a record as a "frame" and fill it with new content. This is often done by recording artists to their own hit records. For example, the Mississippi Sheiks had a hit in 1930 with "Stop and Listen Blues" (Okeh 8807), a song about the death of the singer's girl friend. Later that year they recorded "Stop and Listen Blues No. 2" (Okeh 8859) with the same melody, accompaniment, and theme, but a different text. In 1932 they recorded "The New Stop and Listen Blues" (Paramount 13134), also on the same theme but with a new text again and an altered melody. Little Brother Montgomery followed his 1930 "Vicksburg Blues" (Paramount 13006) with a "Vicksburg Blues No. 2" (Bluebird B6072) in 1935 and a "Vicksburg Blues—Part 3" (Bluebird B6697) in 1936. And Blind Lemon Jefferson followed his 1927 "Black Snake Moan" (Okeh 8455) with a "Black Snake Dream Blues" (Paramount 12510) later that same year and "That Black Snake Moan No. 2" (Paramount 12756) in 1929. Singers also follow up the hit records of other artists in this same manner. Sometimes they compose "answers" to a hit record. For example, Lightnin' Hopkins had a hit in 1947 with "Short Haired Woman" (Aladdin 3005), which begins with the line, "I don't want no woman, if her hair ain't no longer'n mine," and continues on the same theme. In 1953 Willie B. Huff, a female singer, recorded "Beggar Man Blues" (Rhythm 1770), which begins, "I don't want no man, if his money ain't no longer'n mine," thus turning the tables on Hopkins. Another common practice among singers is to provide the tune, and perhaps the accompaniment also, of a hit record with a new text that is unrelated in theme. Sometimes the original record has a refrain, which another singer uses with a new set of stanzas. For example, Memphis Minnie had a hit in 1930 with "I'm Talking about You" (Vocalion 1476), followed later that year with "I'm Talking about You—No. 2" (Vocalion 1556). Both records have the following refrain:

I'm talking 'bout you; I'm talking 'bout you.
I'm talking 'bout you. I don't care what you do.

In 1967 Houston Stackhouse used the same refrain and tune to create a blues with a different set of stanzas altogether. In addition, he personalized his song by introducing the members of his band in one stanza.[41]

Woodrow Adams's "How Long" serves as a good example of this process of using a record as a frame for a new blues. Adams's song is based on "Baby How Long" (Chess 1575), recorded by Howlin' Wolf (Chester Burnett) in 1954. In the late 1940s Burnett lived near Adams's hometown of Robinsonville, Mississippi, and Adams learned part of his harmonica and guitar style from him. Adams continued to emulate Burnett after the latter became a popular blues recording artist. Burnett's text probably owes its key phrase to Leroy Carr's big hit record of 1928, "How Long—How Long Blues" (Vocalion 1191), but otherwise it is totally different. Here is Burnett's text:

Example 15. "Baby How Long." Howlin' Wolf, vocal and harmonica; Otis Spann, piano; Jody Williams and Hubert Sumlin, guitars; Willie Dixon, string bass; Earl Phillips, drums. Chicago, 1954. Chess 1575, reissued on *Moanin' in the Moonlight*, Chess LP 1434, 12" LP.

INSTRUMENTAL CHORUS.

1. *When you left me this morning, you taken my heart away.*
   When you left me this morning, you taken my heart away.
   That's all right, baby. You gonna come back home someday.

INSTRUMENTAL CHORUS.

2. *How long, baby, how long, how long?*
   How long, baby, how long, how long?
   You know I love you. You steady doing me wrong.

INSTRUMENTAL CHORUS.

3. *Well, when you leave home, you can call me on your phone.*
   Well, when you leave home, you can call me on your phone.
   I'll send you your money. Darling, you come back home.
   Spoken: *Oh, come back.*

INSTRUMENTAL CHORUS.

4. *How long are you gonna do me wrong?*
   How long are you gonna do me wrong?
   Ain't nobody never lived that didn't do somebody wrong, wrong, wrong,
   wrong.

© 1960 ARC Music Corporation. Used by permission.

Woodrow Adams's "How Long" uses the same vocal melody, and he and his band recreate a number of the instrumental figures on Howlin' Wolf's record. Adams's text, however, is quite different, even though he maintains the theme of the singer wishing that his woman would return home and stop mistreating him. Here is Adams's text:

Example 16. "How Long." Woodrow Adams, vocal and harmonica; Curtis Allen, guitar; Fiddlin' Joe Martin, drums. Robinsonville, Miss., Aug.

28, 1967. Recorded by David Evans and Marina Bokelman. Issued on *High Water Blues*, Flyright LP 512, 12″ LP.

INSTRUMENTAL CHORUS.

1. *How long 'fore you gonna bring my loving home?*
   How long, baby, 'fore you gonna bring my loving home?
   Yeah, I been worried about you, darling, ever since that you been gone.

INSTRUMENTAL CHORUS.

2. *How long, baby, how long, how long?*
   How long, baby, how long, how long?
   How long, little girl, 'fore you gonna bring my loving home?

Woodrow Adams. Photo by Marina Bokelman.

3. *How long you gonna keep me feeling like you do?*
   How long, baby, you gonna keep me feeling like you do?
   Yeah, you told me that you love me, and, darling, I don't believe it's true.

INSTRUMENTAL CHORUS.

4. *How long you gonna keep me begging you?*
   How long, baby, you gonna keep me begging you?
   Darling, you ought to be ashamed to treat me the way you do.

INSTRUMENTAL CHORUS.

5. *How long, baby, 'fore you keep on back to me?*
   How long 'fore you come around back to me?
   You know, I'm worried about you, baby, just as worried as I can be.

INSTRUMENTAL CHORUS.

Many blues singers do not base their compositions on particular records but simply "lift" verses from records and insert them into their own songs.[42] Usually they take only one or two stanzas from the original record, setting them to a different melody and accompaniment. Both Roosevelt Holts and Eli Owens, neighbors in Bogalusa, Louisiana, do this with a couple of stanzas from Joe Williams's 1935 recording of "49 Highway Blues" (Bluebird B5996), inserting them in various improvised blues. The following improvised blues by Isaiah Chattman exemplifies this practice:

Example 17. "Cold in Hand." Isaiah Chattman, vocal and guitar in standard tuning, key of E. Baton Rouge, Aug. 18, 1966. Recorded by David Evans and Marina Bokelman. Issued on *High Water Blues*, Flyright LP 512, 12″ LP.[43]

GUITAR CHORUS.

1. *Oh yeah, oh, little girl like you won't treat me now. [sic]*
   Oh yeah, oh, little girl, look like you want to treat me bad.
   Yes, ain't no reason why. Oh baby, don't you see you making me awful mad?

2. *Blues got me in trouble. Oh, little girl, it's all on a cause of you.*
   Blues got me in trouble. Oh, little girl, it's all the cause of you.
   Why don't you make up your mind to settle down? Baby, you know I wouldn't have to run around.

GUITAR CHORUS.

3. *Sun rose this morning. I didn't have my baby by my side.*
   Sun rose this morning. I didn't have my baby by my side.
   Well, I didn't know where she was. I think, riding around with another guy.

4. *Said, blow, cold wind, blow; blow my baby back to me.*
   Blow, blow, cold wind, blow; I said, blow my baby back to me.
   Yes, you know I'm full of trouble, and my heart full of misery.

GUITAR CHORUS.

Isaiah Chattman. Photo by Marina Bokelman.

5. *I said, baby, don't you hear me calling you?*
   Baby, don't you hear me calling you?
   Yes, I want to know what you mean to do to me.

It was unusual for Chattman to improvise a blues like this. Most of the other pieces I recorded from him were fairly close imitations of popular blues records of the previous fifteen years. His orientation towards records and popular blues was shown also by the fact that he had been playing rhythm guitar and taking occasional vocals in the band of Silas Hogan and had played on some of Hogan's records made a few years before I met him. Chattman began "Cold in Hand" in an unusual free rhythmic style on the guitar, which he maintained through the first two stanzas. These stanzas are typical of improvised nontraditional blues in being slightly confused in sense and not rhyming according to one of the standard patterns. Chattman was obviously having some difficulty in putting his song together. The first line is nonsense, but he straightens it out by the second line and even manages to achieve a good rhyme in the third line. The second stanza continues the theme of trouble and mistreatment, but Chattman is unable to rhyme his lines and settles instead for a third line with internal rhyme. At this point he takes an instrumental break, probably to collect his thoughts. His mind ranges through his repertoire, and he comes out with the opening stanza of Muddy Waters's 1953 recording of

"Blow Wind Blow" (Chess 1550), a stanza that fits in well with the
theme that Chattman has established. Since he is now able to fall back
on a familiar set of lyrics, he regularizes his rhythm in the second line
of this stanza. Chattman continues with the third stanza from Muddy
Waters's record. After this he takes another instrumental break, perhaps because he has forgotten the rest of Waters's record. For his final
stanza Chattman opens with a traditional line, but he fails to use one of
the standard rhyming lines, such as, "You're three times seven, and you
know what you want to do." Instead he ends the piece with an improvised unrhymed line. The result of his effort is a moderately coherent blues, but the piece probably would have failed after the second
stanza if he had not been able to lift two stanzas from Muddy Waters's
record.

Some blues singers compose blues that are nothing but combinations of stanzas taken from several records. Perhaps the most outstanding example of this process was pointed out by Odum and Johnson as
early as 1926. A four-stanza blues they collected consisted of a stanza
from one record, a stanza from a second record, a stanza that was a
combination of two more stanzas from the second record, and a final
stanza from yet a third record.[44]

No account of the alteration of records by blues singers would be
complete without the mention of garbling, even though it is not a deliberate process on their part.[45] In most cases garbling produces nonsense. An outstanding example was pointed out recently by Stephen
Calt.[46] In 1926 Ardell Bragg recorded "Bird Nest Blues" (Paramount
12410), a song about a raid on a barrelhouse during Prohibition, containing the following stanza:

*Just as they played "Home Sweet Home," the man stepped up with shinin'
star.*
Say, "You don't need no taxi; I'll take you in my car."

In 1930 Charley Patton recorded "Bird Nest Bound" (Paramount 13070),
a blues which contained three stanzas derived from Bragg's record.
Among them was:

Take me home, sweet home, baby, to that shining star.
Take me home now to that shining star.
Spoken: Lord, you know I'm gonna play it now.
You don't need no telling, mama; take you in my car.

Sometimes garbling can yield startling results, as when Robert
Pete Williams sang, "I go up on the mountain so high, I seen grass
growin' on a dollar bill."[47] The line is derived from a stanza in Leroy
Carr's "The New How Long How Long Blues" (Vocalion 1435):

I can look and see the green grass growin' up on the hill,
But I haven't seen the green back of a dollar bill,
For so long, so long, baby, so long.

A final example of garbling illustrates several of the other processes that we have noted in the alteration of recorded blues. In 1969 I recorded the following blues from Roosevelt Holts:

Example 18. "Matchbox Blues." Roosevelt Holts, vocal and guitar in standard tuning, key of A. Bogalusa, La., Apr. 2, 1969. Recorded by David Evans. Issued on *South Mississippi Blues*, Rounder 2009, 12" LP.

1. *Hey, sitting here wondering would a matchbox hold my clothes.*
   Sitting here wondering would a matchbox hold my clothes.
   Said, I ain't got so many matches, but I got so far to go.

2. *Hey, cold in China, working hard this train.* [sic]
   Cold in China, working hard this train.
   You didn't make me mad, baby, till you broke my diamond ring.

3. *Lord, ain't gon' marry, can't stand settling down.*
   Lord, ain't gon' marry, can't stand settling down.
   Said, I'm gonna act like a preacher, ride from town to town.

4. *Says, I walked from Dallas to the little switch car board.* [sic]
   Yes, I walked from Dallas down to little switch car board.
   Say you hadn't found my good gal. I hadn't done no walk at all. [sic]

5. *Hey, cold in China, working hard this train.*
   Cold in China, working hard this train.
   You didn't make me mad, baby, till you broke my diamond ring.

Holts says that he learned the piece from a record by Blind Lemon Jefferson, but in fact his stanzas come from two records by Jefferson, "Match Box Blues" (Okeh 8455) from 1927 and "Long Lonesome Blues" (Paramount 12354) from 1926. Holts's first and third stanzas are from "Match Box Blues" and the others from "Long Lonesome Blues." Both of Jefferson's pieces used a similar melody and guitar part in open G tuning. Holts tries to duplicate the singing and plays a similar sounding guitar part in another tuning. His stanzas from "Long Lonesome Blues," however, are garbled. Jefferson sings, "So cold in China, the birds can't hardly sing." It is a remarkable line, combining imagery of frigidity, distance, and lack of harmony, all of which tie in with the rhyming line. Holts's version makes little sense at all. Jefferson's other stanza is as follows:

> *I walked from Dallas; I walked to Wichita Falls.*
> *I said, I walked from Dallas; I walked to Wichita Falls.*
> *Had done lost my sugar; Lord, it wasn't no walk at all.*

Holts had probably never heard of Wichita Falls, Texas, but his emendation makes no sense either. Nevertheless, he uses this and his other altered stanza as "floating stanzas" in other improvised blues, apparently satisfied with their meaning or lack of it.

In summary, thirteen processes used by blues singers in dealing with popular records have been noted here. In most cases several of them are used in combination. These processes are:

1. Outright imitation
2. Shortening the record by omitting stanzas or instrumental choruses
3. Repetition of stanzas or instrumental choruses
4. Changing the instrumental accompaniment
5. Concatenation of two or more records or parts of records
6. Personalizing the lyrics
7. Localizing the lyrics
8. Modernizing the accompaniment and/or lyrics
9. Using the record as a jumping-off point and adding new material
10. Using the record as a frame and filling it with new material
11. Lifting lyrics from a record and setting them in a new blues
12. Recombining stanzas from two or more records
13. Garbling lines from a record

Original Compositions: Thematic Texts

Earlier it was noted that commercially issued blues and other blues that are based on records are usually thematic, meaning that they maintain a single theme throughout the text. Such blues, therefore, could be called "story-songs" in the sense that a coherent "story" or a single scene or mood could be reconstructed from the text. With the exception of most of the "classic" female blues singers of the 1920s, the singers on the majority of commercial blues records have also been the composers of their songs or else have altered earlier blues records using the processes described above. Many other singers have learned to perform blues from records or adaptations of them. Some of these singers then go on to compose blues of their own that are story-songs with thematic texts in the manner of commercially recorded blues. These singers may later even get an opportunity themselves to make records.

Most of these thematic blues are performed by an artist virtually the same way every time, except for repetitions and omissions of stanzas and instrumental choruses and perhaps some improvisation in the accompaniment. This tendency is probably largely a result of the stability built into a recorded performance, which never varies from one playing to the next. Often recording artists and their imitators are then expected to reproduce the sounds of records as accurately as possible for their live audiences. Eventually a positive value may be placed upon stability of a recorded blues in the performer's repertoire. This valuation can, in turn, affect the status of other original compositions, even when they have never been recorded. It will be shown later in this study that such a valuation is quite different from that held by most performers of traditional folk blues.

A number of blues singers have expressed the opinion that blues lyrics ought to "tell a story," by which they mean that they should be thematic throughout the song. Usually these are singers who have made commercial recordings. Lowell Fulson, who has composed and recorded over two hundred blues, says, "In the blues it's the words. It's the story. No, but it's facts though. Any time you come over with a slow blues, they'll listen to the story, see what you're talking about." He contrasts this thematic approach to composition with that of singers who are "just out there saying something," in other words, improvising their lyrics.[48] Brownie McGhee, who has had equally prolific careers as a popular blues singer and as a folk revival artist, conducted a school for blues composers in New York City in the late 1940s and early 1950s. He says,

> It was . . . supposed to have been a production company, to
> develop black singers on how to construct a blues song to tell a
> story. I always believed in telling a story without getting lost on
> three or four different subjects. Some blues are written with three
> or four different things involved. There's nothing! No continuity to
> it! You start to singing about my woman left me; let's see why she
> left me. Then let's see what created leaving me, and what
> happened after she left me. And climax it somewhere. But you can
> add to it if you want to by moving one verse down.[49]

Even Furry Lewis, who usually skips from one subject to another in his blues, expresses this ideal, saying, "You want all the verses to be talking about the same thing."[50]

In a number of cases composers of thematic blues have revealed the stories and events which prompted their compositions. Often these blues are nothing more than recastings of personal experiences. Henry Townsend states that he composed "Poor Man Blues" (Columbia 14491-D) because "I had been broke down and I had been pretty poor at that time."[51] Booker White composed three blues on prison themes in 1940 after he was released from the Mississippi State Penitentiary.[52] Similarly straightforward explanations of their blues texts have been given by Big Bill Broonzy and Sleepy John Estes.[53]

Boogie Bill Webb tells the following story of how he came to compose "Drinking and Stinking":

> I made some songs. One I made was "Drinking and Stinking." It
> may sound funny, but that's what it is. A friend of mine is the
> cause of that. He's in California today. I don't want none of the
> ladies who hear this to get mad with me, but this actually
> happened. We knowed three ladies that had been playing hookey
> for around three days then. I want you to know they wouldn't go
> home. We knowed it was time for a bath or something, you know.
> And so, he's the one that said, "Man, you ought to put a song out
> about 'Drinking and Stinking'." They had been drinking three days
> and nights and stinking. So me and him right then started the
> "Drinking and Stinking."[54]

Webb's lyrics grow directly out of the experience, but they are put in the first and second person for greater vividness. His final spoken interjection is probably taken from "Drunk Again" (Red Robin 130), recorded in 1953 by Champion Jack Dupree, also a New Orleans blues singer. Dupree's song has a similar theme to Webb's, but the lyrics are completely different. Webb recorded this song for me in 1969 and 1970. The two versions are virtually identical textually and musically except for the addition of accompanists and the repetition of more stanzas in the later recording. The text of the 1970 version is as follows:

Example 19. "Drinking and Stinking." Boogie Bill Webb, vocal and guitar in standard tuning, key of E; Roosevelt Holts, guitar; Robert Rucker, drums. New Orleans, Aug. 27, 1970. Recorded by David Evans. Issued on *Roosevelt Holts and His Friends*, Arhoolie 1057, 12" LP.[55]

1. *You've been drinking and stinking all night long.*
   You've been drinking and stinking all night long.
   Well, I'm gonna sing, babe, I'm gonna sing to you.
   Girl, you smell like a garbage can, and I don't know what I'm gonna do.

2. *You smell like a garbage can late at night.*
   If I tell you what you been doing, it make you want to fight,
   When you've been drinking and stinking all night long,
   And you've been drinking.
   Girl, you've been drinking, pretty babe, and stinking all night long.

INSTRUMENTAL CHORUS.

3. *You smell like a garbage can late at night.*
   If I tell you what you been doing, it make you want to fight,
   When you've been drinking and stinking all night long,
   When you've been drinking.
   You've been drinking, pretty babe, and stinking all night long.

INSTRUMENTAL CHORUS.

4. *You don't want to never brush your teeth, but you always want to be up*
       in my face.
   You smell like something I never smelled before,
   When you've been drinking and stinking all night long,
   When you've been drinking.
   You've been drinking, pretty baby, and stinking all night long. .

INSTRUMENTAL CHORUS.

5. *You smell just like a garbage can late at night.*
   If I tell you what you been doing, it make you want to fight,
   When you've been drinking and stinking all night long,
   When you've been drinking.
   You've been drinking, pretty baby, and stinking all night long.

6. *You don't want to never brush your teeth, but you always want to be up*
       in my face.
   You smell like something I never smelled before,
   When you've been drinking and stinking all night long,
   When you've been drinking.
   You've been drinking, pretty baby, and stinking all night long.

Spoken: *Kiss me, baby!*

© 1972 Tradition Music Co.

In studying the stories that blues singers tell about their songs, we must guard against accepting explanations that were made up after a recording simply in order to satisfy a need for coherence in the lyrics. Tommy Johnson, for example, told such a story after recording his "Cool Drink of Water Blues" (Victor 21279) in 1928. The tune and Johnson's guitar part are printed below for purposes of comparison later in this study. His singing is especially interesting for its frequent leaps into falsetto. In all stanzas after the first he drops the opening line (measures 1–4). In some of these later stanzas he plays a variant guitar figure in measures 7 and 8. Johnson's guitar part is sometimes difficult to distinguish on the record from that of his accompanist, Charlie McCoy. The "fairo" in stanza 4 is a term used by many blues singers with the meaning of "sweetheart." Its etymology is uncertain. Perhaps it is from "fair" used as a substantive, from "fairy" in the manner of love poetry, from the Scottish *fere*, meaning "mate" or "consort," or from "farrow," a young pig, as in the expression "pigmeat" for a young woman. Whatever the word's derivation, its meaning has always been clear to blues singers and audiences.

Example 20. "Cool Drink of Water Blues." Tommy Johnson, vocal and guitar in standard tuning, key of E; Charlie McCoy, guitar. Memphis, Feb. 3, 1928. Victor 21279, reissued on *Country Blues Encores*, Origin Jazz Library 8, 12″ LP.

1. *I asked for water, and she gave me gasoline.*
   I asked for water, gave me gasoline.
   I asked for water, and she gave me gasoline. Lord, Lordy, Lord.

2. *Crying, Lord, I wonder will I ever get back home.*
   Crying, Lord, I wonder will I ever get back home. Lord, Lordy, Lord.

3. *I went to the depot, looked up on the board.*
   I looked all over. "How long has this east-bound train been gone?"

4. *"It's done taken your fairo, blowed its smoke on you."*
   "It's done taken your fairo, blowed its smoke on you." Lord, Lordy, Lord.

5. *Lord, I asked the conductor, "Could I ride the blinds?"*
   Spoken: *Want to know, can a broke man ride the blinds.*
   "Son, buy your ticket, buy your ticket, 'cause this train ain't none of mine."

6. *"Son, buy your ticket; train ain't none of mine."*
   "Son, buy your ticket, 'cause this train ain't none of mine." Lord, Lordy, Lord.

7. *"Train ain't none of mine."*

Johnson claimed that this song was based on an actual experience. He was walking along a railroad track and met a woman whom he asked for a drink of water. She gave him gasoline instead. This caused him to want to return home. He went to the depot, asked the

agent how long the train had been gone, and received the answer given in the lyrics. Then he asked the conductor to let him hobo ("ride the blinds"), but the conductor told him to buy a ticket.[56] This makes a nice story, but it is almost certainly untrue or highly exaggerated. All of the stanzas are traditional and have been used by many other blues singers. It is even possible that their arrangement was improvised by Johnson at the time he made his recording.

Some blues singers compose thematic songs which celebrate somebody's character or attributes, often their own. Blues of boasting, frequently with a sexual meaning, are quite common. For example, Bo Carter boasted that he was an "All Around Man" (Bluebird B6295), and Muddy Waters announced, "I'm Your Hoochie Coochie Man" (Chess 1560). Many other blues celebrate the good or bad points of a person of the opposite sex. Some blues simply celebrate another person in the singer's community. Robert Wilkins's "New Stock Yard Blues" (Vocalion 03223) describes the singer's boss, a Mr. Owens, and urges listeners to buy their mules at his auctions.[57] Some of the most remarkable blues of this sort were composed by Sleepy John Estes. His "Lawyer Clark Blues" (Bluebird B8871) describes a white lawyer in Estes's hometown of Brownsville, Tennessee. "Liquor Store Blues" (Decca 7491) similarly describes the proprietor of such an establishment. Estes composed many other blues like these in which he gave a profusion of details in a matter-of-fact way about local people who could have been of very little interest to most of the buyers of his records.[58] Nevertheless, he recently explained these compositions, saying, "Well, I got to thinking about them people and I figured they would make great hits out of songs about people I known, make it sell good. We made songs about all them white folks around Brownsville. Oh, they would sell. They had a store down there, you know. . . ."[59]

Occasionally a blues celebrates a place rather than a person. In 1967 I recorded such a piece, "Doodleville Blues," from Cary Lee Simmons. Doodleville is a section in the southern part of Jackson, Mississippi, where Simmons was living. The correct name of this section is Duttoville after Father Louis A. Dutto, a Catholic priest. Simmons and Bubba Brown composed this piece in the 1930s and performed it to the great amusement of friends in Jackson.[60]

Example 21. "Doodleville Blues." Cary Lee Simmons, vocal and guitar in standard tuning, key of C. Jackson, Miss., Sept. 4, 1967. Recorded by David Evans and Marina Bokelman. Issued on *High Water Blues,* Flyright LP 512, 12" LP.

1. *I got a girl in the Bamas. I got one that lived out on Bailey Hill.*
   I got a girl in the Bamas, and I got one that lived out on Bailey Hill.
   But don't none of them suit me like that one I got down here in Doodleville.

2. *The womens on Farish Street shakes until they can't be still.*
   I said, the womens on Farish Street shakes until they can't be still.
   But they cannot shake like these gals live down here in Doodleville.

3. *Turn your lamp down low. Somebody done shot poor Bud, Buddy Will.*
   Turn your lamp down low. Somebody done shot Buddy Will.
   I told him to stay off of Mill Street and get him a gal in Doodleville.

4. *I wouldn't have a gal on Farish Street, wouldn't speak to one that lived on Mill.*
   I wouldn't have a gal on Farish Street. I wouldn't speak to one that lived on Mill.
   'Cause the next woman I got, she got to live in Doodleville.

5. *They get the meat from the slaughterhouse and the wood from Grimm Stage Mill.*
   They get the meat from the slaughterhouse and the wood from Grimm Stage Mill.
   And if you want to live easy, easy, get you a girl in Doodleville.

6. Spoken: *I got a secret for you though.*
It's a mad dog out, and, boys, and it ain't been killed.
It's a mad dog out, and, boys, and it ain't been killed.
And you better be careful, careful, careful how you doodle in Doodleville.

137

THE BLUES
SINGER

The thematic blues discussed up to this point have all been based on some actual experience or observation of the singer, which is reflected imaginatively in the lyrics. Some singers, however, take the experiences of others and make them their own in blues. Victoria Spivey's "T. B. Blues" (Okeh 8494) and Booker White's "High Fever Blues" (Vocalion 05489) and "Fixin' to Die Blues" (Vocalion 05588) were all sung in the first person but were inspired by the illnesses of other people known by the singers.[61] Robert Wilkins's "Nashville Stonewall Blues" (Brunswick 7168) was based on the prison experience of a friend.[62] Big Bill Broonzy has described other such compositions.[63] Jimmy Rogers combined an experience of someone else with one of his own to compose "That's All Right" (Chess 1435). He tells the following story about the song's origin:

> It came from really a fight in a club that I were playin' in. And this fellow and his wife, or his lady or whoever it was, they were fightin' and talkin' and he was tryin' to get his point over. She had mistreated him, see, and he was sayin', tellin' her it was all right, you know, what she did and so on. And then fellows that really knew him, we would laugh about it and they just kept singin' about the way he was sayin', "I know you don't love me no more but that's all right." And that was something that stuck in my mind. And then my life started, and I was havin' trouble myself, and I just build from one day to day, time after time, until I got started. And after that number, after I built it, it wasn't no problem to me then to build a story, from then on. . . . I built it, put it together and lined it out with harmony and built the music around it, and then we recorded it. . . . I build 'em from different stories, of my past life and people that I've known. Quite a few people have come to me with their problems, you know, and I would give 'em the best advice that I could, help 'em out, because I have lived kind of rough myself, you know.[64]

The kind of solidarity with his audience that Rogers describes is one of the important factors in a blues singer's popularity. "That's All Right" was Rogers's first record and proved to be quite a big hit.

In a similar manner, a number of other blues singers have composed blues based on "something that stuck in their mind."[65] Often it is a chance remark, which the blues singer reflects upon until he develops all of the idea's possibilities into a blues. John Lee Hooker has told how he composed "Boom Boom" (Vee Jay 438), a hit for him in 1961, in this fashion. He says,

> It's a funny thing: you can say a word—it wouldn't mean anything to you—I can take that one word and write a whole song. Rhyme it right down the line, just rhyme it from word to word—just one word you speak. The songs have to tell a story. Just like "Boom Boom": I used to come into a bar and there was a

*barmaid used to come in nights—she was a very nice kid, a friend
of mine—some nights, you know, I would come in late, she'd say,
"Uh oh, boom boom!" Just like that, "The boss gonna get you." She
kept saying that over and over and I just put one and two
together:*

> *Boom! Boom! Boom! Boom!*
> *Gonna shoot you right down,*
> *Right offa your feet,*
> *Take you home with me,*
> *Put you in my house.*
> *Boom! Boom! Boom! Boom!*

*Maybe we be sitting here and talking, me and you. You can seem
worried. Now I may not say anything about it right then, but it's
right here [taps forehead]; it don't leave here. I keep it in mind.
We can be just having a conversation; hear something I like, make
a song out of it, or a title. I just take it and keep it up here until
you leave. Then I get up from bed—I don't know what time of
night it is—and get my guitar.*[66]

Big Bill Broonzy illustrated a similar process of composition by
taking the simple subject of a knife and exhausting its possibilities
through the application of the imagination. He said, "Now take a knife.
How many things can you do with a knife? You can cut fish, you can
cut your toenails, I seen guys shave with it, you can eat beans with it,
you can kill a man. There. You name five things you can do with a
knife, you got five verses. You got yourself a blues."[67]

Most of the thematic blues that have been discussed so far are
performed by their composers nearly the same way every time except
for repetitions, omissions, and some improvisation in the instrumental
accompaniments. Undoubtedly the concentration on a single theme
helps to maintain stability. The built-in stability of blues whose texts
are fixed on records has been noted too. In addition, some blues singers
use writing as an aid to the memory for their own compositions and
pieces learned from records, and a few even write out blues which they
give to other singers.[68]

By comparing recordings made over a year apart, we note that
"Drinking and Stinking" (Example 19) has a stable status in Boogie Bill
Webb's repertoire. Sleepy John Estes also performed his pieces in the
1960s and 1970s virtually unchanged from his records made in the
1930s. Many other examples of such stability could be cited. But sometimes there can be variation from one performance to another of a
thematic blues. Son House's "Preachin' Blues" has been a stable item in
his repertoire since his rediscovery in 1964, but his nine-stanza version
recorded in 1965 (issued on *The Legendary Son House, Father of Folk Blues,*
Columbia CL 2417, 12" LP) has only three stanzas in common with his
eleven-stanza version recorded in 1930 (Paramount 13013).[69] Thus he
would appear to have settled on a stable combination of stanzas sometime between 1930 and 1964.

Probably many thematic blues have a similar partly stable status in singers' repertoires over periods of many years. It would appear, therefore, that dissatisfaction, which is such a prominent attitude in blues lyrics, also plays a role in the attitudes of many singers toward their lyrics. A number of singers have told me that they hadn't "finished" composing songs which they had been performing for years. The improvisational tendency, which pervades all blues performance to a greater or lesser extent, can thus play a part in undoing the stability of thematic compositions. Undoubtedly the factors which make for complete or partial stability of a thematic blues are very complex. Certainly they are deserving of a more thorough treatment than can be given here, where our primary interest is in the more traditional blues. Most of these thematic blues are original compositions and are performed only by their composers, except when they are learned from records made by the composers. Not too many of these original compositions are spread strictly through the processes of oral tradition without the medium of records. Even when thematic blues are spread orally, one can usually trace them ultimately to recorded sources.

I do not mean to suggest in the preceding statements that traditional elements are virtually absent in thematic blues. Indeed, many of them have melodies and accompaniments that were learned orally. Some are also comprised entirely of traditional stanzas woven together by the singer to tell a story. Son House's "Preachin' Blues," in fact, is a combination of traditional stanzas on the theme of a backsliding preacher. Earlier we noted texts of this sort in the reports of the first collectors and observers of blues (cf. Example 2). Many more thematic blues have one or two traditional stanzas combined with others that are original. For example, we noted earlier that the second stanza of Johnnie Temple's "Hoodoo Women" (Example 12) was traditional. Even the processes of imitating and changing blues from records represent a kind of tradition, although it is not completely an oral one. Furthermore, most original texts are still concerned with traditional themes.[70] The use of traditional elements by creative composers of thematic blues deserves greater attention. It could constitute a major study in itself, for which the discussion here serves only as an introduction.

Before we leave the subject of original thematic blues, we must look at those which are created spontaneously at the time of performance. Usually they are performed only the one time and then forgotten. Such totally improvised blues tend to be extremely loose in their structural features. Often there is a great variation from one stanza to another in the melody, instrumental part, number of measures, and number of lines. The lines tend to be unrhymed, and sometimes the singing turns into speech. The texts of such improvised blues are usually thematic, although they often depart on unusual tangents and sometimes become surrealistic, as thoughts crowd one another in an effort to find expression. Some of the finest as well as some of the most confused blues have been composed in this manner, and often it is only a thin line that divides the one from the other. Basically such blues are an inspired outpouring of the mind of the singer with a minimal reliance upon external structure. Whether his state of mind is clear or clouded, it will be reflected in the blues he produces.

John Lee Hooker is one of the few blues singers to make a great number of commercial recordings in this manner. Since his pieces are so freely improvised, he is almost impossible to accompany and is at his best when singing alone with his guitar. Contrary to his assertion quoted earlier, most of his lines are unrhymed, a practice which often seems deliberately designed to force the listener away from his own expectations and toward greater concentration on the singer's personal message. Hooker says of this style of composition,

> On my records, lots of times I just make up the words right on the spot, right there, like I do in clubs. "Democrat Man"—I made that up as I went along:

> Democrats put us on our feet; these crazy women they voted them out.
> Democrats put us on our feet; these crazy women they voted them out.
> But I don't think they'll make the same mistake, won't make that same mistake again.

> They told them, "I'll send your sons home." They did just that: they sent them home without a job.
> I declare they won't make the same mistake again.
> Democrats put us on our feet; these crazy women voted them out.

> You know, though, I'm pretty good at those things, doing things like that. I don't know how I do it, but I do.[71]

Booker White composed his "sky songs" in this manner.[72] His lines were usually unrhymed, but his improvised stanzas tended to be set to a limited number of fairly regular musical structures. Sometimes he wrote out notes to himself for future reference in composing these blues, but the actual composition itself was always extemporaneous. White said, "I have an imaginary mind to do things like that. Well, I made 24 songs. Didn't have nary a word written down. I just reached up and got 'em. When I got through, though, I couldn't go back over them if you gave me a thousand dollars."[73]

A great number of freely improvised blues have been recorded in Louisiana by Harry Oster, who has printed their texts in his *Living Country Blues*. Oster's greatest informant is Robert Pete Williams, whom he first met in the state penitentiary at Angola.[74] Williams is a composer with a remarkably poetic gift and a seemingly unlimited inventive capacity. I was fortunate enough to have him as a guest for a week in 1966, not long after he had been released from prison through Oster's efforts and allowed to travel out of Louisiana by his parole board. Williams had been brought to California for a series of concert and coffeehouse appearances. It was the longest he had been away from his home and family since his release from prison. My house was on the Pacific coast at the base of a canyon, and it was the first time he had seen the ocean or been near mountains. By the fifth day of his visit he was quite homesick, afraid that the mountains would fall, and worried about taking his first airplane flight to Europe in a few months for a concert tour. He was far away from home, unable to get around by himself, and caught between a desire to return to a simpler life with his family and the need to make money from his music. Early in the morning he rose and began practicing on the guitar in a new tuning, a variation of standard tuning in the key of B but with the sixth string tuned from E down to B. I asked him to perform a song, and he composed the following piece. It is extremely loose, with each line of text followed by a long instrumental passage. I have separated the lines into stanzas, but it might be just as correct to conceive of the piece as a series of single lines. Some of these lines themselves have fairly lengthy instrumental passages in the middle.

Example 22. Untitled blues. Robert Pete Williams, vocal and guitar in EBGDAB tuning, key of B. Malibu, Calif., July 13, 1966. Recorded by David Evans and Marina Bokelman.

1. *I'm gonna buy me a mule. I can ride him and plow him too.*
   I'm gonna buy me a mule. I can ride him and plow him too.
   You better believe what I say.
   I'm gonna buy me a mule, baby, something I can ride and plow too.

2. *I can walk to my woman's house, if I want to, or either ride my mule.*
   Yeah, I can either walk to my woman's house or either ride my mule to
       my woman's house.
   Yeah, you better believe just what I say.
   Mmmm, mmmm, here I go again. Hey now, me and my woman.

3. *Well, I'm all 'round . . . the mountains all around me. I never seen so*
       many mountains before.
   Ah, the mountains all around me. I never had so many mountains around
       me this way before.
   Oh, they so tall and high, I'm scared they gonna tumble over on me.

4. *Mmmm, I wish you could see, baby, how tall these mountains out west.*
   Oh, I wish you could see, darling, how tall these mountains are out west.

5. *I'm gonna tell all of my friends how tall these mountains out west.*
   I'm gonna tell all of my friends how tall these old mountains are out west.

6. *Now they got me going with the wind, and now here I go again.*
   Mmm hmm, here I go again, baby.
   Aaaaaaah, here I go again.

This blues may appear disjointed and nonthematic, but given our knowledge of Williams's thoughts at the time, it makes perfect sense. He felt both trapped (represented by the mountains) and always on the move from one concert appearance to another ("Here I go again"). His chief desire was to return to his family and community and a simpler way of life, symbolized by the mule. This blues, then, tells a single story, but only a knowledge of the circumstances under which it was spontaneously composed allows us to understand this.

Another blues singer who composes many of his pieces spontaneously is Napoleon Strickland. Like Robert Pete Williams's blues, his are often unrhymed, structurally loose, and apparently a direct expression of what is on his mind. In fact, sometimes they are incomprehensible, a jumble of thoughts and phrases that flow out in a stream of consciousness. When he is able to organize his thoughts while singing, he is apt to produce a blues of great beauty and striking imagery. One of his better spontaneous pieces is "Black Sam," a blues about a stubborn mule. Strickland is a farmhand on a white man's plantation, where he has lived all his life. He feeds and milks cows, plows, harvests, and does any other tasks that are deemed necessary in return for a small salary and a rent-free house for himself and his mother. "Black Sam" grows directly out of his life-style and his reflections upon his life-style.

Example 23. "Black Sam." Napoleon Strickland, vocal and D harmonica, played in the key of A. Como, Miss., June 27, 1971. Recorded by David and Cheryl Evans.

HARMONICA CHORUS.

1. *Come over here, Black Sam. You know I want to plow your hams down.*
   Come over here, Black Sam. Believe I'm gonna plow your black hams down.
   You know, your legs so long, Lord, you gonna run my short legs down.

2. *You ain't gonna hold your line in the wagon, and your plow's all down on the ground.*
   Lord, I plowed Black Sam so long, till the old coot, he done got straightened wrong.

HARMONICA CHORUS.

Robert Pete Williams. Photo by Marina Bokelman.

3. *Lord, when Black Sam got hungry, Lord, I had to take him out and carry
   him to the barn.*
   Lord, I carried him to the trough. Lord, he sure didn't want no water.

4. *Lord, his bell was ringing all day long. Lord, Black Sam would holler up
   and hoot.*
   Lord, I'm leaving here. Black Sam, good day!
   *What Black Sam will do—he wouldn't eat, he wouldn't eat, he wouldn't
   eat when he got hungry.*

Napoleon Strickland. Photo by Cheryl T. Evans.

Robert Pete Williams, Napoleon Strickland, and others like them can and do sing traditional blues and blues learned from records, although they tend ordinarily to perform blues like the examples given above. Basically their spontaneous, improvisatory approach is applied to almost all of their blues to some extent, transforming even traditional and commercially recorded blues into something quite personal. Singers who perform in this style do so mainly for their own benefit, and their blues are direct personal responses to the conditions of their lives and their feelings. Nowhere is the therapeutic function of blues more evident than in pieces of this sort. Singers who specialize in this kind of blues often have difficulty adjusting to society. Booker White, Robert Pete Williams, and most of Oster's other informants who performed in this style have spent time in prison for murder and other crimes. Napoleon Strickland is tongue-tied in speech, and John Lee Hooker has a slight stammer. I have noticed also that a number of heavy drinkers compose in this style. The style seems to be characteristic of a certain range of personality types. Yet we must beware of facile generalizations. There are many blues singers who exhibit similar personal traits, who do not compose in this manner. Guitar Welch, whom Oster also recorded in prison, performed traditional blues and pieces from records. Tommy Johnson was an alcoholic and had a slight speech impediment, yet most of his blues were nonthematic and were constructed from traditional elements. John Lee "Sonny Boy" Williamson had a slight speech impediment, yet his many commercially recorded blues are usually well structured thematic compositions.[75] Certainly the relationship of the more spontaneous, highly personalized blues to the personalities of their singers is a subject worthy of further attention. Many of these singers are very interesting people, often brilliant lyricists and instrumentalists. It is a tribute to the blues genre that it allows them a medium of expression for their personal artistry. John Lee Hooker has had a successful career in commercial recordings, while Robert Pete Williams has won worldwide acclaim and made many concert appearances before highly appreciative audiences.

Traditional Blues Compositions

Most of the blues that we have examined so far in this chapter have been thematic. Some, like "Drinking and Stinking," are deliberate compositions on a topic of interest to the singer and remain fairly stable items in the singer's repertoire over long periods of time. Others, like some of the blues of Robert Pete Williams and Napoleon Strickland, are direct expressions of the singer's thoughts at the time of performance and are usually never performed by him again. Many blues singers, however, have little interest in such deliberate compositions or in the expression of their momentary thoughts in song form. Instead, they rely on a vast body of traditional lines, stanzas, vocal melodies, and instrumental parts for composing many of their blues. A few dozen to a few hundred of these elements may comprise the bulk of a performer's blues repertoire. To compose a blues he combines perhaps five or six of these stanzas with a tune and instrumental part. Usually the stanzas are only loosely related in theme or even inconsistent and contradictory. Basically such blues are not story-songs and are quite different from the texts we have discussed so far. Most of the traditional stanzas and lines that make up these blues treat some aspect of the man/woman relationship or a few other common topics. Usually they express thoughts which could have application to almost anyone's life experience, rather than strictly to that of the singer or some acquaintance of his. Consequently, these verses are known by many blues singers and are quickly recognized by their audiences, whereas the more thematic blues texts are inevitably more closely associated with their composers.

As we noted in the previous chapter, many writers have mentioned this approach to blues composition, often using such terms as *formula* or *commonplace* to describe the basic traditional elements used by the performers in constructing their pieces. Even the more deliberate composers of thematic blues and the spontaneous improvisors often reach into this storehouse of elements for help in their compositions. This is particularly the case in the musical portion of their blues. Few performers have a different melody and instrumental accompaniment for each of their blues. Instead, they work with a limited number of musical patterns to which they set many different texts. Often these patterns owe much to tradition. Many singers like Kokomo Arnold, Peetie Wheatstraw, and Elmore James have composed dozens of different thematic texts to only a few melodic and instrumental patterns each.[76]

There are thousands of traditional textual and musical elements altogether, and no comprehensive attempt has ever been made to organize this body of material for study. Fahey has pointed out five "tune families" used by Charley Patton, while Titon has described four that are in more general use in folk and popular blues.[77] Wolfe has proposed an index of blues lyric formulas, and Taft has begun work on a concordance to blues texts.[78] But with perhaps thirty thousand blues on phonograph records alone and many more in field recordings, the task is enormous, and it will be a long time before useful results can be achieved. Thus, when we state that a certain verse or tune is traditional, we are not able to cite all of the other recorded examples of it for comparative purposes. Yet anyone who has listened to a few thousand blues can begin to recognize traditional elements without the need for a list of all the known cases in which they have been used. Our goal should be to go beyond the mere establishment of the traditionality of a performance and to reach a point where we understand the nature of the relationship between performers who use the same traditional elements. It is for this reason that I have chosen to study in the next chapter a group of folk blues singers from a single local tradition.

We observed in the previous chapter that some writers have criticized the singers who rely on traditional verse elements, calling them unimaginative or lazy, because they sing blues made out of prefabricated pieces. However, a few writers have praised the imagery and the poetic and dramatic qualities of many of these stock expressions. Indeed, these qualities are found in abundance in traditional folk blues. Not only is there art and beauty in many of the lyrics but the melodies and instrumental parts frequently contain these qualities too. When performed with feeling, the traditional blues can be just as powerfully moving as the more original compositions. Certainly the blues singers who use good taste in selecting the best of these traditional verses and musical elements and who perform them with sincerity and conviction deserve praise for their efforts.

Writers have also criticized traditional folk blues for lacking textual coherence. Basically they object to the fact that these blues are nonthematic. Only a few writers have recognized any underlying logic or structural unity in these blues. Francis Lee Utley noted the "poetic logic" in a blues that was on the surface textually incoherent.[79] Samuel Charters and Harry Oster have recognized the "emotional association" that can connect stanzas that seem otherwise unrelated, although they claim that a good many blues still remain incoherent.[80] Yet if we grant that *contrast* is a basic structural principle in folk blues, many seemingly incoherent texts make sense and reveal an underlying structure.

Earlier I attempted to show the structural patterns in four examples of nonthematic folk blues, "Baby, You Sho' Lookin' Warm" (Example 3), "Mississippi Jail House Groan" (Example 4), whose text Charters had called "confused,"[81] "Sorrowful Blues" (Example 6), and "Got the Blues" (Example 8). Many other texts could be similarly analyzed (cf. Example 14). Here we shall look at only one additional example which a writer has specifically criticized for its incoherence.[82]

John Fahey has at some length pointed out the "disconnection, incoherence, and apparent 'irrationality'" in the blues texts of Charley Patton, claiming that Patton usually selected his verses "at random from a large storehouse of them in his mind."[83] As an example of these characteristics Fahey cites "Pony Blues." Certainly Patton was not the most coherent folk blues singer, but his blues were by no means unstructured, random compositions. They could be analyzed in the same way as our previous examples, and their structures would be seen to be only slightly less clear than the others. "Pony Blues," in fact, can serve as a good example. The melody and guitar part are printed here along with the text, since these will be important later in this study for comparative purposes. Actually, Patton uses three melodies and guitar parts, which have some elements in common. He uses the first of these patterns in stanza 1, the second in stanzas 2, 3, and 5, and the third in stanzas 4 and 6. Unfortunately, all available copies of the original record are in poor condition, making transcription of both the text and music difficult.

Example 24. "Pony Blues." Charley Patton, vocal and guitar in standard tuning, key of E. Richmond, Ind., June 14, 1929. Paramount 12792, reissued on *Charley Patton, Founder of the Delta Blues,* Yazoo L-1020, 12" double LP.

1. Hitch up my pony, saddle up my black mare.
   Hitch up my pony, saddle up my black mare.
   I'm gonna find a rider, baby, in the world somewhere.

2. Hello, Central, the matter with your line?
   Hello, Central, matter now with your line?
   Come a storm last night, tore the wires down.

3. Got a brand new shetland, man, already trained.
   Brand new shetland, baby, already trained.
   Just get in the saddle, tighten up on your reins.

4. And a brownskin woman like something fit to eat.
   Brownskin woman like something fit to eat.
   But a jet black woman, don't put your hands on me.

5. Took my baby to meet the morning train.
   Took my baby, meet that morning train.
   And the blues come down, baby, like showers of rain.

6. I got something to tell you, when I gets a chance.
   Something to tell you, when I get a chance.
   I don't want to marry; just want to be your man.

The structure of this piece is by no means clear, and one may question, with Fahey, whether Patton is indeed incoherent. Nevertheless, if we may be allowed to interpret the meaning of the more obscure stanzas, we shall be able to discern a structure in their selection and arrangement. The piece opens with a powerful statement of the singer's determination to obtain a woman (a "rider"). But in the next stanza he is unable to place a telephone call. Whom is he calling? If our principle of contrast holds, he is trying to call his woman. Certainly an attempted call to a lover was what W. C. Handy had in mind when he used variants of these lines in his "The Hesitating Blues":

> *Hello Central, what's the matter with this line?*
> *I want to talk to that High Brown of mine.*
>
> . . . .
>
> *What you say, can't talk to my Brown!*
> *A storm last night blowed the wires all down.*[84]

Patton, then, is contrasting his inability to get in touch with a woman with his determination to do so. This contrast is dealt with in a more direct fashion in stanzas 3 and 5. On the surface the third stanza seems to be about a pony and offers a thematic connection with the first stanza. But almost certainly the riding of the Shetland is metaphoric for lovemaking, or, in a more abstract sense, for easy, contented living. In stanza 5, however, the singer has taken his woman to meet a train, giving him the blues. One must assume, therefore, that she is leaving on the train and breaking up their relationship. Stanzas 4 and 6 contain internal contrasts concerning the singer's relationships with women.

In the fourth stanza he contrasts brown and black women, partly through the use of a startling simile. In the sixth stanza he contrasts the permanent relationship of marriage with a more temporary alliance. Perhaps it is also significant that these two stanzas, which each contain a contrast compressed into their couplet form, both greatly emphasize the neutral third in the guitar part (pattern 3), the fundamentally ambiguous note of the blues. Basically, then, this piece, although it is non-thematic, deals with the problems of establishing relationships with women.

Five years later, Patton recorded a second version of this song with an interesting new development in the text. The piece was called "Stone Pony Blues," which means more or less a "real pony" or a "good pony." For the melody and guitar part he used variations on the three patterns of his earlier recording. The first stanza is set to the first pattern but with a minor or neutral seventh in the vocal instead of the major sixth (measures 1 and 5). The second pattern is used for stanzas 2, 5, and 6, though in the last stanza Patton begins singing on the neutral third above high E and comes down to high E by the end of the first measure. He uses a variant of the third pattern for stanzas 3 and 4, in which the second melodic line is the same as the first line of the second pattern.

Example 25. "Stone Pony Blues." Charley Patton, vocal and guitar in standard tuning, key of E. New York, Jan. 30, 1934. Vocalion 02680, re-issued on *Charley Patton, Founder of the Delta Blues*, Yazoo L-1020, 12" double LP.

1. *I got me a stone pony, and I don't ride shetland no more.*
   I got me a stone pony, don't ride shetland no more.
   You can find my stone pony hooked to my rider's door.

2. *Vicksburg's my pony; Greenville's my grey mare.*
   Vicksburg's my pony; Greenville, Lord, is my grey mare.
   You can find my stone pony down in Lula town somewhere.

3. *And I got me a stone pony, don't ride shetland no more.*
   Got a stone pony, don't ride shetland no more.
   And I can't feel welcome, rider, nowhere I go.

4. *Vicksburg's on a high hill, and Natchez just below.*
   Vicksburg on a high hill, Natchez just below.
   And I can't feel welcome, rider, nowhere I go.

5. *Well, I didn't come here to steal nobody's brown.*
   I didn't come here to steal nobody's brown.
   I just stopped by here, well, to keep you from stealing mine.

6. *Hello, Central, the matter with your line?*
   Hello, Central, matter now with your line?
   Come a storm last night and tore the wires down.

This blues opens with a line that serves to remind the listener of Patton's earlier "Pony Blues," which was a minor hit, and also suggests that the singer has improved his lot since he recorded it. Then he goes on to say that his new pony can be found tethered to his woman's door. In the next stanza the singer seems to be saying that he has women in Vicksburg and Greenville, but that his best woman is in Lula. In fact, not long after he recorded his earlier version of this song, he met his wife, Bertha Lee, in Lula. In the first two stanzas, then, the singer seems to be welcome everywhere. But in the next two he is welcome nowhere. The contrast between these two pairs of stanzas is heightened by Patton's repetition of several lines and phrases. Finally, he returns to an earlier concern of "Pony Blues." In the fifth stanza he states that he wants to maintain his relationship, but in the sixth stanza, which he used in the earlier piece also, he is unable to get in touch with his woman. Basically, then, this blues deals with states of being welcome and unwelcome and moves on to a concern with the maintenance of a relationship with a woman.

We can not be certain whether Charley Patton had established these two songs as stable items in his repertoire or whether he simply arranged his verses in a structured manner at the time of performance. We can say, however, that the arrangements were not "random," even if the singer was unaware of their structure. Blues singers, in fact, perform traditional nonthematic blues which are stable from one performance to another, ones which are improvised at the time of performance, and ones which are partly stable. Most of them have structures built on principles similar to those of the blues discussed above.

An example of a stable blues is Roosevelt Holts's "Red River Blues." I recorded this piece from him on August 31, 1965; February 3, 1966; and August 28, 1966. Each time, the piece contained the same four stanzas and the same melody and guitar part, except for rhythmic changes in the latter and variable ordering and repetitions of stanzas. The text of the second version is as follows:

Example 26. "Red River Blues." Roosevelt Holts, vocal and guitar in standard tuning, key of E. New Orleans, Feb. 3, 1966. Recorded by David Evans and Marc Ryan. Issued on *Presenting the Country Blues: Roosevelt Holts,* Blue Horizon 7-63201, 12" LP.

> 1. *Which a way, which a way do the Red River run?*
>   *Which a way, which a way do the Red River run?*
>
> 2. *Well, some says east, and some says west.*
>   *But I know, sweet mama, it run by the rising sun.*
>
> 3. *Says, I asked for a nickel, and she give me a dime.*
>   *I don't see what make why she do it every time.*
>
> 4. *Which a way, which a way do the Red River run?*
>   *Which a way, which a way do the Red River run?*
>
> 5. *Well, some says east, and some says west.*
>   *But I know, sweet mama, it run by the rising sun.*
>
> 6. *Hey, sweet mama, don't hold your head so high.*
>   *Every living soul got to lay down and die.*

© 1968. Goodie Two Shoes Music, Inc. All Rights Reserved. International Copyright Secured. Used by Permission.

The first two stanzas are cryptic, to say the least. They have no clear meaning, but they do have a power to trigger a number of associations for the singer and his listeners. Basically these stanzas convey a mood of mystery. Some say that the Red River flows east and others say west. The singer knows that it flows by the rising sun. But who has ever been there to check? The Red River in this song seems more mythological than terrestrial. It also may create an ominous mood by being a blood-red river, a river of death. If so, it fits well with the song's final stanza. In fact, in another version of this blues, which enjoys a widespread distribution in oral tradition, Blind Boy Fuller sings:

> *Which a way, which a way do that Blood Red River run?*
> *Run from my window to that rising sun.*[85]

Fuller's two subsequent stanzas both deal with the subject of death. Holts's Red River, then, probably has a similar significance. His other two stanzas draw a sharp contrast between an overly generous woman and an overly conceited one, ending with a warning to the latter of her impending doom.

Why do these four different stanzas along with their tune and guitar accompaniment constitute a stable unit in Roosevelt Holts's repertoire? One could state that it is because they form a well structured blues, but so do many verses that are put together at the time of performance and never sung again in the same combination. I think that the answer lies in the way that Holts learned this blues. He associates the song with Harrison Smith, an older blues singer near Holts's hometown of Tylertown, Mississippi, from whom Holts learned it in the late 1920s. Other traditional nonthematic blues that Holts learned from specific singers like Smith and Tommy Johnson have also remained stable in his repertoire. I have noticed this same tendency among other blues singers in their handling of traditional blues which they associate with particular singers. Somehow a certain sanctity seems to grow up around such pieces, so that those who learn them are reluctant to alter them. This is not a universal rule, however, or otherwise the folk blues tradition as a whole would exhibit more stability than it actually does. Undoubtedly important factors in the stabilizing process are the personality and talent of the original singer and the impression they make on the learner. We shall see these factors exemplified further in chapter 4 in the case of a blues learned by many singers from Tommy Johnson.

Many nonthematic blues are improvised at the time of performance and never performed the same way again. Talented singers are often adept at drawing extemporaneously from a storehouse of traditional verses and musical elements and composing well structured blues. Sometimes they also draw verses or tunes from phonograph records, thereby reincorporating them into the folk tradition. Fred McDowell, a Mississippi folk blues singer, has described this process of composition, saying:

> I made up a lot of the songs I sing. It's like you hear a record or something; well, you pick out some words out of that record that you like. You sing that and add something else onto it. It's just like if you're going to pray, and mean it, things will be in your mind; as fast as you can get one word out, something else will come in there. Songs should tell the truth.[86]

The comparison with the highly formulaic prayers offered in fundamentalist black churches is a very apt one.

Roosevelt Holts composes many of his other blues in this spontaneous manner, employing a repertoire of several dozen mostly traditional stanzas, a few melodies, and some guitar parts in standard tuning in the keys of E, G, and A. So heavily does he rely on this manner of composition that once, when I was recording him, he said that he wanted to end the session because he had "run out of verses." "Let's Talk It All Over Again" is a typical blues composed in this manner. Holts composed it on the spot in 1966 and has never to my knowledge performed it since, although he has used all of its separate elements in other blues.

Example 27. "Let's Talk It All Over Again." Roosevelt Holts, vocal and guitar in standard tuning, key of G. New Orleans, Feb. 3, 1966. Recorded by David Evans and Marc Ryan. Issued on *Presenting the Country Blues: Roosevelt Holts,* Blue Horizon 7-63201, 12″ LP.

GUITAR CHORUS.

1. *Well, come on, baby. Let's talk it all over again.*
   Well, come on, baby. Let's talk it all over again.
   'Cause you know we love each other. Let's try to hold out to the end.

2. *Well, wake up in the morning feeling sad and blue.*
   Well, wake up in the morning feeling sad and blue.
   Well, I woke up this morning, didn't hardly know what to do.

3. *Well, I got a red rooster, crow every morning 'fore day.*
   Well, little red rooster, he crow every morning 'fore day.
   Well, I can always tell when my baby gone away to stay.

4. *Well, the lead in my pencil done gone dead on me.*
   Lord, the lead in my pencil done gone dead on me.
   Well, that's the worst old feeling that a poor man ever had.

In this blues the structure is built not so much on contrast as on *association*. The singer begins by asking his woman to try to talk things over and make their relationship work. Then he states that he has been waking up regularly with the blues. The third stanza is suggested by the preceding one through the idea of something occurring every morning. It also may suggest that the woman's leaving is the cause of his being blue. The fourth stanza could refer back to the first as an attempt to reestablish contact in a broken relationship, or, more likely, it could be a metaphoric description of impotence, which might have caused her leaving. In either case, it fits well within the general context of the song. This blues is not really thematic, because there is no underlying story to it, although Holts once told me that he associates the first stanza with the breakup of his own first marriage many years ago. Despite this stanza's personal association, a listener would have no reason to think that the song as a whole had any basis in a particular personal experience, and it is highly doubtful that Holts himself thought so either. He has simply constructed a nonthematic blues that maintains an emotional continuity.[87]

Babe Stovall was another singer who composed some of his blues spontaneously from traditional elements. He called them simply "regular old blues." He knew about as many verses and melodies as Holts and played guitar parts in standard tuning in the keys of C, G, and A. In 1966 I recorded one of these blues from him. In it Stovall sometimes used a device he was fond of, singing the final line of the preceding stanza over a guitar chorus (stanzas 3 and 5).

Example 28. Untitled blues. Babe Stovall, vocal and guitar in standard tuning, key of A. New Orleans, Jan. 26, 1966. Recorded by David Evans and Marc Ryan.

GUITAR CHORUS.

1. *Well, run here, brown. See what you done done.*
   Eeehooo, see what you done done.
   Says, you made me love you; now your man done come.

2. *Says, the woman that I'm loving, woman that I crave to see.*
   Well, the woman that I'm loving, woman that I crave to see.
   Says, she lives in Memphis. She won't write to me.

3. *Says, she lives in Memphis. She won't write to me.*

4. *Says, the woman that I'm loving done been here and gone.*
Says, the woman that I'm loving done been here and gone.
I ain't got nobody carry my loving on.

5. *I ain't got nobody carry my loving on.*

6. *Well, the woman that I'm loving, mouth chock full of gold.*
Well, the woman that I'm loving, mouth chock full of gold.
When she begin to love me, makes my blood run cold.

GUITAR CHORUS.

7. *I hear a rumbling way down in the ground.*
I hear a rumbling way down in the ground.
Says, it must have been the devil turning his people around.

GUITAR CHORUS.

Although Stovall's arrangement of these traditional verses is spontaneous, they do exhibit a structure. The first stanza makes a complaint against the singer's unfaithful woman. Stanzas 2 through 6 then describe a woman, using the principle of contrast. In stanzas 2 through 5 she has left the singer alone, but in stanza 6 she and the singer seem to be together. All of these stanzas are linked through association by their description of "the woman that I'm loving." Finally, after an instrumental break, there is a stanza describing the devil's activities, carrying an implied threat to the woman.

After performing it, Stovall said that he had no title for this "regular old blues." Then he showed me a guitar part in the key of C which he could also use for composing such blues, and I asked him the following series of questions:

> Evans: *Do you sing the same words to that song [in C] that you just sang in the last one [Example 28]?*
> Stovall: *No, I just mix the words up. I just sing, you know, just mix 'em up, make 'em correspond with the music.*
> Evans: *How do you know which words you're going to sing?*
> Stovall: *It just come into my mind.*
> Evans: *When does it come in?*
> Stovall: *It come in my mind whilst I'm singing.*[88]

Stovall's statement shows that such blues represent not so much what is *on* the singer's mind at the time of performance as what comes *to* his mind while singing. Most songs composed in this manner have no name, because a name would designate them as objects of some permanence and stability. Singers give titles, if requested, after they have performed the song, but these are drawn from a verse they have just sung, are fanciful and unrelated to the words of the song, or are generic titles such as "Worried Blues," "Lonesome Blues," or "Midnight Blues" (used for some of Babe Stovall's compositions).[89]

Sometimes a group of traditional blues elements remains fixed in a performer's repertoire. Usually this group of elements consists of the melody, instrumental part, and a single stanza of the text, normally the

opening stanza. These elements form a stable unit which we shall **155**
henceforth call a *core*. Usually the core stanza is traditional, though in- THE BLUES
SINGERcreasingly singers have tended to take their cores from phonograph
records.[90] To the core the singer adds stanzas drawn from his repertoire
of traditional formulas at the time of performance. These added stanzas
vary with each performance by the singer. He sings as many of them as
he feels inclined to at the time. If he is playing for a dance and everyone is having a good time, he might extend the song considerably, perhaps to twenty stanzas. The core is given a name by the singer and
audience who are familiar with it, and all subsequent performances
which use it are considered by them to be versions of the same song.
The core, then, becomes an element in the singer's repertoire, just like
the other elements of individual stanzas, melodies, and instrumental
parts. It may be transmitted as a core to other singers through the processes of oral tradition. It may even have a story connected with it by
the singer, although such stories tend to be made up after the fact and
attached to traditional stanzas. For example, Tommy Johnson told his
sister-in-law a story about the core stanza of his "Maggie Campbell
Blues" (Victor 21409):

> *Crying, who's that yonder coming down the road, coming down the road?*
>   *Mmmm.*
> *Who's that yonder coming down the road?*
> *Well, it looks like Maggie, baby, but she walks too slow.*

Johnson said that the song (actually only the core stanza) was about his
first wife, Maggie. Johnson was visiting a sporting house, when his
wife approached unexpectedly. One of the women inside looked out a
window and said, "Who's that yonder coming down the road?" Johnson took a look himself and answered, "She walks like Maggie, but she
walks too slow."[91] Since the stanza is a traditional one, Johnson's story
was almost certainly untrue. As we shall be looking at a number of
blues cores in the next two chapters, I shall refrain from printing here
any further examples of their use.

Blues Duets

Until now I have avoided mention of an interesting type of blues, the
kind performed by two singers alternating stanzas between them.
Blues of this sort have not often been recorded, but there are probably
enough of them to make a separate study worthwhile. We can give
only a few examples here, however. Most of the available recordings
are highly commercialized performances by man and woman vaudeville teams from the 1920s, such as Butterbeans and Susie or Coot Grant
and Kid Wesley Wilson. Pieces somewhat closer to the folk blues have
been recorded by Memphis Minnie and Kansas Joe, Lonnie Johnson
and Victoria Spivey, Guitar Slim and Jelly Belly, and a number of other
artists. In the field the practice has been reported by John W. Work and
William Ferris, and the latter prints an example showing its use as a
form of verbal competition between the singers in order to see which
one can sing the largest number of traditional obscene stanzas.[92]

Such blues need not always be competitive, however. In 1966 I recorded a twenty-stanza blues by Babe Stovall and O. D. Jones lasting almost nine minutes, which would have to be described as highly co-operative. The two singers had played together for years around their hometown of Tylertown, Mississippi, and had similar repertoires and styles, but this was their first time together in several years since each had moved separately to different sections of New Orleans. They were glad to be playing together again and were obviously enjoying themselves. They exchanged verses on several other blues, giving the impression that this had been a common practice with them. The instrumental pattern on this piece is one that Stovall played for "regular old blues." Each singer used his own melody. The stanzas are all traditional, and their arrangement was improvised at the time of performance. An S or J preceding each stanza indicates whether it was sung by Stovall or Jones.

Example 29. Untitled blues. Babe Stovall and O. D. Jones, vocals and guitars in standard tuning, key of G. New Orleans, Aug. 14, 1966. Recorded by David Evans and Marina Bokelman.

GUITAR CHORUS.

GUITAR CHORUS.

GUITAR CHORUS.

S 1. *Well, I'm going up the country. Don't you want to go?*
Well, I'm going up the country, brown. Don't you want to go?
Says, I'm going to a place, brown, Lord, never been before.

S 2. *Says, I'm going to a place, brown, Lord, never been before.*

J 3. *Baby, don't worry, because the stuff is here.*
Baby, don't have to worry, 'cause the stuff is here.
'Cause the more you cry, baby . . .

S 4. *Well, it's your time now, brown, be mine some old day.*
Well, it's your time now, brown, be mine some old day.
When I leave this time, brown, Lord, going away to stay.

J 5. *Just take me, baby, do the best you can.*
Now take me, baby, do the best you can.
'Cause, even though you loving me, you still got another man.

S 6. *Says, the woman that I'm loving, woman that I crave to see.*
Well, the woman that I'm loving, woman that I crave to see.
Says, she lives in Memphis; Lord, she won't write to me.

GUITAR CHORUS.

J 7. *Now take me, baby, do the best you can.*
Take me back, baby, do the best you can.
'Cause I know you in love, baby, and I know you in love with
*   another man.*

S 8. *Don't never let, Lord, one woman worry your mind.*
Don't never let, Lord, one woman worry your mind.
Says, she'll keep you worried, Lord, and bothered all the time.

S   9. *Well, you don't want me, give me your right hand.*
       Well, if you don't want me, give me your right hand.
       Says, I'll get me a woman. Lord, get you another man.

J   10. *Says, now, baby, that's all right, that's all right for you.*
      Now that's all right, babe, that's all right for you.
      You can treat me low down and dirty, babe. It's all coming home to
            you.

S   11. *Well, it's late in the evening, when the sun goes down.*
      Well, it's late in the evening, when the sun goes down.
      I'm gonna take my brown, Lord, Lord, and leave this lonesome town.

S   12. *I'm gonna take my brown, Lord, Lord, and leave this lonesome town.*

J   13. *Now you don't have to worry, 'cause the stuff is here.*
      Now, my baby, don't worry, 'cause the stuff is here.
      'Cause the last word I remember her saying, "You don't have to go."

S   14. *Well, she don't want to go, I'm gonna leave her here.*
      Well, if she don't want to go, I'm gonna leave her here.
      I'm gonna find me a brown, Lord, Lord, in the world somewhere.

J   15. *I know my babe. Did you ever think of me?*
      Yes, I know my baby. Wonder do she ever think of me.
      I want you to remember one thing, baby. Just got to remember O. D.

S   16. *I ain't never loved, Lord, three women in my life.*
      I ain't never loved, Lord, three women in my life.

Babe Stovall (left), Dink Brister (center), O. D. Jones (right).
Photo by Marina Bokelman.

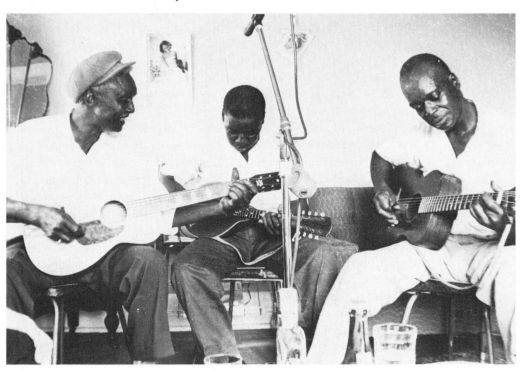

Says, the one my mother, sweetheart and my wife.

J   17. *Now I'm gonna ask the Lord to forgive me all the wrong I did.*
         Yes, I ask the Good Lord forgive me all the wrong I did.
         'Cause I know it's a crying shame, stealing and I know it's hid.

J   18. *Ummmmh hmmmm.*

S   19. *Well, some folks say, Lord, worried blues ain't bad.*
         Well, it's some folks say, Lord, worried blues ain't bad.
         Says, it must not have been the, Lord, worried blues I had.

J   20. *Lord, the blues was whisky, stay drunk all the time.*
         If the blues was whisky, stay drunk all the time.
         'Cause if I don't go crazy, you know, I've got to lose my mind.
         Spoken (S): Have mercy on the people!

If we eliminate from consideration stanzas 2, 12, and 18, which do nothing to advance the text, we are left with seventeen stanzas or statements, nine by Stovall and eight by Jones. The singers generally alternate stanzas. The ordering of the stanzas exhibits the principle of contrast clearly in only the first five stanzas and between stanzas 16 and 17, which present boastful and remorseful attitudes toward the singers' adultery ("stealing"). A more remarkable feature of the text, however, is the overall contrast of moods between the two singers. Of Stovall's nine statements, all except stanzas 6 and 19 express an optimistic mood or one in which the singer purports to be on top of the situation. In contrast, only stanzas 3 and 12 of Jones's eight statements convey this mood. His others are all pessimistic or show the singer as being controlled by an unfavorable situation. The two moods, then, serve to balance each other, and the song as a whole can be called neither optimistic nor pessimistic. In fact, the singers have cooperated to create the ambiguous mood that is so typical of the blues. They each sing a final stanza declaring that they have the blues, as if to confirm this mood, while Stovall's final spoken comment takes the sentiment beyond the two singers to society in general, emphasizing the universality of the blues.

Other blues performed in this manner are truly competitive. A blues recorded by Ferris was a competition in the recall of obscene stanzas. A spirit of competition can be expressed also in the content of the lyrics themselves, as in the case of two blues I recorded by a man and a woman. They had formerly been lovers, but now were married to other people. The woman lived in a large house with her husband and several paying boarders and had pretensions to middle-class respectability. Nevertheless, she liked the blues, which were still played by her two brothers and many of her old friends. She occasionally performed them herself or went out for an evening of fun despite her husband's disapproval. The male singer lived in a small, poor house with his wife and a large family as well as an older woman and her epileptic son whom they had taken in. Apparently the singer still tried to see his old girl friend on the side, although she was ambivalent about these attempts. The recordings were made at the house of the male singer's son by a previous marriage. The woman had left her husband at home passed out from drinking. The male singer was obviously the better guitar player and was trying to make his old girl friend nervous by outplaying her. He was also constantly reminding her of their former relationship and the difficulty he had in seeing her now. The tension had built up considerably, and most of the others who were present felt quite uncomfortable. After several pieces had been played, the man began the following improvised blues. He was very adept at composing in this manner and even prodded the woman into responding to his verses with improvised ones of her own. M and W preceding the stanzas indicate whether they are sung by the man or woman.

Example 30. Untitled blues. Anonymous man, vocal and guitar in standard tuning, key of A; anonymous woman, vocal. Baton Rouge, Aug. 17, 1966. Recorded by David Evans and Marina Bokelman.

M   1. *I'm gonna tell, I wish I had you, little old darling, Lord, all in my home.*
Lord, I wish I had you, darling. You know, I used to love you years ago.

M   2. *Now I want you to tell me now, (Woman's name), why you got it in your mind to put me down.*
I want you to tell me now, (Woman's name), why you got it in your mind to put me down.

W   3. *You asked me the question, (Man's name). That's why I'm telling you why I done.*
You asked me a question, (Man's name). I'm gonna tell you why I done.
You know I'm a married woman. Can't run around no more.

W   4. *Oh, (Man's name), can't run around no more.*
I'm a married woman. I think you're a married man.

M   5. *Well, I know. Still and all, we still can steal away on the side.*
Now I know it all the time, but we can steal away on the side.
But still and all, you don't put yourself in the mood no more.

M   6. *I know it all the time. You done found somebody you love better than me.*
Well, I know it all the time. You done found somebody you love better than me.
Now tell me yes or no. Tell me yes or no now.

W   7. *Yes, (Man's name). Yes, (Man's name). I found somebody that I love better than you.*
Yes, (Man's name), (Man's name). I found somebody that I love better than you.

M   8. *I wish I had my pistol. You wouldn't tell me that to my face again.*
Lord, I wish I had my pistol. You wouldn't tell me that to my face.
Well, I'd shoot you down, woman, then stand over you and dare you to die.

W   9. Spoken: *I don't care. Shoot me down. You can't hit me, but you think. Sing your song.*

M 10. *I don't want to hit you, woman. I'm gonna put you where I know
you'll be all the time.*
That's somewhere in some old lonesome graveyard.

W 11. Spoken: *I don't care if you do. You know what a hump is. Two
humps in the ground. We fight one another. That's when we
together, spirits! Play your stuff. Enough of that juice. I don't
want to hear it.*

M 12. *Now I'm going away to leave you, woman. . . . (W spoken: I don't
care.) I don't want to hear what you say. (W spoken: I don't
care.)*
*Ain't but one thing you can do me now. . . . (W spoken: He had
done once in the ground.) You can spit me if you want to. (W
spoken: They humps in the ground.)*

A blues such as this allows the singers to express thoughts that
could not otherwise be spoken without fear or embarrassment. These
thoughts represent feelings other than those which they act upon in a
normal context. By letting out these repressed feelings, the singers en-
able their present difficult relationship to continue. The man does not
really want to make the woman a "hump in the ground," as he once
did to a man who threatened him (see stanza 12). Otherwise he probably would have killed her long ago. And the woman is not totally committed to her husband, or else she would have stayed at home with
him. The words that they sing and speak in this blues, then, are exaggerated fantasies, which nevertheless help to regulate their actual behavior toward each other in normal contexts.

When this piece ended, there was a feeling of relief and a bit of
laughter. After a round of drinks, the singers performed another blues
together, in which they discussed their relationship in greater detail.
Apparently they had not fully expressed themselves in the previous
piece. The text of their second blues is as follows:

Example 31. Untitled blues. Anonymous man, vocal and guitar in standard tuning, key of A; anonymous woman, vocal. Baton Rouge, Aug.
17, 1966. Recorded by David Evans and Marina Bokelman.

M 1. *I want you to know this the woman I been telling you about, Lord, a
few days ago.*
*Yeah, this the woman I been telling you about with the hair like a
horse's mane.*

M 2. *Yeah, I told you I done knowed it all. I used to couldn't stand to see
this woman out of my sight.*
*Ain't that right, darling? (W spoken: That's what you say.) Well,
talk back in just a little while.*

M 3. *Yeah, she ain't so good looking, and her teeth don't shine like gold.
(W spoken: They my teeth. I ain't got no false teeth.)*
*Let me tell you, darling. She ain't so good looking, people, and her
teeth don't shine like gold. (W spoken: But they mine. They
ain't no false teeth.)*
*But I can't help it. I love that black woman. God knows I do. (W
spoken: Man, I can laugh any day and don't worry about
'em falling out, 'cause they mine.)*

M   4. *I want you to tell me the time, darling, that train run by your door.*
      I want you to tell me, woman, that train run by your door.

W   5. *Six o'clock in the morning. Don't ask me that question.*
      Six o'clock in the morning. Don't ask me that question.
      You already know, I thought, many long times ago.

M   6. *Well, that's the only way we time to tell the time. We don't have no*
         timepiece in our house.
      I know when your man gone, when that old freight train run.

M   7. *When that train run, darling, . . . (W spoken: It's at six.) That's*
         when I head toward your house. (W spoken: He was sick that
         morning and caught you. Outrun the train!)
      I swear I'm off to bed. Then I slam off my hat. (W spoken: Yeah.)
      What did I tell him? That you was kin to me.

M   8. *He told me it was all right.*
      He said, "Looky here, boy. You welcome here any time." (W
         spoken: *It wasn't all right with me.)*

M   9. *Well, tell me now what you want, woman . . . (W spoken: Keep*
         who you got.) Must want me or my dog. (W spoken: I don't
         think you love her. Let me hear a little music.)

M 10. *Mmmmmm. If you love me, darling, . . . (W spoken: You ain't no*
         good.) Please show me the white of your eyes. (W spoken:
         You're looking in 'em now.)

Again, the atmosphere became more relaxed after this piece was performed. However, the woman then went on the offensive and sang a version of "I'm Gonna Ride to Your Funeral in a V-8 Ford."[93] The man followed with his own version of the same piece, even more spiteful than hers, in which he said he would stand by her grave while they "throw dirt in your face." Again the tension was relieved rather than intensified by this performance. The woman then attempted a few pieces on her own, and both of them sang together on a blues called "Big Fat Mama." What actually broke up the session was not the competition in these blues but an argument over the war in Vietnam, which was then at its height. The man improvised a blues denouncing American participation in the war and noting the fact that a black soldier didn't have any rights when he returned to Louisiana. The woman was on the side of the American administration and urged loyalty to its cause. Both of them had relatives serving in Vietnam. When the argument could not be resolved, the man and woman left and went their separate ways.

Composition and Context

Five main types of blues in use among black folksingers have been noted in this chapter. These types differ in the degree of stability of a piece in the performer's repertoire and in whether or not the text is thematic. The five types are:

1. Thematic/Stable (Example 19, "Drinking and Stinking")
2. Thematic/Improvised (Example 23, "Black Sam")

3. Nonthematic/Stable (Example 26, "Red River Blues")
4. Nonthematic/Improvised (Example 27, "Let's Talk It All Over Again")
5. Nonthematic/Partly Stable ("Core" blues—examples to be presented in chapters 3 and 4)

In general, the thematic blues tend to be either original compositions of their singers or pieces derived from phonograph records, and the nonthematic blues tend to be comprised of traditional formulaic elements. But there are exceptions to this rule. Son House's "Preachin' the Blues," as we noted earlier, is thematic but is made up of mostly traditional elements. Nonthematic blues can also be wholly or partly derived from phonograph records, and some can be completely original compositions with no reliance upon traditional elements. In addition, many singers use a few original stanzas, which they have composed themselves, as personal formulas, inserting them into any number of nonthematic blues.[94]

There are also a good number of blues that do not fit neatly into one of the five categories listed above. Indeed, it is probable that stability in blues can be viewed only as a relative characteristic. Improvisation is present to some degree in all blues. We simply recognize that some blues are largely improvised out of traditional elements or original ideas at the time of performance, while others tend to be whole pieces performed largely from memory. The latter, however, may change and evolve slowly over a period of time. More research is needed on the status of "stable" blues in performers' repertoires. It may well be necessary to establish a sixth category of Thematic/Partly Stable blues. Such blues could be the result of one of three conditions: the spontaneous improvisation of original textual material following one or two "core" stanzas; the singing of only a portion of the entire song at any one performance; or simply the performance of the song in successive stages of composition on its way to becoming a stable piece in the performer's repertoire. Since so many stable blues are composed for or derived from phonograph records, the task of investigating their status further is one for the student of popular song as well as for the folklorist.

When we looked at the blues of Blind Lemon Jefferson in chapter 1, it was noted that some of them were "partly thematic." Most of these were shown to represent a transitional stage from nonthematic to thematic blues in Jefferson's recorded output. I have not listed partly thematic blues among the five categories above. Instead, for the sake of simplicity, I have subsumed them under the nonthematic headings. Basically they are nonthematic, in the sense that they do not develop a single theme throughout the full text. Nevertheless, some people may want to establish categories of Partly Thematic blues, which could be either Stable, Partly Stable, or Improvised. Certainly there are many blues that do have two or three stanzas on a single theme with the remainder on different subjects. Charley Patton's "Stone Pony Blues" (Example 25) and Roosevelt Holts's "Red River Blues" (Example 26) could perhaps be considered partly thematic, and many other examples could be given.

Each blues performer usually exhibits a preference for one of the five types of blues listed above, but most can and do compose in more than one way. For instance, most of Roosevelt Holts's blues are Nonthematic/Improvised, but he also performs some which are Thematic/Stable, Nonthematic/Stable, and Nonthematic/Partly Stable. Mott Willis, as we shall see shortly, also prefers to compose Nonthematic/Improvised blues, but he performs some in all of the other categories as well. Napoleon Strickland prefers to compose Thematic/Improvised blues, but he also performs many that are Nonthematic/Stable, Nonthematic/Improvised, and Nonthematic/Partly Stable. And, as noted above, Blind Lemon Jefferson, under the pressure of commercial recording, went from nonthematic to thematic blues. It is important that these options available to the performer be recognized, because some folklorists have tended to categorize performers themselves with respect to their personality type as it affects their overall handling of folklore.[95] Certainly personality is an important factor, especially in cases of Thematic/Improvised blues like those of Robert Pete Williams and Napoleon Strickland. But we must beware of stereotyping performers by assuming that they can handle their material in only one way.

A good description of the options open to a folk blues singer was given to me and John Fahey by the Reverend Rubin Lacy in a discussion of his former blues repertoire. Lacy's blues were all comprised of traditional stanzas and musical elements.

Lacy: (Plays "Long Lonesome Blues" on the guitar.) I don't remember nothing but the tune. You see, music like that, you can make your own words to it easy. Anytime a man can play music like that, he can make his own words to it. If it's a church song, he can make church song words to it. If it's a blues, he can make blues out of it, anything he want.
Evans: When you sang the "Long Lonesome Blues" [Columbia unissued], would you always sing the same words each time?
Lacy: No, I'd sing different things, just put them in, anything that come across my mind to put in it.
Evans: When you were singing "Ham Hound Gravy" [Paramount 12629, issued as "Ham Hound Crave"], would you always sing the same words on that each time?
Lacy: Yeah.
Evans: But on "Long Lonesome Blues" you'd sing it different each time?
Lacy: I'd sing a lot of the same words on "Long Lonesome," but I'd have different things. Different words would come to me, you know. Add to it or sometimes take from it, according to how long I was playing it.
Evans: What about the "Jailhouse Groan" [Paramount 12629, Example 4]? Would you always have the same words to it?

Lacy: *You could add to that or take from it.*

Evans: *But "Ham Hound Gravy" was pretty much the same thing every time?*

Lacy: *I never did add to that or take from it. That's just about the end of it, far as I ever did know about it. These others, according to how long you wanted to play them. Like if I was making a record, I had to quit in three minutes.*

Fahey: *Did you feel constrained? When they told you that you had three minutes, did that make you feel different than when you were on stage or down in the Delta someplace?*

Lacy: *No, I was glad of it. Didn't want to play nohow part of the time. And when they said I didn't have to play but three minutes, the quicker was the better. So I just went to work at it real hard, and I knew I could play anyway three minutes. I don't care how tough it was.*

Fahey: *How long would one of those songs last if you were in the Delta at some show?*

Lacy: *That's what I'm telling you now. You see, if you're playing at some dance or somewhere, you'd make it as long as you wanted, just keep adding things to it. You might run it ten minutes. Yeah, one song, just adding first one thing, then another to it.*

Fahey: *So when you made a record, you were really cutting your songs down?*

Lacy: *Just cutting them down. But that "Ham Hound Gravy," it was just the right length the way I played it.*[96]

There are a number of reasons why improvisation is a characteristic of many blues performances. The simplest explanation is a historical one. Afro-American music and African music before it have always been highly improvisational, so that the blues are hardly unusual in this respect. Furthermore, the blues arose out of hollers sung by black farmers and laborers for the purpose of self-expression and to take their minds off their tedious work. With no particular audience in mind, the singer could holler whatever thoughts came to him. Undoubtedly the freedom to improvise in hollering persisted in the blues, but improvisation also fulfills functions that are peculiar to the blues. We have noted that the Thematic/Improvised blues, like those of Robert Pete Williams, Napoleon Strickland, and the anonymous man and woman, serve mainly the needs of the singers themselves. The singing of these blues provides an individual catharsis of emotions. Improvisation of nonthematic blues undoubtedly serves the singers' needs too, but these songs are just as important to the audience. The blues singer must reach his audience with his words and music or his blues will be unsuccessful. Since the audience is varied and its moods are constantly shifting, a successful blues singer must have considerable variety in his repertoire. His ability to improvise offers him a simple but effective means of achieving this variety. It enables the singer to meet the needs of the moment, to try out new ideas to see if they will be successful, and to abandon unsuccessful ideas. The blues audience is a demanding one, and it needs excitement as well as rhythm for dancing. Improvisation assures that a blues singer's repertoire will not become too familiar to the audience and thus will continue to provide excitement. Finally, the ability to improvise, even when it involves only the recombining of traditional elements, gives the blues singers a feeling of originality. This feeling is highly valued among both performers and audiences. Improvisation allows the singer to be an individualist at the same time that he expresses sentiments which are familiar and relevant to himself and to the audience.

One might ask why so many folk blues are nonthematic and why the principle of contrast is so important in them. Why does Charley Patton sing in one stanza that he has women that will take him in and in another that he can't feel welcome anywhere he goes (Example 25)? The answer lies in the fact that nonthematic blues do not tell stories, provide explanations, or offer solutions to problems. Instead, they state common, even universal, problems, and one way to state a problem is simply to portray two contrasting sides of it. Yet these blues do not simply state problems in a matter-of-fact way. If they did, they would just make people more depressed. Instead, they arouse pleasant sensations, both through their musical setting with its accompanying dancing and through their striking imagery. This imagery often allows the listeners to have several different perspectives on the problems. These blues also make the problems seem more bearable by exaggerating the two contrasting sides of them. Blues lyrics may be truthful, in the sense that they deal with common problems, but they deal with them in an extreme manner. In his blues the singer is extraordinarily boastful and extraordinarily self-pitying. Yet most of the time in reality he is not nearly so successful or so miserable. By stating these extremes for himself and his audience in the form of contrasts, the folk blues singer is able to opt for a state closer to equilibrium. He provides for everyone present a catharsis of extreme emotions, which helps to maintain a steadier state. The blues do not bring about solutions to problems, because the problem areas of life that they deal with are basically universal and will always be present in some form or other. These problem areas exhibit temporary ups and downs, which are stretched to extremes by the singers in what amounts to a celebration of life itself.

The traditional stanzas, which make up the great bulk of nonthematic blues, have been known to incite many reactions in people, but perhaps the most common one in their normal performance context is laughter. When the singer boasts and orders his woman about, or when he tells about the most dreadful troubles, his words are usually met by chuckles and smiles from his audience. Why? Simply because they know that he is not going through these problems at the time of singing. Things couldn't be as extreme as all that, even though the singer and members of his audience may have felt that way at other times. Since the context of the singing contradicts the feelings expressed in the songs, then life with all its problems must have something to recommend it after all.

Many nonthematic folk blues contain within their texts a whole series of contrasts, and adjacent stanzas may contain opposite sentiments. Since these blues have no thematic unity, individual stanzas or pairs of stanzas can often be considered apart from their place in the text as a whole. This, in fact, is what is done by most members of the blues audience. I have observed that most people do not listen attentively to a blues of this sort all the way through. Often they listen to one or two stanzas and then begin talking with someone, perhaps on a tangent developed from the preceding verses. Or they may move further from the singer where it is difficult to hear his words clearly above all the noise. Dancers likewise often do their steps for only a minute or two. The song as a whole may be perceived only by the performer and those of us who later listen to or analyze a recording of it. There are usually many other things going on when traditional folk blues are being performed which compete for the attention of each person present. Consequently the nonthematic structure of these blues is an actual advantage in getting their points across, because these points are contained in small units of one or two stanzas.

Popular blues on phonograph records and in print, which can be contemplated at greater leisure, usually take the entire song to make a single point. These thematic blues can explore that point much more thoroughly than can nonthematic folk blues with their shifting focus. The same contrasting structure is present in the performance of popular blues, but here it simply involves contrasts between the various whole songs that are performed during the course of a session.[97] The audience for popular blues, therefore, must concentrate on the singing for longer periods of time, increasing the risk of dissatisfaction if they do not like the particular piece being performed. They also tend to be more physically removed from the performer, who may be reaching them from a stage or through a phonograph record. Folk blues, particularly the highly traditional kinds, usually reach the audience through live performance in a crowded setting like a house party, picnic, or small juke joint in the country. Their social context and their structure both reflect the small, fairly close-knit community, while the context and structure of popular blues reflect a more complex, technological society, where the distance is greater between spokesman and audience and where the risks of dissatisfaction are greater.

T H R E E

THE LOCAL TRADITION

Regional and Local Aspects of the Blues

SIMPLY to note the processes by which folk blues singers combine traditional elements in composing their songs does not lead to a complete understanding of the nature of their musical tradition. We also need to know the singers' immediate sources for their traditional material and how they utilize, adapt, and combine this material with other elements of their own invention. To gain such knowledge we must place the folk blues tradition in sharper focus and refrain from selecting examples for study in a random manner or from the tradition as a whole. Instead we must examine a portion of the total tradition consisting of the blues of singers with known personal and musical links to one another. Such links are often developed at a regional or local level, so that the blues of a certain limited geographical area come to display their own distinctive characteristics. It is to these levels of the folk blues tradition that we now turn.

As early as 1936 Alain Locke made a naive attempt to characterize black secular music on a regional basis,[1] but it was not until the blues revival of the 1960s that the regional approach gained greatly in popularity among writers. Two recent surveys of country blues performers by Charters are organized by states, and Oliver's study of the history of the blues uses a modified form of this arrangement.[2] More specialized studies of single regions have been made by Leadbitter, Zur Heide, and Bastin.[3] Performers and styles have been grouped geographically on many blues record albums, particularly those on the Origin Jazz Library, RBF, Yazoo, Flyright, and Roots labels. Although in some cases this approach may be no more than a convenient way to give some kind of arrangement to a large body of material, it can have a basis in real stylistic differences. These differences have been summarized succinctly by Welding, Keil and Middleton.[4] They rest primarily on a musical rather than a textual basis.

For the study of the folk blues the most important regional traditions are the Delta, Texas, and the East Coast. Perhaps the main reason for the importance of these traditions is simply the fact that most of the commercial and documentary blues recording activity has taken place in these areas. But they may also be the actual centers of blues activity.

Strictly speaking, the Delta comprises the fertile lowland area between the Mississippi and Yazoo Rivers, but the term is often extended to cover the entire Mississippi Valley from Louisiana to southeastern Missouri. It has traditionally been an area of large cotton plantations, extraordinarily rich in blues activity. This region's black folk music is especially well documented. Its blues are generally the most intense and heavy in the amount of emphasis given to each individual note. A strong beat and a percussive instrumental approach are usually found here. Vocal moaning and instrumental bass drones and ostinato patterns are also characteristic of this region's performance style.

Less is known of the blues further west in Louisiana and Arkansas. Texas and Oklahoma blues are known largely through artists who happen to have been recorded commercially in Dallas, San Antonio, and Houston, and since World War II in California. This regional style is quite difficult to characterize. It too has a good bit of "moaning and droning," but it is less percussive and has a lighter emphasis on individual notes. The melodies and sometimes the instrumental parts are more embellished than they are in the stark Delta style.

Eastward from the Delta lies another vast, poorly documented region of eastern Mississippi and Tennessee and all of Kentucky and Alabama. In the East Coast and Piedmont area of Georgia and the Carolinas the blues are better documented, but in Florida, Virginia, and Maryland recording activity and research have been less extensive. The East Coast blues style is the lightest of all in emphasis. It shows a slight influence from white folk music and a heavy one from ragtime. The blues scene in this region seems to have been dominated by an elite group of blind and otherwise handicapped professional musicians, who have emphasized great instrumental virtuosity at the expense of some of the intensity found in Delta and Texas styles.

There are a good number of performers, however, whose musical styles constitute exceptions to these generalizations. Mississippi John Hurt, with his gentle singing and intricate guitar playing, certainly does not sound like the typical Delta blues singer; Peg Leg Howell, Barbecue Bob, and Charlie Lincoln are a good deal rougher than most other East Coast performers; and musicians as varied as Henry Thomas, Blind Lemon Jefferson, J. T. Smith, and Smokey Hogg hardly give a very firm basis for positing a homogeneous Texas style. Perhaps the rambling life-style of many blues singers explains some of these exceptions. Traveling blues singers pick up and leave songs and musical ideas wherever they go. Other blues singers are highly individualistic performers for reasons of their own.

Despite the many individual exceptions, most folk blues singers display regional characteristics in their musical styles. Many blues singers also develop the major part of their repertoire within a single community, county, or other small area in the context of a local tradition.[5] The importance of studying these local traditions has been affirmed by many writers,[6] but the main studies of blues in such small regions have focused on the cities of Memphis, Atlanta, Chicago, and New Orleans.[7] These cities have tended to attract blues singers from all the surrounding areas and even further afield, so that it is difficult to talk about the distinctive local traits of their blues. Nevertheless, the careful research of Karl Gert zur Heide has shown at least one characteristic feature of New Orleans blues piano playing,[8] and we might hope to learn of more such features in the future.

Perhaps the best documented rural local tradition is the one which is centered in Drew, Mississippi. In order to understand this tradition, we must first discuss the performances and repertoires of the artists who are representative of it. Fortunately this work has already been done for Charley Patton and Tommy Johnson, two of the most important representatives, and for Son House, whose blues were influenced by this tradition.[9] The present chapter will add detailed studies of the blues of Mott Willis and Mager Johnson. As a result of the study of such individual repertoires, it will be possible to determine the elements that were shared by several or all of the artists within the local tradition. These shared elements, in fact, are what constitute the basis of that tradition.

Drew, Mississippi: A Profile

Drew is a town of slightly more than two thousand people, situated in the heart of Mississippi's Delta region in Sunflower County. About five miles east and ten miles west of town flow the Quiver and Sunflower rivers. A railroad line runs north and south through the center of town with shops lining it for a few blocks. Beyond these, farther down the tracks in both directions, are the houses (mostly small shacks) of blacks, while to the west, away from the tracks, is the white residential area. U.S. Highway 49 runs north and south along the eastern edge of town. Physically Drew is typical of Delta towns. Its main buildings are the railroad station and the cotton gin. The population is predominantly black, and for the blacks the centers of public social life are a few cafés and the "Chinaman's grocery" on the east side between the tracks and the highway.

To a great extent, the real focus of life in Drew is not in the town itself but in the surrounding countryside. For miles around there are large plantations, owned by whites and worked by blacks. Most of the land in this area was not settled until the 1890s and early 1900s. Previously it had been a swampy woodland inhabited by bears, "panthers," and alligators. When levees were built along the riverbanks to control the spring floods, lumber companies moved in and cut down the trees, turning the cleared land over to farming. White planters came next, mainly from the surrounding hill country, where land had become eroded and impoverished. With them they brought a train of thousands of poor black workers and a smaller number of poor whites. Between 1910 and 1930, the most important period for our study, the population of Sunflower County grew from 28,787 (80.9 percent black) to 66,364 (70.3 percent black). To a great extent, then, this was still an expanding frontier area in the early twentieth century.

Sunflower County contains some of the best agricultural land in the United States. Until recently cotton was cultivated there almost to the exclusion of anything else, but today soybeans and other crops have largely replaced cotton in the Delta. Before the 1940s most of the plantation work was done by hand through the sharecropping system, making for an economy which supported at subsistence level a large population of resident blacks, supplemented by many more seasonal workers brought in for the fall harvest. Some of these immigrants from the surrounding hill country would stay and become permanent residents, taking the places of others who would leave in search of something better for themselves or for their families. Many of the latter moved into the teeming ghettos of Chicago and other midwestern cities.

Sharecropping was a brutal system, efficient for the white planters and grinding for the black workers. Since the landowner could not

**Sign at Parchman Farm (Mississippi State Penitentiary).
Photo by Cheryl T. Evans.**

Sign, "Welcome to Drew". Photo by Cheryl T. Evans.

possibly work all of his land himself, he contracted with workers on an annual basis, so that each sharecropping family would work a certain portion of the land. In return for providing the sharecropping family with land for farming, the landlord received a portion of the crop, usually one-half. He also furnished a house (generally a shack), farming tools, and sometimes cash advances and food from a plantation-owned store. The cost of these furnishings was deducted from the sharecropper's earnings at the time of his settlement in the late fall, so that he often came out after a year's work with nothing or even owing the landlord money. Some landlords were dishonest, giving their workers a low price for their cotton or charging exorbitant rates for their meager furnishings. The cheated worker had no legal recourse. Punishment was swift and often brutal for those who protested the system. For the worker who came out in debt to his landlord there were two alternatives, to try harder the next year or to leave. Many chose the latter. However, if a sharecropper was a good worker in a good year and had an honest landlord, he could make money in the fall and keep himself and his family going through the rest of the year by doing other odd jobs around the plantation. It was this possibility that lured thousands of blacks to try sharecropping on the Delta's rich soil.[10]

The desire of the planters for increased efficiency finally brought about the decline of the system, just as it had once created it. In the last three decades much of the agricultural work has become mechanized. Tractors now plow fields, and other machines pick crops. As the price of cotton steadily dropped, landowners found that they could be paid for growing nothing through a system of federal subsidies that was sponsored largely by wealthy Mississippi planters in Congress. The unneeded black workers were driven off the land in great numbers. The Civil Rights movement of the 1960s served only to hasten the death of this moribund system. By 1970 the population of Sunflower County was down to 37,047 (62.8 percent black), lower than the figure for 1920, while the number of blacks was slightly lower than the figure for 1910. The black population now consists more and more of the very old and very young. Most of the middle-aged and young adults have gone off to the cities to find work, although some remain to drive the tractors and take various service jobs in the towns. The pattern is similar in other Delta counties.

The Delta has always been one of the strongholds of the blues. Its population has always been overwhelmingly black, and this concentration has produced an intensification of the distinctly black cultural and expressive forms, such as the blues. The region's problems of poverty, illiteracy, and social segregation, factors which surely have contributed to the blues, have been some of the worst in the nation. The migratory character of the black population, its raised expectations, and the unsatisfactory conditions of life encountered in the Delta have made this area a most appropriate one for the development of a rich blues tradition. Many of the Delta's resident black workers have been blues singers, and before the decline of the sharecropping system many more singers used to come there every fall in order to pick up some of the money that was floating about.

With so many blues singers constantly entering and leaving the Delta, it may seem surprising that any distinctly local musical traditions were able to develop there at all. Yet apparently enough singers

Downtown Drew. Photo by Cheryl T. Evans.

Modern juke joint in Drew. Photo by Cheryl T. Evans.

stayed in the same area for a long enough period of time for this process to take place. Much of the movement of the resident black farmers was, in fact, from one plantation to another only a few miles away. Blues singers were thus able to maintain their contacts with each other despite frequent changes of residence. Furthermore, the movements over longer distances were not entirely random but showed a great deal of patterning. As we shall see shortly, a great many of both the black and white settlers in Drew came from Crystal Springs, 160 miles to the south. Similar patterns undoubtedly affected other parts of the Delta, serving to produce more close-knit communities than one would expect to find in the region. Many of those who entered the Delta came from places where the blues were not such a dominant feature of the local folk music, but in the Delta the black audiences wanted mainly to hear the blues.[11] Naturally the incoming musicians tended to learn blues from the local traditions they encountered in the Delta. Those who left the Delta brought the blues traditions back to their home areas or spread them to the cities further north, where they formed the basis for many modern developments in the music after World War II.

The town of Drew provides a convenient name for the local blues tradition that we are studying here. This tradition actually encompassed other nearby towns like Ruleville, six miles to the south, and Doddsville, another six miles below Ruleville. Naturally the Drew tradition flourished also in the surrounding countryside, where most of

Black houses in Drew. Photo by Cheryl T. Evans.

the music was performed at house parties and in small juke houses.
One of the most active centers of blues activity out in the country was
Dockery's plantation about five miles west of Ruleville. This huge
forty-square-mile tract once employed hundreds of black workers, and
even today there are probably several dozen living there. The Drew
blues tradition flourished throughout this region. Many of its representatives also played in other nearby towns such as Boyle, Cleveland, and
Merigold on visits. We know less about the sound of the blues of the
resident singers in these towns and in rural areas further from Drew.
Therefore, unless more research is done in these adjacent areas, we will
be unable to plot the exact boundaries of the Drew tradition. Probably
there was a great deal of overlap between the traditions of adjacent
areas, and we should not really seek to define them precisely in geographical terms. "Local tradition," therefore, is a term of convenience
for discussing the blues of a group of singers who frequently performed with and learned from each other in one small area. It does not
imply that these singers lacked contacts and cross-influences with others from outside the area.

The Drew Blues Singers

The story of the Drew tradition begins around the turn of the century.
In 1903 W. C. Handy heard a man at the Tutwiler railroad station play
the guitar in knife-style and repeat three times the verse, "Goin' where
the Southern cross the Dog." Shortly afterward, Handy heard more
folk music, possibly including some blues, in Cleveland from a string
band made up of guitar, string bass, and mandolin. This trio stole the
show from Handy's own more musically sophisticated orchestra.[12]
Tutwiler is only seventeen miles north of Drew, and Cleveland is only
five miles west of Dockery's plantation. It is even possible that the
singer at Tutwiler was the young Charley Patton, who was able to play
knife-style guitar and who recorded that very stanza twenty-six years

later in his "Green River Blues" (Paramount 12972). Patton was living on Dockery's plantation in 1903 and was already an accomplished blues musician.

Dockery's was founded in 1895 by Will Dockery, and two years later the Patton family moved there. Charley Patton was born in 1881, or possibly a few years later, in the hill country between Bolton and Edwards, Mississippi, about twenty miles west of Jackson and about 120 miles south of Dockery's.[13] There he began learning to play guitar at the age of fourteen with members of the Chatman (or Chatmon) family, a large clan of musicians spanning several generations. In fact, Patton may have been related to the Chatmans, as Sam Chatmon has been quoted as saying that he and Patton were half brothers.[14] After Patton's family moved to Dockery's in 1897, he would frequently return to his native area to visit and make music. At Dockery's he learned to play well by following an older musician named Henry Sloan, who stayed on the plantation until 1918, when he moved to Chicago. Sloan played blues and was probably a major influence on the young Patton. It is quite unlikely that Patton had brought any knowledge of the blues with him to the Delta. The Chatman family at this time and up until World War I were playing string band music mainly for white dances.[15] Patton, too, could play this kind of music and probably learned some of it, rather than any blues, from them. The guitar in string band music plays mostly bass notes and chords, whereas in blues single notes are

Dockery's Plantation. Photo by Marina Bokelman.

picked in various complex ways. Patton's sister says that he "couldn't really pick a guitar until he came to Dockery's."

Charley Patton continued to make Dockery's his home base until 1928 or 1929, but would often make trips to the nearby towns such as Drew, Cleveland, and Boyle to play at parties. Rubin Lacy, who knew Patton well and played music with him around 1927 and 1928, remembers that Patton was a "home boy" who performed mostly in the area near Dockery's. But Patton is known to have made occasional longer trips away from there, not only to his native area between Bolton and Edwards but also to Memphis, Jackson, and the area around Rolling Fork and Hollandale in the Delta south of Dockery's. Millie Torry, one of Patton's wives, who was living in Boyle in 1967, recalled that when he left her he went off to Dermott, Arkansas, with another musician named Tee Nicey Wade. This was sometime before 1910.

Patton was very influential upon the younger local musicians around Dockery's and Drew. One of these was his own brother, Willie "Son" Patton, who learned to strum guitar in accompaniment to Charley. The most important disciple, however, was Willie Brown. He was born sometime between 1890 and 1895, either in Drew itself, in Shaw (about twenty miles to the southwest), or somewhere in Tennessee. In any case, by 1911 he was living near Drew on Jim Yeager's plantation and playing guitar. He told both Son House and Mott Willis that he learned to play guitar from Patton. Exactly when and where this took place is not known, nor is it known whether Brown was influenced by other musicians when he first started playing. One suspects that he was, since he and Patton lived several miles apart, and there were quite a few other musicians in the area. Brown remained on Yeager's plantation until about 1929, playing blues mostly right around Drew, where he was generally considered to be the best all-around blues musician. Apparently he traveled little.

Brown's wife, Josie Bush, was also a very accomplished blues singer and guitarist. She was about seven or eight years older than her husband, to whom she was married by 1911. She was born in Florence, about nine miles southeast of Jackson, but spent much of her youth around Gatesville and Freetown, small settlements to the northeast of Crystal Springs, about twelve miles southwest of Florence. There she learned to play guitar from an uncle known as "Red." She was probably as good a musician as Brown when she married him. They stayed together until around 1922, when they quarreled and broke up. She is said to have died some years ago. Mott Willis, who was a distant cousin, recalls Josie Brown well:

> Her home was in Rankin County, out there from Florence, but she'd be over across the river playing. She was a good guitar player to be a woman. She was playing guitar when I first knowed her, when I was a little old boy. . . . Used to give little old suppers, and we'd go down there. "Riverside Blues," that was her piece. Well, she sure could sing though. Man, she'd have the house

Charley Patton.
Reproduced from Paramount Records publicity photo.

rocking, you know. You see, everybody have a different way of
playing, you know. But Josie could play better than any woman I
ever seed play a guitar. And she could sing so, you know.

And after a while she went to the Delta and come back, and
she told me about a fellow up there, he could play good. And he
learned some of her pieces; she learned some of his'n. And she
married this fellow named Willie Brown, but they didn't stay
together long. They stayed at Drew. And he sure could play too.
They used to play together just like two men, you know. He's a
guy that sure could play some blues. He wasn't much on rags, but

*he sure could, you know, play a lot of blues. Here's a blues here.
His first verse would be about—he know my good gal gonna jump
and shout. He called it "Jumping and Shouting Blues." He had a
good voice, he did. Old Josie'd hit him then when he say that. She
thought he was thinking about some other gal. Well, both of 'em
was jealous of one another. They'd fight, you know. Go to places
that way and play and get to fighting. I used to laugh about it,
you know. And I'd be playing with 'em, and I'd try to part 'em,
you know. Them old things was mean. They both of 'em jealous of
one another. Maybe some man would come up there and tell her,
"Miss Josie, I want you to play me the 'Riverside'." She had a lot
of pieces she played, you know. And if he [Willie Brown] didn't
hear what the man said, you know, those things get mad as a
white-mouthed mule. "Josie, what'd that nigger say to you?" It
started just from that on, you know. They parted, and she went to
Helena, Arkansas, and I ain't never heard from her since.[16]*

Brown's wife was actually part of a large migration of blacks and
whites from the hill country south and west of Jackson to the area
around Drew. Charley Patton's native home was only about twenty
miles west of Jackson, and Will Dockery himself came from a few miles
south of Jackson. Many people moved from Crystal Springs, twenty-five
miles south of Jackson, to Drew. One of the earliest of these was Dick
Bankston. He was born in 1899 at Crystal Springs and began to learn
violin there before moving in 1910 to Lombardy, eight miles northwest
of Drew. His older brother Ben, who also played violin, moved with
him. In 1911 they moved to Drew, and in the following year Dick began
to learn guitar and the blues. His mentors were Willie Brown, Charley
Patton, and Ben Maree. Maree was born around 1887 and was apparently living in Ruleville by 1911 and playing guitar. Bankston was heavily influenced by him, although Bankston thought Brown was the better
musician. Maree and Patton clowned too much for his taste. Maree
played around Ruleville, Drew, and Dockery's for many years and is
recalled as far away as Crenshaw, sixty miles north of Ruleville. He was
reputedly still living in Ruleville as late as 1967 but was crippled and in
a wheelchair.[17]

The young Dick Bankston rapidly became one of the best musicians in Drew. He and his brother played there regularly until the
1950s, when they began to play less often in the face of competition
from jukeboxes. Ben Bankston died in a fire in 1959, and Dick retired to
Memphis in 1962. Mott Willis recalls Dick well from the 1920s:

*Dick would sing so loud. He used to sing, "I got the blues, I can't
be satisfied," and one of them old songs he used to sing about—he
ain't gonna marry and he ain't gonna settle down; he gonna stay
right here until his moustache drag the ground. He kept a lot of
beard on his face biggest of the time, you know. And they used to
call him "Old Santa Claus." He could sing good, but he just would
holler so loud. You know, he'd deafen you near 'bout if you setting
there helping him.[18]*

There were other good musicians around Drew at this early period. Cap Holmes was living there and playing guitar as early as 1916.

Dick Bankston and Jake Martin both recall him as a good musician. He used to travel about to surrounding towns such as Doddsville, twelve miles south of Drew, and play blues with other local musicians. Jim Holloway was another early musician at Drew. He began learning guitar from Bankston, Brown, and Patton not long after 1912. He stayed at Drew at least into the 1930s but eventually became a preacher in Memphis, where he was supposed to be still living in 1967.

Just as people were moving from the area around Crystal Springs to Drew, Dockery's plantation was attracting workers from the hill country around Bolton and Edwards. Among these were several musicians. Jake Martin was born in 1886 and began learning guitar as a child with Charley Patton. He remembers the Chatman family as the

Dick Bankston. Photo by Marina Bokelman.

most prominent local musicians. It was not until 1916 that he moved to Dockery's with his family. He recalls that Will Dockery liked to have musicians on his plantation and would give them the special privilege of missing work in order to play in nearby towns. Besides Patton, Martin remembers Henry Sloan at Dockery's, and Jack Hicks. Hicks was originally from the same area as Martin, the two of them having grown up and learned music together. Another from there who played at Dockery's was Lee Van Robinson, an older man than Martin. Jake Martin would travel up and down the Mississippi River, sometimes going as far as Clarksdale and Memphis, playing mostly for white people at parties. He frequently played at Cleveland and recalls string bands there and at Rosedale, seventeen miles to the west. Martin says that he was never much of a guitarist but could keep good time for dancing, could clown with the guitar, and was a good singer. Most of his songs were designed for white audiences and were not blues, although he says he could play all the songs that Patton, Brown, and the other local blues singers performed. It would appear that Martin was not in the mainstream of the blues tradition and instead was more in the mold of the Chatmans, who played string band music largely for white audiences. Martin was in the army from 1917 to 1919 but returned to Dockery's, where he stayed until 1947. He gave up guitar playing in the 1930s.

Tommy Johnson was born a few miles north of Crystal Springs around 1896. He began learning guitar there, but not blues, from his older brother LeDell, who was born in 1892. Around 1915 Tommy left home with an older woman and went to Rolling Fork in the Delta, also spending some time at Boyle.[19] He was gone for two years and returned to Crystal Springs able to play blues. LeDell said that Tommy met Bankston, Brown, and Patton on this trip and learned from them. This is very likely, although exactly where these meetings took place is a mystery. Boyle is quite near Drew and even closer to Dockery's, but Patton is also known to have frequented the area around Rolling Fork and Hollandale during this period. Bankston does not recall meeting Tommy Johnson at this time but says that Patton and Ben Maree knew him. Both lived closer to Boyle than Bankston and Brown, whom Johnson may have only heard or met briefly at this time. Tommy Johnson returned to Crystal Springs able to play blues in the style of the Drew area musicians. One of the songs he performed opened with the stanza:

> Hitch up my buggy, saddle up my grey mare.
> Hitch up my buggy, saddle up my grey mare.
> I'm gonna find my baby in the world somewhere.

According to LeDell Johnson, Tommy claimed to have learned this song from Dick Bankston. But it should be remembered that Bankston himself had only started to play guitar in 1912. Bankston said that he learned the song from Ben Maree, although all of the other musicians played it too. Tommy Johnson, then, probably learned it from Maree and Patton, who later recorded it as "Pony Blues" (Paramount 12792,

Jake Martin. Photo by Marina Bokelman.

Example 24). LeDell Johnson learned the song from Tommy when he returned and eventually came to perform it far more than Tommy ever did. He associates it with Bankston, whom he later met and heard play it often. LeDell Johnson apparently never knew Ben Maree.

In 1921 LeDell and Tommy Johnson moved to Drew and lived on the plantation of Tom Sanders, a white man who also came there from Crystal Springs.[20] There they played regularly with Bankston, Brown, and Patton. Brown lived on Yeager's plantation, Bankston in town, and Patton at Dockery's. Bankston recalls that Tommy Johnson was not really very good when he came to Drew, but that his music improved quickly. Tommy left after one year, and LeDell returned to Crystal Springs at the end of 1923.

It must have been very stimulating for a blues singer to be around Drew in this early period. There were many musicians there, all playing and learning from one another. It must be borne in mind that all of these men were under forty, and some were only in their teens. Mrs. Maybelle Johnson was born near Crystal Springs in 1900 but moved with her family to Drew and lived there in 1913 and 1914. She returned there around 1917 to marry and stayed until 1940, when she left for Jackson and married the Reverend LeDell Johnson. She recalls what it was like to be a young girl in Drew before 1920:

> I knows Willie [Brown] and them were playing when I knew
> them, both of them, when I was fourteen years old. I was a little
> girl when I went there, but I never did forget Josie and them,
> 'cause I was around them all the time. I remember that "Saddle up
> my pony, and bring me my black mare." He never told me where
> he learned 'em, but he was playing 'em when I seed him, 'cause he
> played for all the parties and suppers, him and his wife. And Dick
> Banks. He was a Bankston, but we just called him Dick Banks. He
> was kin to me. He come from Crystal Springs. That's his home. He
> was born and raised there. They moved to the Delta. He was born
> and then moved up there a long many years ago, before I went up
> there. But I know he sure could play. He played many of 'em, but
> I can't think of 'em. All of 'em was playing then. I think Dick
> Bankston and Willie Brown and Charley Patton was all good.
> There was lots of 'em up there. I knowed one when we moved
> there. We was little old girls, me and my sister, cotton picking. He
> was named Paul Baskett. He left there when Mr. Arnold got
> killed. Mr. Arnold got killed there. All them boys disappeared,
> every one of 'em. They got scared around there with all that
> killing up there. When that man killed that white man, they all
> left.[21]

It is not known when this killing took place, but it was probably around 1918. Jake Martin recalls that when he returned to Dockery's in 1919, most of his former fellow musicians were gone. Among those to leave besides Paul Baskett were Henry Sloan, Jack Hicks, and Cap Holmes. Patton, Brown, and Bankston may have left briefly, but they all remained in the area.

Tommy Johnson.
Reproduced from Victor Records publicity photo.

Reverend LeDell Johnson. Photo by Marina Bokelman.

New arrivals compensated for the loss of these musicians. One of
the most important of these newcomers was Mott Willis. He was born
in 1897 in Crystal Springs and raised nearby in Gatesville. Willis
learned guitar, violin, and mandolin from his older brothers and cousins, who were uncles of LeDell and Tommy Johnson. Before he moved
to Drew in 1919, he was already an accomplished musician. He had
begun to play the guitar at the age of eight, and when he was eighteen
or nineteen he played guitar and other instruments in a minstrel show
led by his cousin Henry Bailey. The performers, all from the Crystal
Springs area, traveled around Memphis and got as far as Texas. Their
band consisted of violin, one or two guitars, string bass, mandolin,
trombone, and tambourine, and they performed popular and sentimen-

tal songs of the day. Bailey's son was the main vocalist, and other entertainers danced and cracked jokes.

Willis was not performing blues at this early period except for
those pieces that he had managed to learn from Josie Bush. All of the
pieces that he played in Henry Bailey's show were the kinds of songs
that were popular among whites at the time. If they played blues at all,
they were probably popular blues derived from sheet music. Henry
Bailey, in fact, was a music reader and an accomplished lead violinist.
But when Willis moved to Drew in 1919, he learned to perform blues.
He stayed there until about 1922 when he left and moved to Nitta
Yuma, a little Delta town about sixty miles south of Drew near Rolling
Fork. Here he played in a band led by Willie Funchia (pronounced
"Fience") for four or five years until Funchia's death. The band played
a variety of songs for both white and black audiences. Then Willis
went to Clarksdale and got in another minstrel show led by a man
called Dirty Baby. He also substituted twice for an ailing Jim Jackson in
a medicine show and played in Clarksdale with other blues recording
stars like Tampa Red and Bessie Smith, who were passing through. He
even spent some time in St. Louis playing with Lonnie Johnson and
claims to have played in one of Johnson's recording sessions. Around
1928 or 1929 he returned to Drew for several more years to farm and
play music. Occasionally he would travel to Nitta Yuma and Hollan-

Mott Willis. Photo by Cheryl T. Evans.

Mott Willis and friend. Photo by Cheryl T. Evans.

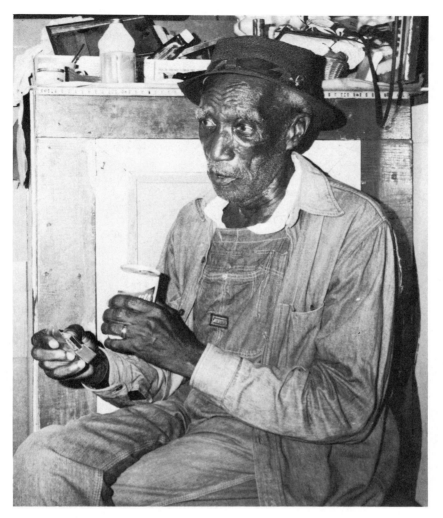

Mott Willis. Photo by Cheryl T. Evans.

dale to play with some of the Chatman brothers, who had moved to
Hollandale and become known as the Mississippi Sheiks. In Drew his
main playing partners were Willie Brown, Dick Bankston, and Charley
Patton. Bankston thought that Willis was the best musician there, although Willis himself preferred Willie Brown.

Willis vividly recalls this period in his life, which is probably the
time that he was most active as a musician:

> *That was directly after World War I ceased, because I used to
> work here at the mill. Well, about a year after it ceased, near as I
> can get at it, that's the year I went up to Drew. I belonged to a
> little old show, you know, before I went up there. That was
> Bailey's show. He used to live here in Crystal Springs, an old
> minister show [sic]. I played mandolin when I first started with
> him, then a guitar, and then sometimes violin, bass a little
> sometimes. But I just, you know, wanted to hear them play some
> [i.e., the musicians at Drew]. You know how it is, a fellow go to a*

*new place, you know. I was up there a long time before they
knowed I could play, you know. They was having them little
suppers, you know, and I'd go to the suppers. And I had an old
guitar, you know, but I'd leave mine at home and go out and listen
at them. And another boy from Gatesville, you know, he says,
"Willie, here's a fellow here. He can play a guitar." And, well,
they kind of worried me, you know, to play some, and I got tied
up with him then. Him [Brown] and Banks was playing together
then and next time Charley Patton. You know, Willie and Tommy
Johnson played together. They'd help them. One would lead one
piece, and the other would second. Tom knowed him before I did.
He had been knowing Willie Brown for about a year 'fore I
knowed him. They had been playing together a lot in the Delta.
They played some pieces alike. But Willie, it just looked like he
played the best music, had the best voice. Charley had a good voice
too, but Willie Brown, you know, he had the date. Well, after a
while Willie and Charley, they had some kind of falling out. And
Charley Patton had a brother called Buster. He commenced
playing with Buster, his brother, you know. He was a great big old
fellow. He couldn't do nothing but drum [i.e., on the guitar
strings], you know, but he was a good seconder. Never would sing.
Charley would do all the singing, you know. I played, you know, a
little with Charley, just at suppers, you know, but we never did go
out nowhere else and play, you know. Played with Dick Bankston
right sharp. I think Charley's the one that learned Willie how to
play. Think it was, you know. And some way or other they got to
arguing there one night, and one told the other, "Well, I ain't
gonna play with you no more." I never did know them to play
together. They had been knowing one another a long time, way
before I ever knowed 'em, but they just had a falling out. I don't
know what it was about, you know. The way it was, Willie say he
could beat Charley. Charley say he could beat Willie. And I think
that's the way it started, you know. And they had this falling out.
But Willie could play better than Charley could, you know. He
could out-note him. He could find more notes, you know. Charley
could holler the loudest. He was a better singer for blues, you
know. Course now, I never knowed him to sing no rags. The only
kind of piece he called a rag was that about "It Ain't Gonna Rain
No More."*

*I stayed up there about three years. Come on down to Nitta
Yuma. That's just above Rolling Fork. That's where I got with
Willie Funchia. Me and him played together until he died. We
played together about four or five years, I reckon. I got acquainted
with him there at Nitta Yuma, and then we moved out there to a
little place out west they called Grace, Mississippi. Willie Funchia
didn't have no show. He just had a little old band. . . . We played
practically all around there, Nitta Yuma, Rolling Fork, and all
through the Delta, you know, Hollandale, Anguilla, and way back
out here at Grace, Mississippi, out there for a white man. He was
the high sheriff out there. Oh, we got them big plays, you
know. . . . We played the biggest along in that time for white.*

*Well, Willie Funchia died, and I played with Dirty Baby up
there in Clarksdale. He had a show, you know. . . . We'd just be
around there in town. And sometimes kind of out in the country,
you know, have a little old tent. You don't never see them little*

*old minister shows now, do you? Oh, we were around Clarksdale
and Tutwiler and all up around in there, Hollandale.*

*After that I went back to Drew and fooled around there a
while, you know. I was just backwards and forwards, you know. I
was farming though when I was staying at Drew. Stayed there a
pretty good while. I stayed in town about three or four months.
Then I worked out for a man, you know, called Mr. Yeager, Jim
Yeager. Made two crops or three crops with Mr. Yeager. He was
a mighty good white man too. He's dead now. I moved around
from place to place, you know, staying with different fellows
playing. I was there off and on from Drew to Hollandale. I played
with the Mississippi Sheiks a while. Come on back to Nitta
Yuma. . . . Well, fact of the business, I've been all over that Delta
just about. Along at that time just here and yonder, you know.
The year after things commenced to getting kind of dull, I just,
you know, come back down here then.[22]*

When Mott Willis returned to Crystal Springs, he became active
in the local blues scene. Elements of the Drew tradition had already
been introduced in Crystal Springs by Tommy and LeDell Johnson.
Two younger Johnson brothers, Clarence and Mager, began to learn
blues in the early 1920s, while Mott Willis helped to teach his nephews
Willis and Charlie Taylor. Many other Crystal Springs musicians
learned some or all of their music from these men, so the Drew blues
tradition could be said to have been transplanted successfully to Crystal
Springs, 160 miles to the south. The Johnson brothers seem to have
been the first musicians in the area to emphasize blues in their music.
Mager Johnson says of this period in the mid-1920s,

*At one while there wasn't but three musicians as I know around
here in Copiah [County], close by where we knew, me and Tommy
and Clarence. We used to make pretty good too at that time,
'cause it wasn't nobody to make no music but us. We'd go
someplace and play probably from seven or eight o'clock up until
twelve o'clock at this place, and leave that place and go to another
one and play till daylight. And then right back that Sunday
evening playing for a party at times.[23]*

LeDell Johnson gave up blues and became a preacher in the late
1920s, and Clarence Johnson was killed in 1945. Of all the brothers,
Tommy was probably most responsible for spreading the Drew tradition. He was influential not only in Crystal Springs but in Jackson,
Tylertown, and in general throughout Mississippi until his death in
1956. Tommy Johnson traveled widely within the state and rarely
stayed in one place very long. Mager Johnson's life was quite different.
He was born December 7, 1905, and has lived nearly all his life around
Crystal Springs. One year around 1930 he and Clarence and their families sharecropped near Yazoo City on the edge of the Delta. Tommy,
Clarence, and Mager also would often go up to the Delta in the fall for
a few weeks. Mager says, "We'd go up there and pick cotton. Sometimes we'd be in Rolling Fork, and Hollandale, Anguilla, and Belzoni.
And I believe there was two towns, Greenville and Greenwood. We'd

Mager Johnson. Photo by Marina Bokelman.

be all up around them places. And it be not raining, that's all we'd do, go from town to town playing old guitars."[24] Mager Johnson has not performed much in recent years, but he still plays for gatherings of friends.[25]

During the 1920s many of the blues singers left the Drew area. Much of this movement was a natural consequence of the oppressive sharecropping system, which drove many black farmers back to the hill country or to the northern cities. World War I had also created dissatisfaction with the status quo among black veterans and had opened up many new jobs for blacks in northern industries. Then the disastrous 1927 Mississippi River flood and the 1929 dry spell proved to be the last straws for many struggling sharecroppers. There was also the problem of racial strife, which was bad throughout the Delta but particularly intense at Drew. We have already noted a racial killing that took place probably around 1918, but perhaps the most spectacular incident took place in 1923. On December 14 of that year Joe Pullen, a black sharecropper and veteran of World War I, killed four white men and wounded eight others near Drew before he was finally brought down by a posse. The incident was a classic case of the surfacing of tensions inherent in the sharecropping system. Pullen and his boss, W. T. "Tom" Sanders, had an argument over Pullen's settlement for his year's work, and Pullen expressed a determination to move off the plantation. According to one oral account, Sanders refused to pay Pullen the money

Mager Johnson. Photo by Marina Bokelman.

that was due him or somehow tried to cheat him. The newspapers, however, state that Pullen was in debt to Sanders, apparently because he had not made enough of a crop to cover his rent and other advances. In any case, Pullen was within his rights in leaving the plantation, and Sanders's attempt to make him stay and work off his debt would have constituted peonage. Oral sources claim that Sanders shot and wounded Pullen first, but the newspapers mention nothing about this. In any case, Pullen went to his house and got his gun, shot and killed Sanders, and then fled to the swamps east of Drew with a pistol, a shotgun, and seventy-five rounds of ammunition. As Pullen holed up in a drainage ditch near the Quiver River, a posse of one thousand men searched the area for him. Some came from as far away as Crystal Springs, when they received the news of the death of Sanders, who had moved from there two years before. The sheriff from Clarksdale arrived with a machine gun. When it got dark, they poured five hundred gallons of gasoline into the drainage ditch and set it on fire in an effort to illuminate the area and drive Pullen out. But his deadly aim brought down one white pursuer after another. Oral accounts say that he killed seventeen and wounded forty, or killed nineteen and wounded thirty-eight, but the newspaper reports of four killed and eight wounded are probably more accurate. Three of the dead were originally from Crystal Springs. Around 1:00 A.M. on December 15, Pullen was brought down by the machine gun. Oral sources and the first newspaper accounts agree that Pullen was taken still alive and dragged by a mob through the streets of Drew where he finally died or was killed. A subsequent news report and the death certificate, however, claim that he died instantly from a hail of bullets. Probably the earlier accounts are more accurate, the story having been altered to protect Drew's reputation.[26]

After this incident Drew became known among blacks as a "bad" town. Tensions increased in Crystal Springs also, where one of Tom

Mager Johnson. Photo by Marina Bokelman.

Sanders's brothers, a policeman, began taking out his revenge on local blacks. Drew instituted a curfew for blacks in town after this, which led to another serious act of violence the following year. An oral account states that one Saturday night a group of blacks at a dance in town failed to observe the curfew quickly enough. The chief of police got in an argument with some people who were leaving the dance hall, and he began shooting without warning. According to my informant, about seven or eight people were killed, including two musicians.[27]

Tension and periodic violence continued in Drew, giving it a reputation as one of the worst towns in the South for race relations. As recently as May, 1971, an eighteen-year-old black girl was shot and killed on the streets of Drew by three drunk white teenagers in a passing car following her high school graduation. During the 1920s and later this unpleasant climate of hostility caused many blacks to leave, including probably some of the best blues singers. Charley Patton and Willie Brown both left in the late 1920s, and others left in the following years. Although Drew continued to attract black workers to its cotton fields, few were inclined to stay for any considerable length of time. This naturally affected the continuity of the blues tradition. The band members killed by the police were apparently not local blues musicians, but the handwriting was still on the wall for the others.

A few of the blues singers who came to Drew in the 1920s stayed long enough to participate in the local tradition. One of the best of these was Nathan Scott, who may have come originally from Blaine, sixteen miles south of Drew. He played guitar and harmonica and began learning from Bankston, Brown, Patton, and Mott Willis in the 1920s. He played in Drew and is recalled as far away as Lambert, about thirty-five miles north of Drew, playing with Charley Patton.[28] A Nathaniel Scott, who may be the same man, made recordings for the Library of Congress of a spiritual and a work song in Parchman Penitentiary in 1936 along with several other convicts, including one named Charlie Holloway.[29] Mott Willis has a clear recollection of Scott:

> Oh, I know Long Nathan. Yeah, he sure had a good voice. He could sing really good. I used to play a little bit with him. He could blow a harp mighty good too, harp and guitar. Played piano a little bit too. He played guitar. He couldn't play all that good, but he had such a good voice. He could outsing any of 'em. Just change his voice like a woman and then sing like a man. He'd sing keen, you know. He had two voices. And he had a stout voice, you know. I can't go that way like him. Old Nathan Scott. He hadn't been long started to playing too. He was a youngster, you know. . . .
>
> He played about—he going away, won't be back till fall; if he take the blues, he won't be back at all. That's one of his pieces, you know. Another one he played about—Come here, baby, let me whisper in your ear; I got something to tell you that I know you want to hear. He was just an old devilish fellow. I think he made up his songs, you know. Nathan's home was out from Drew out

there. He stayed on the high sheriff's place out there. . . . Nathan
didn't stay far from the plantation what I stayed on when I was at
Mr. Yeager's there. Well, I got acquainted with him, you know,
shortly after Willie Brown left, you know. Shortly after Willie
pulled off and left, you know, well, Nathan and this here Banks
boy, you know, Dick Bankston, us three played together a pretty
good while. Willie tried to get me to go with him. He said that he
was going somewhere to record. I think he put out some records,
didn't he?[30]

Another important musician in the area was Chester Arthur
Burnett. He was born in West Point, Mississippi, in 1910 and moved
with his family to Ruleville in 1923. They farmed there and at Drew
and Doddsville. In 1933 Burnett left the area and moved to Arkansas.
He began to learn guitar in 1928 from Charley Patton but was also influenced by Dick Bankston, Nathan Scott, and Jim Holloway. He claims
to have married Willie Brown's sister. He often played on the streets of
Drew, Ruleville, Cleveland, Skene, Boyle, and Mound Bayou, and was
given the nicknames of "Bull Cow," "Foot," and "Howlin' Wolf," the
last of which stuck with him. There were apparently other musicians in
the area with some of the same nicknames. A man called "Bull Cow"
played at Skene, about twenty miles southwest of Drew, and knew
Charley Patton, and there was another "Howlin' Wolf" around Dockery's, whose real name was John Dee.

Other musicians from the 1920s are more obscure. A Lucille Davis
is recalled by Mott Willis, who says, "There was one up there, a one-
eyed woman called Lucille. Well, she could play some nice blues, but
nothing but blues now, sing good too. Called her Lucille Davis. Didn't
have but one eye, you know. She played one piece running up and
down the strings in A."[31] Several of my informants recognized the
name of Kid Bailey but seemed reluctant to talk about him or simply
knew little about him. Perhaps he was involved in some of the violence
at Drew, as Mott Willis referred to him as "Killer Bailey." Sam Williams
and Will Bryant are also recalled from around Drew at this time.
Bryant, who came originally from Schlater, about fifteen miles southeast of Drew, may be confused with Willie Brown in some accounts.
Roebuck Staples began learning guitar around Drew and Dockery's in
the late 1920s, but he played mostly church songs. In the early 1930s he
moved to Chicago and eventually founded a very successful gospel
singing group with his children, the Staples Singers. They have recently begun recording soul music. Some of Staples's brothers also
played guitar around Drew.[32] Charley Patton is known to have played
with many other local musicians. One was Willie Stewart, who was
known for a song with the line, "You country women gonna let my
hambone spoil." Patton also played with both Homer Lewis, an accor-
dion and mandolin player from Symonds, about fifteen miles northeast
of Dockery's, and an otherwise unknown white harmonica player.
Many musicians would visit Dockery's occasionally to play. One was
Joseph Harris, a guitarist from Merigold about ten miles to the north-

west. Another was Fiddlin' Joe Martin, a cousin of Jake Martin, who was born in 1904 near Edwards. He learned guitar, mandolin, and bass violin, and began visiting Dockery's around 1924. Rubin Lacy from Jackson was another guitarist who played there around 1927 and 1928.

Charley Patton left the area around 1928 or 1929. In 1929 he spent some time in Jackson, and later that year he lived in Clarksdale. In 1930 he was living at Lula, further north in the Delta, where he met and married Bertha Lee, also a guitarist and blues singer. Shortly afterwards they moved to Holly Ridge, about twenty miles southwest of Dockery's, where Patton died in 1934. Until his death he played at country parties and barrelhouses, often with Willie Brown and Son House, who visited him from further north.[33]

Willie Brown left Drew around 1929 and moved to Robinsonville, eighty-four miles to the north and only twenty-seven miles southwest of Memphis. By 1935 he was living at Lake Cormorant, eight miles closer to Memphis. From 1930 until about 1943 Brown played often with Son House, a blues singer who had moved to Robinsonville from Clarksdale. Usually House would sing and play lead guitar with Brown seconding, but House managed to learn some of Brown's songs in the process. House moved to Rochester, New York, around 1943 and still lives there, while Brown stayed in Lake Cormorant, where he died in December, 1952.[34]

Chester Burnett (Howlin' Wolf) left Ruleville around 1933 and lived in a succession of small towns, where he farmed and made music on the side. One of these places was Robinsonville, where he played with Son House and Willie Brown. From 1945 to 1947 he again lived about three miles north of Robinsonville in Penton. After that he moved to West Memphis and then to Chicago, where he became one of the most popular blues singers. His recorded music showed the effects of keeping up with forty years of popular trends much more than it did the effects of the Drew tradition. Burnett died in Chicago on January 10, 1976.[35]

A few other blues singers from the Robinsonville area picked up elements from the Drew tradition, mainly from Willie Brown and Howlin' Wolf. Robert Johnson was born around 1912 in Hazlehurst, Mississippi, and raised in Robinsonville, where he began learning guitar from Son House and Willie Brown in the 1930s. He left the area soon after he began learning and traveled about to other Mississippi and Arkansas towns as well as to several northern cities, absorbing elements of many different styles. He was killed in 1938.[36] Fiddlin' Joe Martin, who had visited Dockery's in the 1920s, came to Robinsonville in 1935 and played for many years with Son House and Willie Brown. An injury to his left hand in a fire caused him to switch to drums, which he played for several years with Howlin' Wolf. Martin died in 1977.[37] Woodrow Adams moved to Robinsonville in the 1940s and learned guitar from Howlin' Wolf, although the harmonica remained his main instrument. He continued to play there with Fiddlin' Joe Martin.[38]

The Drew blues tradition did not really take root around Robinsonville in the 1930s and 1940s as it had in Crystal Springs. Probably there were simply not enough representatives of it to effect a successful transplanting. The blues scene there was dominated by the strong personalities of Son House and Fiddlin' Joe Martin, while Willie Brown seemed to remain in the background. Brown did, however, exert some influence over the styles of House and Robert Johnson, while House was further influenced by Charley Patton, with whom he played often from 1930 until Patton's death in 1934. Howlin' Wolf was not really around Robinsonville long enough to exert a strong influence, except on Woodrow Adams. Furthermore, Howlin' Wolf had begun playing in a number of different styles in the 1940s and was concentrating more on the harmonica than the guitar.

Starting in the late 1920s, following the departure of several important performers from the area, a number of the Drew tradition's chief representatives began to make commercial recordings. Tommy Johnson was the first to reach a studio. Between 1928 and 1930 he recorded twelve issued songs and two others that were unissued, although alternative takes of one of the latter have been made available recently. All of his pieces but one were blues. Between 1929 and 1934 Charley Patton recorded fifty-two issued songs and played guitar on six others by Henry Sims and Bertha Lee. Most of these were blues. In 1929 Kid Bailey recorded two blues, and in 1930 Willie Brown recorded four and played second guitar on four of Patton's blues. These early commercial recordings, along with my recent field recordings of Mott

Fiddlin' Joe Martin. Photo by Marina Bokelman.

Willis and Mager Johnson, yield the bulk of the musical evidence for
the study of the Drew blues tradition.

In 1936 and 1937 Robert Johnson recorded twenty-nine blues,
some of which show the influence of Willie Brown. In 1941 and 1942
field recordings were made by Alan Lomax in Robinsonville and Lake
Cormorant for the Library of Congress. Son House recorded fourteen
blues, some of which show the influence of Brown and Patton. House's
earlier commercial recordings in 1930 showed almost nothing of their
influence, as he had just met them shortly before recording. Lomax unfortunately recorded only one song from Brown himself, though
Brown played accompaniments to three pieces by House, two by Fiddlin' Joe Martin, and one by Leroy Williams. Since his rediscovery in
1964, Son House has continued to record some songs which show
Brown's influence. Howlin' Wolf began his recording career in 1948
and continued until his recent death. A few of his early recordings are
representative of the Drew tradition. Woodrow Adams has made a few
commercial recordings since 1952, but only one of them shows the influence of Howlin' Wolf's guitar playing and singing. Various other
blues singers have recorded songs that show the influence of Drew
musicians, especially of Tommy Johnson and Charley Patton. Several of
these recordings will be discussed in this study.

The local blues tradition in Drew in the 1930s and later was apparently much weaker than it had been in the 1920s and earlier. Very
few new local musicians emerged, and most of the older ones eventually left or quit music. Good blues were undoubtedly performed in
the area, but more often by musicians who were just passing through
rather than by local residents. Dick Bankston, Jim Holloway, and probably Nathan Scott remained as the nucleus of the local tradition there.
Willie Farris began playing blues on Dockery's plantation, but he is
now a preacher in Benoit, about twenty miles to the west, and is uninterested in the blues. Robert Johnson (no relation to the Robert Johnson
in Robinsonville) was born in 1917 on a plantation near Dockery's and
began playing guitar in 1928, learning from an uncle. In his youth he
knew Charley Patton, Howlin' Wolf, and Roebuck Staples. When Johnson grew older, he played with Willie Farris and a cousin in Rosedale,
but he gave up blues around 1955 and switched to church songs. He
died in 1974.[39] In 1932 O. M. McGee began playing guitar and singing
blues in Drew. By the 1940s he had moved to Merigold, about ten miles
to the west, and became a preacher. When recorded in 1978, he recalled
only fragments of his old blues, but several of them showed melodic
and instrumental similarities to the songs of Charley Patton even
though McGee never saw Patton. One of McGee's stanzas reflected the
large-scale migration of blacks from Crystal Springs to the Drew area:

> *My home ain't here; baby, my home's in Crystal Springs.*
> *Got a brownskin woman, and I'm scared to call her name.*

Interestingly, McGee himself has never been to Crystal Springs but simply adopted the verse from the local blues tradition of Drew. Many other musicians visited the area during the 1930s, such as Jasper Love, a pianist from Lambert, thirty-three miles to the north.[40] From 1946 to 1953 Boyd Gilmore, a blues singer from Belzoni, fifty miles to the south, played guitar there.[41] Men such as these undoubtedly introduced many new elements into the music of Drew.

There are no known representatives of the local blues tradition currently resident and performing in the Drew area, and a blues scene of any kind appears to be nonexistent there. Dick Bankston says that

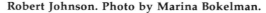

Robert Johnson. Photo by Marina Bokelman.

the jukeboxes began driving him out in the 1950s, although age may also have been a factor. The heavy migrations of blacks out of the Delta since the 1940s have also had a dampening effect on the continuity of folklore traditions there. But even by the late 1920s the local tradition around Drew was breaking up. This was due in part to the particularly intense racial hostility as well as to natural disasters and the normal movements of sharecroppers. Undoubtedly another important factor affecting this and other local traditions was the increasing commercialization of the blues during the 1920s and later. Thousands of different blues records had been produced by black artists from all over the country, representing a great variety of local traditions and personal syntheses of traditional and original elements and styles. Local musicians in Drew must have been affected by the music on these records, although we have no recorded documentation of musical developments there after 1930. Drew was not really isolated enough from outside influences, nor did its black population have a strong enough sense of community, to sustain a viable local blues tradition after the main early musicians left and the sharecropping system declined.

The last known active representative of the Drew blues tradition still in the area was Skeeter Johnson, who used to play guitar and violin with Dick Bankston and Boyd Gilmore. He was playing in Drew recently, but in 1969 he moved to St. Louis, and even before then he had been leaving the area to support himself as a migrant agricultural worker. There is supposed to be a man called "Wolf" who still plays there, although it is not known whether he represents the local tradition. A young man named Peter Bell, whom I recorded near Cleveland in 1967, performed only pieces from recent phonograph records. As a child he had once seen Charley Patton, and he recognized some of the common titles of local blues but called them "real old songs before my time." Another blues singer in Cleveland named Pretty Bell [sic, no relation to Peter Bell] was not actively performing at the time. In any case, he was from Indianola, twenty miles to the south, and was not representative of the local tradition. He played piano and guitar, but his repertoire was heavily influenced by records of such artists as Blind Lemon Jefferson, Muddy Waters, and Little Walter. L. V. Banks from Greenville was playing one night a week at a café in Boyle with a three-piece band, but his blues were in a modern style. Not long afterward he moved to Chicago to try his luck in the blues scene there. Ironically, the best representatives of the Drew blues tradition can be heard today in Crystal Springs, far to the south.

The Drew Tradition: An Overview

In the Drew tradition there are too many obscure figures like Henry Sloan, Ben Maree, and Nathan Scott to allow us to establish exact origins and lines of relationship. In the preceding discussion I have indicated that certain performers learned from certain others. This might lead us to expect that the blues of the learners would be derived from those of their particular teachers. Yet, when we examine the songs, we find that this is true only to a limited extent. It will be shown that the blues of the Drew area were in many respects a communal product and can not be plotted in lines of relationship like those of a family tree. The learners, once they became established musicians, probably affected their teachers' music as much as they themselves had been affected by it.

The best way to study the workings of the Drew tradition is to begin with an examination of the blues repertoires of the individual performers. For this purpose we have adequate recorded samples by four artists, Mott Willis and Mager Johnson from field recordings and Tommy Johnson and Charley Patton from early commercial recordings. The few recordings by Willie Brown and Kid Bailey represent just a fragment of their repertoires, while only a few of Howlin' Wolf's records show the influence of the Drew tradition.[42]

One of the most striking facts about the blues of these men is that almost all of them are nonthematic. Blues like Patton's "High Water Everywhere" (Paramount 12909), about the 1927 Mississippi River flood in the Delta, and Tommy Johnson's "Canned Heat Blues" (Victor V38535), about the drink he loved so well, are quite exceptional. Furthermore, the blues lyrics of these men are highly traditional, containing many verses found in folk blues by other performers. Their blues are also little influenced by phonograph records. Nine of Patton's thirty-two extant blues show the influence of records, but in most cases he made considerable departures from his sources so that their overall influence is slight. The other Drew singers also reworked recorded sources in terms of their own tradition. Tommy Johnson, for example, is known to have set the lyrics and melody of Leroy Carr's "Prison Bound Blues" (Vocalion 1241) to a guitar part well-known in his own tradition. He could perform several blues derived from commercial records, but he never recorded any of them. Finally, there is little evidence that the records made by representatives of the Drew tradition had an influence on that local tradition. Instead, the records mainly serve for us as documents of the tradition. We are fortunate, then, to be able to study an almost purely oral tradition, which, nevertheless, has a rich history of commercial documentation.

The Blues of Mott Willis

Mott Willis is in some ways one of the most traditional of the Drew performers, yet his music also has the distinct stamp of his personality upon it. His blues repertoire may appear quite limited to us, but Dick Bankston considered him to be the best of all the musicians at Drew. Houston Stackhouse, who has performed with almost all of the greatest blues singers in Mississippi and Arkansas since the 1920s, including Tommy Johnson, Charley Patton, Robert Johnson, Robert Nighthawk, and Sonny Boy Williamson (Rice Miller), has recently stated that Mott Willis is one of the very best guitarists he has ever heard.[43] Willis displays his skill on the instrument by taking fairly frequent guitar choruses, in contrast to most of the other Drew musicians, who rarely took them. Willis sings rather short texts and does not really consider himself a good singer. Actually he is not bad but he is simply a much better instrumentalist. His instrumental emphasis is perhaps conditioned by the fact that he played for many years in string bands. He is more than competent on guitar, violin, and mandolin, and is able to fill in on harmonica, piano, string bass, and trombone. In recent years, however, he has concentrated almost entirely on the guitar. His string band background is probably responsible also for the breadth of his repertoire, of which blues are only a part and not even his favorite kind of music. He prefers to play ragtime and sentimental pieces, although his years as a professional or semiprofessional entertainer have made him ready to oblige any kind of request.

One of the features of Willis's guitar playing is his use of a variety of tonal effects. He plays overtones and mandolin-style trills, bends strings, snaps them, strokes them, taps them against the neck, and plays in the bottleneck style. He usually plays quite a few variant figures from one chorus to another. A further feature of his playing is that he usually strikes only one note or chord at a time, instead of "pinching" bass and treble notes simultaneously. This is characteristic of the playing of all the Drew musicians. It enables Willis to play his pieces with a flat pick or plectrum, although he usually picks with the thumb and first two fingers.

Willis's singing also has certain distinctive characteristics. Perhaps because of his instrumental emphasis, he sometimes drops the last word or phrase from his lines and occasionally drops a whole line altogether. A number of black folk musicians do this, and the practice is usually deliberate. Musicians and their audiences both consider it a sign of high competence if a musician can make his instrument "talk." This is what performers like Willis are doing when they use the guitar to complete a vocal line. Willis also speaks some of his lines or phrases rather than singing them. This is simply a personal idiosyncrasy of his style. Sometimes, for humorous effect, he even paraphrases traditional verses or his own original pieces in prose, delivering his speech over the guitar accompaniment. Traits like these give his otherwise highly traditional music a great deal of originality.

In six sessions between 1967 and 1973 I recorded sixty-five musical performances by Willis and accompaniments by him to several more pieces by other singers. Some of his pieces were recorded more than once. He played guitar on all but four performances. Two of these performances featured him on violin and the other two on harmonica. None of these four pieces contained any singing. Forty-nine of his performances were blues, while the remainder were sentimental popular songs, instrumental waltzes, nonblues lyric folksongs, and a religious song. Undoubtedly the percentage of nonblues pieces would have been higher if I had not so often specifically requested blues from him. His popular songs were "Would You Care?," "On My Way to Mexico,"

"The Grizzly Bear," "Just Because," and "I Have the Blues When It Rains." The waltzes were "Tennessee Waltz" and a piece called "Mexican Waltz," which he learned in Mexico on one of his trips with a minstrel show. "It Ain't Gonna Rain No More" is the only nonblues piece he associates with the Drew area. His guitar accompaniment is played in standard tuning in the key of C and employs several variant choruses. He says that he learned the piece from Charley Patton.[44] Jake Martin has independently confirmed that both he and Patton used to perform this piece. Willis's other nonblues lyric folksongs are "Careless Love," a piece that his older brothers used to play, and "Tear It Down, Bed Slats and All," a ragtime piece. The only religious song he performed was "You Got to Reap Just What You Sow." Five of these nonblues pieces were recorded twice, but none of them showed any significant variation from one performance to another.

The Drew tradition has been the main source of inspiration for Willis's blues. In fact, he had little exposure to blues before he first went to Drew in 1919. Instead he had concentrated on ragtime pieces and the current popular songs for his work with minstrel shows. All he brought to the Drew blues scene initially was musical talent and experience, but eventually he reached the point where he could create blues of his own within the local tradition.

Twenty-five of his forty-nine recorded blues performances are not noticeably representative of the Drew tradition. Most of these are derived from popular phonograph records or are showcase pieces for his instrumental talent. The pieces derived from records are "Baby Please Don't Go," "Come Back Baby," "M & O Blues," "44 Blues" (guitar solo), and "Wintertime Blues" (played on the violin).[45] His other strictly instrumental blues are "Flat Foot Boogie," "Hoboing Blues" (played on the harmonica), and a couple of guitar patterns for accompanying twelve-bar blues, one in open G tuning in knife style and the other in standard tuning, key of G. Another instrumental showpiece is a twelve-bar blues pattern with several variant choruses in standard tuning, key of E, with a spoken commentary. In it Willis describes a professional wrestler whom he has seen on television. The guitar makes the sounds of blows and bodies falling on the canvas. Willis originally called the piece "Joe Louis,"[46] but by 1970 it had become the "Wrestling Match Boogie." In 1971 it was "The Spoiler," and by 1973 it was in the process of being transformed to "Doctor X," his latest hero. Another boogie instrumental piece, to which he sometimes improvises humorous spoken monologues about his encounters with strange men and women, is played in the unusual tuning of DBGDAD in the key of D. He also has a piece whose lyrics are more chanted than sung. The text consists of the following stanza only:

> Yes, wasn't for the trees, be no leaves.
> I said, wasn't for the trees, wouldn't be no leaves.
> Wasn't for the dog, wouldn't be no fleas.

The instrumental accompaniment, which is really the heart of the piece, can be the part for "The Spoiler" in the key of E, his part in the DBGDAD tuning, or other parts in the keys of C and G in standard tuning.

Mott Willis has composed at least one blues with a totally original thematic set of lyrics, which he calls either "Bad Night Blues" or "Strange Woman." He claims that the song is based on an incident in his life, explaining it simply by saying, "that's the way one done me once sure enough." Neither the melody nor the guitar part nor any of the song's stanzas occur in any of his other blues or in blues by other Drew musicians. The guitar part contains numerous variations and special effects. The singing in the first version he recorded becomes speech by its third stanza, although the guitar part continues to fulfill a responsorial function to the lines, and rhyme is maintained. His text is as follows:

Example 32. "Bad Night Blues." Mott Willis, vocal and guitar in standard tuning, key of C. Crystal Springs, Miss., July 14, 1971. Recorded by David and Cheryl Evans. Issued on *Big Road Blues*, Advent 2815, 12" LP.

1. *I was out one bad night, baby. I was traveling through the land.*
   Spoken: *Real lonesome.*
   I was out one bad night, mama. I was traveling through the land.
   I was looking for a woman, say she didn't have no man.

2. Spoken: *Yeah, I found one, you know.*
   I found a lady. She said she's by herself.
   Yes, I found a lady. She said she was by herself.
   I got to loving that woman. Up popped someone else.
   Spoken: *People, I'm gonna tell you that.*

[Remainder of piece spoken]

3. *Yeah, I asked her . . . Asked her what he was there for. Yeah. She looked*
       at me and smiled.
   I asked her what he was there for. She looked at me and smiled.
   You know by that, gentlemen, . . . Listen. . . . she was making up a lie.
       [Laughter]

4. *I wasn't too much out on her, you know.*
   I told her, "Listen. . . ." Times was tight. I said, "Give me that gum I
       bought you, baby, and put it in my hand."
   I said, "Give me that gum I bought you 'fore I hurt you, and put it, put it
       in my hand."
   That old thing tried to be smart.
   I said, "You just strictly welcome unto your other man."
   Good night, baby, and good bye too.

In a second version of this piece, recorded in 1973, the accompaniment remained essentially the same, and the stanzas stuck to the same subject matter, but the piece became totally a prose monologue by the second stanza, and even the opening stanza was only half sung.[47] The piece was performed at a party among friends and relatives at Willis's house after a great deal of liquor had been consumed. Willis's spoken text elicited uproarious laughter from the audience.

The blues that we have briefly surveyed up to this point display mainly the creative side of Mott Willis's repertoire and the influence of commercial records and other traditions he encountered after leaving Drew. Willis's twenty-four remaining blues performances show clear connections with the Drew tradition. They fall into ten patterns, some of which he recorded several times. Most of these patterns Willis claims to have learned from other Drew musicians, but a few he says he made up himself. Several of the patterns share some common elements, either lyrics, melodic phrases, or instrumental ideas. Of these shared elements the reader will be able to recognize easily the many lyric stanzas used in more than one blues. Willis also uses exactly the same melody for blues with accompaniments in the key of A in standard tuning (Examples 33–35) and in open G tuning (Examples 36–37). Furthermore, the second and third lines of this melody correspond in part with those of his "Dresser Drawer Blues" (Examples 42–44). His "Big Road Blues" (Examples 64–67) and one of the melodies sung to a guitar part in the key of C (Example 39) share the first phrase of their first lines with "Dresser Drawer Blues." In both "Big Road Blues" and his guitar parts in the key of C and open G tuning he snaps the guitar's sixth string. The rhythmic pattern of snaps in each is very similar. Another instrumental idea that Willis favors is a change from the tonic chord to subdominant seventh and back to the tonic at the ends of his second and third lines. This chord change can be heard in his "Riverside Blues" (Example 41), "Big Road Blues," "Dresser Drawer Blues," and one of his guitar parts in the key of C. The fact that so many elements are shared in these ten blues patterns would indicate that Willis has drawn upon a personally created repertoire of lyric, melodic, and instrumental elements in composing his blues or else that he has drawn upon a traditional repertoire of such elements. As we shall see, after examining each of these patterns, most of his elements are traditional and are found particularly in blues performed by other representatives of the Drew tradition.

When I first recorded him, Willis sang the following nonthematic blues with traditional lyrics and a guitar accompaniment in standard tuning, key of A. The guitar part is especially interesting for its use of a movable fingering position on the first three strings (measures 1–3, 7–8, 11), which Willis plucks with the first two fingers of his right hand. (See Figure 4, p. 206).

Example 33. Untitled blues. Mott Willis, vocal and guitar in standard tuning, key of A. Terry, Miss., Sept. 7, 1967. Recorded by David Evans and Marina Bokelman.

GUITAR CHORUS.

1. *Know my good gal, she gonna jump and shout, she gonna jump and, jump and shout.*
   Know my good gal, she gonna jump and shout.
   Train roll up, I come walking out.

2. *What you gonna do, baby, when your trouble get like, trouble get like, like*
     mine?
   What you gonna do, baby, trouble . . .
   Get your pick and shovel, ease on down the line.

3. *Black woman squalled, scared my brown to death, scared my brown,*
     brown to death.
   Black woman squalled, scared my brown to death.
   Hadn't had my cannon, I'd a run my . . . [Spoken: *run my little self.*]

4. *Quit your shouting, gal; let your happy come down, let your happy come*
     down.
   Quit your shouting . . .

Willis said that he learned this piece from Willie Brown. The repetitions in the first line of the vocal part may represent the influence of
quartet singing style at some point in the tune's history. The "cannon"
in stanza 3 is simply a term for a powerful gun.

String   E   A   D   G   B   E

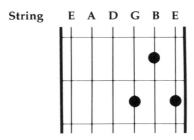

Figure 4. Movable fingering position on the guitar in standard tuning

Three years later, using the same melody and guitar part, Willis sang the following words. On this occasion he played the guitar with a flat pick. It should be noted that the two pieces have no lyrics in common, despite their being virtually identical musically.

Example 34. "Who Is That Yonder Coming Down the Road?" Mott Willis, vocal and guitar in standard tuning, key of A. Crystal Springs, Miss., Aug. 31, 1970. Recorded by David Evans. Issued on *Big Road Blues*, Advent 2815, 12" LP.

GUITAR CHORUS.

1. *Yeah now, who is that yonder coming down the, coming down the, down the road?*
   Who is that yonder coming down the road?
   She got a stocking full of dollars and mouth chock full of gold

2. *Yeah now, reason I like her, she's so nice and, she's so nice and, nice and brown.*
   Reason I like her, she's so nice and brown.
   Good Lord made her; tell me the angels sent her down.

3. *Oh now, hey, hey, baby, me whisper in your, want to whisper in your, in your ear.*
   Hold your head down low, gal; whisper in your ear.
   I've got something to tell you, know you like to hear.

Two days later Willis sang another set of verses to the same tune and guitar part, which overlaps with portions of both of the above texts. His final guitar chorus contains some variations from the guitar part printed above.

Example 35. "Jumping and Shouting Blues." Mott Willis, vocal and guitar in standard tuning, key of A. Crystal Springs, Miss., Sept. 2, 1970. Recorded by David Evans.

GUITAR CHORUS.

1. *Know my good gal sure gon' jump and, sure gon' jump and, jump and shout.*

Know my good gal, she gonna jump and shout.
Train roll up, I come walkin out.

2. *Hold your head down low, gal, let me whisper, let me whisper in your ear.*
   Hold your head down, want to whisper . . .
   I got something to tell you, know you like to hear.

3. *Says, she's so nice and, she's so nice and brown.*
   Reason I like her, she's so nice and brown.
   Good Lord made her, angels sent her down.

GUITAR CHORUS.

The first of these three nonthematic texts was built on the principle of contrast, while the other two were developed through association. Looking at these three examples, which are nearly identical musically, one might assume that each was a fragmentary version of a blues which in its full form contains the seven different stanzas that the three pieces employ altogether. This view becomes untenable, however, when we examine the rest of Willis's blues and see how he composes them in a traditional manner.

In some of his other blues Willis uses a melody almost identical to the one above but with a guitar part in open G tuning. An interesting feature of this guitar part is the snapping of bass notes on the sixth string in a descending phrase (measures 1–3). These snaps are indicated by an asterisk printed over the note in the transcription below. On the guitar chorus following stanza 2 Willis plays a variant high part with a distinctive phrase in measures 1–4, 7–8, and 10, which is also printed below. He sang the following words in 1967, using the same melody as that of Examples 33–35.

Example 36. Untitled blues. Mott Willis, vocal and guitar in open G tuning (DBGDGD). Terry, Miss., Sept. 7, 1967. Recorded by David Evans and Marina Bokelman. Issued as "Pick and Shovel Blues" on *Big Road Blues*, Advent 2815, 12" LP.

1. *What you gonna do when your troubles get like, troubles get like, get like*
        mine?
   What you gonna do, troubles get like . . .
   Get your pick and shovel, ease on down the line.

2. *Hey, bye and bye, baby, baby, bye and, baby, bye and, bye and bye.*
   Baby, bye, baby, bye and bye.
   Oh now, bye and bye . . .

GUITAR CHORUS.

3. *Mmmm, know my good gal, she's gonna jump and, she's gonna jump and,*
        jump and shout.
   Know my good gal sure gonna jump and shout.
   Train roll up, I come walking out.

The first and third stanzas above were also used in blues with the guitar part in the key of A (Examples 33 and 35). Three years later each of these stanzas became the first stanza for a blues with accompaniment

in open G tuning as in the above example. Yet the two new blues did not have any verses in common, even though they were recorded at the same session. In 1973 Willis recorded a fourth blues with this same tune and accompaniment pattern.

Example 37. "Who's That Yonder?" Mott Willis, vocal and guitar in open G tuning. Crystal Springs, Miss., Aug. 16, 1973. Recorded by David and Cheryl Evans.

1. *Going away, baby now; won't be back till, won't be back till, back till fall.*
   Going away, baby; won't be back till fall.
   If I don't find my good gal, won't be back at all.

2. *Yeah now, what you gonna do, baby, trouble get like mine?*
   Spoken: *Eyes full of tears.*
   I say, what you gonna do, gal, trouble get like mine?
   Get your pick and shovel, ease on down the line.

3. *Yeah now, who is that yonder coming down the road, coming down the, down the road?*
   Who is that yonder coming down the road?
   She got a stocking full of dollars, mouth chock full of gold.
   Spoken: *That old thing must have looked very well, but I don't know.*

The four blues with accompaniment in open G tuning contain altogether only three stanzas not found in blues with accompaniment in the key of A (Examples 33–35). Furthermore, Willis uses the single "jump and shout" stanza in a blues with accompaniment in the key of C in standard tuning with a totally different melody. (The same melody and guitar part are used in Example 39.) He considers these three guitar parts, two melodies, and eight sets of lyrics (containing ten different stanzas) to be all the same song. The song is Willis's concept of what the various blues singers were performing at Drew when he lived there. In fact, he felt that the two guitar parts in the key of A and open G tuning should be played together in order to make it "prettier." The other Drew musicians did, in fact, cross these two parts. Willis's attitude is illustrated in the following interview with him and his nephew Willis Taylor:

> Evans: *Do you remember any of Nathan Scott's songs?*
> Willis: *He played this here.* [Plays in the key of A.] *Willie* [Brown] *learned him. He played that piece, but he'd tune his guitar in Spanish* [open G tuning] *and play that.*
> Evans: *Could you show me how?*
> Willis: *Have to retune it though. Have to run that E down. See, Willie would get with him. But me and you* [Taylor] *used to play that way. We chord it kind of cross, you know. See, I'm crossed, and that would leave him straight.*
> Taylor: *That's the way Tom composed his, in that tune you got there, Tom Johnson. That's the way he composed his, right in that tune you got there.*
> Evans: *You mean the one he just played or the one he's about to play?*
> Taylor: *The one he just played a while ago and the one you're on now.*
> Willis: [Plays a blues in open G tuning.] *I done forgot it. That's the same piece but just in a basser tune. One would be picking it that way, and the other would be picking it. It go prettier that way.* [Taylor and Willis perform "Mama Do Right." See Examples 33 and 36 for the melody and guitar parts.]

Example 38. "Mama Do Right." Willis Taylor, vocal and guitar in open G tuning (DBGDGD, with capo on second fret); Mott Willis, guitar in standard tuning, key of A. Crystal Springs, Miss., Sept. 2, 1970. Recorded by David Evans. Issued on *Big Road Blues*, Advent 2815, 12" LP.

1. *Yeah, I ain't gonna be here, baby, when the morning come soon.*
   I'm gonna get up early in the morning. Believe I'll ease on down the line.

2. *I got something to tell you, woman, make the springs cry on your bed.*
   Yeah, I got something to tell you, make the springs cry on your bed.
   I'll tell you again in the morning, baby now; I ain't gonna be here long.

3. *Yeah, my woman, she got ways like a fox squirrel in a tree.*
   Yeah, my woman got ways like a fox squirrel in a tree.
   Now she see me coming, baby; she run and hide from me.

4. *And I ain't gonna be your, your riding horse no more.*
   Mmmmm, I be your riding horse no more.
   Just tighten up on my reins, baby, baby, . . .

5. *Hold your head down low, baby; let me whisper in your ear.*
   Hold your head down low; let me whisper in your ear.
   Says I got something to tell you, baby, I know you really want to hear.

GUITAR CHORUS.

6. *I believe I'll leave here, but I sure don't want to go.*
   But I believe I'll leave here, but I sure don't want to go.

Willis: *How do you like them doubled up there together?*
Evans: *Beautiful! What do you want to call that?*
Willis: *Let me see. What you gonna name that?*
Taylor: *"Mama Do Right." Ha ha ha ha. "Mama Do Right." Ha ha ha ha ha ha.*
Willis: *Ha ha. That's the name of it.*
Taylor: *Yeah, "Mama Do Right." Ha ha ha ha ha ha ha ha.*
Willis: *He's the one that have to name it. He's doing the singing, you know. Mama have to do right!*
Evans: *Do you know any more of Willie Brown's songs?*
Willis: *I did know some of them. They have to come to me sometimes. Here's one of the same pieces, but it's just, you know, another way of playing. He says,* [Sung] *"Who's that yonder coming . . ."*
Evans: *Now this is one of Willie Brown's pieces?*
Willis: *Yes.* [Sung] *". . . down the road?" You can just put anything in it. I can't sing it too good. I got such a cold.* [Plays in the key of C.]
Evans: *What's that piece called?*
Taylor: *That was the "Riverside," but I'm gonna give it another name at the end of it.*
Willis: *What did they call that? What did Willie Brown call that?*

Willis Taylor. Photo by Cheryl T. Evans.

Taylor: *Just name it when you get to the end.*
Willis: *Yeah, just name it something.* [Taylor and Willis perform "The Trashy Gang Blues."]

211
THE LOCAL
TRADITION

Example 39. "The Trashy Gang Blues." Willis Taylor, vocal; Mott Willis, guitar in standard tuning, key of C. Crystal Springs, Miss., Sept. 2, 1970. Recorded by David Evans. Issued on *Big Road Blues*, Advent 2815, 12" LP.

1. Who is that yonder coming down the road?
   Wonder who is that yonder, baby, coming down the road.
   She got a stocking full of dollars, mouth chock full of gold.

2. You can lose your money. Please don't lose your mind.
   You can lose your money, but, partner, don't lose your mind.
   You can lose your friend girl. Please don't you mess with mine.

3. I had trouble 'bout you. Trouble always been ups and down.
   I had trouble with you, Trouble has been ups and down.
   If you lose your baby, please don't you mess with mine.

GUITAR CHORUS.

4. *When I woke up this morning, got up with a worried mind.*
Well, I woke up this morning. Babe, I had a worried mind.
If your mind worried like mine, don't want you to mess with mine.

5. *I ain't got no money, got no station home.*
I ain't got no money, baby, no station way home.
If you lose your gal, please don't you mess with mine.

The remarks of the two men reveal their awareness that they are performing within a tradition, that songs from this tradition may contain overlapping elements, and that the songs do not exist as distinct entities apart from their performance. This last point is most effectively demonstrated by Taylor, who waited until the songs were over before naming them "Mama Do Right" and "The Trashy Gang Blues," names that he simply pulled out of the air. These blues were entirely improvised, but all of their component parts were traditional. Close variants of the melody and guitar parts of "Mama Do Right" were used by many of the Drew musicians, and the guitar parts were recorded together by Charley Patton and Willie Brown. All of the lyrics are traditional, and many of them are associated with Tommy Johnson and Charley Patton, while Mott Willis also used some of them in examples already printed (33–37). Willis uses the guitar part of "The Trashy Gang Blues" with other sets of lyrics. It has a few phrases similar to ones he plays in "Bad Night Blues" (Example 32), and its snapped sixth string (measures 1 and 2) displays a technique found also in his guitar part in open G tuning (Example 36). Willis's guitar part in the key of C also has some similarity to Charley Patton's guitar part in the same key used in "Down the Dirt Road Blues" (Paramount 12854) and "34 Blues" (Vocalion 02651). In fact, in 1967 Willis stated that his guitar part in C was one that Patton also played. Taylor's melody is almost identical to the one that Willis uses with this accompaniment, and it shares phrases with melodies used by other Drew performers. Two of Taylor's five stanzas are used in variant form by Mott Willis, Tommy Johnson, and Charley Patton in some of their blues, while Taylor's other stanzas are all drawn from the larger folk blues tradition.

Willis Taylor regularly thought up fanciful titles for his traditional folk blues, while his nonblues songs and blues derived from phonograph records were all given conventional titles. Mott Willis himself once produced a fanciful title to a blues he played in the key of D in the tuning DBGDAD (his own invention). All three of its stanzas are used in various combinations in his other blues, while some phrases in the melody and guitar part also have similarities to ones in his other blues.[48] After he had performed it, he called the piece "Wild Western Blues," because, as he put it, it was a song that would "make your good gal catch something wild" and because I had come from the West. He said, "I got some what I play in this new tune. I ain't never named 'em nothing yet, you know, Just holding 'em there a while, you know."

Willis improvised another blues in 1973 that is similarly a combination of various elements from the Drew tradition. Its guitar part is in the key of E in standard tuning and contains phrases and ideas drawn from many sources. These sources include his "Riverside Blues" (Example 41) and another guitar part which he associates with Tommy and Mager Johnson and which is similar to the one used by Tommy Johnson in his "Cool Drink of Water Blues" (Example 20).[49] It also has similarities to guitar figures in Charley Patton's "Pony Blues" (Example 24) and draws an idea for a walking bass figure from Willis's accompaniment to his "Big Road Blues" (Example 65) played in the key of D, an idea which Tommy Johnson also used in his "Canned Heat Blues" (Victor V38535). Willis speaks rather than sings some of his lines, but the first line of his melody is almost identical to the second line of the melody of "Big Road Blues" as sung by himself, Tommy, and Mager Johnson (Example 60). His five stanzas are all found in variant form in blues by Tommy and Mager Johnson, Charley Patton, Willie Brown, and Kid Bailey. We have encountered some of them in previous examples by Willis. The text is as follows:

Example 40. "Traveling Man Blues." Mott Willis, vocal and guitar in standard tuning, key of E. Crystal Springs, Miss., Aug. 16, 1973. Recorded by David and Cheryl Evans.

GUITAR CHORUS.

1. *I'm a traveling man, baby, and I got a traveling mind.*
   Yeah, I'm a traveling man, baby, and I, I got a traveling mind.
   I'm gonna buy me a st . . . [Spoken: *a ticket or steal it, one.*] *. . . ease on down the line.*

2. *Oh, who is that yonder coming down the road?*
   I say, who is that yonder coming down the road there?
   Yeah, she got a stocking of dollars, mouth chock full of gold.

3. *Yes, reason I like her, she's so nice and brown.*
   Heeey suh! Reason I like her, she's so nice and brown.
   She got . . . [Spoken: *No, it ain't, but I was starting to say there.*] *. . . just need a heaven of her own.*

4. *Hello, Central, matter with the line?*
   Spoken: *Telephone line out of shape.*
   Yeah, hello, Central, matter with your line?
   He said, "The wires done blowed down, and your best gal is gone."
   Spoken: *That made me mad then.*

5. *Oh, what you gonna do, suh, when your trouble get like mine?*
   I say, what you gonna do, baby, trouble get like mine?
   Says, she gonna get a pick and shovel, ease on down the line.

Willis was unable to think of any words to "Riverside Blues" both times he played it. He says that he first heard it played by a man named

Willie Love from Gatesville, near Crystal Springs. Love taught it to Josie Bush before she went to Drew, and she later taught it to her husband Willie Brown. It has a few phrases in common with Charley Patton's "Pony Blues" (Example 24) and Tommy Johnson's "Cool Drink of Water Blues" (Example 20) as well as with Willis's other pieces in the key of E. Some of its most notable features are its slow tempo, the alternation of duple and triple rhythms, the unusual blue notes (between the major sixth and minor seventh and between the major second and minor third), the use of bass string drones, and the almost complete lack of any "pinching" of bass and treble strings simultaneously. This last trait is also characteristic of all of Willie Brown's recorded guitar playing and is found in most of the playing of the other Drew musicians. Willis uses variant figures in some measures, which are transcribed here.

Example 41. "Riverside Blues." Mott Willis, guitar solo in standard tuning, key of E. Crystal Springs, Miss., Sept. 2, 1970. Recorded by David Evans. Issued on *Big Road Blues*, Advent 2815, 12" LP.

Another piece that Willis associates with Josie Bush is "Joking Blues." He learned it from her before either of them went to Drew. He speaks the verses and adds a good number of asides. His twelve-bar guitar part in standard tuning, key of C, is reminiscent of one used by Charley Jordan (in the key of E) in his 1930 recording of "Keep It Clean" (Vocalion 1511), also a humorous song which contains variants of two of Willis's stanzas. This piece is not known to have been played by any other Drew artists besides Josie Bush and Willis, but a variant of Willis's first stanza was used in Willie Brown's "Future Blues" (Paramount 13090).[50]

Willis's "Dresser Drawer Blues" uses the "core" technique described in the previous chapter. He claims that this piece is an original composition. Three texts are printed below along with the melody and guitar part of the first performance. The "Santy Claus" in the opening stanza, according to Willis, represents the woman's money, but quite likely it is also a metaphor for the pubic area, since there is an evident play upon the word "drawers." In fact, some black women customarily keep their money, along with various lucky charms and other valuables, in a "nation sack" (i.e., a bag made in Oklahoma, the "Indian Nation") tied around their waist.[51] It is clear that the core of this blues is the melody, guitar part, and first stanza, while the remaining stanzas are drawn at the time of performance from Willis's repertoire of traditional stanzas. Some of the most significant variations in the guitar part of the first version are transcribed below. Actually there are slight variations throughout all three versions in both the melody and guitar part from one chorus to another. In the guitar part these include additional mandolin-like trills (as in measure 4 below) and the playing of overtones. The third version is played with a flat pick. The unusual tuning is Willis's own invention, and he claims it was not used by any of the other Drew artists.

Example 42. "Dresser Drawer Blues." Mott Willis, vocal and guitar in EBADAD tuning, key of D. Terry, Miss., Sept. 7, 1967. Recorded by David Evans and Marina Bokelman.

GUITAR CHORUS.

1. *My babe was a dresser, I'd search all through her drawers.*
   Say, my babe was a dresser, I'd search all through her drawers.
   Yes, I wouldn't stop rambling until I found her Santy Claus.

2. *Who is that yonder coming down the road?*
   I said, who is that yonder coming down the road?
   She's got a stocking of dollars, mouth chock full of gold.

3. *Reason I like her, she's so nice and brown.*
   Reason I like her, she's so nice and brown.
   Guess the Good Lord made her, angels sent her down.

4. *I ain't never loved but four women in my life.*
   Ain't never loved but four women in my life.
   That's my mama and my sister, kid gal and my wife.

Example 43. "Dresser Drawer Blues." Mott Willis, vocal and guitar in EBADAD tuning, key of D. Crystal Springs, Miss., Aug. 31, 1970. Recorded by David Evans. Issued on *Big Road Blues*, Advent 2815, 12'' LP.

GUITAR CHORUS.

1. *My babe was a dresser, I'd ramble all through her drawers.*
   I said, my babe was a dresser, I'd search all through her drawers.
   I wouldn't stop searching till I found her Santy Claus.

2. *Long tall woman, she wears a turned up hat.*
   Long tall woman, she wears a turned up hat.
   I love that woman. What do you know 'bout that?

3. *Quit your shouting, gal; let your happy come down.*
   I said, quit your shouting . . . [Spoken: *Kind of mean old gal.*] *. . . and let*
       your happy come down.
   Told you, baby, . . .

Example 44. "Dresser Drawer Blues." Mott Willis, vocal and guitar in
EBADAD tuning, key of D. Crystal Springs, Miss., July 14, 1971. Recorded by David and Cheryl Evans.

1. *If my babe was a dresser, I'd search all through her drawers.*
   Say, if my babe was a dresser, I'd search all through her drawers.
   I wouldn't stop searching until I found her Santy Claus.

2. *Reason I like her, she's so nice and brown.*
   I said, reason I like her, she's so nice and brown.
   I reckon the Good Lord made her, angels sent her down.

3. *Hold your head down low, gal; want to whisper in your ear.*
   I said, hold your head down low; I want to whisper in your ear.
   I got something to tell you I know you like to hear.

4. *Hey, hey, baby, . . .* [Guitar chorus.]

Willis thinks of these three performances as variants of the same
song and gives them all the same title. They share basically the same
guitar part and melody, but in their lyrics, except for a shared stanza in
Examples 42 and 44, they have only the initial core stanza in common.
This is the stanza that gives these blues their title. All of the other
stanzas are traditional, as is this core stanza, and we have encountered
four of them in previous examples of Willis's blues. All of the melodic
phrases are also found in other blues by Willis. Measure 1 is similar to
the first measure of "The Trashy Gang Blues" (Example 39) and "Big
Road Blues" (Example 60). Measures 2, 5, and 9 are similar to the same
measures of Example 33, and measure 10 is similar to the second measure of Example 33. Measure 6 is similar to the same measure of "Bad
Night Blues" (Example 32). Willis's guitar part is more distinctive, but
measure 11 is similar to the same measure in "Big Road Blues," while
the variant part for measures 7 and 8 is similar to measures 7–8 and 11–
12 of "Big Road Blues." Measure 3 is also reminiscent of the same measure in "Bad Night Blues" (Example 32), which also contains a number
of guitar trills, while the slow tempo in triplets and the bass string
drones are reminiscent of "Riverside Blues" (Example 41).

It should be clear from the three examples and the discussion
printed above that "Dresser Drawer Blues" is hardly as original as
Willis claims it is. In fact, it can be considered original only in the very
limited sense that all three versions represent Willis's own combination of largely traditional elements. Yet in 1973 he gave another performance of it that was much more distinctive. He used a different
fourteen-bar guitar part in DBGDAD tuning and paraphrased the lyrics

in prose. We noted a similar process in the case of "Bad Night Blues" (Example 32), but there the song text was fixed and thematic. In "Dresser Drawer Blues" only the first stanza is fixed, and none of the three previous examples could have been called thematic. Nevertheless, Willis manages to tell a reasonably coherent story, building it largely around traditional verses. ("Uncle Snapper" in stanza 5 is Willis's nickname.)

Example 45. "Dresser Drawer Blues." Mott Willis, speech and guitar in DBGDAD tuning, key of D. Crystal Springs, Miss., Aug. 16, 1973. Recorded by David and Cheryl Evans.

GUITAR CHORUS.

1. *I said, my baby was a dresser, search all through her drawers, suh. Eeeh!*
   I said, my baby was a dresser, search through her drawers. Old thing, they
       say, got the money, you know.
   And I wouldn't stop rambling until . . . found her Santy Claus. Found a
       great big old purse.

2. *She said, "Mott, is you searching through my drawers?" I said, "What*
       kind of drawers, suh?"
   Say, "You been rambling all through my dresser drawer. Is there some
       clothes in there you like or something or other?" I said, "I don't
       know, suh."
   Said, "You ain't gonna stop rambling till you find my Santy Claus." Called
       her money her Santy Claus.

3. *I said, "Farewell, suh." Thing commenced beating me up, you know. I tried*
       dodging good licks.
   I said, "Baby, I ain't gonna try to search through your dresser drawers no
       more." Eeeh, suh!

4. *She was a gal dressed all in green, named Josephine.*
   Old thing looked pretty well, you know.
   She was the prettiest woman that I ever seed, Mr. Evans.

5. *Oh, had another one stay up on the hill, you know, long tall woman.*
   Oh, that old thing had quit me. I tried to get her back, you know.
       Oh, woman stay up on the hill.
   That old thing done quit me. Uncle Snapper loves her still.

6. *She got out in the road. I said, "Who is that yonder coming down the*
       road?" They say, "You know her."
   I said, "I don't know that thing. Tell me her name." She was named
       Martha Mae.

7. *I said, "Martha Mae, you better take me back." I said, "You ain't looking*
       for a little trouble, is you?" She said, "No, not a bit more than a
       snake got hips, sir. I ain't looking for no trouble."
   Say, "You must be looking for trouble." I said, "You don't take me back,
       you can call it trouble, suh." She said, "Yes, sir, I'll take you back,
       Mr. Willis." I said, "Take me back now, suh."
   Old gal pulled out four hundred dollars. Laid it in my hand. Eeeh, suh!

We have now completed our survey of the blues repertoire of Mott Willis, except for his versions of "Big Road Blues," which will be examined in the next chapter. It is clear that there are two main forces operating on this repertoire. One is the force of tradition and familiarity. Willis frequently uses traditional elements in his blues, particularly in the lyrics. The latter are ready-made building blocks which can be used in a great variety of new combinations. Willis usually doesn't know beforehand what combination he will use. "Dresser Drawer Blues" has a fixed opening stanza, but otherwise Willis builds his traditional blues texts spontaneously according to the structural principles of contrast and association. For instance, the first two stanzas of Example 33 illustrate the principle of contrast (arrival and happiness/departure and sadness), while the last two illustrate the principle of association (squalling/shouting). Another pair of stanzas linked by association is found in Examples 34 (stanzas 1 and 2), 40, and 42. Most of these stanzas, however, occur as individual elements in other examples. Willis also uses ready-made melodies and guitar parts, which contain many phrases found in his other blues as well as phrases which are part of the larger blues tradition. His blues, then, are highly traditional, and in a sense his repertoire seems very limited. Offsetting these limitations is the second force that affects his repertoire, that of variation and creativity. As if to compensate for his meager supply of traditional verses (though many of them are quite striking), he frequently improvises spoken texts, usually very humorous ones, or delivers a running prose commentary on his singing. These spoken sections often employ favorite phrases, which he uses also in ordinary conversation, such as "prettier than a white mouthed mule," "catch something wild," "not a bit more than a snake got hips," and "eeeh, suh!" These phrases may be part of traditional folk speech, but they do not occur in the blues lyrics of other singers. Such phrases help to personalize Willis's songs, and the humorous way in which he delivers them makes his songs more entertaining to his audience. Willis also plays a number of small variations within his guitar part for any piece and sometimes has alternate parts for the same piece. Thus, even when drawing upon traditional material, his guitar playing is very inventive, so that it transforms any piece into something distinctly his own. Mott Willis is by no means a servant of tradition. Instead, he uses tradition creatively for his own ends.

The Blues of Mager Johnson

Mager Johnson is, if anything, even more traditional in his blues than Mott Willis. In fact, practically his entire repertoire could be considered traditional. He does not display Willis's tendency to improvise prose lyrics, nor is there as much overt humor in his blues. He is also a less spectacular guitarist than Willis, though still very capable. Johnson, however, is a more strongly rhythmic guitar player and a more powerful singer, with a somewhat larger repertoire of traditional verses. He also introduces more variation into his singing, whereas Willis tends to vary his guitar playing. Like Willis, Johnson often lets the guitar "talk" words at the ends of lines or sometimes even whole lines. He often extends his musical lines by repeating short guitar phrases or "riffs" at their end. Consequently his blues are seldom an even twelve bars in length. Like Willis, he picks with the thumb and first two fingers and seldom "pinches" bass and treble strings simultaneously. Occasionally he plays a kazoo, held between his teeth. He calls this instrument a "jazz horn."

All but three of Mager Johnson's forty-three recorded performances are blues. The others, all nonblues lyric folksongs, are "Rabbit on a Log," learned from his older sister Idella, and two songs with a ragtime chord progression (I-VI-II-V-I) played in the key of C, "How Come You Do Me Like You Do" and "Sally, Take Your Time."[52] Thirty-eight of the forty remaining blues display traits of the Drew tradition. The two exceptions are "St. Louis Blues," a 1914 composition of W. C. Handy, and "Special Rider Blues," whose guitar part in the key of G resembles parts played by Ishmon Bracey, Charlie McCoy, and Rubin Lacy, all friends of Mager's brother Tommy in Jackson. All of Mager's thirty-eight blues from the Drew tradition fall into a very few musical patterns, although each pattern has sufficient variety to make any performance distinctive. Mager Johnson's repertoire may, like Mott Willis's, seem quite limited on the surface, but this has not affected the high esteem in which other blues singers hold his music. Houston Stackhouse considers him to be a fine performer, and Ishmon Bracey and Roosevelt Holts considered him to be even better than his brother Tommy, who was regarded by many musicians as one of the finest blues singers in the state of Mississippi.[53]

Mager Johnson's manner of handling traditional textual and musical material is basically like that of Mott Willis, in the sense that there is considerable variation from one performance of a piece to another. The only blues which exhibits any stability in Johnson's repertoire is "Catfish Blues." His two performances of this song, recorded in 1966 and 1969, use the same guitar part, melody, and text. The only significant differences are the use of the kazoo and the playing of instrumental choruses in the 1966 version. The guitar part contains a phrase used by Charley Patton in his "Green River Blues" (Paramount 12972) and "Circle Round the Moon" (Paramount 13040), and the text contains the core stanza of Mott Willis's "Dresser Drawer Blues" (Examples 42–45). "Catfish Blues" is known outside the Drew tradition. Versions of it have been recorded by many blues singers, especially those from Mississippi.[54] It is one of those rather uncommon traditional blues which maintain a fairly stable form over a wide expanse of territory and time. Johnson's melody, guitar part, and first two stanzas are found in slightly variant form in most other versions of the song.

Johnson's other blues usually contain a stable core consisting of a guitar part, a melody, and one or perhaps two stanzas. The remaining stanzas are drawn from his repertoire of traditional stanzas and lines. It will be easiest, then, to discuss each core separately and to point out the cases of overlap in the lyrics.

One of Mager Johnson's blues cores is called "Bye and Bye Blues," a variant of a song that his brother Tommy recorded in 1928 as "Bye-Bye Blues" (Victor 21409). The versions by the two singers have much in common musically, but Tommy sang only the first stanza of Mager's version printed below, and in it Tommy repeated the first line three times. Mager Johnson's version, however, contains some lines in stanzas 2 and 6 that were used in Tommy's 1930 recording of "Slidin' Delta" (Paramount 12975). Mager preceded his performance with the statement, "I may play it my way there," making it clear that he was not copying his brother's version. Mager's text is built out of traditional verses mainly on the principle of association. The song deals mostly with problems of leaving. His opening verse is probably adapted from a lullaby, but it also has a second meaning of bidding farewell. It was used not only by his brother Tommy but also by Mott Willis (Example 36), Charley Patton ("Poor Me," Vocalion 02651), and Dick Bankston.[55] The reference to "black spasm" in stanza 7 is obscure, and Mager Johnson could offer no explanation for it. Several times Johnson drops vocal lines or parts of lines and adds extra measures on the guitar, as in measure 12 below. Sometimes he drops the third measure, a characteristic found on his brother Tommy's recorded version, which consistently has stanzas of eleven measures in length. Tommy also consistently sang the variant first-line melody of Mager's stanza 8, which is printed below. In fact, this variant melodic line also appeared in Charley Patton's "Pony Blues" (Example 24, stanza 2) and several of Patton's other recordings. Mager Johnson's usual first melodic line (stanza 1 below, measures 1–3) is like the one used in the first line of stanza 1 of Patton's "Pony Blues," while Johnson's second melodic line (measures 4–7) is like the second line of Patton's second stanza. The most prominent guitar figure of Johnson's piece (measures 1–3, 7, 11–12) is also similar to the figure used in Patton's stanza 1, measures 3, 9, and 11, and stanza 2, measure 6, and is found in Tommy Johnson's "Bye-Bye Blues" and "Cool Drink of Water Blues" (Example 20, measures 1 and 9), Willie Brown's "M and O Blues" (Paramount 13090), Kid Bailey's "Rowdy Blues" (Brunswick 7114), and other blues by Patton and Mott Willis. The pieces by Brown and Bailey also have melodic similarities to Mager Johnson's piece. The ninth measure of Johnson's guitar part is similar to the ninth measure of Mott Willis's "Riverside Blues" (Example 41), while measures 1 and 2 of Johnson's guitar part for stanza 4 are similar to the first two measures in the second chorus of Willis's piece. Mager Johnson's blues, then, is thoroughly within the Drew tradition, though it remains his own distinctive combination of elements.

Example 46. "Bye and Bye Blues." Mager Johnson, vocal and guitar in standard tuning, key of E. Crystal Springs, Miss., Sept. 5, 1966. Recorded by David Evans and Marina Bokelman. Issued on *The Legacy of Tommy Johnson*, Matchbox SDM 224, 12″ LP.

1. *Hey, bye and bye and, baby, bye and bye.*
   I said, bye and bye and, baby, won't you bye and bye.
   If I never more see you, mmm, baby, you'll be on my mind.

2. *Says, I'm leaving town, woman, to wear you off . . .*
   Says, I'm leaving town, mama, to wear you off my mind.
   Hey, the way you treat me, woman, I, baby, can't live here no more.

3. *Mmmm, Lord, have mercy now.*

4. *Now I said, bye and bye and, baby, won't you bye and bye.*
   If I never more see you, baby, you'll be on my mind.

5. *Babe, how can I stay here; all I got is gone?*
   Baby, Lord, have mercy, baby, on my . . .

6. *Take me . . .*
   Take me out of the bottom, baby, 'fore the water rise.
   When the water rise, . . .

7. *Hey, bye, black spasm, and I know you going home to die.* [sic]
   I said, bye, black spasm, baby, going home to die.
   If I never more see you, crying, baby, you'll be on my mind.

8. *Mmmm, run here, woman, and sit down on my knee.*
   I said, run here, woman, baby, sit down on my knee.
   Says, I just want to tell you, baby, how you treated me.

9. *Says, it's fare you well, baby, won't you fare you well.*

Three years later Mager Johnson recorded two versions of "Bye and Bye Blues," each with different sets of lyrics which only partially corresponded with the earlier version. The first of these two new versions has only one new stanza. It is very close musically to the earlier version except for the second line in stanzas 1 and 5, which has a new melody and a guitar part that alludes to the chord of the subdominant. Stanzas 2 and 6 actually begin with the second musical line, apparently using the final line of the preceding stanzas as their first line. Thus, one might consider them to be continuations of the previous stanzas.

Example 47. "Bye and Bye Blues." Mager Johnson, vocal and guitar in standard tuning, key of E, Crystal Springs, Miss., Mar. 30, 1969. Recorded by David Evans.

1. *Crying, bye and bye and, baby, bye and bye.*
   Bye and bye and, baby, bye and bye.
   If I never more see you, you'll be on my mind.

2. *I said, bye and bye and, baby, won't you bye and bye.*
   If I never more see you, baby, you'll be on my mind.

3. *Says, I'm leaving town to wear you off my mind.*
   Says, I'm leaving town to, baby, wear you off my mind.
   Says, the way you treat me, . . .

4. *Mmmmmm, mmmmmmm.*
   Says, fare you well now, baby, won't you fare you well.
   If I never more see you, baby, you'll be on my mind.

5. *Never seen no trouble like my bosom friend.*
   Never had no trouble like my bosom friend.
   Says, she keep me worried, bothered all the time.

6. *Says, she keep me worried, baby, bothered all the time.*

The next version was recorded immediately after the above, yet the two have only the opening stanza in common. Variants of stanzas 3 and 4 below were sung also in Tommy Johnson's "Bye-Bye Blues" (Victor 21409). The version below contains no new musical elements.

Example 48. "Bye and Bye Blues." Mager Johnson, vocal and guitar in standard tuning, key of E. Crystal Springs, Miss., Mar. 30, 1969. Recorded by David Evans.

1. *Hey, bye and bye and, baby, bye and bye.*
   Hey, bye and bye and, . . .
   If I never more see you, you'll be on my mind.

2. *I said, bye and bye and, baby, won't you bye and bye.*
   If I never more see you, baby, you'll be on my mind.

3. *Mmmm, two trains running, running side by side.*
   Says, there's two trains running, baby, running side by side.
   You done taken my fairo. Baby, guess you satisfied.

4. *Mmmm, going away, mama, and I won't be back 'fore fall.*
   Says, I'm going away, won't be back 'fore fall.
   If I get lucky, baby, I won't be back at all.

5. *Says, I'm stone barefooted, mama, and I ain't got no shoes to wear.*
   Says, I'm stone barefooted, baby, got no shoes to wear.

The musical portion of the above three examples of "Bye and Bye Blues" is fairly stable, but in the lyrics only the first stanza remains stable. This stanza, then, and the melody and guitar part with their variations printed above constitute the song's core. Yet Mager Johnson by no means feels bound to use these elements in this single fixed combination, for elsewhere he freely uses this core's musical elements with different lyrics. A few minutes after he recorded Example 46, I asked him if he could perform his brother's "Cool Drink of Water Blues" (Example 20). He stated that it was just like his own "Bye and Bye Blues" and played a brief fragment, which was indeed identical musically. Then Mager performed the following untitled piece, remarking that "it's the same thing." Musically it is the same as "Bye and Bye Blues," except for the last two lines of the first stanza, which use the falsetto melody of "Cool Drink of Water Blues" (Example 20). The lyrics, however, contain only a few similarities to the above versions of "Bye and Bye Blues" and none at all to his brother's "Cool Drink of Water Blues." Yet textual variants of the first four stanzas were used in Tommy Johnson's 1928 recording of "Big Fat Mama Blues" (Victor V38535, Example 55), which has a completely different melody and guitar part.

Example 49. Untitled blues. Mager Johnson, vocal and guitar in standard tuning, key of E. Crystal Springs, Miss., Sept. 5, 1966. Recorded by David Evans and Marina Bokelman.

GUITAR CHORUS.

1. *Hey, big fat woman, the meat shaking on her bones.*
   Says, a big fat mama, the meat shaking on her bones.
   Every time shakes, it's a fat mama lost her home.

2. *Every time she shakes, mama, baby, fat mama lost her home.*
   Hey, Lord, have mercy, baby, on the wicked soul.

3. *Lord, I'm going away, and I won't be back 'fore fall.*
   Lord, I'm going away, baby, and I won't be back 'fore fall.
   If I meet my rider, baby, won't be back at all.

4. *Mmmm, quit . . . ; got to murmur low.*
   Lord, I done quit hollering, baby; baby, got to murmur low.
   Mmmm, Lord, have mercy, baby, on my wicked soul.

5. *I'm a poor boy traveling, been a long ways from home.*
   Says, I'm a poor boy traveling, baby, long ways from home.
   Says, I ain't got no money, either no way to go.

6. *Mmmm, stone barefooted, woman, got no shoes to wear.*
   Says, I'm stone barefooted, baby, got no shoes to wear.
   Hey, why you treat me, baby, like you do do do?

7. *Hey, Lord, ain't got no special rider here.*
   Hey, Lord, I ain't got no special rider here.

Mager Johnson states that this melodic and guitar pattern was also used by his brother LeDell as part of a blues core called "Hitch Up My Buggy, Saddle Up My Grey Mare." In fact, this was the only blues with a title that LeDell Johnson performed. All of his other pieces were apparently untitled in the manner of some of the pieces by Mott Willis and the above example by Mager Johnson. LeDell's blues, as performed by Mager Johnson, is simply a variant of the first stanza of Charley Patton's "Pony Blues" (Example 24), which was probably constructed from a core also. The text printed below is set to a guitar part like that of Mager Johnson's "Bye and Bye Blues" and employs the melodic variant printed with Example 47. The second stanza is simply a continuation of the first, as in some stanzas of Example 47.

Example 50. "Hitch Up My Buggy, Saddle Up My Grey Mare." Mager Johnson, vocal and guitar in standard tuning, key of E. Crystal Springs, Miss., Sept. 4, 1966. Recorded by David Evans and Marina Bokelman.

GUITAR CHORUS.

1. *Lord, hitch up my buggy, saddle up my grey mare.*
   Now hitch up my buggy, saddle up my grey mare.
   I'm gon' find my baby in the world somewhere.

2. *Lord, hitch up my buggy, baby, saddle up my grey mare.*
   I'm gon' find my baby . . .

This piece by Mager Johnson demonstrates the concept of the blues core and the importance of the singer's naming of the core. The name serves to identify the song and becomes a trademark of the singer, even though the various elements in the song's core may be performed separately by other members of the local tradition. In fact, Mager states that all of the Johnson brothers could perform blues using this core or its separate elements, although it was used most of all by LeDell, who had named it. By naming it he gave it an existence of its own and a certain degree of permanence in his repertoire. Mott Willis has similarly named a "Dresser Drawer Blues" (Examples 42–45), even though many of its elements are used by other members of the Drew tradition. Naming a blues is an important step and marks a different level of awareness by the blues singer of himself as a creative artist. Mager Johnson describes this process in discussing the ways in which his brother Tommy composed blues. He says,

> *I didn't never know him to just have something special he wanted to make up. He'd just get to playing something or other, and just the way it sound to him it ought to go—maybe he'd just start to singing it. And maybe the next time he may say something else or carry it a little different way. But now if he didn't finally name it, it's just named that. Whatever you're singing in it, it's just named that.*[56]

Tommy Johnson, then, did not set out deliberately to compose blues. They simply came to him as air music. If a blues kept coming to him in the same way with a recognizable core of stable elements, he would name it and give it permanence in his repertoire. Mager Johnson and Mott Willis also operate in this manner, as did probably most of the other Drew blues singers.

Mager Johnson performs another blues constructed around a core, which he calls "Traveling Blues." It has a guitar part in open G tuning that is rather like the one used by Mott Willis in that tuning (Example 36). It features a descending bass figure played on the guitar's sixth string, but, unlike Willis, Johnson does not snap this string. Other variants of the guitar part were recorded by Willie Brown and Charley Patton, both with snapped bass strings. These will be discussed in greater detail later. Johnson's melody is also somewhat similar to the one used by Willis (see Example 33), but it is even closer to the melody of Tommy Johnson's "Maggie Campbell Blues" (Victor 21409), which

used a similar guitar part. Mager Johnson uses a variant melody, which
consists mostly of humming, for the first two lines of the fifth stanza in
the version printed below. His text has nothing in common with the
text of his brother's "Maggie Campbell Blues," although a variant of
stanza 4 was sung in Tommy's "Big Fat Mama Blues" (Victor V38535,
Example 55), which uses the same melody but a different guitar part.
This stanza, however, was also used by Mager Johnson in Example 49,
and variants of stanzas 5 and 6 below were used in one of his versions
of "Bye and Bye Blues" (Example 46). In addition, Johnson's first two
stanzas have been encountered previously in blues by Mott Willis (Examples 33, 36, 37, and 40). Thus, "Traveling Blues" is thoroughly within the Drew tradition.

Example 51. "Traveling Blues." Mager Johnson, vocal and guitar in open
G tuning. Crystal Springs, Miss., Sept. 4, 1966. Recorded by David
Evans and Marina Bokelman. Issued on *Goin' up the Country*, British
Decca LK 4931, 12" LP (reissued on Rounder 2012).

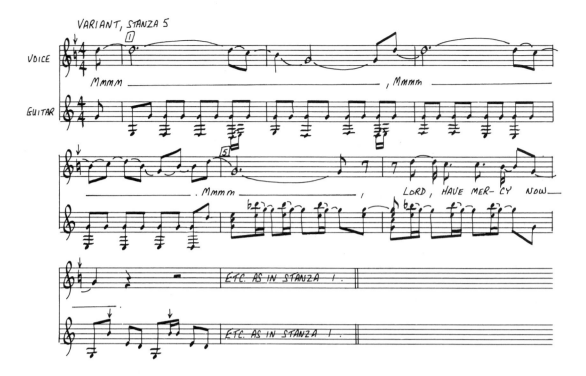

1. *I's a traveling man, mama, 'n I sure got a traveling, sure got a traveling mind.*
   I's a traveling man, mama, 'n I sure got a traveling mind.
   I'm gon' buy me a ticket, mama, gon' ease on down the road.

2. *Mmmm, what you gon' do, rider, when your trouble gets like, trouble gets like mine?*
   Hey, what you gonna do, rider, when your trouble gets like mine?
   Get your pick and shovel, woman; let's ease on down the line.

3. *Got the blues so bad till it hurts my feet to, hurts my feet to walk.*
   Got the blues so bad till it hurts my tongue to talk.
   Done settled on my brain, woman, . . .

4. *Hey, big fat mama, the meat shaking on her, meat shaking on her bones.*
   Hey, a big fat mama with the meat shaking on her bones.
   Every time she shake, it's a fat mama lost her home.

5. *Mmmm, mmmm.*
   Mmmm, Lord, have mercy now.
   If the Good Lord don't help you, the devil will damn your . . .

6. *Take me out of the bottom, mama now, 'fore the water rise.*
   Take me out of the bottom, mama now, 'fore the water rise.

    The following day Johnson recorded a vastly different version of this blues. Only the first two stanzas of the lyrics are the same, yet, as in the earlier version, some of the other stanzas correspond to ones he sang in "Bye and Bye Blues." Stanzas 4, 8, and 9 below are found in variant form in Examples 47, 48, and 49. Johnson's guitar playing is similar to that of the earlier version, although in several stanzas he

plays the figure used in measures 7 and 8 as a riff throughout the first
three measures. In the first four stanzas he sings a variant melody,
which is printed below. His kazoo choruses offer further variations on
this new melody. In stanzas 5 and 8 he returns to the standard melody
of Example 51 above. The first line of his final stanza is like that of the
new melody, while the last line is sung to the falsetto part that Johnson
also used in Example 49.

Example 52. "Traveling Blues." Mager Johnson, vocal, kazoo, and guitar
in open G tuning. Crystal Springs, Miss., Sept. 5, 1966. Recorded by
David Evans and Marina Bokelman. Issued on *Big Road Blues*, Advent
2815, 12" LP.

GUITAR CHORUS.

1. *I'm a traveling man, mama, and I sure got a traveling mind.*
   I'm a traveling man, mama, and I sure got a traveling mind.
   I'm gonna buy me a ticket, woman, and gon' ease on down the line.

2. *Hey, what you gonna do, mama, when your trouble gets like mine?*
   Hey, what you gonna do, woman, when your trouble gets like mine?
   Get your pick and shovel, woman; let's ease on down the line.

3. *Crying, mmmm, mmmm.*
   Lord, I ain't gon' be here long.
   Says, the way you treat me, woman, I can't live here no more.

4. *Says, I'm stone barefooted, mama, and I got no shoes to, got no shoes to*
   wear now, woman.
   Crying, . . .

GUITAR AND KAZOO CHORUS.

GUITAR AND KAZOO CHORUS.

5. *Hey, sit down, woman; let me shine your, let me shine your shoes.*
   Aaah, sit down, woman; let me shine your shoes.
   If I shine your shoes, I'm sure gonna feel your leg.

6. *She's got great big legs. Sometimes I could, sometimes I could sigh.*
   She's got great big legs, man, and sometimes I could sigh.

7. *I had a dream last night, and I hope my dream come, hope my dream*
   *   come true.*
   I had . . .
   Yes, I dreamed last night, woman, that I spent the night with you.

GUITAR AND KAZOO CHORUS.

8. *Hey, fare you well, mama; baby, fare you well.*
   Hey, fare you well, mama; baby, fare you well.
   If I never more see you, crying, you'll be on my mind.

9. *Hey, what makes you do me, mama, like you do do do?*
   Hey, Lord, ain't gon' be here long.

Johnson's text printed above is an interesting example of folk blues structure. The first four stanzas all contain images of travel and departure, linked through the principle of association, with the additional suggestion of mistreatment in stanza 3. Then Johnson has someone put the kazoo into his mouth for him, and he plays two instrumental choruses. The next three stanzas are sung through the kazoo, which distorts the sound of the singer's voice. All three of these stanzas deal with sexual desire of the singer for his woman. Thus they contrast with the imagery of the first four stanzas, although the subject of shoes links stanzas 4 and 5. Then Johnson plays another instrumental chorus and returns to the imagery of departure and mistreatment in the last two stanzas. He drops the kazoo after the first line of stanza 8. The kazoo, then, serves in an important structural role as a vehicle for introducing a contrastive section of the text as well as a means for disguising the normal voice during the singing of sexually suggestive lyrics.

In 1967 and 1969 Mager Johnson recorded three more versions of "Traveling Blues." All contain the same opening stanza as the two earlier versions. Some of the subsequent stanzas occur in more than one version, but each text is quite distinctive on the whole. The three later versions offer little that is new musically, but instead contain various combinations of the melodic and instrumental elements used in Examples 51 and 52.

A comparison of the five versions of "Traveling Blues" illustrates the difficulty of trying to describe a folk blues singer's notion of what constitutes one of his songs. We could state that the core of this song appears to consist of a single guitar part in open G tuning but with variant figures for a number of measures, a pair of alternative melodies which can be used either singly or together in the same performance and which also have occasional variations in certain measures and lines (e.g., the falsetto part), and two lyric stanzas. One of these stanzas is used as the opening stanza in all five versions, and the other is the second stanza in four versions. Two more stanzas, however, occur in three versions each, and another two are found in two versions each. Yet three of these recurring stanzas are found in other blues by Mager

Johnson. Furthermore, certain lyric stanzas show an affinity for certain melodic lines. For example, the partially hummed stanza 3 in Example 52 is always sung to the same melody in the three versions in which it occurs. Likewise, the text of the final falsetto lines of two versions is similar (see Example 52). Stanzas 3 and 5 of Example 51 are found in only one other version, one which uses the same tune. Finally, we should note that all five texts contain imagery of travel and departure. Some of the texts contrast this with imagery of sexual desire and reconciliation. Yet we must be very cautious in generalizing about the characteristics of "Traveling Blues." Each new version of the five has presented further surprises and variations, so it is likely that even more would be disclosed by continued recording of the piece and our conclusions would have to be modified accordingly. Consequently, it is only with some difficulty that we can speak of "Traveling Blues" as a distinct song at all.

Mager Johnson's discussion of the piece's origin, in the following interview, helps to explain its diffuseness:

> Evans: *Did you or Clarence ever help Tommy make up any of his songs?*
> Johnson: *No, sure didn't.*
> Evans: *Or did you and Clarence have songs different from the ones Tommy played?*
> Johnson: *Some of 'em. Now you take this I recollect, that "Maggie Campbell" he [Tommy] got. When we was playing one just like it, well, that's where that come from. It was near about like it in a way, but it had a lot more changes.*
> Evans: *Which one came from which?*
> Johnson: *I'm fixing to tell you now. See, he had the "Maggie Campbell Blues," and we had the "Rambling Blues." And we had it with two names, the "Rambling Blues" or the "Traveling Blues."*
> Evans: *And which one came first?*
> Johnson: *Tom. Tom put that on the air, you know [in 1928, Victor 21409].*
> Evans: *Oh, he made "Maggie Campbell" first?*
> Johnson: *That's right. And we played his music of "Maggie Campbell" until—well, we have laughed about it a right smart of times—we got off one night, and I guess we got to feeling too good, and it kind of changed up from the "Maggie Campbell Blues." We just carried it a different way, and it looked like everybody liked that. And so it wasn't the "Maggie Campbell Blues." We called it the "Rambling Blues."*
> Evans: *Is the "Rambling Blues" the same as the "Traveling Blues?"*
> Johnson: *It's a little different, but it's nearly about in the same tune in spots.*[57]

It is probable that "Rambling Blues" was Clarence Johnson's title, since Mager always calls his own piece "Traveling Blues." Apparently these two younger brothers did not care for Tommy's initial stanza about his former wife. Therefore, they substituted their own core stanzas and made a few additional changes in the melody and guitar part in order to personalize the song.

Mager Johnson performs two other pieces in open G tuning. One is a blues guitar solo learned from his brother Tommy, which shares some figures with "Traveling Blues." The other is called "Shaking That Thing" and has the same guitar part as that used by Arzo Youngblood in a piece learned from Tommy Johnson called "The Old Folks Doing It and the Little Ones Trying."[58]

Mager Johnson performs three blues with guitar parts in the key of D with a tuning produced by lowering the bass sixth string (E) of standard tuning to D. "Big Road Blues," which is formed around a core somewhat in the manner of "Traveling Blues," will be discussed in the next chapter. "Canned Heat Blues" was never a regular part of Mager's repertoire, and he performs only fragmentary versions of it. He considers it to belong to his brother Tommy, who recorded it in 1928 (Victor V38535). Mager's few verses are all similar to ones on Tommy's record, as are his melody and guitar part. The lyrics deal with the devastating effects of a cheap alcoholic drink made of Sterno, a cooking fuel called "canned heat," to which Tommy was addicted.[59]

Mager Johnson's third blues in the key of D has no title and has little identity of its own in the lyrics, although the melody and guitar part are distinctive. Five of his six performances contain vocals. They have a total of eighteen stanzas, only five of which do not occur in some of his versions of "Bye and Bye Blues" and "Traveling Blues." Three of these five are, in fact, the same stanza. This stanza, the first in Example 54 below, was used in variant form as the opening stanza of Kid Bailey's "Rowdy Blues" (Brunswick 7114) and is said by Mott Willis to have been sung by Dick Bankston. There is one line, "I'm leaving town, mama, to wear you off my mind," which occurs in four of the five versions, and another line, "Lord, have mercy on my wicked soul," is found in three. Perhaps these two lines could be considered the song's lyric core, yet both have been encountered already in versions of "Bye and Bye Blues" and "Traveling Blues." Johnson usually plays the same guitar part in each chorus with only minor variations. A different solo guitar chorus following stanza 1 of Example 54 is printed below. In measures 7–9 this chorus is like the guitar part of "Big Road Blues" (Example 60). He sings two alternative melodies, using the second of these in all but four stanzas. These melodies differ only in their first line. Often he omits the last line of his stanzas. The first two of his five texts and the musical parts are printed below. The texts deal mainly with the subjects of leaving and mistreatment, although in two of them the singer expresses a contrasting determination to stay put (see Example 54).

Example 53. Untitled blues. Mager Johnson, vocal and guitar in EBGDAD tuning, key of D. Crystal Springs, Miss., Sept. 5, 1966. Recorded by David Evans and Marina Bokelman.

GUITAR CHORUS.

1. Lord, I'm leaving town, woman, to wear you off my mind.

Mmmm, leaving town, woman, to wear you off my mind.
Says, the way you treat me, woman now, make me lose my mind.

2. *Crying mmmm.* [Guitar Chorus.]

GUITAR CHORUS.

Example 54. Untitled blues. Mager Johnson, vocal and guitar in EBGDAD tuning, key of D. Crystal Springs, Miss., Sept. 5, 1966. Recorded by David Evans and Marina Bokelman. Issued as "Moustache Blues" on *Big Road Blues,* Advent 2815, 12″ LP.

GUITAR CHORUS.

GUITAR CHORUS.

1. *Lord, I ain't gon' marry, mama now, either settle down.*
   Lord, I ain't gon' marry, mama now, either settle down.
   I'm gon' stay right here, woman, till my moustache drag the ground.

GUITAR CHORUS.

2. *Mmmm, Lord, have mercy on my wicked soul.*
   If the Good Lord don't help me, the devil will damn my soul.

3. *Take me out of the bottom 'fore the water rise.*

The remainder of Mager Johnson's blues fall into two groups which have guitar accompaniments in the key of A in standard tuning. These guitar parts share a couple of figures with each other, one of which was used also in Tommy Johnson's "Lonesome Home Blues" (Victor unissued).[60] One of Mager's patterns is a typical three-line blues, while the other, which he calls simply a "Boogie," consists largely of strummed chords in the accompaniment with a couplet substituted for the first line of each stanza. The seven recorded versions of these pieces, some of them brief or fragmentary, contain twenty stanzas, only one of which is not used in one of Johnson's other blues. Although most versions have one or more lines or stanzas in common, no single line or stanza occurs in all seven. The line, "I'm leaving town, woman, just to wear you off my mind," is used in four versions, and "How can I stay here, all I got is gone?" is found in three. Even if we were to consider these lines to be the textual core of this group of blues, we would have to note that one of them occurs in the core of another group (see Example 53). For the most part, in these blues Johnson simply picks stanzas out of his repertoire as he goes along, most of them on themes of leaving and mistreatment, and arranges them loosely by association.

Mager Johnson, then, performs about the same number of blues melodies and guitar accompaniments as Mott Willis. For both artists, one guitar part with its variant figures tends to be associated with one melody and its variant figures. There are some exceptional cases, however, where a single guitar part serves two altogether different melodies (Examples 51 and 52) or where a single melody is used with two different guitar parts (Examples 33–37). The texts of these artists' blues, particularly those of Willis, display a great amount of overlap. In fact, it is not really possible to discuss some of Willis's blues as "songs" having an existence of their own outside of their performance. Most of Mager Johnson's blues, however, and Willis's "Dresser Drawer Blues" are constructed around a core consisting of a melody, guitar part, and one or two stanzas or lines, to which are added more lyrics from the singer's repertoire as he sees fit at the time of performance. Johnson's use of a blues core is rather flexible, and occasionally he performs only part of it in a blues. Mott Willis obtains flexibility sometimes by paraphrasing his lyrics in prose (Example 45). Both performers, in addition, use a number of minor variations in the melody and accompaniment of a blues from one chorus to another, so that it is altogether difficult to discuss their "version" of any blues title except in the context of a particular performance.

The Blues of Tommy Johnson

The only other artists in the Drew tradition whose blues outputs are large enough to be considered representative samples of their repertoires are Tommy Johnson and Charley Patton. I have refrained from analyzing their recorded blues thus far because, unlike those of Mott Willis and Mager Johnson, they were recorded for commercial companies, and we have few alternate versions of their songs recorded on different occasions. The record companies were seeking originality in each blues performance they issued, so they could be expected to suppress or not record performances which greatly resembled each other, especially in the lyrics. H. C. Speir, the talent scout who discovered both Patton and Johnson, stated that the companies required every singer who was to be recorded to have at least four original and different songs.[61] There is no way to tell how many fine folk blues singers were rejected by Speir and the record companies because their blues did not meet these requirements. Mott Willis, for instance, would probably not be able to produce four "different" blues in a short audition, while Mager Johnson's blues would not seem original to the listener who had already heard those of his brother Tommy. Yet Willis and

Mager Johnson were both judged to be fine performers by other blues singers. The record companies and the singers were simply applying different sets of standards to the same music.

Indeed, Tommy Johnson himself was nearly rejected on account of these standards. Speir stated that at Johnson's first audition he could perform only two different songs. Only by working diligently together were Speir and Johnson able to increase this number to the required four songs. This statement might seem incredible for an artist of Johnson's stature, but, when it is viewed in the light of what we know about the blues of his brother Mager and of Mott Willis, it becomes more plausible. In fact, an examination of Tommy Johnson's blues output reveals that Speir did not entirely correct these "faults," so that there is still considerable overlap among his extant blues.

I will merely summarize Tommy Johnson's recordings here, since they have already been discussed elsewhere in some detail.[62] Ten of his eleven extant recordings are blues. One of them, "Lonesome Home Blues" (Victor unissued) exists in two takes recorded consecutively at the same session. They are virtually identical and are treated here as a single version for statistical purposes. It is impossible to ascertain whether Johnson performed this song the same way every time, since we lack recordings of it on other occasions. A later recording by Johnson with the same title (Paramount 13000) is altogether different.

Except for the guitar part of "Slidin' Delta" (Paramount 12975), all ten of Johnson's blues display similarities in their lyrics, melodies, and accompaniments to one or more recorded blues by other artists in the Drew tradition. He uses a different guitar part for each blues, although there are partial similarities between some of them. For example, "Big Fat Mama Blues" (Victor V38535, Example 55) and "Black Mare Blues" (Paramount 13000) employ almost identical guitar parts, except that they are in the keys of A and G in standard tuning, respectively. This happens to be a guitar part which can be transposed, with slight modifications, to any key. The guitar parts of "Big Road Blues" (Victor 21279, Example 60) and "Canned Heat Blues" (Victor V38535), which are both played in EBGDAD tuning in the key of D, share some phrases, as do the parts of "Big Fat Mama Blues" (Victor V38535, Example 55) and "Lonesome Home Blues" (Victor unissued), both in the key of A in standard tuning. Johnson plays one additional guitar part in open G tuning and four different ones in the key of E in standard tuning. His melodies display even greater overlap. He uses the same melody for three of his blues, "Maggie Campbell Blues" (Victor 21409), "Big Fat Mama Blues" (Victor V38535, Example 55), and "Black Mare Blues" (Paramount 13000), while "Lonesome Home Blues" (Victor unissued) is similar to them in its first melodic line. The last line of the latter piece is similar to the last line of "Big Road Blues" (Victor 21279, Example 60) and "Canned Heat Blues" (Victor V38535). These last two pieces also have similar second melodic lines. Finally, Johnson uses portions of the falsetto melody of "Cool Drink of Water Blues" (Victor 21279, Example 20) in "Big Road Blues" (Victor 21279, Example 60), "Canned Heat

Blues" (Victor V38535), and "Slidin' Delta" (Paramount 12975). Almost all of Johnson's verses are traditional. In his texts Johnson uses two stanzas and six single lines in slightly variant form in more than one song. This represents less overlap between songs than in the blues of his brother Mager and indicates that Tommy may have had a wider repertoire of lyrics. Yet the two brothers might well display equal amounts of overlap if only we possessed other versions of Tommy's songs.

We cannot know for certain whether Tommy Johnson always performed his blues the same way, but our evidence strongly suggests that he did not. Instead, he probably composed most of his blues in the manner of his brother and Mott Willis, who were part of the same tradition. Ishmon Bracey, Johnson's playing partner in Jackson for many years, said, "He would always mostly sing the same tune but a different time, slow or fast, you know. He'd change his words. He just put some more verses to it and on and on like that."[63] Other singers who knew Johnson have said substantially the same thing about his songs. Evidence to support Bracey's statement also comes from the performances of other blues singers who learned songs from Johnson. I have several dozen field recordings by such artists of blues which they learned from Johnson *in person* rather than from his records. In almost all instances where it is possible to compare these versions with the blues recorded by Johnson himself, we find that they have only the guitar part, melody, and one or perhaps two stanzas in common with Johnson's record. In other words, the versions share only a blues core. Almost invariably they reproduce the first stanza of Johnson's record and then continue with stanzas not on the record but apparently sung by Johnson in person. Furthermore, each of these singers has his own version of the lyrics to Johnson's songs, unlike the version of any other singer except for the first stanza, which belongs to the song's core.[64]

An examination of versions of "Big Fat Mama Blues" by Tommy Johnson, Roosevelt Holts, Houston Stackhouse, and Arzo Youngblood reveals the fact that they share only a core in common. This core consists of the guitar part, melody, and first stanza of Tommy Johnson's version, which is printed below. The other three versions were all learned from Johnson in person.[65] Besides the core stanza they contain between them three additional stanzas and two single lines used in other recorded blues by Johnson and the other Drew artists. The core stanza is also used occasionally by Mager Johnson as a "floating" stanza (Examples 49 and 51). All four versions of "Big Fat Mama Blues" use essentially the same melody and guitar part with only minor variations. The melody is like one of those used by Mager Johnson for his "Traveling Blues" (Example 51), and the guitar part is similar to the one used by Mott Willis in Example 33.

Example 55. "Big Fat Mama Blues." Tommy Johnson, vocal and guitar in standard tuning, key of A. Memphis, Aug. 31, 1928. Victor V38535, reissued on *Blues Roots/Mississippi*, RBF 14, 12" LP.

1. Crying, big fat mama, meat shaking on her bones.
   Time the meat shake, it's a skinny woman lose a home.

2. Well, I'm going away, mama, won't be back till fall, won't be back till fall,
      mmmm.
   Going away, mama, won't be back till fall.
   Big fat mama with the meat shake on her bones.

3. Well, aaah, mmmm, got to murmur, got to murmur low, mmmm.
   No need to holler; I got to murmur low.
   Big fat mama, Lord, meat shake on her bones.

4. Every time the meat shake, fat mouth lose a home, fat mouth lose a home,
      mmmm.
   Time the meat shakes, it's a fat mouth lose a home.
   Time the meat shakes, it's a fat mouth lose a home.

5. Mmmm, what's the matter, rider? Where did you stay last, where did you
      stay last night, mmmm?
   What's the matter, rider? Where did you stay last night?
   Hair all down, baby, and you won't treat me right.

6. *Mmmm, big fat mama, meat shakes on her bones, meat shakes on her*
     bones, mmmm.
   Big fat mama, meat shaking on her bones.

For this blues Tommy Johnson must have had a stable core consisting of the guitar part, melody, and first stanza of his recorded version. The other performers learned this core from Johnson and added to it stanzas of their own, some of which they probably learned from Johnson and others which they drew from the larger blues tradition. The additional verses that Johnson himself sang in 1928 must have been improvised on the spot from his repertoire of traditional lyrics. If Johnson had had a stable text of this song in his repertoire, we should expect the texts of the other performers to show greater similarity than they do. In the next chapter we shall be able to draw a similar conclusion in regard to Johnson's performance of "Big Road Blues."

The Blues of Charley Patton

Charley Patton's recordings have also been discussed in some detail,[66] so that again I shall only summarize their characteristics. Patton recorded fifty extant songs, among which are thirty-two blues. The remainder consist of three blues ballads, ten religious songs, three non-blues lyric folksongs, and two versions of popular songs. In addition, he played guitar on four pieces by Henry Sims and on two by his wife Bertha Lee. All but one of these pieces are blues. Six of his thirty-two blues texts are thematic throughout, and a few others are partly thematic or contain highly personal or topical references. Most of these texts are from the latter half of his recording career, indicating an increasing self-consciousness typical of recorded blues singers. Even so, Patton's percentage of thematic blues (18.75 percent) is quite low. At least nine of his blues show some discernible influence from earlier blues records, but in most cases these sources have been drastically altered or utilized only in part by Patton. All but six of his blues show some similarity to one or more blues recorded by other members of the Drew tradition. Seventeen of Patton's thirty-two blues texts share at least one line with a blues by another Drew artist, and twenty-two tunes and twenty-one guitar parts also share elements with the tradition. One of his accompaniments for Bertha Lee is also within the Drew tradition.

Most of Patton's guitar parts and melodies fall into a small number of groups. The largest of these comprises ten blues in two subdivisions. All ten use the same basic melody, which has two alternate strains for the first line.[67] Nine of them have a similar guitar part in open G tuning, which features the snapping of the bass sixth string in a descending figure. This part has some similarities to those of Mott Willis and Mager Johnson printed in Examples 36 and 51. Patton's nine blues that use this guitar part are "Screamin' and Hollerin' the Blues" (Paramount

12805), "Heart Like Railroad Steel" (Paramount 12953), "High Water Everywhere—Parts 1 and 2" (Paramount 12909), "Moon Going Down" (Paramount 13014), "Bird Nest Bound" (Paramount 13070), "Jersey Bull Blues" (Vocalion 02782), "Love My Stuff" (Vocalion 02782), and "Revenue Man Blues" (Vocalion 02931).[68] The tenth blues in this group, "Devil Sent the Rain" (Paramount 13040), has a different guitar part in the key of A in standard tuning similar to that of Mott Willis in Example 33 and Tommy Johnson in Example 55. Patton's second group of blues also has two subdivisions. The first of these consists of "Pony Blues" (Paramount 12792, Example 24), "Rattlesnake Blues" (Paramount 12924), "Dry Well Blues" (Paramount 13070), and "Stone Pony Blues" (Vocalion 02680, Example 25), which all use a group of three closely related melodies and guitar parts in the key of E in standard tuning.[69] One of these melodies and one of the guitar parts are also used in the other subdivision, which consists of "Circle Round the Moon" (Paramount 13040) and "Green River Blues" (Paramount 12972).[70] These two pieces each contain another alternative melody and guitar part. A third group of Patton's blues contains some slight similarities to this second group in the guitar part. It consists of "Mean Black Cat Blues" (Paramount 12943) and Patton's accompaniment to Bertha Lee's "Yellow Bee" (Vocalion 02650). Patton's "Joe Kirby" (Paramount 13133) contains an interesting mixture of musical elements found in the first three groups. The melody uses variants of the tunes associated with the first group above. The guitar part, however, shares a number of phrases with the second and third groups above. It also contains the movable chords that Patton played in the key of A in "Devil Sent the Rain" (Paramount 13040). A fourth group by Patton includes "Down the Dirt Road Blues" (Paramount 12854), "34 Blues" (Vocalion 02651), and "Poor Me" (Vocalion 02651). All three pieces have a similar guitar part in the key of C in standard tuning, which shares figures with the part played by Mott Willis in Example 39.[71] The first two pieces in this group also share a similar melody. "Magnolia Blues" (Paramount 12943) and "When Your Way Gets Dark" (Paramount 12998) share the same melody and guitar part in open G tuning, played in knife-style, and have three stanzas in common. Similarly, "Tom Rushen Blues" (Paramount 12877) and "High Sheriff Blues" (Vocalion 02680) share the same melody and knife-style accompaniment in open G tuning with parts of three stanzas in common. They are both influenced in their melody and lyrics by Ma Rainey's 1924 recording of "Booze and Blues" (Paramount 12242). Patton's "Mean Black Moan" (Paramount 12953) has a distinctive melody, but its guitar part was also used in his accompaniments to Henry Sims's "Farrell Blues" (Paramount 12912), "Come Back Corrina" (Paramount 12912), and "Tell Me Man Blues" (Paramount 12940). The remainder of Patton's blues all have distinctive melodies and guitar parts.

From the brief analysis above it is clear that there is considerable overlap in the musical portion of Patton's blues performances. Overlap is exhibited in his texts also. Patton sings fifteen stanzas or single lines in more than one blues. In addition, he recorded four pairs of blues, each of which could be considered a set of two alternative versions of a single blues. Each pair shares a melody, guitar part, and two or three stanzas. We have already noted that "Stone Pony Blues" (Example 25) seems to be simply an updated version of "Pony Blues" (Example 24). "Tom Rushen Blues" and "High Sheriff Blues" have a similar kind of relationship, both dealing with different jailhouse experiences. As noted above, their close relationship derives from the fact that each is influenced by an earlier record by Ma Rainey.[72] Patton's "Magnolia Blues" and "When Your Way Gets Dark" are simply two takes of the same piece recorded consecutively but given different titles. The similarities between "Bird Nest Bound" and "Revenue Man Blues" are ascribable to the fact that both are influenced by Ardell "Shelly" Bragg's 1926 recording of "Bird Nest Blues" (Paramount 12410). The textual differences in these four pairs lead one to think that Patton also had blues cores in his repertoire, rather than whole songs, and that he used these cores as the basis for many of the blues that he recorded. In addition, most of his blues are not thematically coherent but are composed mainly from traditional stanzas which Patton knew and used in any number of different combinations. It is quite likely that most of these combinations were made at the time of performance. Son House has said of Patton, "Charley, he could start singing of the shoe there and wind up singing about that banana."[73]

Shared Elements in the Drew Tradition

We have noticed considerable overlap within the blues outputs of each of the four singers in the Drew tradition who have been recorded extensively. A singer might use the same melody and/or guitar part for many different sets of lyrics, or, conversely, he might use the same line or stanza with different melodies and guitar parts. In addition, two or more melodies or guitar parts might have a single musical phrase or line in common. These singers' blues repertoires each consist of a number of lyric stanzas and lines, melodies and melodic phrases, and guitar parts and phrases. Their repertoires also contain larger fixed combinations of these elements. Such combinations may be either blues cores, each consisting of a guitar part, a melody, and usually one or two lyric stanzas, or they may in some cases be whole songs performed as set pieces. The vast majority of the blues by these four singers draw heavily upon traditional lyrical and musical material and could be classified as Nonthematic/Improvised or Nonthematic/Partly Stable.

Each member of the Drew tradition also displays considerable overlap in his blues repertoire with the repertoires of other members. In fact, the amount of overlap is so great that I have been able to mention only selected instances in this chapter. It has been noted previously that all ten of Tommy Johnson's blues share at least one element with a blues by another singer from the local tradition, as do twenty-six of Charley Patton's thirty-two blues, thirty-eight of Mager Johnson's forty blues performances, and twenty-four of Mott Willis's forty-nine. Furthermore, all three of the recordings by Willie Brown and both of those by Kid Bailey share elements with the local tradition. Of the thirty-three blues by these performers that do not contain elements drawn from the local tradition, nine have their origins in popular phonograph records. Only Howlin' Wolf, who began his recording career many years after he left the Drew area and who was continually subject to commercial influences, displays little indebtedness to his original local tradition. In general, each singer from the Drew tradition draws upon that tradition in at least half of his blues recordings and often in a much higher percentage. These percentages might well be raised even further if we possessed more recordings by these and other local performers. Many of the lyrics and musical ideas which now appear unique to individual singers might be found to be traditional at Drew.

Despite these great similarities in the repertoires of the Drew blues singers, no two of them have recorded a blues in exactly the same way using all the same elements. There are, however, five blues cores performed by more than one of the Drew singers. One of these, "Big Road Blues," will be discussed in the next chapter. Another, "Canned Heat Blues," was invented by Tommy Johnson and is performed only by Mager Johnson among the other artists in the local tradition, and even he prefers not to perform it. This piece has also been learned from Tommy Johnson by a number of artists outside the Drew tradition.[74] The three other shared blues cores from the Drew tradition, "Pony Blues," "Bye and Bye Blues," and "Cool Water Blues," are so closely connected that they can be discussed separately only with difficulty.

The "Pony Blues" core has been recorded by Charley Patton (Examples 24–25), Mager Johnson (Example 50), and Howlin' Wolf (Chess 1515), all major participants in the Drew tradition. It was reportedly performed also by Willie and Josie Brown, Dick Bankston, Ben Maree, and the other Johnson brothers, especially LeDell. Tommy Johnson used a textual variant of the core stanza in his "Black Mare Blues" (Paramount 13000). The three recorded versions employ a total of five different melodic lines among them, rather than the usual two or three of most blues. Patton sings three different three-line melodies in his "Pony Blues" (Paramount 12792, Example 24), which have the forms AAB, CDB, and EAB. Mager Johnson's two stanzas have the forms AAA and DA, while Howlin' Wolf sings the lines CCB, except in his last stanza which has a couplet in place of his first line. Thus the melodies of Mager Johnson and Howlin' Wolf have nothing in common, although each is sung by Patton. Mager Johnson's guitar part is the same as the one that he uses for "Bye and Bye Blues" (Examples 46–47). Its similarities to Patton's guitar part have already been noted. Howlin' Wolf's guitar part is, like the others, in the key of E in standard tuning but is in other respects considerably different. It features a figure containing movable chords played on the treble strings. This was played by many of the other Drew artists, but usually in the key of A (cf.

Examples 33 and 55), though Patton played it in the key of E in his "Joe Kirby" (Paramount 13133). The first two stanzas of Howlin' Wolf's text are found in Patton's "Pony Blues," and the opening couplet of his third stanza is found in variant form in Patton's "Heart Like Railroad Steel" (Paramount 12953) and "Rattlesnake Blues" (Paramount 12924).[75]

Closely connected with the "Pony Blues" core is the "Bye and Bye Blues" core. It has been recorded by Tommy Johnson as "Bye-Bye Blues" (Victor 21409) and by Mager Johnson (Examples 46–48), but it is also said to have been performed by Dick Bankston and Ben Maree at Drew. Variants of its core stanza were also used by Charley Patton in "Poor Me" (Vocalion 02651) and by Mott Willis in Example 36. Tommy Johnson sings the CDB melodic pattern of Patton's "Pony Blues" (Example 24) throughout his piece, while Mager Johnson favors an ADB pattern, though he also sings CDB and AAB tunes. The close similarities in the guitar parts of these pieces have already been discussed (see Example 46). Except for one stanza Tommy Johnson's text is close to Mager Johnson's in Example 48.[76]

It is apparent that the "Pony Blues" and "Bye and Bye Blues" cores share the same melodies and guitar parts. The only thing that differentiates them is the presence of one or the other of the core stanzas, which gives the particular blues performance its title. As we have already noted, all of the elements in both of these cores have been used separately in other blues recordings by Charley Patton, Willie Brown, Kid Bailey, Tommy Johnson, and Mott Willis.

Mager Johnson considers "Pony Blues," "Bye and Bye Blues," and "Cool Water Blues" essentially the same piece, and indeed his versions of all three are musically the same. The latter piece has been recorded by Tommy Johnson as "Cool Drink of Water Blues" (Victor 21279, Example 20) and by Howlin' Wolf as "I Asked for Water" (Chess 1632, Example 56). It was also performed by Ben Maree and Robert Johnson at Drew. The versions by Tommy Johnson and Howlin' Wolf, however, really have only a guitar figure in common with "Pony Blues" and "Bye and Bye Blues." Otherwise, their versions of "Cool Water Blues" are quite different. Much of Johnson's melody is sung in falsetto, though Howlin' Wolf employs the technique only in his third line. His first two melodic lines are not found in the blues of the other Drew singers. Mager Johnson used the falsetto melody in a piece (Example 49) that was otherwise musically the same as his "Bye and Bye Blues," as well as in some of his other blues (see Example 52). Falsetto singing is also featured in various songs by Drew artists associated with the "Big Road Blues" core, as will be shown in the next chapter. Howlin' Wolf's guitar part for "Cool Water Blues" is a simplified version of the one used by Tommy Johnson and is notable for its very slow tempo. It seems to have independent bass and treble lines. It is not known for certain whether there are one or two guitarists and whether Howlin' Wolf is one of them. The part could easily be played on one guitar, and if Howlin' Wolf does not play on the record, he almost certainly taught

the part to his accompanist(s). He definitely plays the harmonica, however. If it is a single guitar, the playing is unusual for a Drew artist on
account of the "pinching" simultaneously of bass and treble strings.[77]
His text has only the initial core verse in common with Tommy Johnson's text. It should be noted that Howlin' Wolf has said that he never
met Johnson or heard his record. The similarities in their pieces are
ascribable to the fact that both participated in the same local tradition.[78]

Example 56. "I Asked for Water." Howlin' Wolf (Chester Burnett), vocal,
harmonica, and guitar in standard tuning, key of E; Hosea Lee Kennard, piano; Earl Phillips, drums. Chicago, May, 1956. Chess 1632, reissued on *Moanin' in the Moonlight*, Chess LP 1434, 12" LP.

1. *Oh, asked her for water. Oh, she brought me gasoline.*
   Oh, asked her for water. Oh, she brought me gasoline.
   That's the terriblest woman that I ever seen.

2. *Oh, the church bell toning. Oh, the hearse come driving slow.*
   Oh, the church bell toning. Oh, the hearse come driving slow.
   I hope my baby don't leave me no more.

3. *Oh, tell me, baby, oh, when are you coming back home?*
   Oh, tell me, baby, oh, when are you coming back home?
   You know I love you, babe, but you been gone too long.

© 1956 ARC Music Corporation. Used by permission.

Besides these blues cores there were other important shared elements among the Drew blues singers. These include two closely associated guitar parts. One of these, in the key of A in standard tuning, features a series of movable seventh chords played as a repeated figure on the three treble strings. Variants of it were performed by Tommy Johnson ("Big Fat Mama Blues," Victor V38535, Example 55), Charley Patton ("Devil Sent the Rain," Paramount 13040), Kid Bailey ("Mississippi Bottom Blues," Brunswick 7114), Mott Willis (Examples 33–35), and Willie Brown (in his accompaniments to Patton's "Moon Going Down," Paramount 13014, and "Bird Nest Bound," Paramount 13070, and Fiddlin' Joe Martin's "Fo' Clock Blues," a field recording made in 1941 for the Library of Congress, AFS 4781-A-2). The other guitar part is played in open G tuning and features a descending bass figure played either on the sixth string or on the fourth and sixth strings, which are tuned an octave apart. The former variation has been recorded by Charley Patton in nine blues, by Mager Johnson in his "Traveling Blues" (Examples 51–52), and by O. M. McGee, while the latter variation has been recorded by Tommy Johnson ("Maggie Campbell Blues," Victor 21409), Willie Brown ("Future Blues," Paramount 13090)[79] and Mott Willis (Examples 36–37). These guitar parts in the key of A and open G tuning are the two that Mott Willis feels "go prettier together." They are played together on Willis Taylor's "Mama Do Right" (Example 38, Taylor in open G, Mott Willis in A) and on Charley Patton's "Moon Going Down" and "Bird Nest Bound" (Paramount 13014 and 13070, Patton in open G, Willie Brown in A). In all cases where a singer's repertoire includes both of these guitar parts, he sings the same melody with each. Yet, altogether, three different melodies are used by the Drew artists with this pair of guitar parts, one by Brown, one by Patton and Kid Bailey, and one by Mott Willis and the Johnson Brothers. The melody used by Patton and Bailey is heard also in Tommy Johnson's "Lonesome Home Blues" (Paramount 13000, Example 57), which has a different guitar part in the key of E in standard tuning.

A large number of textual lines and stanzas were also shared by the Drew blues singers. Many have already been noted, and to list them all would be tedious, but a few of the more spectacular cases of the usage of traditional lyrics will be noted here in order to show the degree to which singers could rely on the local tradition for material. Mott Willis relies on it to a very high degree in some of his blues. For instance, in Example 36 his first stanza is found in some versions of Mager Johnson's "Traveling Blues" (Examples 51–52), while his second stanza is found in Tommy and Mager Johnson's versions of "Bye and Bye Blues" (Examples 46–48) and Charley Patton's "Poor Me" (Vocalion 02651). Only Willis's third stanza is not found in the recordings of another Drew singer, although Willis claims that Willie Brown sang it often. In this piece Willis also uses the guitar part in open G tuning, variants of which were recorded by Patton, Brown, O. M. McGee, and the Johnson brothers. Willis's playing is most like Brown's. His melody, however, is like that of Tommy Johnson's "Maggie Campbell Blues" and Mager Johnson's "Traveling Blues" (Example 51). Mott Willis and the Johnson brothers, all from Crystal Springs, naturally show the greatest overlap with each other, but they could also overlap in their lyrics with the other Drew artists. For instance, in Example 54 by Mager Johnson the first two lines of stanza 1 are found in Kid Bailey's "Rowdy Blues" (Brunswick 7114), while the first line of stanza 2 is found in Patton's "Screamin' and Hollerin' the Blues" (Paramount 12805). Johnson's final stanza is found in variant form in his brother Tommy's "Slidin' Delta" (Paramount 12975). Patton's "Screamin' and Hollerin' the Blues" also contains two stanzas sung by Kid Bailey and another stanza similar to one of Tommy Johnson's.

There are also a number of interesting musical stylistic features that the Drew singers share. For instance, they all normally pick the guitar with the thumb and first two fingers, although Willie Brown and Mott Willis sometimes play with a flat pick. In their picking style they usually play only one string or chord at a time, rarely "pinching" two strings simultaneously with the thumb and finger in the manner of blues singers in many other local traditions.[80] Their guitar lines are usually quite distinct from the vocal lines, as an examination of any of the transcriptions in this study will show. In most other folk blues guitar styles the instrument plays in rough unison with the voice or plays simple chords or rhythmic patterns behind the singing. The basic rhythmic pattern in almost all blues in the Drew tradition is a series of eighth notes (/ ♫ ♫ ♫ ♫ /) or quarter-and-eighth note triplets (/ ♩♪ ♩♪ ♩♪ ♩♪ /). Sixteenth notes (except as slides) and eighth-note triplets (♫♪) are rare in the blues of all the Drew performers except Mott Willis. Furthermore, the thumb and finger rarely play alternate beats (T f T f . . . etc.), as in the styles of so many folk blues guitarists in other local traditions. The thumb, in fact, rarely strikes the third or seventh beat in a measure, even though these are onbeats, which we might expect to be accented in a bass note played by the thumb. In fourteen guitar parts by Tommy and Mager Johnson, Charley Patton, and Mott Willis printed in this study (Examples 20, 24, 33, 36, 39, 41, 42, 46, 51, 53, 54, 55, 57, and 60), plus eight guitar parts by Patton, Willie

Brown, and Tommy Johnson printed by Grossman,[81] there are 556 occasions for striking the third or seventh beat of a measure. Only 173 of these beats, or 31.1 percent, quite a low figure, are played by the thumb. Instead of picking patterns on the order of /T f T f T f T f/, the Drew musicians frequently play such patterns as /T f f f T f f f/, /T f f f f f f T/, and /T f f f T f f T/.

The Drew musicians were also great "clowns" with the guitar, often playing it behind their heads, between their legs, on the floor, tapping it with their knuckles, and using any number of other tricks and special effects. Among the Drew artists who were noted for clowning are Charley Patton, Tommy Johnson, Mager Johnson, Mott Willis, Howlin' Wolf, Ben Maree, and Jake Martin.[82]

One of the most interesting shared stylistic characteristics is the tendency of many of the Drew singers to drop the first vocal line of the opening stanza, playing the line as a guitar solo and beginning the singing with the second line. This was done by Willis Taylor (Example 38), Mager Johnson (in a version of "Traveling Blues" not printed here), Tommy Johnson ("Lonesome Home Blues," Victor unissued; "Big Fat Mama Blues," Victor V38535, Example 55; "Slidin' Delta," Paramount 12975; and "Lonesome Home Blues," Paramount 13000, Example 57), Charley Patton ("Mean Black Moan," Paramount 12953), Willie Brown ("Future Blues," Paramount 13090), and Kid Bailey ("Mississippi Bottom Blues" and "Rowdy Blues," Brunswick 7114).

Individualism and the Creative Use of Traditional Elements

In spite of all these stylistic similarities and the great amount of overlap of elements in their repertoires, all of the Drew singers display considerable individuality, even when they perform related lyrics, guitar parts, melodies, or blues cores. It would be impossible to say that one performer is imitating another. Their melodic or instrumental lines are never *exactly* the same. This can be seen easily by examining any of the comparisons that have been made throughout this study of blues by any two of the Drew singers (e.g., Examples 33 and 55). The performers do not learn and transmit musical phrases, lines, or parts note for note. Instead, the learner acquires, through repeated listening and observation, a musical idea which is more or less an approximation of what his source is performing. He then goes about the task of trying to recreate and sometimes reshape this musical idea until it becomes his own. That the performers are aware of both the resultant similarities and differences is revealed in their comments. Mager Johnson said of his "Bye and Bye Blues" (Example 46), "I may play it my way there," thus noting that it was a bit different from his brother's version. Many other blues singers differentiate their own performances from those of others in their local tradition by saying that one version has "more beats," "a different beat," or "more notes." Some singers also favor certain tones in the scale and not others. For example, Tommy Johnson tended to sing the major sixth degree of the scale in places where Charley Patton favored the minor or neutral seventh.[83]

New guitar parts and figures were sometimes developed from other parts and figures already in the local tradition by the processes of *transposition, patterning,* and *experimentation.* For instance, the guitar part featuring a series of seventh chords (Examples 33 and 55) can be transposed to any key, although it is generally played in standard tuning in the key of A, as in performances by Willie Brown, Charley Patton, Mott Willis, and Tommy Johnson. Johnson, however, also played it in the key of G on one of his recordings, and Charley Patton and Howlin' Wolf played variants of it in the key of E. Other artists who learned from Tommy Johnson have also played this part for me in the key of E. It can be transposed so easily because its featured figure is played entirely on the three treble strings of the guitar in a movable chord position (Figure 4). Tommy Johnson's guitar part to "Canned Heat Blues" (Victor V38535) displays the same characteristics. Johnson himself played it in the key of D in EBGDAD tuning, but I have observed other artists who learned it from him playing it transposed to the keys of E and G in standard tuning. Probably these transpositions were originally made by Johnson himself or by others in the Drew tradition. Portions of Tommy Johnson's guitar part for "Lonesome Home Blues" (Paramount 13000, Example 57), played in the key of E in standard tuning, are used by Mager Johnson in the key of D in EBGDAD tuning (Examples 53–54). Tommy Johnson is also said to have used this guitar part in D for his version of "Prison Bound Blues."

An example of the process of patterning in the creation of guitar figures would be Mott Willis's use of snapped bass strings in his performances of "Big Road Blues" (Examples 64–67). This was probably suggested to him by the string snapping that is usually done in the guitar part in open G tuning, as in performances by Charley Patton, Willie Brown, O. M. McGee, Tommy Johnson, and Willis himself (Example 36). In both tunings the fourth and sixth strings are an octave apart. In the EBGDAD tuning of "Big Road Blues" the bass pattern ascends on alternating strings in parallel fashion (Example 60), while in open G tuning it descends in the same manner. Willis also snaps his bass string in the key of C in standard tuning (Example 39). In all three patterns the majority of snaps are on the offbeat.

Experimentation resulting in new ideas may have been stimulated partly by the need to develop second guitar parts for ensemble playing. But many of the artists must also have felt a desire to vary their own playing occasionally. We have already noted a number of examples of such variations in the playing of several Drew artists. Tommy Johnson is said to have had variations in his guitar parts, depending on whether he was performing for dancing or listening. For example, he played his guitar part to "Maggie Campbell Blues" in open G tuning with the descending bass pattern on either one or two strings, one for dancing at parties and two for listening and on his record (Victor 21409)[84]

Similarly, in their lyrics the Drew singers display subtle differences when singing obviously related lines or stanzas. In "Pony Blues," for example, Mager Johnson gives a command to hitch up his "buggy" (Example 50), whereas the other singers call for a "pony." Mager Johnson calls for a "grey" mare, Charley Patton for a "black" mare (Example 24), and Howlin' Wolf for a "brown" mare. In an unissued field recording Woodrow Adams, who learned the song from Howlin' Wolf, calls for a "white" mare.[85] Seemingly minor differences in wording, such as in the opening stanzas of Tommy Johnson's "Big Fat Mama Blues" (Example 55) and Mager Johnson's Example 49, can convey major differences in meaning. Often several singers share only one line of a stanza, singing a completely different rhyming line. For instance, Mott Willis sings in example 42 (cf. Examples 34, 35, 40, and 44):

> *Reason I like her, she's so nice and brown.*
> *Reason I like her, she's so nice and brown.*
> *Guess the Good Lord made her, angels sent her down.*

Kid Bailey sings in "Rowdy Blues" (Brunswick 7114):

> *And I love you, baby. You so nice and brown.*
> *And I love you, baby, You so nice and brown.*
> *'Cause you put it up solid, so it won't come down.*

And Willie Brown sings in "Make Me a Pallet on the Floor" (Flyright LP 541):

> *Oh, I love you, babe, 'cause you so nice and brown.*
> *Now babe, I love you, babe, 'cause you so nice and brown.*
> *Now I love you, babe, 'cause you so nice and brown.*
> *'Cause you tailor made, and you ain't no hand-me-down.*

Undoubtedly these differences could be explained in part by differences in the personalities and life experiences of the singers who have created and used these lines, but they are also due in part to the play of individual imaginations upon traditional material. Such individual traits as these demonstrate the strength and flexibility of the tradition and make its study endlessly fascinating for anyone who is willing to listen for its subtleties.[86]

Singers in the Drew tradition sometimes created new blues cores from elements already in the tradition. Such was the case with Mott Willis's "Dresser Drawer Blues" (Examples 42–44). He considers this blues to be his own original composition, and other members of the tradition would probably support his claim. Nobody else in the tradition has recorded this blues core, although many of its separate elements have been recorded in various blues with different titles by other Drew singers.

Creativity was displayed also by the composition of totally original elements, cores, or even whole songs. Charley Patton recorded many verses which only he could have made up from events in his own life or from his observations of life around him. In his blues are a good number of references to his jailhouse experiences, towns he visited, and people he knew, as well as his accounts of the 1927 flood of the Mississippi River and the 1929 dry spell.[87] Tommy Johnson composed "Canned Heat Blues" (Victor V38535) about his own drinking habits, and Mott Willis composed "Bad Night Blues" (Example 32) about a woman because "that's the way one done me once sure enough."

Even though we may never determine the original inventors of particular elements, it is possible to show how certain ideas and themes were developed by blues singers within the Drew tradition. Each singer seems to have had favorite themes which he emphasized when drawing upon traditional lyrics or when creating original ones. Charley Patton, for example, frequently builds an image of toughness and aggressiveness; Mott Willis comments on the physical characteristics of women; Tommy Johnson describes his drunkenness in two blues and in others often expresses an urge to return home (see Examples 20 and 57). On the other hand, his brother Mager often sings about a desire to leave home. We must be careful, however, in drawing conclusions about the behavior and life-styles of the singers from the themes that they emphasize in their blues. While it is true that Patton was by most accounts a very aggressive person and Tommy Johnson was an alcoholic, we must keep in mind that Tommy Johnson rarely fulfilled his pledge to return home. Instead, he had four brief marriages and was a rambler all his life.[88] Mager Johnson, on the other hand, although he likes to portray himself in his blues as a victim of mistreatment and "a traveling man with a traveling mind," has spent almost his entire life in his native Crystal Springs and recently celebrated his golden wedding anniversary. In some cases, then, traditional blues lyrics would seem to serve the singers as a vicarious outlet for behavior they cannot otherwise engage in. Yet no blues singer concentrates on one or even a few lyric themes exclusively. They all tell us of their actual experiences, the experiences of others they have known, and the projections of their rich imaginations.

Even though many elements of the Drew tradition were shared, the idea for each must have originated somewhere. Since the Drew tradition is about as old as the blues themselves, it is possible that some of the elements originated there, particularly since some are found nowhere else. Yet our knowledge of the overall blues tradition in the South is too sketchy to permit us to say that something was invented at Drew simply because it has been recorded only by Drew singers.

We do know that new elements were constantly being introduced into the Drew tradition from outside. Many were brought by musicians who were just passing through or staying for a season to pick cotton, but others were brought by musicians who stayed longer, such as Jake Martin, who was already an accomplished performer before he arrived at Dockery's. We know too that Josie Brown brought the "Riverside Blues" (Example 41) to Drew from her native Florence, where she had learned it from Willie Love, a local musician. Her song took root at

Drew and was learned by her husband Willie Brown and by Mott Willis. Tommy Johnson also learned it but changed the guitar part into the one he played on "Lonesome Home Blues" (Paramount 13000), which is printed below. Mott Willis says of Johnson's transformation,

Old "Riverside Blues," Tom Johnson just kind of changed it. That was her piece, you know, in E minor [sic]. Me and Tommy Johnson, we was raised up together. Tom, he's about a couple years older than me. And we'd get together and play, you know. He said, "I'm gonna play some of Josie." We called her Josie Bush, you know. Play some of Josie's pieces.[89]

Example 57. "Lonesome Home Blues." Tommy Johnson, vocal and guitar in standard tuning, key of E. Grafton, Wis., ca. Mar., 1930. Paramount 13000, reissued on Jackson Blues, 1928–1938, Yazoo L-1007, 12" LP.

1. *Lonesome place don't seem like it's home to me.*
   Lord, this old lonesome place don't, mama, seem like it's home to me.

2. *I rose this morning, blues all 'round my bed.*
   Mmmm, rose this morning, the blues all 'round my bed.
   Had them blues so bad, mama, till I couldn't raise up my head.

3. *If you want to live easy, pack your clothes with mine.*
   Mmmm, want to live easy, pack your clothes with mine.
   If you want to live easy, babe, pack your clothes with mine.

4. *Mmmm, soon one morning blues come falling down.*
   Mmmm, soon one morning the blues come falling down.
   Well, they fell so heavy that it caused my heart to mourn.

5. *Well, I'm going back home, gon' fall down on my knees.*
   Mmmm, going back home, gonna fall down on my knees.
   Says, I'll 'knowledge now, pretty baby, that I treat you mean.

Johnson's text, which is made up almost entirely of traditional lines and stanzas, is quite interesting from a structural point of view. The first and last stanzas provide a framework featuring imagery of homesickness. Contrasting with this is the middle stanza, in which the singer attempts to establish a satisfactory domestic relationship in his present location. These three stanzas are separated by two others that describe the effects of the blues. Stanzas 2, 4, and 5 additionally present the singer as being under the weight of a heavy force, the blues. Johnson's melody shares some phrases with the tune that he sang in his "Maggie Campbell Blues" (Victor 21409), "Big Fat Mama Blues" (Victor V38535, Example 55), and "Black Mare Blues" (Paramount 13000). It is also like a tune used in several blues by Charley Patton and in Kid Bailey's "Mississippi Bottom Blues" (Brunswick 7114). Johnson's first two melodic lines are even closer to the first line in the third tune pattern of Charley Patton's "Pony Blues" (Paramount 12792, Example 24). Johnson's third melodic line is quite like the second line of Patton's "Magnolia Blues" (Paramount 12943) and "When Your Way Gets Dark" (Paramount 12998). But it is Johnson's guitar part that interests us the most. Several of its phrases are indeed related to ones in Mott Willis's "Riverside Blues" (Example 41), which Willis says he learned from Josie Brown. Johnson has shortened the part, however, from twelve to eleven measures and plays a duple instead of a triple rhythm. Measures 1, 2, 7, and 8 of Johnson's guitar part are simply variants of Willis's measures 1, 2, 8, and 9. Johnson's measures 4, 5, and 9 are also variants of Willis's measures 5, 6, and 10, but they are transposed an octave lower. Johnson's third measure is a variant of the figure that Charley Patton used in the fifth measure of the third pattern of his "Pony Blues" (Example 24). Measures 6 and 10 of Johnson's piece are transpositions of the figure played by Mager Johnson in the key of D in measures 7 and 11 of Examples 53 and 54. Tommy Johnson is also reputed to have played this part in the key of D. Tommy Johnson, then, in his guitar part for "Lonesome Home Blues," varied and transposed some of the phrases in Josie Brown's part and filled in the rest of the piece with phrases drawn from the Drew tradition.

Other newly introduced songs were also adapted to the Drew tradition. Charley Patton learned "Some These Days I'll Be Gone" (Paramount 13110), a song popularized by Sophie Tucker, but his guitar part consists mostly of parallel sixths played on the first and third strings, a device similar to one which he used in "Devil Sent the Rain" (Paramount 13040) and which was also used by other Drew artists. Mager Johnson performs "Catfish Blues," a song widely known among Mississippi blues singers, but in his guitar part he alludes to the subdominant chord in a figure similar to one he uses in "Bye and Bye Blues" (Example 47) and which is also used by other Drew artists. Tommy Johnson is known to have adapted several blues from records to his style in the Drew tradition. He set "Don't You Lie to Me," a blues learned from a record by Tampa Red (Bluebird B8654) or Fats Domino (Imperial 5123), to a guitar part similar to that of his own "Maggie Campbell Blues" (Victor 21409).[90] He also set Leroy Carr's "Prison Bound Blues" (Vocalion 1241) to a guitar part in the key of D quite like the one Mager Johnson plays in Examples 53–54.[91]

Several of the Drew musicians made commercial records of their own, and a few of those by Tommy Johnson and Charley Patton enjoyed moderately good sales and popularity. Nevertheless, these records seem to have had virtually no effect on other performers in the Drew tradition, so that internally the tradition remained almost purely oral-aural. The effect of the records was mainly on blues singers outside the local tradition, who learned some of these songs, sometimes as set pieces and sometimes with modifications and adaptations. Most of these singers were from Mississippi and had at one time or another met Charley Patton, Tommy Johnson, or Howlin' Wolf in person. Each Drew recording artist, however, may have been affected by his own records. If a man made a blues record that enjoyed some popularity, it was likely that people would request him to perform the same song in person. Recordings, then, may have helped to stabilize some blues cores or even some set pieces in singers' repertoires, blues which at the time of recording may have been simply spontaneous combinations of various single elements, although the evidence for this actually happening is not very conclusive. Such blues cores as "Pony Blues" and "Big Road Blues" are recalled as being already known to Drew musicians and their audiences many years before they were ever recorded.

The Learning Process in the Drew Tradition

It has been noted frequently in this chapter that musical and textual elements used by one singer are shared with other singers in the Drew tradition. We cannot always say which element was learned from which singer, but we can reconstruct in a general sense the ways in which singers learned the blues. All of the singers in this tradition probably underwent essentially the same learning process. This would have begun with the potential blues singer recognizing that there was something "in the air" and would have ended in his being able to make this air music manifest in the form of blues performances. Of course, what was in the air was largely determined by what the singer heard performed by the other blues singers around him. Probably most folk blues singers have begun by listening to other *local* blues singers.

This was certainly the case among most of those who participated in the Drew tradition. The beginning blues singer at Drew heard many combinations of lyrics, melodies, and guitar parts but hardly ever the same combination from one performance to another. At most, he might have perceived that some singers had blues cores to which they had given titles. But he also might have noticed that all of these men performed many of the same melodies, lyrics, and guitar parts, and even used some of the same blues cores. When Mott Willis first went to Drew, he noticed that the blues singers there "played some pieces alike." Maybelle Johnson, who first came to Drew in 1913 and listened to the blues there, though never learning to sing them herself, has said, "Everyone I know, they did the same thing." Her husband, LeDell Johnson, who learned blues there a few years later, said, "I never did see no difference in 'em. They was all good musicianers. Each one could play the same songs. But some could, I reckon, beat the other ones playing."[92] What these people mean when they say the Drew musicians performed some songs "alike" or "the same" is that they shared many of the same elements in their song performances—lyrics, melodies, guitar parts, and blues cores. They shared them simply because they played most of the time with or in the presence of each other and because they learned from each other and from previous blues singers in their locality.

The novice folk blues singer in a tradition like that of Drew usually learns a blues composing style, even if he thinks that he is learning individual songs from individual singers. Such was the case with Mott Willis and the Johnson brothers and probably with the men who preceded them at Drew: Charley Patton, Willie Brown, Dick Bankston, and the others. While learning to compose in this style, the singer usually assimilates each of the elements separately. He may, therefore, claim his own performances as original compositions. But if he learns a blues core, he may attribute it to another singer in the tradition. Tommy and LeDell Johnson attributed the "Pony Blues" core to Dick Bankston, although LeDell admitted that Willie Brown and Charley Patton also performed it. LeDell actually learned it from Tommy first and only later heard Bankston perform it, but Tommy had told LeDell that he had learned it from Bankston. Bankston himself, however, attributed the piece to Ben Maree, while Mott Willis, who apparently did not know Maree, considers it to be Charley Patton's song. Mager Johnson, who never knew Patton or Bankston, associates the song with his brother LeDell (Example 50), yet LeDell's wife, Maybelle, thinks of it primarily in connection with Willie Brown. Since Charley Patton was the only member of the Drew tradition to make an early commercial recording of the song (Example 24), most people outside the local tradition have associated "Pony Blues" with him. But obviously the song was common property long before Patton ever sang it into a microphone. In fact, Patton and Willie Brown used to fight with each other over the right to perform the piece, with the crowd usually siding with Brown, whom they considered to be the better musician.[93]

The novice folk blues singer, then, learns many of the lyrics, melodies, guitar parts, and blues cores, which are part of the local tradition, but he may add to them elements from outside the tradition. These he may learn from other blues singers who come into his area or whom he meets on his travels, or he may learn them from phonograph records. All of this learning is selective and determined by the appeal that each of the elements and whole songs has for the singer. No single blues singer knows or ever performs all of the elements that constitute the local tradition. Instead, each singer builds up a personal repertoire of favorite elements and songs from the local tradition and outside sources. He may be able to play other guitar parts if requested or if accompanying another singer from the local tradition, but he does not normally perform them on his own. Mager Johnson, for instance, can perform a version of his brother Tommy's "Canned Heat Blues," but he doesn't like to do so. He knows the song only because he heard Tommy perform it so often. Surviving members of the Drew tradition all agree that the blues singers at Drew could perform almost anything from each other's repertoire, although some were better performers than others. Charley Patton, for example, is said to have been able to sing falsetto like Tommy Johnson, although he never sang this way on any of his fifty extant recordings. The recorded evidence of the singers reveals instead definite personal preferences for certain elements. Tommy Johnson, for example, used the same melody in three out of ten blues recordings and sang falsetto in four others. Charley Patton used the same guitar part in open G tuning in nine of his thirty-two blues recordings. And Mott Willis and Mager Johnson each sang certain favorite lines or stanzas in many of their blues performances. All of these elements, however, were used to a lesser extent by other performers in the local tradition.

The Influence of the Drew Artists

Many of the individual verses and melodic and instrumental figures of the Drew artists are traditional over much of the South. Drew, therefore, represents a tradition within another larger blues tradition. The important fact is that the Drew performers play and sing many of the same things, while in other areas these usually occur as isolated elements. Whether these elements spread from other areas to Drew or vice versa, we cannot always say. We are too far removed in time from their origins. Even if we could speak to Charley Patton and Willie Brown, we would probably not learn the origins of the elements they employed in their blues. For Brown learned much from Patton, and Patton followed Henry Sloan. Here our trail reaches a dead end.

There would be little point in trying to cite all of the cases in which elements known in the Drew tradition are used by performers from other areas. Fahey has cited a number of elements in Charley Patton's recorded blues repertoire that are shared with the larger tradition,[94] and other examples will be given in our study of "Big Road Blues" in the next chapter. These examples can be considered typical of the Drew tradition as a whole. Although it is only an impression based on extensive listening, it would seem that variants of elements found in the Drew tradition occur most frequently in performances by other artists from the Delta and its immediately surrounding territory and that they occur less frequently among musicians who have had little or no contact with Mississippi and its blues singers. This is as we might expect in a situation where one local tradition gradually fades into a neighboring one. Among the many blues singers who share occasional elements with the Drew tradition are Delta artists Freddie Spruell, John Hurt, and Booker White, and Memphis artists Furry Lewis, Will Shade, and Tom Dickson. In no case can the similarities be attributed exclusively to phonograph records or direct personal contact. Instead they are the result of more complex processes of diffusion.

There are a good number of instances where it is possible to state that elements or songs from the Drew tradition directly influenced performances by other blues singers. The latter are musicians whose initial learning was in another local tradition but who later came under the influence of a Drew blues singer, or else they are those who learned initially from one of the Drew musicians along with several other musicians representing different traditions. In either case, one or more elements or songs from the Drew tradition have become part of their personal repertoire and may even have entered into the local tradition in which they participate.

Charley Patton had a number of disciples from outside the local tradition, and his records appear to have been even more influential.[95] One such disciple was Son House. As previously discussed, House adapted "Pony Blues" to his own style from Patton's record. House's "Special Rider Blues" also uses guitar figures that are heard in Patton's "Banty Rooster Blues" (Paramount 12792) and "Pea Vine Blues" (Paramount 12877). House's blues were much more influenced by Willie Brown, with whom he played for many years after Brown moved to Robinsonville. House's "The Jinx Blues" and "Empire State Express" use a close variant of the guitar part in open G tuning that Brown played in his "Future Blues" (Paramount 13090). House played a variant of the guitar part of Brown's "M and O Blues" (Paramount 13090) in his "Depot Blues" and "Louise McGhee" and sang a variant of Brown's melody in his "Dry Spell Blues" (Paramount 12990). House's "Walking Blues" contains the guitar part featuring a series of movable seventh chords that was played by Brown in several accompaniments to other singers and by other Drew artists, usually in the key of A in standard tuning. On "Walking Blues" House plays this part in the key of G, although he can also play it in A and E. It should be recalled that this guitar part can be transposed to any key. In view of this considerable musical influence from Brown and Patton, it is surprising how few lyrics from the Drew tradition House sings.[96]

Willie Brown also had some influence on Robert Johnson during the 1930s in Robinsonville. Johnson even sang about "my friend Willie

Brown" in his "Cross Road Blues" (ARC 7-05-81). Johnson was a very creative singer and lyricist, and most of Brown's influence was on his guitar playing. Brown, in fact, did little singing around Robinsonville, preferring instead to accompany Son House. Johnson played a rather distant variant of the guitar part featuring movable seventh chords in the key of A on seven blues: "Kind Hearted Woman Blues" (ARC 7-03-56), "Phonograph Blues" (ARC unissued), "32-20 Blues" (ARC 7-04-60), "Dead Shrimp Blues" (ARC 7-04-81), "Little Queen of Spades" (Vocalion 04108), "Me and the Devil Blues" (Vocalion 04108), and "Honeymoon Blues" (Vocalion 04002). On "Malted Milk" (ARC 7-10-65) and "Drunken Hearted Man" (ARC unissued) he played a variant of the guitar part in the key of D in EBGDAD tuning, which Mager Johnson played in Examples 53–54.[97] Mager Johnson probably learned this guitar part from his brother Tommy, who is reputed to have played it, and Tommy and Robert Johnson both probably learned it at different times from Willie Brown. Robert Johnson's playing also shows some influence of a guitar part used on many blues records by Lonnie Johnson. Interestingly, Mager Johnson claims that Lonnie Johnson was a relative on his father's side, while Robert Johnson's death certificate reveals that he was a native of Hazlehurst, a town only ten miles south of Crystal Springs, the home of Mager and Tommy Johnson. Robert Johnson is also said to have told his audiences that he was a brother of Lonnie Johnson.[98] The relationships between the blues played by all of the Johnsons may thus be rather complex. Robert Johnson and his records had a considerable influence on other blues singers from Mississippi and Arkansas, and his songs can be found in the repertoires of such performers as Muddy Waters, Robert Lockwood, Elmore James, Houston Stackhouse, and Johnny Shines.

Woodrow Adams at Robinsonville never played with Son House or Willie Brown, but he was influenced by the blues of Howlin' Wolf in the 1940s. In his "Pretty Baby Blues" (Checker 757) Adams uses a similar melody and guitar part to those heard in Howlin' Wolf's "I Asked for Water" (Example 56). Adams has also used this guitar part in field recorded blues, including a version of "Pony Blues."[99]

Tommy Johnson was by far the most influential of the Drew blues singers. The handling of one of his blues cores (Example 55) by other singers has already been discussed, and further examples will be printed in the next chapter.[100] Some blues singers, however, have shown a tendency to recombine smaller elements learned from Johnson to form new compositions. One performer who has done this is Roosevelt Holts from Tylertown, Mississippi, a cousin of one of Johnson's wives, Rosa Youngblood. When Johnson married her around 1935, they moved to Tylertown and stayed in the area about two years. Holts learned several blues cores and smaller elements from Johnson when he and Rosa lived in Tylertown and during the next year in Jackson where Holts moved with them. Holts's "Sundown Blues," printed below, is a combination of several elements learned from Johnson, which Holts put together in 1969. The melody is very similar to that of Johnson's "Lonesome Home Blues" (Paramount 13000, Example 57), while measures 1–3, 5–6, 8–9, and 12 of Holts's guitar part are also found in variant form in Johnson's piece. Measures 7 and 11 of Holts's guitar part are found in variant form in Johnson's "Slidin' Delta" (Paramount 12975) and measures 4 and 10 in Johnson's "Bye-Bye Blues." Close variants of stanzas 2 and 4 of Holts's text are found in Johnson's "Big Fat Mama Blues" (Victor V38535, Example 55) and "Cool Drink of Water Blues" (Victor 21279, Example 20). Variants of the first two lines of stanza 1 are found in Willie Brown's "Future Blues" (Paramount 13090), and a variant of stanza 5 is found in Charley Patton's "Poor Me" (Vocalion 02651). Holts's piece is unusual for the slight deceleration of tempo. His text is also interesting for its use of contrast. In the first two stanzas images of a "little bitty woman" and a "big fat mama" are contrasted. Then the singer changes the subject, stating that he has done everything he could to make his relationship with his woman work, and follows this with a contrastive statement that he has been trying to leave by any means possible, including hoboing ("riding the blinds"). Finally, he presents an image of his woman leaving him.

Example 58. "Sundown Blues." Roosevelt Holts, vocal and guitar in standard tuning, key of E. Bogalusa, La., Apr. 2, 1969. Recorded by David Evans. Issued on *Big Road Blues*, Advent 2815, 12" LP.

GUITAR CHORUS.

1. *Aah, little bitty woman right down on the ground.*
   Yeah, little bitty woman right down on the ground.
   Yeah, sometimes she think she's too doggone cute to die.

2. *Crying, big fat mama, meat quivering on her bones.*
   Yeah, big fat mama, meat quivering on her bones.
   Says, every time she quiver, fat mouth leaving home.

3. *Well, I rolled and I tumbled, trying to get along with you.*
   Crying, I rolled and I tumbled, trying to get along with you.
   Well, I done done everything that a poor old man can do.

4. *Crying, went to the depot. "Please let me ride the blinds."*
   Says, I asked the depot agent, "Please let me ride your blinds."
   "Well, you got to buy you a ticket, 'cause the train ain't none of mine."

5. *Well, don't the sun look lonesome shining down through the trees?*
   Well, the sun look lonesome shining down through the trees.
   Don't your baby look lonesome packing up her trunk to leave?

Immediately after Holts performed this piece, I recorded the following interview:

Evans: *You learned that from Tommy?*
Holts: *Yeah. That's his famous big blues.*
Evans: *Did he have a name for that?*
Holts: *No, but you can play it, I'll say, the "Sundown Blues."*
Name it something like that. "Don't the sun look lonesome shining down through the trees?" Well, you can say "Sundown Blues."

Holts was not recreating a core or a set piece by Johnson, since he claimed that Johnson did not have a name for this song. Obviously then, Holts combined various elements that he had learned separately from Johnson with the result that he created a new, yet familiar, blues. One year later Holts recorded virtually the same guitar part with a different melody, one that he uses in some of his other blues. Except for the last stanza, the text of this later recording consists of a completely different set of traditional verses.[101] It is clear, then, that these blues were composed from separate melodic, lyric, and instrumental elements in Holts's repertoire.

We have already seen that Willis Taylor is similarly able to combine elements from the Drew tradition (Examples 38–39) learned from such performers as his uncle Mott Willis, the Johnson brothers (his second cousins), and Charley Patton. Most of Taylor's blues, however, show no relation to the Drew tradition. His brother Charlie Taylor is similarly outside the mainstream of the Drew tradition, although he can perform an occasional blues drawn from it. The following piece is such a blues. Taylor's guitar playing consists of little more than the

strumming of chords, as is the case in most of his accompaniments, while his uncle plays guitar in the bottleneck style. Taylor's melody, however, and his first stanza are found in very similar form in Tommy Johnson's "Maggie Campbell Blues" (Victor 21409). His second stanza was sung in various blues by Mager Johnson and Mott Willis (Examples 40, 51–52), while his third stanza was used by Tommy Johnson in "Bye-Bye Blues" (Victor 21409). Taylor's final stanza consists of lines that he uses as a personal signature in many blues. These lines are not found in the repertoires of other artists in the Drew tradition. This piece, then, is a composite of personalized elements and elements from the Drew tradition.

Example 59. "Who's That Yonder?" Charlie Taylor, vocal and guitar in standard tuning, key of G; Mott Willis, guitar in open G tuning. Crystal Springs, Miss., Aug. 16, 1973. Recorded by David and Cheryl Evans.

GUITAR CHORUS.

1. *Aah, who's that yonder, baby, coming down the road?*
   Aah, who's that yonder now, baby, coming down the road?
   Aah, she walks like my baby now; swear she walks too slow.

2. *Oh, I'm a traveling man now, sure got a traveling mind.*
   Now I'm a traveling man now. Poor me sure got a traveling mind.
   I'm gonna buy me a ticket, darling. I'm gonna ease on down the line.

3. *Now the Good Book'll tell you, got to reap just what you sow.*
   Oh, the Good Book'll tell you, you got to reap just what you sow.
   Now if you don't reap it now, baby now, you going to reap it now, baby,
       bye and bye.
   Spoken: *Look out, Jimmy kid, now. Look out. . . . (?)*

4. *Oh, cried this morning. Babe, I sure ain't gonna cry no more.*
   I'm gonna quit my ways. I'm gonna even move on even out of town.

In some cases it is not possible to trace exact links between a member of the Drew tradition and a singer outside the tradition, although we know that such links must have been present. For instance, a singer named Otto Virgial recorded "Bad Notion Blues" (Bluebird B6213) in 1935, using a melody heard in several of Charley Patton's blues. Four of Virgial's six stanzas are sung by various Drew singers (Patton sings three). Virgial's guitar part, however, is unlike that used by any Drew musician. All four of Virgial's recorded guitar parts are strongly percussive and betray a connection with the blues of the hill country east of Drew. Big Joe Williams, who recorded at the same session as Virgial, has stated that Virgial came from Columbus, Mississippi, near the Alabama border, a fact which would be consistent with his style of guitar playing.[102] Virgial recorded two other blues called "Little Girl in Rome" (Bluebird B6213) and "Got the Blues about Rome" (Bluebird B6279). In the latter he sang, "Got the blues about Rome, but Rome is not my home." There is a town of Rome about twelve miles north of Drew. People there told me in 1969 that Otto Virgial had lived in Rome for some years but had moved around 1960 to a place further south, somewhere near Belzoni or Yazoo City. From these clues it would appear that Virgial had come to Rome from somewhere further east before 1935 and had been influenced by one of the nearby Drew musicians. Possibly he could not adapt to the Drew style of guitar playing and was able to learn only a melody and some lyrics; or perhaps he simply preferred his own style of guitar playing and decided to incorporate other elements from the Drew tradition into his own repertoire. Other blues singers whose relationships to the Drew tradition remain unclear are Floyd Jones, Mattie Delaney, and J. D. Short. Their songs will be discussed in the next chapter.

It can be seen from the preceding discussion and examples (58–59) that a number of different things can happen as songs and elements from a local tradition become diffused elsewhere. There is no way of predicting the results. Different musicians who learned from Tommy Johnson, for instance, do different things with his songs. Roosevelt Holts performs a number of Johnson's blues cores to which he usually adds the same group of stanzas in every performance, but he has also created "Sundown Blues" (Example 58) from separate elements in Johnson's repertoire. The majority of Holts's other blues performances, however, are unique combinations of elements from his own repertoire (see Example 27). This repertoire is mostly a collection of musical and lyrical ideas that Holts learned in his native Tylertown and in Jackson in the 1930s from various blues singers, including Tommy Johnson. Holts, then, is not in the mainstream of the Drew tradition, but his repertoire has been influenced by it. His contact with the tradition is Tommy Johnson, and he has selectively incorporated elements from it into his own repertoire.

There may be several reasons why the Drew tradition exerted considerable influence on other blues singers, more influence than most other local traditions have had. One reason is the fact that Drew is located in the heart of the Delta and was, until fairly recently, constantly attracting newcomers to its cotton fields, including many musicians who would subsequently leave and carry off songs and ideas with them. Drew could thus be considered a musical crossroads. But many other Delta towns were like Drew, and yet the influence of their local blues traditions was not nearly as profound. Probably the history of intense racial violence at Drew caused its tradition to spread more than was usual even in the Delta. Most of the important blues singers had left there by 1930. Another very important factor was the dynamic personalities of men such as Charley Patton and Tommy Johnson, spectacular musicians both to see and hear. Even long after their deaths they are well remembered by fellow musicians and members of their audiences alike. The prestige of these men must also have been increased by their having made early commercial recordings. There may also have been factors within the Drew tradition itself which aided its diffusion. Several of its most popular melodies are highly distinctive and memorable tunes, which tend to stand out from the folk blues tradition as a whole. The instrumental style of the Drew musicians is also very complex and sophisticated and must have had special appeal for guitar players. It features movable and transposed guitar parts, which offer great opportunity for flexibility and creativity. Blues from the Drew tradition also contain clearly differentiated guitar and vocal lines, in contrast to most other folk blues styles, where the guitar either plays the same notes as the vocal melody or plays chords or simple rhythmic patterns behind the vocal. The Drew musicians must have considered other styles to be crude by comparison.

The Place of the Local Tradition in Folk Blues

In this and the previous chapter I have tried to show how folk blues are composed, what elements they consist of, where they come from, and how singers and songs are related to each other to form a tradition. Since these subjects can sometimes be bewilderingly complex, it will be useful at this point to recapitulate some of the general conclusions which have been reached.

If someone were to look upon the body of folk blues as a collection of songs and attempt to put it in order, he would probably become quite frustrated. Texts would appear inconsistent in their meaning, and the songs would not fall into neat groupings and types. Indeed, frustration and exasperation have been bywords in most attempts to classify and categorize folk blues. But if, instead, one views blues as *performances* generated by *performers,* a different picture emerges.

The individual blues singer should be viewed as the first level of the folk blues tradition. He has a repertoire comprised of lyric lines and stanzas, melodies, and instrumental parts, which he can combine in a number of different ways in order to produce blues performances. Some combinations of these elements recur in performances as blues cores, usually groups consisting of an instrumental part, a melody, and one or two lyric stanzas. Finally, there may be some complete songs in a performer's blues repertoire which recur in virtually the same form in every performance.

The blues performer shares many of these elements and combinations with other performers in his locality with whom he makes music. The blues of these performers can be viewed as products of a local tradition. This is the second level of the folk blues tradition. Of course, each local tradition shows considerable overlap with other neighboring local traditions, so that there may be somewhat vaguely defined broader regions of tradition, such as the Delta, Mississippi, Texas, the East Coast, the Carolina Piedmont, and so forth. These broad regions represent the third level of the folk blues tradition. The fourth and final level is the folk blues tradition as a whole, consisting of a number of these broad regional traditions, many local traditions, and countless individual blues singers. These four levels simply reflect the levels of contact between blues singers. One finds greater variety in the blues at each successive level.

I realize that this model of four levels inevitably distorts our view of a tradition which involves individual creativity as well as acceptance, rejection, and reinterpretation of particular elements and songs from other singers. Yet I believe that the present chapter has shown that this model can be a useful one for analyzing a tradition or an aspect thereof, which may appear hopelessly confusing at first. It should be clear, however, that every level of the tradition is crosscut by the influence of popular blues phonograph records as well as by the influence of individual performers, who can and do spread their blues anywhere. Indeed, a major part of the Drew blues tradition itself was transplanted to Crystal Springs, 160 miles away, where its main representatives are to be found today. Some of these crosscutting factors will be considered in the next chapter in our study of "Big Road Blues," a song which originated within the Drew tradition but which was diffused far beyond it. It is my hope, therefore, that this model of a tradition with four levels will not be considered by others as an end in itself, but will instead lead to an increased understanding and appreciation of a dynamic blues tradition and to a greater feeling for the music and the people who make it.

I have already pointed out that many musicians in other localities besides Drew compose blues using the same processes as Mott Willis, Charley Patton, the Johnson brothers, and others in the Drew tradition. I have also pointed out that many blues singers are highly creative and individualistic and show little influence from their local traditions, while other singers show roughly equal degrees of individuality and indebtedness to tradition. But the question may arise as to whether there are other local traditions comparable to that of Drew, or whether I have described here a curiously isolated phenomenon. The answer is that there are other local blues traditions, but they do not all work the same way as the Drew tradition. It must always be kept in mind that the Drew tradition was remarkably free of commercial influences and values, in spite of the fact that it is well documented on commercial recordings. It is doubtful whether any other local tradition has been equally well documented.

It is not easy to find a largely oral blues tradition today after more than fifty years of commercial recordings and influences. However, it can be done if the researcher is willing to venture into some of the more isolated regions of the rural South as well as to follow leads that may carry him all over the country. Around Bentonia and Satartia, Mississippi, for example, I have found a local blues tradition, which exhibits most of the same general characteristics and processes as the Drew tradition but which has different elements.[103] In dealing with the local blues tradition of Tylertown, Mississippi one would have to take into account such factors as the enormous outside influence there of Tommy Johnson in the 1930s and the importance of string band music and other instruments besides the guitar.[104] Another quite different local tradition exists around Como and Senatobia, Mississippi. There one would have to consider the closeness of the blues to field hollers and the subordination of most other instruments to the drums. The blues there are not so well defined as a separate musical genre, so that one would have to investigate the entire local musical tradition rather than simply the blues tradition.[105] In the Carolinas many of the local manifestations of the blues tradition have been obliterated or modified by the great influence, both in person and through commercial records, of a number of highly mobile professional folk blues singers like Blind Boy Fuller, Buddy Moss, Josh White, Brownie McGhee, and Sonny Terry.[106] Similarly, in the study of blues traditions where the piano is an important instrument, one must take into account the extraordinary mobility and greater sense of professionalism and sophistication of most blues piano players.[107] Finally, one might choose to view the blues in some of the urban centers as products of local traditions, but one would have to consider the fact that the cities have always attracted musicians from the surrounding rural areas and from further away, whose blues are representative of many different local traditions, and that the urban environment tends to promote a greater sense of individualism and professionalism in the blues singers.[108] There are thus many factors to be considered in the study of local and regional blues traditions and the relationship of the individual performer to them. If we keep all these factors in mind, we can achieve a greater understanding and appreciation of individual folk blues performances.

THE TRADITIONAL BLUES SONG

Blues and the Comparative Study of Folksongs

I N the previous chapter we established a model of the folk blues tradition with four levels: the individual repertoire, the local tradition, the regional tradition, and the folk blues tradition as a whole. For convenience we might view these as four concentric circles, the smallest one representing the individual repertoire and each successive circle representing a larger segment of the tradition. The workings of this model prescribe ideally that blues elements and songs diffuse gradually outward from the individual performer through successively larger circles and conversely that elements and songs reach the individual performer from the outside through successively smaller circles. Several songs cited in the last chapter have exemplified various steps in this diffusionary process. Yet we have also noted that two or more levels or circles can be traversed easily by a single influential blues singer, either through his travels or through phonograph records. There is nothing, for example, to prevent a song or element developed by a singer in North Carolina from spreading directly to another singer in Mississippi through personal contact or through a record. Therefore, in order to understand fully the workings of the folk blues tradition, we must take into account the effect of such influential performers. One way to do this is to study how a blues song with a known composer was spread in the overall blues tradition as a result of the influence of its composer. A comparative study of the variants resulting from the diffusion of such a song can help us to understand better the processes of the blues tradition that are not fully explained by the study of individual repertoires and local and regional traditions.

The comparative approach has long been used in the study of narrative folksongs. Its aims have been stated succinctly by W. Edson Richmond as "(1) to establish lines of development, (2) to show how each text is related to every other text, and (3) to suggest what the major and early form or forms of any particular ballad must have been."[1] Richmond adds that the approach "proceeds from the basic assumption that there was once an ur-text, a basic form, whence all known texts have descended,"[2] and that "to the comparativist it is the song rather than the singer that has importance."[3] Using the comparative method, folklorists over the years have achieved an impressive list of findings concerning the origins and dissemination of a number of individual ballads.[4]

Richmond's summary of the aims and assumptions of the comparative approach to ballad study is applicable to the study of most other forms of folklore, and, in fact, many studies of prose narratives, riddles, proverbs, games, and items from other genres have been carried out using a comparative method.[5] There has, however, been little comparative study of nonnarrative folksongs.[6] Blues have been especially neglected by scholars interested in this approach. The reasons for this neglect are not difficult to detect. For one thing, blues lack the unifying story line of ballads, and, as we have noted, a great many folk blues lack even a thematic unity. The very diffuseness of their texts has discouraged comparative scholarship. Furthermore, there are virtually no indices of blues lyrics, musical parts, or song titles, such as exist for the comparative study of ballads and prose narratives. In fact, indices of blues lyrics and musical parts would be extremely difficult to compile, while song titles often give little indication of a blues's content or relationship to other blues. Yet problems even more serious than these confront the comparativist interested in folk blues. As our findings in the previous two chapters have indicated, the very concept of an *Urtext* is inapplicable to the majority of folk blues. Except for those pieces which are stable in a performer's repertoire, most folk blues are either totally improvised at the time of performance from original or traditional elements or are constructed by adding verses to a blues core. With such songs, therefore, the comparativist can at best hope only to study the diffusion and life history of a single verse or stanza, melody, instrumental part or figure, or blues core. And in order to carry out such a study, he must pay particular attention to the lives and repertoires of the performers. Even ballad scholars have come to recognize the usefulness for comparative research of studying the singers, but for the comparative study of blues it is absolutely essential.

There has been only one comparative study of a blues that attempts to be comprehensive. This is Paul Oliver's fine piece of research on "The Forty-Fours" and the related "Rollin' and Tumblin' " complex.[7] The "Forty-Fours" is essentially a group of associated instrumental figures, usually played on the piano, which have attracted to themselves two melodies and several lyric themes. Its component elements are traditional, and the originators of many of them are unknown, but versions of the piece have been recorded commercially many times and the piece tends to be associated with its three most prominent and earliest recorded performers. Although his study leaves several admittedly unanswered and perhaps unanswerable questions about this musical and lyric complex, Oliver concludes,

> The Forty-Fours, *at any rate, demonstrates the complex family-tree of the blues. Its basic instrumental theme provides the groundwork for two major vocal tunes and a number of subsidiary ones; the instrumental theme itself is also subject to many variations. The blues shows the degree to which a singer's individual style may influence the way in which a tune is interpreted by others; it exemplifies the passing on of traditional verses and lines, the dropping of some and the grafting of others in the process of evolution. The association of certain verses only hinted at by a line, or non-existent in the earliest recordings, with a blues suggests the importance of personal transmission; the copying of verses or even the whole blues likewise emphasizes the importance of transmission by recordings.*[8]

Oliver has made other useful, but less extensive, comparative studies of four off-color blues types, "Sweet Patunia," "Shave 'Em Dry," "Dirty Mother Fuyer," and "The Dirty Dozens,"[9] and has compared four versions of the very old folk blues, "Poor Boy Long Ways from Home."[10] Bob Groom has also done an admirable job of bringing together the many recordings, mostly commercial, of "Kokomo Blues" and its subsidiary and derivative forms such as "Sweet Home Chicago," but his brief study is more in the nature of an outline than a thorough exposition of the subject.[11] Elsewhere I have outlined the materials that could be used for the comparative study of several folk blues.[12] Further comparisons, most of them sketchy, incomplete, or impressionistic, have been made by many blues writers in record album notes and in articles in specialist magazines. In most cases the authors simply cite the titles and release numbers of the blues being compared with the assumption that the reader will obtain and listen to copies of the performances. The reasons for such comparisons are usually to indicate sources or parallel versions of a particular performance under discussion (as in album notes) or to suggest possible contact or influences between two or more performers on the basis of such similarities, rather than to study the life history of a particular blues type for its own sake or for a greater understanding of the processes of transmission. Nevertheless, it is to be hoped that a number of these sketchy comparisons, outlines, and incomplete introductory studies will be expanded into comprehensive studies of important and well-known blues types. It would be especially useful to study some blues with strong thematic unity as they persist and undergo change in transmission. There are also several traditional nonthematic blues types that would well repay comparative study, such as "Catfish Blues," performed mostly by Mississippi singers, and "Red River Blues," known throughout the folk blues tradition (see Example 26). Almost all of the widespread blues types began to develop only after the advent of phonograph records, so that the earliest versions are commercially recorded ones. These have often influenced some or all of the later versions. A few types, however, like "Poor Boy Long Ways from Home," "Baby, Take a Whiff on Me," and "See See Rider," were first documented in early printed sources, while "Hesitation Blues" made its debut in sheet music. These types too are worthy of further comparative study.[13]

"Big Road Blues" is like most other widespread folk blues types in the fact that it was first documented in a commercial recording. Records have continued to play an important role in the song's history and development, but it has also enjoyed an active life in purely oral tradition, and most versions can not be explained solely by the influence of phonograph records. Such factors as personal influence, approaches to blues composition, individual repertoires, and local traditions have had an important effect on "Big Road Blues." The study of this blues type will, like Oliver's study, leave some unanswered questions, but it will help to demonstrate the importance of the above factors in the growth of a blues type and their relationship to phonograph records. The following study differs from Oliver's, however, because it is a study of a distinct blues core and because it is based largely on field recorded versions, whereas Oliver's was based mainly on commercial records.

D. K. Wilgus has stated that for the comparative study of lyric folksongs "the first step is to select the identifying element in the song, which may be melodic or textual, and thus to limit the material."[14] In the study of "Big Road Blues," therefore, our attention will be concentrated on the song's core, which consists of a single stanza, an internal refrain, a melody, and a guitar part (see Example 60). This core is our "identifying element." It shows an ability to persist in tradition with only minor variations in its component elements, whereas the stanzas that are added by different singers to this core show great variation. We must be aware, however, that our decision to concentrate on this identifying element, which does not constitute a complete song performance, is to a certain extent arbitrary and poses a danger of rejecting other blues performances which might provide insights into the origins and development of the pieces that we choose to study. In order to minimize this danger, we shall survey in some depth the elements that have contributed to this core as well as blues which have drawn elements from it. We shall also examine the place of various performances in individual repertoires, local and regional blues traditions, the blues tradition as a whole, and the corpus of commercial blues recordings.

Tommy Johnson and "Big Road Blues"

There have been a few previous attempts to study the versions of "Big Road Blues." All of them have recognized that the song was first documented in a 1928 commercial recording of that title by Tommy Johnson (Victor 21279, Example 60). Simon Napier, in a survey of Johnson's influence in the blues tradition, listed most of the recorded versions of the song up to 1966 and stressed the importance of the related "Stop and Listen Blues" (Okeh 8807, Example 70) by the Mississippi Sheiks.[15] Two years later Paul Oliver made a superficial attempt at textual and musical comparison of a few versions, but his ignorance of the piece by the Mississippi Sheiks led him to several false conjectures.[16] My own survey of the materials in 1971 in *Tommy Johnson* could be considered a prospectus for the present more detailed study, although I have supplemented it with some new examples.[17]

There can be little doubt that Tommy Johnson was the man who first conceived of the "Big Road Blues" core. Mott Willis, Mager Johnson, and almost all other performers claim to have learned the song from him, and his was the earliest recording. It was also Tommy Johnson's favorite piece and the one best liked by his audiences.[18] The comparative study of versions by many singers will indicate strongly that "Big Road Blues" existed in Johnson's repertoire as a blues core, to which he added different stanzas at each performance, rather than as a stable song. Johnson was probably the first performer to construct this core, but its elements already existed separately in the folk blues tradition and particularly in the local tradition of the Drew area. Through his travels, his record, and his personal influence on many other blues singers, Johnson spread this blues core far beyond the Drew tradition.

Our first step in this song study is to print and discuss Tommy Johnson's 1928 recording of the piece, his only extant version. Then we shall note its place in the folk blues tradition as a whole, the Mississippi regional tradition, and particularly the local Drew tradition. Performances by Mott Willis and Mager Johnson will be used to illustrate how Tommy Johnson probably handled the song in various performances. Next we shall list and discuss the later commercial recordings of this and related pieces and their influence. Finally we shall discuss the remaining documentary and field recorded versions of the song and the effects that Johnson's personal influence and various phonograph records have had upon them.

Tommy Johnson's version of the song is printed below.[19] The first stanza with its accompaniment constitutes the song's core. Johnson's guitar part is somewhat difficult to transcribe because of the second guitar part played by Charlie McCoy, which often varies only slightly from Johnson's. A variant melody is sung for the first two lines and refrain of stanza 3. Johnson's final line of stanza 6 switches to the falsetto that he used in "Cool Drink of Water Blues" (Example 20), the piece on the other side of his record of "Big Road Blues."

Example 60. "Big Road Blues." Tommy Johnson, vocal and guitar in EBGDAD tuning, key of D; Charlie McCoy, guitar. Memphis, Feb. 3, 1928. Victor 21279, reissued on *Blues Roots/Mississippi*, RBF 14, 12" LP.

GUITAR CHORUS.

1. *Crying, ain't going down this big road by myself.*
       Now don't you hear me talking, pretty mama? [refrain]
   Lord, ain't going down this big road by myself.
   If I don't carry you, gon' carry somebody else.

2. *Crying, sun gonna shine in my back door someday.*
       Now don't you hear me talking, pretty mama?
   Lord, sun gon' shine in my back door someday.
   And the wind gon' change, gon' blow my blues away.

3. *Baby, what makes you do me like you do do do, like you do do do?*
       Don't you hear me now?
   What makes you do me like you do do do?
   Now you think you gon' do me like you done poor Cherry Red.

4. *Taken the poor boy's money now; sure, Lord, won't take mine.*
       Now don't you hear me talking, pretty mama?
   Taken the poor boy's money; sure, Lord, won't take mine.
   Taken the poor boy's money now; sure, Lord, won't take mine.

5. *Crying, ain't going down this big road by myself.*

Now don't you hear me talking, pretty mama?
Lord, ain't going down this big road by myself.
If I don't carry you, gon' carry somebody else.

6. *Crying, sun gon' shine, Lord, my back door someday.*
    Now don't you hear me talking, pretty mama?
    Lord, sun gon' shine in my back door someday.
    And the wind gon' change, blow my blues away.

Like most traditional blues cores, "Big Road Blues" is distinctive both in its lyric imagery and in its music. It is also rather unusual in having an internal refrain after the first line. This particular combination of elements stands out from the more ordinary traditional blues elements so that this blues core remains memorable and instantly recognizable. Johnson's text as a whole is nonthematic, but it is held together in loose association as the singer asserts his determination to overcome various problems. Although the core stanza is traditional, Johnson claimed that it referred to a real experience. According to his friend and musical partner Ishmon Bracey, "He was at a supper once, and his girlfriend wouldn't let him take her home. And he told her, well, he'd get somebody else. He wasn't going down that big road by hisself. When he got him another girl, he made a song of it."[20] The story may be true, but quite likely Johnson had more than some country road in mind and the stanza is an assertion about his whole lifestyle. This suspicion is strengthened by the cosmic imagery of the second stanza. The third and fourth stanzas appear to be linked thematically and deal with a more specific problem. The identity of "poor Cherry Red" in stanza 3 is unknown. Johnson's two final stanzas repeat the two opening stanzas. He may have employed repetition for emphasis or unconsciously in order to achieve a structural balance in his text, but it is also possible that he had simply run out of verses after the fourth stanza yet had to keep singing in order to complete the record. Johnson did the same thing on several of his other records (cf. Example 55). In person he was known for singing short songs.

Through the first line and the refrain the melody constantly climbs from the major sixth (B) to the tonic note above (D), while in the second and third lines it gradually reaches a state of repose an octave lower. The feeling of climbing is resumed in the last line of the song with the falsetto leaps in the melody. The song's final note manages to reach the high tonic, providing a great sense of relief. The feeling of climbing is also found in the guitar part with its ascending bass pattern behind the first vocal line and refrain (measures 1–4), which leads from the tonic up to the major third. This is followed by a suggestion of the IV chord in the second line (measures 5–6). The musical feeling of climbing correlates perfectly with the overall sense of the text, which expresses a determination to rise above problems. At the end of the second and third line (measures 7–8, 11–12) there occurs a guitar figure that alternates between the major and minor third, expressing strongly the ambiguity of the blue note usually found at that pitch. Johnson's conception of this song, then, even if he did not work it out consciously, is magnificent, and his performance is of a standard to match it. The singing is impassioned throughout and the instrumental work faultless. Additional excitement is provided by the emphatic refrain, the rather rapid tempo, and Charlie McCoy's splendid second guitar work, which becomes more complex and improvisational as the piece moves along. The rhythm of the singing and guitar playing drives relentlessly forward, often with a slight suggestion of triplets. This piece, then, must be considered one of the finest folk blues ever recorded.

Traditional Elements in Tommy Johnson's "Big Road Blues"

All of the elements in Johnson's "Big Road Blues" appear to be traditional. The intensifying refrain is probably derived ultimately from unaccompanied solo or quartet blues singing, where it would have served to fill in the space at the end of the first line. Johnson's opening stanza was widely used in other blues that contain none of the other elements of his "Big Road Blues." Among the many pieces containing this stanza are Garfield Akers's 1930 recording of "Jumpin' and Shoutin' Blues" (Vocalion 1481), Arthur "Big Boy" Crudup's 1945 "Dirt Road Blues" (RCA Victor 20-2757), Big Maceo's 1945 "Big Road Blues" (RCA Victor 20-1870), and John Lee Hooker's 1960 "Dusty Road" (Vee Jay 366). Johnson's second stanza is also widespread in the blues tradition. The first line of his third stanza is drawn from a popular song of 1924, "How Come You Do Me Like You Do?," composed by Gene Austin and Roy Bergere. Tommy Johnson is said to have performed this song with guitar accompaniment in the key of C in standard tuning, using ragtime figures. Mager Johnson still performs the piece. Tommy Johnson's third and fourth stanzas are like a stanza of a work song collected in Georgia, printed by Howard W. Odum in 1911:

Well, you can't do me like you do po' Shine.
You take Shine's money, but you can't take mine.[21]

Melodic phrases similar to ones sung by Johnson are found in Jack Kelly's 1933 "Red Ripe Tomatoes" (Banner 32844). Kelly was a Memphis resident. The bass figure in the first line of Johnson's guitar part (measures 1–4) is heard also in Big Bill Broonzy's versions of "Joe Turner Blues" (Vogue 131; Folkways FA 2326; Folkways FG 3586; Verve MGV 3001). Broonzy was originally from Scott, Mississippi, in the Delta, and he claimed that this was one of the earliest blues he knew, dating it before the turn of the century.[22] Broonzy's guitar is in open D tuning (DAF#DAD). Furry Lewis, a Memphis singer born and raised in the Delta at Greenwood, also uses the same bass figure in "Creeper's Blues" (Vocalion 1457), "I Will Turn Your Money Green" (Prestige/Bluesville BVLP 1037), "Shake 'Em On Down" (Prestige/Bluesville BVLP 1036), and "White Lightnin'" (Prestige/Bluesville BVLP 1036). Lewis's guitar is played in the key of E in EBGEAE tuning. Tommy McClennan, also from Greenwood, played the figure in the same key and tuning as Tommy Johnson (EBGDAD, key of D) in his "New 'Shake 'Em On Down'" (Bluebird B8347). In all three tunings the fourth and sixth strings are tuned an octave apart, and it is on these two strings that the ascending bass figure is played. Others who play guitar figures like some of those in "Big Road Blues" are Blind Boy Fuller from North Carolina in "Been Your Dog" (ARC 7-10-56) and "Crooked Woman Blues" (Vocalion 05527) and Tom Dickson from the Memphis area in "Happy Blues" (Okeh 8590).

Elements from "Big Road Blues" are especially common in the blues of the Drew musicians. Versions of the song itself are performed by Mott Willis and Mager Johnson. These will be discussed later. A variant of Tommy Johnson's first stanza was sung by Charley Patton in "Down the Dirt Road Blues" (Paramount 12854). Mager Johnson sang a variant of the second stanza in one of his versions of "Traveling Blues." Mager also sang a variant of the first line of the third stanza in Examples 49 and 52. The initial melodic phrases in each line of Tommy Johnson's performance are similar to those of Willis Taylor's "The Trashy Gang Blues" (Example 39), a melody also sung by Mott Willis. "Big Road Blues" has some melodic similarities to Examples 40 and 42–44 by Mott Willis and to Examples 53–54 by Mager Johnson. Examples 42–44 and 53–54 also have some similarities to "Big Road Blues" in their guitar parts. Guitar parts in the key of D are heard only on the records of Drew artists who were natives of Crystal Springs. Charley Patton, Willie Brown, Kid Bailey, and Howlin' Wolf did not play in this key on their extant records. We noted earlier, however, that Robert Johnson of Robinsonville, Mississippi, recorded two blues in this key and tuning with an accompaniment that was probably learned from Willie Brown. The other Robert Johnson from the Drew area said in 1967 that he and other local musicians had played in this tuning, and Jake Martin said that he, Willie Brown, and Charley Patton also played a guitar part similar to that of "Big Road Blues." Mott Willis, too, says that Brown and Patton played this guitar part. Maybelle Johnson claimed that Willie and Josie Brown were both playing the guitar part at Drew as early as 1914, and her guess was that Tommy Johnson learned it from them. She said that they "played it all the time" and that Josie was better than Willie. Maybelle Johnson's husband, LeDell, admitted that his brother Tommy didn't begin playing the piece until he returned from his first trip to the Delta, but he believed that Tommy invented it himself and "learnt them on his own self."[23] The ascending bass figure in measures 1–4 is, in fact, similar in conception to the descending bass figure in open G tuning played by Mott Willis (Examples 36–37), Willie Brown ("Future Blues," Paramount 13090), and Tommy Johnson ("Maggie Campbell Blues," Victor 21409). Both figures are played in parallel octaves on the fourth and sixth strings, which are tuned an octave apart.

Two pieces recorded by Howlin' Wolf, "Crying at Daybreak" (RPM 340) and "Smoke Stack Lightning" (Chess 1618), use the melody of the first line and refrain of "Big Road Blues." They also contain a falsetto moaning line and a guitar part found in variant form in Tommy Johnson's "Cool Drink of Water Blues" (Victor 21279, Example 20) as well as lyrics sung by Johnson and other Drew artists in various blues. Stanza 3 of "Crying at Daybreak" is printed below as a typical stanza, although there are slight variations from one stanza to another, particularly in the guitar playing. The first two stanzas lack the refrain. It is not certain whether the guitar is played by Howlin' Wolf or by Willie Johnson, but if it is by Johnson, it was almost certainly learned from Howlin' Wolf. It is quite similar to the part heard on Howlin' Wolf's "I Asked for Water" (Chess 1632, Example 56). In some stanzas the guitarist plays a figure similar to one found in Mager Johnson's "Catfish Blues." A variant of stanza 6 was sung in Kid Bailey's "Rowdy Blues" (Brunswick 7114) and in Mager Johnson's Example 54. The lyrics of stanzas 2–4 appear to be derived from the Mississippi Sheiks' "Stop and Listen Blues" (Okeh 8807, Example 70), recorded in February, 1930, which is itself based on "Big Road Blues." Howlin' Wolf was a great admirer of the music of the Mississippi Sheiks and probably had heard their record.[24] A variant of his stanza 3, however, was also sung by Charley Patton in "Moon Going Down" (Paramount 13014), recorded in May, 1930. Tommy Johnson is also said by Bubba Brown to have performed a blues in the key of D with the phrase, "Smoke like lightning," repeated over and over, mostly in falsetto.[25] Quite possibly, then, this verse with its obscure yet evocative imagery, was well-known in the Drew tradition before it was first recorded in 1930. The problem is complicated even further by the fact that the Mississippi Sheiks came originally from Bolton, Mississippi, the native home of Charley Patton, although by 1928 they had moved to Hollandale in the Delta, about sixty miles southwest of Drew.

The original single issue of Howlin' Wolf's piece was cut off after stanza 5, but it was issued in full on an LP.

Example 61. "Crying at Daybreak." Howlin' Wolf, vocal and harmonica; Willie Johnson or Howlin' Wolf, guitar in standard tuning, key of E; unknown artist, piano; unknown artist, bass guitar; Willie Steel, drums. Memphis or Los Angeles, 1951. RPM 340, reissued in full as "Crying at Daylight" on *Howling Wolf Sings the Blues*, Crown CLP 5240, 12" LP.

1. *Oh, tell me, baby, what's the matter now.*
   Oooh, oooh, oooh.

2. *Oh, today have been a long old lonesome day.*
   Oooh, oooh, lonesome day.

3. *Oh, smokestack lightning shining just like gold.*
      Oh, don't you hear me crying?
   Oooh, oooh, oooh.

4. *Oh, today have been a long old sad old day.*
      Oh, don't you hear me crying?
   Oooh, oooh, oooh.

5. *Oh, look here, baby. What you got on your mind?*
      Oh, don't you hear me crying?
   Oooh, oooh, oooh.

6. *Oh, ain't gon' marry, ain't gon' settle down.*
      Oh, don't you hear me crying?
   Oooh, oooh, oooh.

7. *Oooh.*

In 1956 Howlin' Wolf recorded another version of this piece entitled "Smoke Stack Lightning" (Chess 1618).[26] The melody is virtually identical to that of the earlier version, but the guitar part features two slightly variant figures from the one heard in measures 1–4, 7, and 9–10 above. These variant figures are printed below. Again, it is not certain whether or not a guitar is played by Howlin' Wolf. Two guitars are heard on the record playing almost in unison. The first two stanzas were sung in the earlier version, but the last four are new. Stanza 3 was sung by Tommy Johnson in his "Big Fat Mama Blues" (Victor V38535, Example 55). The fourth stanza may be derived from Floyd Jones's "Dark Road" (JOB 1001 or Chess 1498, Example 63), recorded in 1952. In the final stanza a second rhyming line is substituted for the refrain.

Example 62. "Smoke Stack Lightning." Howlin' Wolf, vocal and harmonica; Howlin' Wolf or unknown artist, guitar in standard tuning, key of E; Hubert Sumlin, guitar; Hosea Lee Kennard, piano; Earl Phillips, drums. Chicago, 1956. Chess 1618, reissued on *Moanin' in the Moonlight,* Chess LP 1434, 12" LP.

1. *Oh, smokestack lightning shining just like gold.*
    Oh, don't you hear me crying?
  Oooh, oooh, oooh.

2. *Oh, tell me, baby, what's the matter here.*
    Oh, don't you hear me crying?
  Oooh, oooh, oooh.

3. *Oh, tell me, baby, where did you stay last night.*
    Oh, don't you hear me crying?
  Oooh, oooh, oooh.

4. *Oh, stop your train. Let a poor boy ride.*
    Oh, don't you hear me crying?
  Oooh, oooh, oooh.

5. *Oh, fare you well; never see you no more.*
    Oh, don't you hear me crying?
  Oooh, oooh, oooh.

6. *Oh, who been here, baby, since I been gone?*
  Little bitty boy, derby on.
  Oooh, oooh, oooh.

The rather lengthy foregoing discussion has been designed to show that all of the elements in Tommy Johnson's "Big Road Blues" core were probably drawn from the Drew blues tradition. It is likely that Johnson himself was the first to combine these elements to form the core, since the only other recordings of this core from the Drew tradition are by artists who are natives of Crystal Springs and who learned it from Johnson. Nevertheless, there remains the problem of the exact relationship of Howlin' Wolf's two performances to the Drew tradition and to earlier records by Johnson and the Mississippi Sheiks.

Some Problematic Cases

Elements of "Big Road Blues" occur also in performances by Floyd Jones, Mattie Delaney, and J. D. Short, three singers whose relationship to the Drew tradition remains unclear. In 1952 Jones recorded two almost identical versions of a blues called "Dark Road" (JOB 1001 and Chess 1498). His text is constructed mostly out of traditional lines. Variants of the core stanza and refrain of "Big Road Blues" are found in Jones's first and fourth stanzas respectively. The first two lines and refrain of Jones's fourth stanza are also sung to a variant of the melody of "Big Road Blues." Jones's third stanza is found in variant form in Tommy Johnson's "Cool Drink of Water Blues." (Victor 21279, Example 20) as well as in Howlin' Wolf's "Smoke Stack Lightning" (Example 62). In the last line of each stanza Jones sings a falsetto melody similar to the one sung by Tommy Johnson throughout "Cool Drink of Water Blues." Jones's guitar part is also similar to that of "Cool Drink of Water Blues" and the pieces by Howlin' Wolf discussed above. Tommy Johnson's "Cool Drink of Water Blues" and "Big Road Blues" were issued on the same record (Victor 21279), so it is possible that Jones has cleverly combined elements from both sides. There is, however, a good possibility that he learned "Dark Road" in person from Tommy Johnson, Howlin' Wolf, or another Drew musician. Jones was born in Marianna, Arkansas, in 1917, and during the 1930s he met Tommy Johnson, Charley Patton, and Howlin' Wolf in Arkansas and Mississippi.[27] The fact that in his first three stanzas he repeats the last phrase of the first line argues for an oral derivation of his song. This sort of repetition was a characteristic of the Drew tradition and is found in various recordings by Tommy Johnson (see Example 55), Charley Patton, Willie Brown, Mott Willis (see Examples 33–37), and Mager Johnson (see Examples 51–52), yet it did not occur on either of Tommy Johnson's pieces on Victor 21279. Floyd Jones's text is as follows:

Example 63. "Dark Road." Floyd Jones, vocal and guitar in standard tuning, key of E; Moody Jones, guitar; Sunnyland Slim, piano; Elgin Evans, drums. Chicago, 1952. JOB 1001, reissued on *Chicago Blues, The Early 1950's*, Blues Classics 8, 12" LP.

1. *Ooh, I can't go down this dark road by myself, this dark road by myself. Gonna be early in the morning, oooh; it's gonna be early in the morning, oooh, gon' carry somebody else.*

2. *Ooh, my mother died and left me, oooh, when I was quite young, when I was quite young.*
   Said, "Lord, have mercy, oooh;" said, "Lord, have mercy, oooh, on my wicked son."

3. *Ooh, stop the train, conductor. Conductor, let me ride, let the poor boy*
   ride.
   "You have to buy your ticket, oooh; you have to buy your ticket, oooh.
   Son, the train ain't none of mine."

4. *Ooh, I started walking down this lonesome road.*
   Now don't you hear me crying?
   I started walking down this long old lonesome road.
   Gonna be early in the morning, oooh, boys, you'll see me go.

Mattie Delaney's "Down the Big Road Blues" (Vocalion 1480) contains the core stanza of "Big Road Blues" as well as a line used by Willie Brown in "M and O Blues" (Paramount 13090) and another line sung in several blues by Mott Willis and Mager Johnson. Her "Tallahatchie River Blues" (Vocalion 1480) has a melody rather like that of Charley Patton's "High Water Everywhere—Part II" (Paramount 12909), which has lyrics on a similar flood theme, while her guitar part in the key of D in standard tuning shows a slight resemblance to that of "Big Road Blues." Nothing whatsoever is known about Mattie Delaney except that she recorded in Memphis in 1930, but she may well have had some acquaintance with the Drew tradition, since the Tallahatchie River flows only about fifteen miles from Drew.

In 1962 J. D. Short recorded two versions of "Sliding Delta," each containing the melody and refrain of "Big Road Blues."[28] Short's text differs somewhat in the two versions, but basically it is about a railroad train called the "Sliding Delta." Tommy Johnson also recorded a "Slidin' Delta" in 1930 (Paramount 12975) with the same opening verse as Short's song. One version of Short's song also contains a line sung by Tommy Johnson in "Bye-Bye Blues" (Victor 21409). Johnson sings the initial line of each stanza of "Slidin' Delta" in falsetto, while Short uses this technique for his final melodic line of each stanza. Short had met Charley Patton in Hollandale, Mississippi, before 1925 and may have learned "Sliding Delta" from him.[29] But Tommy Johnson, a more likely source for the song, was spending a great amount of time in 1924 in Rolling Fork, only twenty miles south of Hollandale.[30] Short never revealed whether he knew Johnson.

Versions by Mott Willis and Mager Johnson

Performances of "Big Road Blues" by Mott Willis and Mager Johnson help us greatly to understand how Tommy Johnson varied his song from one performance to another. Mott Willis has recorded four versions of the song plus a violin accompaniment without vocal, which shows some influence of Lonnie Chatmon's style. Chatmon was the violinist on the Mississippi Sheiks' 1930 recording of "Stop and Listen Blues" (Okeh 8807, Example 70), and Willis often performed with him and some of the other Chatmon brothers. Willis's first vocal version in 1967 contains only two stanzas, the same two with which Tommy Johnson began his 1928 recording (Example 60). Willis uses Johnson's melody, singing the final line in a falsetto voice. Although he plays basically Johnson's guitar part, he introduces some interesting variations, which are printed below. During both vocal choruses he snaps some of the bass notes in the song's first line. These snapped notes are indicated by an asterisk above the note. Willis also snapped bass strings in Examples 36 and 39, and the practice can be heard in blues by Willie Brown, Charley Patton, O. M. McGee, and Tommy Johnson. Walter Vinson of the Mississippi Sheiks also snapped bass strings on "Stop and Listen Blues" (Okeh 8807, Example 70), but his snaps were played on both the fourth and sixth string of the guitar, while the Drew artists all snap the sixth string only. The Drew artists also snap mainly on the offbeat, giving a strong syncopated feeling, while Vinson snapped equally on the onbeat and offbeat. Willis, therefore, probably derived his snapping pattern from the Drew tradition rather than from the Mississippi Sheiks. Willis's other variant pattern, played in the first line of a closing guitar chorus, is also printed below.

Example 64. "Big Road Blues." Mott Willis, vocal and guitar in EBGDAD tuning, key of D. Terry, Miss., Sept. 7, 1967. Recorded by David Evans and Marina Bokelman.

The fact that Willis in the above example sang only the first two stanzas from Tommy Johnson's recorded version might lead one to think that he learned this blues from Johnson's record, but subsequent versions by Willis show that he was capable of considerable variation and that he sings only the core stanza consistently. In a version from 1971 printed below, Willis's second stanza is one that is said by others to have been sung often by Tommy Johnson, though Johnson never recorded it. Willis sang his third stanza elsewhere in Examples 33 and 43. The last line in his second and third stanzas is sung in falsetto. His guitar playing contains snapping in the first line, as in the previous example, but he introduces a new figure, printed below, at the end of the second line of each stanza (measures 7–8) and also at the end of the third line of the first stanza (measures 11–12). A variant of this guitar figure was also used by Tommy Johnson in his 1928 recording of "Canned Heat Blues" (Victor V38535). Willis transposed it into the key of E in standard tuning in his Example 40.

Example 65. "Big Road Blues." Mott Willis, vocal and guitar in EBGDAD tuning, key of D. Crystal Springs, Miss., July 14, 1971. Recorded by David and Cheryl Evans.

STANZA 1

GUITAR

1. *Ain't going down the big road by myself.*
       Now don't you, you hear me talking, pretty mama?
   Ain't going down the big road by myself.
   If I don't carry you, mama, take me someone else.

2. *Yeah, I wish I was in East Colorado Springs.*
       Now don't you, you hear me talking, pretty mama?
   Wish I was in East Colorado Springs.
   Yeah, sun don't shine; it hardly ever rains.

3. *Yeah, quit your shouting, baby; let your happy come down.*
       Now don't you, you hear me talking, pretty mama?
   Hey, quit your shouting, gal; let your happy come down.
   Hey, quit your shouting, and let your happy come down.

Willis's final two versions offer no significant variations in the melody or guitar part from his first two, but they do contain new textual material. The texts are printed below. Willis's "Diddy Wah Diddy" seems to be a remote, mythical place, comparable to East Colorado Springs as someplace far away from the singer. Zora Neale Hurston defines "Diddy Wah Diddy" as "a far place, a measure of distance. (2) another suburb of Hell, built since way before Hell wasn't no bigger than Baltimore. The folks in Hell go there for a big time."[31] Stetson Kennedy describes it as an afterworld place reserved for blacks, similar to the Land of Cockaygne.[32] In his 1955 recording of "Diddy Wah Diddy" (Checker 832) Bo Diddley (Ellas McDaniel) said that it "ain't no town, ain't no city." In Blind Blake's 1929 "Diddie Wa Diddie" (Paramount 12888), however, it served as a code word for sexual intercourse.

Example 66. "Big Road Blues." Mott Willis, vocal and guitar in EBGDAD tuning, key of D. Crystal Springs, Miss., Aug. 13, 1973. Recorded by David and Cheryl Evans.

1. *Ain't going down that big road by myself.*
   Spoken: *That's old Tommy Johnson.*
   Ain't going down that big road by myself.
   If I don't carry you, baby, I'll take me someone else.

2. *Yes, asked her for . . . one woman for water; she give me gasoline.*
       Now don't you, you hear me talking, pretty mama?
   Asked for water; give me gasoline.
   Spoken: *Liked to killed me too, you know.*
   And I asked for water; she give me gasoline.

3. *Yes, Diddy Wah Diddy, baby, place I want to go.*
      Now don't you, you hear me talking, pretty mama?
   Diddy Wah Diddy, place I want to go.
   Tell me the sun don't shine there, and it hardly ever rain.

Example 67. "Big Road Blues." Mott Willis, vocal and guitar in EBGDAD tuning, key of D. Crystal Springs, Miss., Aug. 16, 1973. Recorded by David and Cheryl Evans.

1. *Ain't going down the big road by myself.*
      Now don't you, you hear me talking, pretty mama?
   Ain't going down that big road by myself.
   If I don't carry you, baby, I'll take me someone else.

2. *Yeah, going, baby, . . .*
   Spoken: *I forgot what he say again, you know.* [Laughter]
   Wants to go, baby, to East Colorado Springs.
   Spoken: *That one or the one next to it.*
   Tell me the sun don't shine, it hardly ever rains.

3. *Oh, Diddy Wah Diddy, baby, place I wants to go.*
      Now don't you, you hear me talking, pretty mama?
   Oh, Diddy Wah Diddy [Laughter], *place I want to go.*
   Spoken: *Reckon I'm gonna go.* [Laughter]
   Tell me the sun don't shine, it hardly ever rain.

4. *Hey, what you gonna do, suh, eeh!, trouble get like mine?*
      Now don't you, you hear me talking, pretty mama?
   Oh, what you gonna do, suh, eeeeh!, trouble get like mine?
   Spoken: *Just go to work, that's all.*
   Get your pick and shovel, you ease on, eeeh, down the line. [Laughter]

Willis's spoken asides in his last two versions indicate that he was trying to sing verses that he recalled from Tommy Johnson. Both versions, in fact, were performed in the context of discussions about Johnson's music and personality. The second stanza of Example 66 is, of course, the core stanza of "Cool Water Blues," while the fourth stanza of Example 67 has been encountered many times before in blues by Willis and Mager Johnson. None of Willis's stanzas in all four versions, except for the core stanza and the second stanza of Example 64, are in Tommy Johnson's recorded version of the song. It would appear, therefore, that Johnson varied his text considerably in actual performance. It is interesting to note that Johnson's recording develops the idea of the singer overcoming various problems, while Willis's texts tend to contrast the determination of the singer in the core stanza to travel in the company of some woman, with an image of being alone in some faraway place. Willis's remaining stanzas lie somewhat outside this contrastive structural pattern and simply describe various troubles.

Mager Johnson's five versions of "Big Road Blues" are similarly varied. Johnson cut short his first version after the third stanza, saying, "If you want to make a bigger record out of it, you can make it, and then if you want it to be short, it can be short." When I asked him to complete the song, he added the three remaining stanzas. He had shortened it because he thought that the piece was so familiar from his brother's playing that I would not want a full version. The first half of this performance was issued on an LP record. Mager Johnson plays essentially the same guitar part as his brother, except for a rhythmic variation in measures 7–8 and 11–12, which is printed below. He sings the minor or neutral seventh, however, in the places where Tommy sang the major sixth. He also makes a falsetto leap to the keynote (D) on the last note of the second line in stanzas 1 and 2. The single line in stanza 3 is sung entirely in falsetto, like the last line of his brother Tommy's record. Mager's final stanza is sung to an entirely different melody, which is printed below.

Example 68. "Big Road Blues." Mager Johnson, vocal and guitar in EBGDAD tuning, key of D. Crystal Springs, Miss., Sept. 5, 1966. Recorded by David Evans and Marina Bokelman. Issued in part on *Goin' up the Country*, British Decca LK 4931, 12" LP (reissued on Rounder 2012).

GUITAR CHORUS.

1. *Lord, ain't going down the big road by myself.*
    Don't you hear me talking, pretty mama?
   Lord, ain't going down the big road by myself.
   If I can't carry you, gon' carry somebody else.

2. *Mmmm, stealing back to my same old used-to-be.*
    Now don't you hear me talking, pretty mama?
   Lord, I'm stealing back to my same old used-to-be.
   Says, I can't stay here, baby now, worried and blue no more.

3. *Crying, Lord, mama, I ain't gon' be here long.*

BREAK.

GUITAR CHORUS.

4. *Hey, a big fat mama, the meat shaking on her bones.*
    Now don't you hear me talking, pretty mama?
Lord, a big fat mama, the meat shaking on her bones.
Every time she shakes, Lord, fat mama lost her home.

GUITAR CHORUS.

5. *Hey, I'm traveling back to my same old used-to-be.*
    Now don't you hear me talking, pretty mama?
Lord, I'm traveling back to my same old used-to-be.
Says, the way you treat me, woman, I can't live here no more.

6. *Says, you treat me wrong, mama, 'n' you sure gon' see 't again now,*
    woman, crying, soon one morning, crying,
Mmmm, sure gon' see 't again.
Crying, Lord, have mercy, mmmm, on your wicked soul.

GUITAR CHORUS.

Later the same day, Mager Johnson recorded another version of "Big Road Blues." Melodically and instrumentally it is quite like his first version, but the two share only two stanzas of their lyrics. Mager's second version contains instead three of the four stanzas found in his brother's 1928 recording (Example 60), probably because I played him a tape recording of his brother's record between the earlier performance and this one.

One year later Mager Johnson recorded a third version of "Big Road Blues." It contains no new musical elements, but its text is quite different from the texts of his earlier versions.

Example 69. "Big Road Blues." Mager Johnson, vocal and guitar in EBGDAD tuning, key of D; Houston Stackhouse, guitar; James "Peck" Curtis, drums. Crystal Springs, Miss., Sept. 14, 1967. Recorded by George and Cathy Mitchell.

INSTRUMENTAL CHORUS.

1. *Lord, ain't going down the big road by myself.*
    Now don't you hear me talking, pretty mama?
Lord, ain't going down the big road by myself.
If I can't carry you, gon' carry somebody else.

2. *Hey, sun gon' shine in my back door someday.*
    Now don't you hear me talking, pretty mama?
Lord, sun gon' shine in my back door someday.
And the wind gon' change . . .

3. *Now you big fat mama, the meat shaking all on her bones.*
    Now don't you hear me talking, pretty mama?
Lord, you big fat mama, meat shaking on her bones.
Every time she shakes, it's a fat mama lost a home.

4. *Mmmm, Lord, have mercy now on my wicked soul.*
    Now don't you hear me talking, pretty mama?
Lord, have mercy on my wicked soul.
If the Good Lord don't help me, the devil will damn my soul.

5. *Take me out of the bottom, mama now, 'fore the water rise.*
   Now don't you hear me talking, pretty mama?
   Take me out of the bottom now, mama, 'fore the water rise.
   When the water rise, want to be on the other side.

6. *Mmmm, mmmm, mmmm, mmmm.*
   Mmmm, Lord, have mercy now.
   Hey, Lordy, I ain't gon' be here long.

Johnson's final two versions were recorded one after the other in 1969. Again they contain no significant new musical elements. The first of them has a text comprised of stanzas 1, 4, and 5 of Example 69 above. The second version contains two of these stanzas followed by two new stanzas.

Although the stanzas of one of his five texts are all found in another text, and although another of his texts is quite like that of his brother's record, there is still considerable textual variation in Mager Johnson's versions of "Big Road Blues." His basic technique of composition is to add traditional stanzas and lines from his repertoire to the core stanza at the time of performance. He shows a tendency to favor certain lines and stanzas in this blues. One stanza, for example, occurs in three versions, while two stanzas occur in two versions, and two single lines occur three and four times respectively. Yet all but one of these recurring stanzas and lines are found in other blues by Mager Johnson. Indeed, almost all of his stanzas except the core stanza were used by Johnson in his other blues (Examples 46–54). In fact, Example 69 above has more lyrics in common with Example 51 ("Traveling Blues") than it does with some of his other versions of "Big Road Blues." Johnson generally chooses lyrics for "Big Road Blues" that explore various possibilities of travel: travel with a woman, travel away from a woman, and travel to see a woman. Often these ideas are contrasted in the same performance. Most of his remaining verses deal with mistreatment, self-pity, and censure. Tommy Johnson, Mott Willis, and Mager Johnson, then, each tend to emphasize different subjects in their texts of "Big Road Blues."

Commercially Recorded Versions

Versions of "Big Road Blues" by Mott Willis and Mager Johnson help us to understand how Tommy Johnson probably varied his performances of the song. It was, in fact, through listening to Tommy Johnson's various live performances, rather than to his record, that most other artists learned versions of "Big Road Blues." Some artists sang verses learned from Johnson, while others went on to compose new verses. A number of these pieces were commercially recorded, and some of these records in turn influenced later versions of "Big Road Blues," including probably Johnson's own performances.

By far the most important and influential blues derived from Johnson's song was "Stop and Listen Blues" (Okeh 8807), recorded by the Mississippi Sheiks in 1930. The Sheiks consisted of Walter Vinson, who sang and played guitar, and Lonnie Chatmon, who played violin.

They came originally from the country west of Jackson, near Bolton
and Edwards, but by the 1920s they were playing in Jackson, where
Vinson undoubtedly heard Tommy Johnson perform "Big Road Blues."
During his singing Vinson plays Johnson's guitar part, adding the
snapping of the bass strings in the first line, which he probably copied
from Johnson's live performance. In the opening instrumental chorus
Vinson plays a different guitar part, mostly on the treble strings. His
melody is essentially Johnson's with falsetto singing on the last line of
stanzas 1, 3, and 5. Except for the refrain, Vinson's text is completely
different from that of Johnson's record. Although it is constructed
largely of traditional lines, it is thematic and deals with the singer's
sadness at the death of his girl friend. Despite the musical similarities,
the mood of "Stop and Listen Blues" is in total contrast to that of Johnson's record.

Example 70. "Stop and Listen Blues." Mississippi Sheiks: Walter Vinson,
vocal and guitar in EBGDAD tuning, key of D; Lonnie Chatmon, violin.
Shreveport, La., Feb. 17, 1930. Okeh 8807, reissued on *Jackson Blues,
1928–1938,* Yazoo L-1007, 12" LP.

INSTRUMENTAL CHORUS.

1. *Yeah, today have been, baby, long old lonesome day.*
   Now don't you hear me talking, pretty mama?
   Yeah, today have been a long old lonesome day.
   Crying, seem like tomorrow be the same old way.

2. *Crying, smokestack black, baby; the bells, it shine like gold.*
   Now don't you hear me talking, pretty mama?
   Oh, smokestack black; bells, it shining like gold.
   Crying, I found my baby laying on the cooling board.

3. *Don't the hearse look lonesome, mama, rolling 'fore your door?*
   Now don't you hear me talking, pretty mama?
   Don't the hearse look lonesome rolling 'fore your door?
   Crying, she's gone, she's gone, won't be back no more.

4. *Oh, stop and listen; hear how the bells in tone.*
   Now don't you hear me talking, pretty mama?
   Oh, stop and listen; hear the bells in tone.
   I had a sweet little fairo, but she's dead and gone.

5. *Crying, followed my baby down to the burying ground.*
   Now don't you hear me talking, pretty mama?
   I followed my baby to the burying ground.
   It was hacks and horses standing all around.

Although sales figures are not available, it is clear that "Stop and
Listen Blues" was a big hit for the Mississippi Sheiks, much bigger than
Johnson's "Big Road Blues" had been. Later in 1930 the Sheiks recorded
a "Stop and Listen Blues No. 2" (Okeh 8859) and in 1932 "The New
Stop and Listen Blues" (Paramount 13134), both with new lyrics on the
theme of the girl friend's death. Such follow-up recordings are a sure
indication that the original was a popular hit.

Apparently sometime in the 1930s Tommy Johnson needed money and was given a payment of fifty dollars by the Mississippi Sheiks in return for selling his rights to make records. Perhaps the Sheiks, who had been collecting royalties for "Stop and Listen Blues" and were enjoying considerable popular success, were concerned that Johnson would try to collect some money from the record company for their borrowing of his tune. This verbal agreement was not legally binding, but Johnson took it seriously and told many of his friends and relatives about it. He never made an effort to record again after 1930.[33]

Over the years many blues singers have made recordings of songs derivative of "Stop and Listen Blues," and several versions of "Big Road Blues" have been influenced by it as well. Blues based on the record by the Mississippi Sheiks have been recorded by Fred McMullen (1933), Kokomo Arnold (1935), Jesse James (1936), Lightnin' Hopkins (1947 and 1962), Horace Sprott (1954), Leon Strickland (1959), Eddie Lee Jones (1965), Robert Pete Williams (1966), Thomas Shaw (1971), and Willie Morris (ca. 1972).[34] Several of the texts, particularly those of McMullen, James, Jones, and Williams, make considerable departures from Walter Vinson's text. The versions by Arnold and Strickland contain several stanzas from the Sheiks' record along with the core stanza of "Big Road Blues." Ishmon Bracey recalled that Kokomo Arnold visited Jackson in the 1930s and listened attentively to Johnson's music.[35] Perhaps it was at this time that he added Johnson's stanza to his version of the Mississippi Sheiks' song. Nothing is known about Strickland's life that would explain his use of Johnson's stanza in this song. His version is not influenced by Kokomo Arnold's earlier commercial record. Perhaps he had heard versions of both "Stop and Listen Blues" and "Big Road Blues" and decided to combine them on the basis of their similar tunes. Thomas Shaw's version contains a variant of Tommy Johnson's third stanza along with three stanzas derived from "Stop and Listen Blues" and three other traditional stanzas. Shaw, too, probably had heard both songs and decided to combine portions of each. It is possible, however, that Shaw learned this combination from Sam Chatmon (cf. Example 71), with whom he often performed in recent years for folksong revival audiences in San Diego, California. The version by Robert Pete Williams contains a guitar part similar to that of Howlin' Wolf in Examples 56, 61, and 62. Williams also recorded two similar versions of this piece for me. In an interview he claimed that he had learned the guitar part from a record by "the gasoline man, Howlin' Wolf." Williams said, "I just thought I could mix some songs up with it."[36] Undoubtedly the connection between the songs by the Mississippi Sheiks and Howlin' Wolf was made by Williams on the basis of their similar use of falsetto as well as their sharing of a refrain and two verses. Williams has had no personal contact with the Drew tradition or any of its members. The version by Willie Morris is the only one which recreates the guitar part of Walter Vinson and Tommy Johnson. This is not surprising, since Morris is a native of Bolton, Mississippi, the home town of Vinson, whom he undoubtedly knew. None of the other artists who play versions of "Stop and Listen Blues" is from Mississippi.

Sam Chatmon has also continued to perform "Stop and Listen Blues." He was one of the Mississippi Sheiks, although he did not perform on any of their commercial records of this song. He attributes its composition to Walter Vinson and his brothers Lonnie and Bo Chatmon. In 1966 Sam recorded a version of "Stop and Listen Blues" containing the melody and guitar part used by the Sheiks and Tommy Johnson, and variants of four stanzas found in the original recording by the Sheiks (Example 70). An additional stanza, however, is a variant of the third stanza of Tommy Johnson's record of "Big Road Blues" (cf. Example 71, stanza 2, below).[37] Sam Chatmon knew Johnson and undoubtedly heard his record or live performances of "Big Road Blues." Apparently Chatmon, like so many other artists, combined elements of both songs on the basis of their musical similarity.

In the last few years Chatmon has been commuting between Mississippi and San Diego, California, where he has had successful concert and coffeehouse engagements for folksong revival audiences. As a result of this new interest in his music, he has composed many new songs and revived others from his old repertoire. "Stop and Listen Blues" has undergone a transformation and is now called "Brownskin Woman Blues," a composition which Chatmon considers at least partially his own. He still retains the distinctive melody and refrain, but the guitar part contains some new figures in measures 7–8 and 11–12. The version printed below contains two stanzas from the Sheiks' "Stop and Listen Blues" (Example 70) and a variant of a stanza from their "Stop and Listen Blues No. 2" (Okeh 8859). Chatmon retains the stanza 2 from "Big Road Blues" that he had used in his older version of "Stop and Listen Blues" but adds the core stanza of "Big Road Blues" at the end. Chatmon's opening stanza, although it is traditional (see Example 45), gives his new composition much of its individuality.[38]

Example 71. "Brownskin Woman." Sam Chatmon, vocal and guitar in EBGDAD tuning, key of D. San Diego, Calif., June 6, 1971. Recorded by Frank Scott.

1. *Hey, brownskin woman live up on a hill.*
       Now don't you hear me telling you where she stay?
   I got a brownskin woman, live on that hill.
   And that fool quit me, swear I love her still.

2. *How come you want to do me like you do do do?*
       Now don't you hear me telling you, pretty mama?
   How come you want to do me like you do do do?
   How come you want to treat me, woman, like you do do do?

3. *When I left town this morning on my way back home—*
       Now don't you hear me telling you, pretty mama?
   Left town this morning on my way back home.
   Ah well, the people met me and told me, "Your rider dead and gone."

4. *Ah, don't the hearse look lonesome rolling to your door?*
   Now don't you hear me telling you, pretty mama?
   Hey, hearse look lonesome rolling to your door.
   It's taken that woman you love, and she can't get back no more.

5. *Crying, smokestack lightning, bell what shine like gold.*
   Now don't you hear me telling you, pretty mama?
   Smokestack lightning, bell shine like gold.
   I found that woman I'm loving on her cooling board.

6. *Crying, I ain't going down this big road by myself.*
   Now don't you hear me telling you, pretty mama?
   Oh, ain't going down this big road by myself.
   And if I can't take you, woman, I'm gon' take somebody else.

Sam Chatmon. Photo by Cheryl T. Evans.

Chatmon, like so many other blues singers, has combined textual elements from both "Big Road Blues" and "Stop and Listen Blues," two songs which express quite different moods. Yet he manages to achieve an effective synthesis through the structural device of contrast. The first five stanzas express the singer's devotion to a woman despite the fact that she leaves him, mistreats him, and even dies on him. In the final stanza, drawn from "Big Road Blues," he breaks away dramatically from this idea and states that he can find another woman. This blues, then, deals with the problem of a one-way love relationship by contrasting extreme devotion with rejection.[39]

Other artists besides the Mississippi Sheiks composed new texts to the tune of "Big Road Blues." In 1934 Bumble Bee Slim (Amos Easton) recorded "Sad and Lonesome" (Bluebird B5563) and "Rough Road Blues" (Vocalion 02829), both using the tune and refrain of Tommy Johnson's song. The text of "Rough Road Blues" was almost certainly inspired by the core stanza of "Big Road Blues." Easton's piece may be a remake of his 1931 "Rough Rugged Road Blues" (Paramount 13132), of which there is no extant copy. Easton is known to have performed in Jackson in 1937.[40] Perhaps he was there earlier as well and heard Tommy Johnson sing, or else he may simply have heard Johnson's record.

In 1935 Willie "Poor Boy" Lofton recorded two songs based on Tommy Johnson's "Big Road Blues." Lofton was a barber on Pascagoula Street in Jackson with a talent for entertainment and blues singing. He played often with Ishmon Bracey and Tommy Johnson in Jackson, but by 1934 he had moved to Chicago, where he remained until about 1942. Then he moved back to Jackson, where he died about 1962.[41] The first of his two recordings that interest us, "Dirty Mistreater," has a thematic text about a mistreating woman, which is built out of both traditional and original verses. Lofton squeezes a rhymed couplet into the first four measures and uses the remainder of the stanza for a two-line refrain. His melody and guitar part are basically those of Tommy Johnson, but each chorus contains several extra beats. Either Lofton had learned the part imperfectly or was unable to compress his long verses into the standard twelve-measure format. In the first line of stanza 4 he plays a guitar part similar to that of the opening chorus of the Mississippi Sheiks' "Stop and Listen Blues." Probably this part originated with Tommy Johnson.

Example 72. "Dirty Mistreater." Poor Boy Lofton, vocal and guitar in EBGDAD tuning, key of D. Chicago, Jan. 9, 1935. Decca 7049.

GUITAR CHORUS.

1. *Crying, I give you my money, mama, when you was all out and down.*
   Soon's you got up on your foots, Good God, mama, you wouldn't even 'low
      me around.
   Crying, dirty mistreater, Lord, have mercy, mistreat me all the time.
   Crying, dirty mistreater, mistreat the poor boy all the time.

2. *Crying, dirty mistreater, mistreat me all the time.*

3. *Crying, I was laying down on my sickbed, laying at the point of death.*
   Here come the dirty mistreater, Good God, mama, trying to start some
   mess.
   Crying, dirty mistreater, Lord, have mercy, mistreat me all the time.
   Crying, dirty mistreater, mistreat the poor boy all the time.

4. Spoken: *Play it, boy. Hey! Don't blame me, boys, because I'm gonna make*
   G below the hole.
   Crying, dirty mistreater, mistreat the poor boy all the time.

5. *Crying, you remember the morning I knocked upon your door.*
   You say, "Go 'way, you dirty skunk, Good God, mama, don't want you no
   more."
   Crying, dirty mistreater, Lord, have mercy, mistreat me all the time.
   Crying, dirty mistreater, mistreat the poor boy all the time.

6. *Crying, Lord, have mercy on my wicked soul.*
   Says, I wouldn't get in trouble now, Good God, mama, to save no black
   woman's soul.
   Crying, dirty mistreater, mistreat me all the time.
   Crying, dirty mistreater, mistreat the poor boy all the time.

Lofton's record was not really a hit, but it must have sold moderately well, for ten months later he recorded another blues that was musically similar but had a different text. This new piece, "Dark Road Blues," is nothing more than a version of "Big Road Blues," the only version of the song besides Tommy Johnson's that was recorded commercially for sale to the black record-buying public. Its melody is the same as Johnson's except for a falsetto leap to the keynote (D) at the end of the second line of some stanzas, a trait also found in Mager Johnson's versions and one that Lofton probably learned from Tommy Johnson in person. The guitar part is extended for a few beats, as in Lofton's earlier record, and he snaps the bass strings in the first line like Walter Vinson and Mott Willis, another trait probably learned from Tommy Johnson. Lofton's text, however, contains only two stanzas found on Johnson's record (Example 60). Nevertheless, the remaining stanzas were almost certainly all learned from Johnson in person. Lofton's stanza 2 is a variant of the opening stanza of Johnson's "Maggie Campbell Blues" (Victor 21409), and further variations of this stanza were sung by Mott Willis and Willis Taylor in various blues (Examples 34, 37, 39, 40, 42, and 45). Stanza 5 was sung in variant form by the Mississippi Sheiks in "Stop and Listen Blues" (Example 70), but we have also noted variants of it in use among Drew artists such as Charley Patton and Howlin' Wolf, and Tommy Johnson himself is said to have sung it. Variants of stanza 7 were sung by Mager Johnson (Example 54), Kid Bailey ("Rowdy Blues," Brunswick 7114), Howlin' Wolf (Example 61), and allegedly by Dick Bankston, all from the Drew tradition. Tommy Johnson, then, almost certainly sang it. Stanzas 6 and 8 are widespread in folk blues tradition and were probably known by Johnson. In fact, a variant of the first line of stanza 8 was used in Charley

Patton's "Jim Lee Blues—Part 2" (Paramount 13133). With the possible exceptions of the first verse in stanza 5 and the snapping of the bass strings, Lofton's blues shows no discernible relationship to the Mississippi Sheiks' "Stop and Listen Blues," whereas it shows many signs of having been learned from Tommy Johnson in person.

Example 73. "Dark Road Blues." Willie Lofton, vocal and guitar in EBGDAD tuning, key of D. Chicago, Nov. 1, 1935. Bluebird B6229, reissued on *Jackson Blues, 1928–1938,* Yazoo L-1007, 12″ LP.

GUITAR CHORUS.

1. *Crying, I ain't going down this dark road by myself.*
    Now don't you hear me talking to you, pretty mama?
   Oh, ain't going down that dark road by myself.
   Crying, if I don't carry you, carry me somebody else.

2. *Crying, who's that yonder coming up the road?*
    Now don't you hear me talking to you, pretty mama?
   Oh, who's that yonder coming up the road?
   Crying, it look like my fairo, but she walk too slow.

3. *Crying, won't let you do me, do me, like you did poor Shine.*
    Now don't you hear me talking to you, pretty mama?
   Oh, won't let you do me like you did poor Shine.
   Crying, you taken the poor boy's money; gon' have to kill me 'fore you
       take mine.
   Spoken: *Yeah!*

4. *Crying, you gon' have to kill me 'fore you take mine.*

5. *Crying, smoke like lightning, shine like pearly gold.*
    Now don't you hear me talking to you, pretty mama?
   Oh, smoke like lightning, shine like pearly gold.
   Crying, I wouldn't get in trouble, save nobody's soul.

6. *Crying now, spider, spider, climbing up the wall.*
    Now don't you hear me talking to you, pretty mama?
   Oh, spider, spider, climbing up the wall.
   Crying, I asked the spider, did he want his ashes hauled.

7. *Crying, I ain't gonna marry, ain't gon' settle down.*
    Now don't you hear me talking to you, pretty mama?
   Oh, ain't gonna marry, ain't gonna settle down.
   Crying, I'm gon' stay right here till my moustache drag the ground.

8. *Crying, where was you when the Frisco left the yard?*
    Now don't you hear me talking to you, pretty mama?
   Where was you, Frisco left the yard?
   Crying, I was standing right there. Police had me barred.

The structural pattern of Lofton's text is quite interesting and represents a new emphasis in comparison to the texts of Tommy Johnson, Mott Willis, and Mager Johnson. Stanzas 1, 5, and 7 express in various ways the singer's unwillingness to give special consideration to any one woman, while stanza 2 similarly expresses the inability of the singer to recognize his "fairo." Stanzas 3 and 4, however, contain the singer's declaration that he is unwilling to be treated like every other man and that he needs special consideration. The term "Shine" is probably not a reference to a specific person but a symbol for the black male. It is often used in this way, sometimes with a derogatory sense, but it also occurs as the name of a folk hero in a rhymed narrative toast about the only black man aboard the ship Titanic, a sort of black Everyman.[42] The concluding eighth stanza of Lofton's song seems to be a question addressed by the singer to himself. It presents an image of the singer's inability to move or act and seems to highlight the impossibility of reconciling the attitudes expressed in the previous stanzas. Only stanza 6 with its humorous sexual imagery fails to fit into this pattern, although it may function as a sort of comic relief. An additional thematic contrast that runs through the text is that of unrestricted travel in stanzas 1, 2, 6, and the first line of stanza 8, and the singer's unwillingness or inability to travel in stanza 7 and the last line of stanza 8. Lofton's blues, then, deals with problems of mobility and the establishment of relationships of trust with members of the opposite sex.

Although there were no other commercially recorded and issued versions of "Big Road Blues" after Willie Lofton's 1935 recording, there have been three commercial records by Mose Andrews, Jazz Gillum, and Frankie Lee Sims that display a possible influence from Tommy Johnson's song. In 1937 Mose Andrews recorded "Ten Pound Hammer" (Decca 7338), a blues which contains the melody, guitar part, and refrain of "Big Road Blues" but has a thematic text in which the singer's hammer is obviously a phallic symbol. This song and the piece on the other side of Andrews's record, "Young Heifer Blues," appear to have been inspired by the text of Charley Patton's 1934 "Jersey Bull Blues" (Vocalion 02782). One of the stanzas in "Young Heifer Blues" also occurs in variant form in Willie Brown's "M and O Blues" (Paramount 13090). In 1935 Andrews recorded two unissued pieces, "Mississippi Storm," indicating a probable connection of the singer with that state, and "I Love My Stuff," possibly a version of Charley Patton's "Love My Stuff," the song on the other side of the record of Patton's "Jersey Bull Blues." No biographical information on Andrews has ever been reported. Probably he had heard Patton's record and had somewhere encountered a form of "Big Road Blues" or "Stop and Listen Blues" and decided to combine elements of each. On the other hand, his connection with the Drew tradition may have been more intimate.

Harmonica player William "Jazz" Gillum recorded "One Letter Home" (Bluebird B8943) in 1941, a blues that contains variants of the melody and refrain of "Big Road Blues." Gillum may have simply borrowed these elements from an earlier commercially recorded version of "Big Road Blues" or some other related piece such as "Stop and Listen Blues," but he was a native of Mississippi and thus could have learned them through personal transmission. Gillum was born in Indianola, just thirty miles south of Drew, and began performing by 1918 on street corners in Greenwood, about thirty miles southeast of Drew.[43]

In 1953 Frankie Lee Sims recorded "Lucy Mae Blues" (Specialty
459) using several guitar figures commonly associated with "Big Road
Blues." Sims was from Dallas, Texas, and recorded there, but the man
who recorded him, Johnny Vincent, had his office in Jackson, Mississippi. Furthermore, Sims's blues is a version of Ishmon Bracey's "Saturday Blues" (Victor 21349). Bracey was a friend of Tommy Johnson in
Jackson and played with him for many years. It is possible, therefore,
that Frankie Lee Sims had spent some time in Jackson before 1953 and
had heard the music of Bracey and/or Johnson.[44]

Field Recorded Versions

Even though Tommy Johnson's "Big Road Blues" inspired only one additional version on a commercial record, Willie Lofton's "Dark Road
Blues," the song was transmitted by Johnson to many other artists, several of whom have been recorded under field conditions since the
1950s. Some of their versions of "Big Road Blues" show a degree of
influence not only from Johnson's commercial record of the song but
also from the Mississippi Sheiks' "Stop and Listen Blues" and from the
two pieces by Willie Lofton discussed above, yet all of the field recorded versions show signs of Johnson's personal influence also. We
have already discussed versions by Mott Willis and Mager Johnson.
These two artists are representatives of the Drew tradition, and they
learned the song before Tommy Johnson recorded it in 1928. The remaining field recorded versions were all learned from Johnson during
or after 1928. They will be discussed below in the probable order in
which they were learned from Johnson. This arrangement will be followed so that we may better understand the elements that have been
introduced into this song over the years.

Houston Stackhouse began to learn guitar in 1927 from his neighbors, the Johnson brothers of Crystal Springs. He has remained in
touch with the Johnson family ever since while pursuing a career as a
semiprofessional blues singer and guitarist in various parts of Mississippi, Arkansas, and Tennessee. In 1967 Stackhouse recorded two
versions of "Big Road Blues." The first of these contains only the
stanzas found in Tommy Johnson's 1928 recording.[45] The second version contains these same stanzas with one additional final stanza, a
variant of a stanza sung by Mager Johnson in a number of blues.[46]
Stackhouse's performances are musically almost identical to Tommy
Johnson's recorded version, including even the melodic variation in
Johnson's third stanza. It would appear, then, that Stackhouse learned
this blues from the Johnson brothers in person but modeled his own
performance closely on that of Tommy Johnson's record, which was
released when Stackhouse was first learning the blues and would have
been most impressionable. Such an explanation would be consistent
with the overall pattern of Stackhouse's repertoire. Out of fourteen
blues that I recorded from him in 1967, all but four were modeled
closely upon phonograph records. Several of these records were made

by artists whom Stackhouse had known personally and with whom he had performed.[47]

Cary Lee Simmons moved to Jackson from nearby Luckney in 1928 and began playing guitar with Tommy Johnson. Simmons continued performing into the 1960s. His version of "Big Road Blues," recorded in 1967, contains only lyrics found in Johnson's recorded version and, except for a fast triplet rhythm, a modern feature, is musically very similar to it.[48] Probably Simmons heard the record when it

Houston Stackhouse. Photo by Cheryl T. Evans.

was first released in 1928 and modeled his performance, which he had learned from Tommy Johnson in person, on it.[49]

Another artist who gives evidence of having heard Tommy Johnson's record is Shirley Griffith. He was living in Jackson in 1925 when he met and began playing blues with Tommy Johnson. At the end of 1928, a few months after Johnson's record of "Big Road Blues" was released, Griffith moved to Indianapolis, where he lived until his recent death. When he first moved there, he took pride in performing "Big Road Blues" in the music stores, exactly as it sounded on Johnson's record.[50] Griffith recorded "Big Road Blues" twice. His first version from 1961 contains all but the sixth stanza of the later version printed below.[51]

Example 74. "Big Road Blues." Shirley Griffith, vocal and guitar in EBGDAD tuning, key of D. Indianapolis, Mar., 1973. Issued on *Shirley Griffith: Mississippi Blues,* Blue Goose 2011, 12″ LP.

GUITAR CHORUS.

1. *Crying, I ain't going down that big road by myself.*
    Now don't you hear me talking, pretty mama?
 Lord, ain't going down that big road by myself.
 If I don't carry you, baby, I'm gon' carry somebody else.

2. *Crying, the sun gon' shine in my back door someday.*
    Now don't you hear me talking, pretty mama?
 Lord, the sun gon' shine in my back door someday.
 And the wind gon' change and gon' blow my blues away.

3. *Baby, what makes you do me like you do do do, like you do do do?*
    Don't you hear me now?
 What makes you do me like you do do do?
 Now you think you gon' do me like you done poor Cherry Red.

4. *Taken the poor boy's money now; sure, Lord, won't take mine.*
    Now don't you hear me talking, pretty mama?
 Taken the poor boy's money now; sure, Lord, won't take mine.
 Taken the poor boy's money now; you sure, Lord, won't take mine.

5. *Crying, ain't gon' be your low down dog no more.*
    Now don't you hear me talking, pretty mama?
 I ain't gonna be your low down dog no more.
 Mama, I ain't gon' be, be your low down dog no more.

6. *I'm gon' tell you, fairo, like the sparrow told the wren.*
    Now don't you hear me talking, pretty mama?
 Gonna tell you, fairo, like the sparrow told the wren.
 "Well, I'm going away, baby, but I'll be back again."

7. *Crying, what good is a bulldog, he won't bark or bite?*
    Now don't you hear me talking, pretty mama?
 What good is a bulldog, he won't bark or bite?
 What good is a woman, if she won't let you stay all night?

Griffith's performance shows that he was a good disciple, for it is very close to the sound of Johnson's record. His first four stanzas are the same ones that Johnson sang on his record (Example 60), but

Griffith has decided to carry on with the mood that they express, whereas Johnson merely repeated his first two stanzas. Stanzas 5 and 6 of Griffith's version continue the singer's assertions of independence in thought and action and of his ability to overcome problems. He concludes the song with a denunciation of the woman who will not let him have his way, comparing her to a useless domestic animal. This final stanza should be compared to the fifth stanza, where the singer states that he will no longer be like such an animal. Separating these two stanzas is a stanza that uses the imagery of wild birds and seems to describe the ideal relationship from the point of view of the singer, one in which he can come and go as he pleases. Griffith's text, then, adds further depth to the one that Tommy Johnson recorded. His additional stanzas, however, are probably ones that Johnson himself sang in performances of this and various other blues. Both stanzas 5 and 7 are commonly used by other performers in blues that they claim to have learned from Johnson.

Bubba Brown is another blues singer who came to Jackson in 1928 and began shortly thereafter to perform with Tommy Johnson. In his long career as an entertainer Brown composed many original poems, blues, and other songs, including a piece called "Going to St. Louis," which used the guitar part and melody of "Big Road Blues," but he also performed a version of "Big Road Blues" itself. His three recordings of the song in 1967 all contain the same three stanzas and differ only in

John Henry "Bubba" Brown. Photo by Marina Bokelman.

their ordering and repetitions. This stability of text is characteristic of Brown's other blues. His version of the song contains the core stanza of "Big Road Blues" and variants of two stanzas from "Stop and Listen Blues." His "smokestack black" stanza is greatly changed from any of its other more cryptic forms and makes good sense without any great loss of the power in its imagery. Musically Brown's version is close to Tommy Johnson's except for an interesting variation in the guitar figure in measures 7–8 and 11–12, in which some of Johnson's notes are reversed. This guitar figure, printed below, is probably Brown's own invention, as nobody else plays it.

Example 75. "Big Road Blues." John Henry "Bubba" Brown, vocal and guitar in EBGDAD tuning, key of D. Los Angeles, July 17, 1967. Recorded by David Evans and Marina Bokelman.

1. *Well, I ain't going down the big road by myself.*
   And don't you hear me talking, pretty mama?
   Well, I ain't going down the big road by myself.
   If you don't go with me, I'm gonna carry somebody else.

2. *Well, it's stop and listen; hear those church bells tone.*
   And don't you hear me talking, pretty mama?
   Well, it's stop and listen; hear them church bells tone.
   She's been a mighty nice woman, but now that woman's dead and gone.

3. *Well, I ain't going down this big road by myself.*
   And don't you hear me talking, pretty mama?
   Well, I ain't going down this big road by myself.
   If you don't go with me, I'm gonna carry me somebody else.

4. *She's smokestack black, and her teeth don't shine like pearls.*
   And don't you hear me talking, pretty mama?
   She's smokestack black, teeth don't shine like pearls.
   Guess that nice disposition carries the woman right on through the world.

Brown stated that "just about all" of his version was learned from Tommy Johnson. If this is so, it means that Johnson incorporated stanzas from the Mississippi Sheiks' 1930 recording of "Stop and Listen Blues" into his song. We shall see that other singers who learned "Big Road Blues" from him make similar claims.[52]

Tommy Johnson married Rosa Youngblood in 1935 and moved with her to her home in the country southeast of Tylertown, Mississippi, where they farmed until 1937. Although he often commuted to Jackson and Crystal Springs during this period to play at house parties, Johnson also played with the local Tylertown musicians and had a profound influence on them.[53] Many of them learned his songs, especially "Big Road Blues." A comparison of their versions of this piece affords a good opportunity to see how different blues singers from the same local tradition react to and reshape newly introduced blues elements. The comparison also highlights the importance of such factors as personality, performance context, and the influence of commercial phonograph records.

Of all the Tylertown musicians, Johnson probably performed the most with Isaac Youngblood, his wife's cousin. Youngblood was already an accomplished folk blues musician and singer and considered himself to be Johnson's musical equal. Each learned songs from the other. When I recorded Youngblood in 1966, he had been performing church songs with a quartet and played blues for me only with some reluctance. His first version of "Big Road Blues" contained only two stanzas. He performed it two more times and each time added another stanza, though he claimed that each version was as long as Tommy Johnson ever sang the piece. Youngblood's longest recorded version is printed below. Yet when he heard the playback of it, he stated that the song

Isaac Youngblood. Photo by Marina Bokelman.

also contained the "stop and listen" stanza. This stanza, of course, comes from "Stop and Listen Blues," but it is likely that Johnson himself was singing it during the 1930s in his "Big Road Blues." The remainder of Youngblood's stanzas undoubtedly come from Johnson. The second stanza was known in the Drew tradition and is found in Charley Patton's "Pony Blues" (Paramount 12792, Example 24). Stanza 3 has been encountered already in Shirley Griffith's "Big Road Blues" (Example 74), and stanza 4 was sung by Johnson himself in "Maggie Campbell Blues" (Victor 21409). Youngblood's melody and guitar part are like Johnson's, except for the fact that there is no falsetto singing and that Youngblood plays the variant guitar figure in measures 7–8 and 11–12 that was used by Mager Johnson (Examples 68–69).

Example 76. "Big Road Blues." Isaac Youngblood, vocal and guitar in EBGDAD tuning, key of D; Herb Quinn, mandolin. Tylertown, Miss., Aug. 25, 1966. Recorded by David Evans and Marina Bokelman. Issued on *The Legacy of Tommy Johnson*, Matchbox SDM 224, 12" LP.

INSTRUMENTAL CHORUS.

1. *Well, I ain't going down the big road by myself.*
       Don't you hear me talking to you, mama?
   Oh, going down the big road by myself.
   If I don't carry you, I'm gon' carry me someone else.

2. *Well, I got a riding horse; she's already trained.*
       Don't you hear me talking to you, mama?
   Oh, got a riding horse; she's already trained.
   If you want to ride easy, tighten up on your reins.

3. *Hey, what good is your bulldog, he won't bark or bite?*
       Don't you hear me talking to you, mama?
   Oh, good is your bulldog, he won't bark or bite?
   Well, what service is your woman, she won't let you in at night?

4. *Hey now, see, see, rider, see what you done done.*
       Don't you hear me talking to you, mama?
   Oh, see, see, rider, see what you done done.
   You done made me love you. Now your man done come.

Roosevelt Holts was also a cousin of Tommy Johnson's wife. He was not as accomplished a performer as Isaac Youngblood when Johnson first arrived in the Tylertown area. Holts learned quickly, however, and when Tommy and Rosa left for Jackson in 1937, Holts accompanied them and lived with them there for a year. Holts recorded "Big Road Blues" seven times between 1965 and 1969. Musically the performances are close to Tommy Johnson's version, though Holts extends the ascending bass figure in the first line of the guitar part by about two measures and plays the variant figure at the end of the second and third lines that is used also by Mager Johnson and Isaac Youngblood. Five of Holts's texts are identical. They consist of the core stanza of "Big Road Blues" followed by stanzas 4, 2, and 3 of the Mississippi Sheiks' "Stop and Listen Blues" (Example 70). In one of his other versions

Holts substituted Isaac Youngblood's final stanza above for his last stanza, and in his last version Holts added a fifth stanza, a traditional one that Tommy Johnson is said to have sung on occasion.[54] Holts's version of this blues, then, is basically stable in his repertoire but contains slight room for textual modification toward the end. He was familiar with the record by the Mississippi Sheiks but stated that Johnson himself adopted their verses and sang them in "Big Road Blues." Holts sings the song as he remembers Tommy Johnson singing it.[55]

Arzo Youngblood was seventeen years old when Tommy Johnson married his aunt and came to live on his father's farm. Arzo was so impressed by his uncle's status as a famous blues singer that he began to learn blues from him. Today he still performs many of his uncle's songs. I recorded "Big Road Blues" from him five times between 1966 and 1970. Each version is textually very different, yet all of them draw from a pool of verses that he and other blues singers commonly associate with Tommy Johnson. This diversity of Youngblood's performances is similar to that found in the versions by Mott Willis and Mager Johnson (Examples 64–69). Willis and Johnson treated this song in the manner of other blues from the Drew tradition. Youngblood was never exposed to the breadth of that local tradition, yet his first and most intense learning experiences in the blues were directly under Tommy Johnson. It would appear, therefore, that he assimilated not only Johnson's songs but also much of his approach to creating blues, whereas the other Tylertown performers had already learned to play some blues

Roosevelt Holts. Photo by Cheryl T. Evans.

before Johnson arrived there and were more content to assimilate his blues as whole songs.

Two of Arzo Youngblood's texts are printed below to illustrate the diversity of his performances. They are especially interesting in view of the fact that Youngblood had heard Johnson's record. Despite this, he sings only one stanza from it besides the core stanza. Youngblood knew that his own performances differed from the one on his uncle's record, a fact which he attributed to his learning this blues from Johnson in person. Two of his stanzas are reworkings of ones associated with "Stop and Listen Blues," in which Youngblood contributes some striking imagery. The remainder of his stanzas are all ones which were sung in various blues by Johnson or other artists associated with him. Undoubtedly Youngblood learned them from his uncle. In general, Youngblood's texts contrast assertions of independence with complaints about mistreatment. His performances also exhibit some musical diversity. The second example printed below was performed with an electric guitar and is musically very close to Tommy Johnson's recording. His other performances, however, played on an acoustic guitar, contain some of the variant figures used by Mager Johnson and Walter Vinson, and Youngblood sometimes makes a falsetto leap in the melody at the end of the second line. He knew that Tommy Johnson's record did not contain these features, but he stated that Johnson employed them in various performances of the song.

Arzo Youngblood. Photo by David Evans.

Example 77. "Big Road Blues." Arzo Youngblood, vocal and guitar in EBGDAD tuning, key of D. New Orleans, Sept. 16, 1966. Recorded by David Evans and Marina Bokelman.

GUITAR CHORUS.

1. *Well, going down that big road by myself.*
   Don't you hear me talking, pretty mama?
   Now I ain't going down that big road by myself.
   If I don't carry you, baby sure gon' carry somebody else.

2. *Well, stop and listen what I'm gonna say.*
   Now don't you hear me talking, pretty mama?
   Now stop and listen what I'm going to say.
   It's a mean black snake, Lord, been treating my babe thisaway.

3. *Well, what you gonna do, trouble get like mine?*
   Now don't you hear me talking, pretty mama?
   Now what you gonna do, trouble get like mine?
   Hey, get your pick and shovel, Lord, fall on down the line.

GUITAR CHORUS.

4. *Mmmm, going away now; won't be back till fall.*
   Now don't you hear me talking, pretty mama?
   Now I'm going away; won't be back till fall.
   If I don't find my brownskin, won't be back at all.

5. *Well, you took all the poor boy's money; sure, God, won't take mine.*
   Don't you hear me talking, pretty mama?
   Now took the poor boy's money; sure, God, won't take mine.
   Well, took the poor boy's money, but you sure, Lord, won't take mine.

GUITAR CHORUS.

Example 78. "Big Road Blues." Arzo Youngblood, vocal and guitar in EBGDAD tuning, key of D. New Orleans, Aug. 27, 1970. Recorded by David Evans.

1. *Hey, you see me coming, woman, hoist your window high.*

2. *Well now, ain't going down that big road by myself.*
   Now don't you hear me talking, pretty mama?
   Now I ain't going . . . big road by myself.
   If I don't carry my fairo, Lord, I'm sure gon' somebody else.

3. *Well now, you ain't gonna do me like you done poor Shine.*
   Now don't you hear me talking, pretty mama?
   Now you ain't gonna do me like you done poor Shine.
   Have the poor boy's money, but you have to kill me before you get mine.

GUITAR CHORUS.

4. *Well now, it smoke like lightning, shower down just like rain.*
   Now don't you hear me talking, pretty mama?
   Now smoke like lightning, shower down just like rain.
   You happen to see my woman, please don't call my name.

GUITAR CHORUS.

Another version by Youngblood from 1966 contained the core stanza followed by the second stanza of Example 77 and the fourth stanza of Example 78.[56] In 1969, however, he recorded two radically different versions of this song. At the time of recording he was quite tired, a factor that was compounded with several drinks. Consequently he was unable to concentrate fully on his performances. His texts were extremely garbled and full of dissociated imagery drawn from stanzas that he usually sang in this song as well as additional traditional lyric material. The texts are not worth printing in full, but the following stanza can be taken as typical:

> *Well now, smokes like lightning, showers down just like rain.*
> *Now don't you hear me talking, pretty mama?*
> *Now smokes like lightning, showers down just like rain.*
> *Crying, Lord, Lord, she ain't never, my mama ain't no thing.*

Such performances as these are typically produced in situations where the singer is unable to concentrate fully on his music. They are also typical of the kinds of blues performed at the close of house parties and other engagements where the singers are operating on their last reserves of energy after a long night of drinking and carrying on. I have a fair number of such performances on tape, but they are not representative of the best that the folk blues has to offer. Nevertheless, they are interesting illustrations of the effect of context and the singer's state of mind on his performance.

Relatives of Tommy Johnson's wife were not the only Tylertown musicians who learned from him. Herb Quinn, a fine musician who played a variety of stringed instruments, often accompanied Johnson in playing for both white and black audiences. Quinn's repertoire, however, was already well developed within the local tradition, and he never took much time to incorporate Johnson's songs into it. Instead, he simply worked out accompaniments to them on various instruments. His version of "Big Road Blues," accompanied on the mandolin, contains only the first line of the core stanza repeated twice. This was the only verse that he could remember.[57]

Perhaps the most interesting version of "Big Road Blues" by a Tylertown artist is that by Babe Stovall. He did not perform too often with Tommy Johnson and learned only this one song directly from him, but Stovall was for many years a mainstay of the local blues scene and performed with many other artists who knew Johnson better. Stovall recorded the song eight times in 1965 and 1966. Musically his version is close to Tommy Johnson's, but his text differs greatly. Basically Stovall has a stable text of seven different stanzas, which he always sings in exactly the same sequence, although he omits some stanzas in all but one of his performances. The one complete version is printed below. In only one performance did Stovall sing an additional stanza at the end.[58] In two performances, however, he concatenated "Big Road Blues" with other songs in his repertoire. One of these performances began with four stanzas from the traditional folksong "Careless Love," followed by five stanzas of "Big Road Blues" and one stanza of "Big Leg Woman," a 1938 hit record by Johnnie Temple (Decca

7547).[59] The other performance contained six stanzas of "Big Road Blues" followed by three from "Big Leg Woman." Stovall elsewhere has performed all three of these songs separately They have different melodies and guitar parts, though the latter are in the same key and tuning, and "Careless Love" and "Big Road Blues" share a few musical elements. Their concatenation in some performances is a personal characteristic of Stovall's style and should not be attributed to Tommy Johnson's influence. Stovall concatenates other songs in his repertoire as well.

It is interesting to note that the seven stanzas Stovall sings to the melody and guitar part of "Big Road Blues" represent a composite of verses drawn from at least three different songs that use this musical pattern. Three of the stanzas apparently come directly from Tommy Johnson. In the text printed below stanza 7 is the song's core stanza, and stanza 4 was sung in Johnson's "Maggie Campbell Blues" (Victor 21409), while stanza 9 was known in the Drew tradition (see Example 38). The first two stanzas, however, are ultimately from "Stop and Listen Blues" (Example 70), although Stovall insists that they were sung by Johnson himself in person. Probably this is correct, since other artists have said the same thing. Stovall's final two stanzas are derived from Poor Boy Lofton's record of "Dirty Mistreater" (Decca 7049, Example 72). In fact, Stovall often used Lofton's title for this song. Arzo Youngblood insisted that Tommy Johnson never sang these stanzas, and Stovall admitted that he "added one or two verses" himself, so that these must be the ones to which he referred. Lofton's record was made in 1935, the same year that Tommy Johnson moved to the Tylertown area. It must have seemed natural to Stovall to associate and combine the two songs.[60]

Example 79. "Dirty Mistreater." Babe Stovall, vocal and guitar in EBGDAD tuning; Marc Ryan, guitar. Boston, Apr. 3, 1965. Recorded by David Evans.

GUITAR CHORUS.

1. *Well, today have been a long old lonesome day.*
    Now don't you hear me talking, pretty rider?
   Well, today have been a long old lonesome day.
   Says, I believe tomorrow be the same old way.

2. *Well, stop and listen; hear the church bells in tone.*
    Well, don't you hear me talking, pretty rider?
   Well, stop and listen; hear the bells in tone.
   Says, I had a little fairo, but she's dead and gone.

3. *Says, I had a little fairo, but she's dead and gone.*

4. *Crying, who's that yonder coming down the road?*
    Now don't you hear me talking, pretty rider?
   Lord, who is that yonder coming down the road?
   Well, walk like Mattie, hey, but she walk too slow.

5. *Hmmm, mmmm, mmmm, mmmm.*
   Hmmm, mmmm.
   Hmmm, mmmm, mmmm.

6. *Hmmm, mmmm, mmmm.*

7. *Well, I ain't going down . . . big road by myself.*
   Now don't you hear me talking, pretty rider?
   Lord, I ain't going . . . big road by myself.
   If I don't carry you, rider, carry somebody else.

8. *If I don't carry you, rider, carry somebody else.*

9. *Says, my baby got ways like a fox squirrel in some tree.*
   Now don't you hear me talking, pretty rider?
   My baby got ways . . . fox squirrel in some tree.
   Well, she see me coming, hey, run and hide from me.

10. *Well, see me coming, hey, run and hide from me.*

11. *Crying, Lord, have mercy on my wicked soul.*
    Wouldn't get in trouble, Lord, to save no black woman's soul.
    Crying, dirty mistreater, mistreats me all the time.
    Crying, dirty mistreater, mistreats me all the time.

12. *I was laying on my sickbed trying to take my rest.*
    Here come the dirty mistreater trying to start your mess.
    Crying, dirty mistreater, mistreats me all the time.
    Crying, dirty mistreater, mistreats me all the time.

GUITAR CHORUS.

Eli Owens, another musician from the Tylertown area, learned "Big Road Blues" from Babe Stovall, although he knew that it was originally Tommy Johnson's song. Owens's three short versions are all different. The first, from 1970, contains the core stanza and the ninth stanza of Stovall's version above, separated by a stanza drawn from the often recorded popular blues "Rock Me."[61] Owens sings the typical melody and refrain of "Big Road Blues," but his guitar is played in the key of E in standard tuning and uses a walking bass figure, which he says he learned from records by Jimmy Reed. Owens claimed that it was his own idea to use this guitar part with "Big Road Blues." Immediately following this he performed "Big Road Blues" with the guitar part as he learned it from Babe Stovall in EBGDAD tuning. Owens again sang Stovall's ninth stanza above, but he preceded it with a variant of the eighth stanza of Willie Lofton's "Dark Road Blues" (Bluebird B6229, Example 73).[62] Three years later Owens recorded a piece with the same melody and guitar part, which contained close variants of the fifth and eighth stanzas of Lofton's record. Owens called this piece "Dark Road," saying, "Tommy Johnson put out the 'Big Road Blues,' and I changed it."[63] This record by Willie Lofton was also made in 1935, the year of Johnson's arrival in Tylertown, and it is almost certain that Eli Owens heard it and incorporated some of its verses into "Big Road Blues." It is also a possibility that Arzo Youngblood heard Lofton's record, as his

Eli Owens. Photo by Cheryl T. Evans.

third stanza in Example 78 is actually closer to Lofton's third stanza than to the way Tommy Johnson sang on his record (Example 60).

If we examine all of the performances of "Big Road Blues" by the Tylertown artists, we can discover no clear pattern that distinguishes them as a group from the performances of this song by any other single artist or group. Instead, each performer acts individually. The versions strengthen our suspicion that Tommy Johnson did not perform this song the same way on every occasion and that his recorded performance is only one version out of many that he sang. The Tylertown versions also show that Johnson had incorporated some or all of the verses of the Mississippi Sheiks' "Stop and Listen Blues" into his performances of "Big Road Blues," and they reveal the effect of Willie Lofton's two commercial recordings on the folk tradition. Yet all of the texts by different performers are quite dissimilar. Furthermore, Isaac Youngblood, Roosevelt Holts, and Babe Stovall achieved relatively stable versions of the song in their repertoires, whereas Arzo Youngblood and Eli Owens display considerable variation from one performance to another. Despite the stability of his version, Babe Stovall achieves variety by concatenating it with other songs. The versions by Stovall and Owens (with one exception) are musically similar to Tommy Johnson's, while those of Holts and the Youngbloods contain musical variations not found on Johnson's record but heard in the performances by Mager Johnson. The versions by each artist are thoroughly traditional, yet each reveals a strong element of individual creativity in shaping traditional material, while several performances also reveal the effects of commercial phonograph records, context and the singer's personal stylistic idiosyncrasies and state of mind at the time of performance.

The importance of personal factors and context is nowhere more dramatically illustrated than in the following version of "Big Road Blues" by a singer whom we shall call J. D. It was recorded in Franklinton, Louisiana, but the singer probably learned it from Tylertown musicians, such as Roosevelt Holts and Babe Stovall, who had lived in Franklinton at various times. It is undoubtedly the worst performance of "Big Road Blues" ever recorded. The singer had appeared at several of my recording sessions with his cronies, always drunk and disorderly, and had had a hand in turning the sessions into what I have called "mob scenes" as a result of his insistence on performing and being the center of attention. J. D. was not only drunk from cheap wine but he was one of the filthiest people I have ever met. The near incoherence of his singing was accentuated by the fact that he was missing all of his front teeth, having probably lost them in a fight. His guitar playing and singing were execrable, although allusions to the song's more typical musical patterns revealed the fact that he might once have been a competent performer. His text displays a mixture of alienation, defensiveness, and hostility that is typical of so many alcoholics. Unfortunately, this sort of singer, who seldom gains any respect from his own community, has become in some circles the stereotype of the blues singer and has done much to give an unsavory reputation to the blues. J. D.'s text is printed below. His performance was ended abruptly as another slightly more sober crony clapped a hand over the guitar strings when J. D. showed signs of falling off his chair.

Example 80. "Big Road Blues." J. D., vocal and guitar in EBGDAD tuning, key of D. Franklinton, La., Aug. 26, 1966. Recorded by David Evans and Marina Bokelman.

> 1. *Hey, gon' quit walking. I ain't gon' walk no more.*
>   *I ain't gon' walk down this big road all by myself.*
>
> 2. *Crying, Lord, have mercy. I ain't harmed a man.*
>   *Ain't harmed a man.*
>   *Hey, I ain't goin' down, down this big road by myself.*
>
> 3. *Hey, church bell toning.*
>   *Hey, don't you hear me talking?*
>   *Hey, if I was you, woman, hey, I'd find somebody else.*

4. *It ain't no use, baby. You keep me worried all the time.*
   If I was you, baby, hey, find you somebody else.

5. *I been walking, hey, by myself.*
   I been walking, hey, by myself.
   If I was you, woman, find you somebody else.

6. *I don't want you, baby; I don't want you no more.*
   Hey, don't have to worry . . .

The remaining versions of "Big Road Blues" add only a little to our knowledge of the song's life in oral tradition. Because, for the most part, they confirm observations that we have already made, they will be treated here only briefly.

Blind James Brewer was born in 1921 in Brookhaven, Mississippi, about thirty miles south of Tommy Johnson's home town of Crystal Springs. Before moving to Chicago around 1940 he learned a version of "Big Road Blues" from Johnson. Brewer has made two recordings of the song, which differ only in one line of the text, an indication that the piece is quite stable in his repertoire.[64] His melody displays a few individualized variations from the standard one, while his guitar playing has a triplet rhythm, a modern touch, and employs several extra beats, a characteristic we have noted in the performances of several other artists and one that is probably a result of the difficulty of fitting the first line of text and the refrain into four measures. Brewer's snapping of the bass strings was probably learned from Tommy Johnson. His text is thoroughly the product of oral tradition. It contains variants of the following five stanzas: the core stanza of "Big Road Blues"; the opening stanza of the Mississippi Sheiks' "Stop and Listen Blues" (Example 70); the second stanza in Tommy Johnson's recording of "Big Road Blues" (Example 60); the opening stanza of Johnson's "Big Fat Mama Blues" (Example 55); and the first stanza in one of Arzo Youngblood's performances of "Big Road Blues" (Example 78). Probably all of these stanzas came to Brewer from Tommy Johnson.[65]

K. C. Douglas came to Jackson from Canton, Mississippi, in 1940 and lived there until 1945, when he moved to California. During his stay in Jackson he played frequently with Tommy Johnson and learned "Big Road Blues" from him.[66] Douglas recorded the song three times.[67] Three stanzas are found in all three performances, and one stanza is found in two performances. Each performance, however, contains one unique stanza. All of Douglas's stanzas are traditional, and most have been encountered already in this study. Like many other artists, he extends the ascending bass figure in the guitar part beyond the normal four measures in order to accommodate the first line and refrain. In his instrumental breaks he plays some original figures. Douglas, then, has a largely stable version of this song in his repertoire, though he allows some room for improvisation at the time of performance. In this respect he is reminiscent of Roosevelt Holts.

Boogie Bill Webb has lived most of his life in New Orleans, but he stayed in Jackson sporadically between 1942 and 1951. There he met Tommy Johnson and other local musicians and learned many of their songs, including "Big Road Blues." Webb's version contains the first two stanzas from Tommy Johnson's recorded version (Example 60) followed by two stanzas from "Stop and Listen Blues." He stated that Tommy Johnson played it both a slow and a fast way, but Webb's two performances actually differed little.[68] His text confirms the fact that Johnson was still singing verses from "Stop and Listen Blues" in the 1940s.[69]

J. B. Lenoir was born in Monticello, Mississippi, about forty miles southeast of Crystal Springs, in 1929 and lived there until the late 1940s, when he moved to Chicago. He never knew Tommy Johnson, though he did know Babe Stovall from nearby Tylertown. In 1960 Lenoir played the guitar part of "Big Road Blues" as a solo demonstration for Paul Oliver of his father's style of guitar playing.[70] Five years later, while on a tour of England, Lenoir performed a version of "Big Road Blues" at an informal gathering. For this he borrowed a guitar that was tuned in an open tuning and played the piece partly in bottleneck style, apparently improvising as he went along. He sang the first two stanzas of Tommy Johnson's recorded version (Example 60), followed by a stanza with the line, "See me comin', put your man outdoors."[71] Probably he learned the song from his father, who may have known Tommy Johnson.[72]

Conclusions

Versions of "Big Road Blues" have been recorded a number of times in recent years by white folk music revival and rock performers, but these versions will not be considered in this study, since they are representative of different traditions and different social groups. Nevertheless, they do illustrate the continuing broad appeal of the song. Undoubtedly more versions will also be recorded in black tradition in the years to come. Despite this probability of new versions appearing, we can make a number of conclusions on the basis of the present study, which are unlikely to be altered, since they are confirmed by many specific examples. These conclusions are listed below.

1. The comparative approach can be used successfully in the study of folk blues. The examples studied, however, must be supplemented with information about the performers and the circumstances under which their versions were learned and performed. The investigator should also have an understanding of the processes of blues composition by individual performers, the workings of local traditions, and the effects of commercial recordings.

2. There was no *Urtext* of "Big Road Blues," only Tommy Johnson's blues core, consisting of a single stanza, an internal refrain following the first line, a melody, and a guitar part. Johnson's commercial recording of the song was only one performance out of

many that he gave in his career. In each performance he probably added different stanzas to the song's core.

3. All of the elements comprising the "Big Road Blues" core are traditional and were drawn from the local blues tradition of Drew, Mississippi. They were first combined into this core by Tommy Johnson, who spread the core far beyond the Drew area.

4. Blues by Floyd Jones, Mattie Delaney, and J. D. Short use elements found in the "Big Road Blues" core. The relationship of these songs to "Big Road Blues" and the Drew tradition is not fully explained by the information at hand.

5. The basis of the appeal of "Big Road Blues" probably lies in the striking imagery of its core stanza and its highly distinctive melody and guitar part as well as the song's association with its composer, Tommy Johnson, a greatly admired and widely traveled folk blues singer.

6. This study illustrates the effect of a single influential performer in crosscutting local and regional traditions and leaving versions of one of his songs in the repertoires of many other performers over a wide area.

7. The comparative study of versions of "Big Road Blues" by other artists reveals musical and textual elements that must have been performed by Tommy Johnson in person but which are not heard on his record.

8. The core of "Big Road Blues" shows an ability to persist in tradition, while the stanzas that are added to it by different singers show great variation.

9. All but a few versions of "Big Road Blues" were learned from Tommy Johnson in person in the state of Mississippi, but a number of them were also influenced to a greater or lesser extent by Johnson's commercial record or the records of others.

10. Several new texts have been composed by various artists to the tune and refrain, and sometimes also the guitar part, of "Big Road Blues." The most important of these songs is "Stop and Listen Blues" by the Mississippi Sheiks.

11. "Stop and Listen Blues" has been transmitted primarily by means of the phonograph record. It has, however, crossed many times with "Big Road Blues," and some or all of its verses were incorporated by Tommy Johnson himself into his performances of "Big Road Blues." Johnson helped to spread these verses among other artists in versions of "Big Road Blues" that they learned from him. Willie Lofton's commercial records of "Dirty Mistreater" and "Dark Road Blues" have also crossed with "Big Road Blues" in tradition.

12. Versions of "Big Road Blues" learned from Tommy Johnson around 1928 often show the influence of his record, which was issued in that year. Versions learned in 1930 or later often show the influence of the Mississippi Sheiks' "Stop and Listen Blues," which was recorded in that year. Versions learned around 1935 sometimes show the influence of Willie Lofton's two records made in that year.

13. Most performers have achieved stable or largely stable texts of "Big Road Blues" in their repertoires, but there is considerable textual improvisation from one performance to another by Mott Willis and Mager Johnson from the Drew tradition and by Arzo Youngblood, who learned blues directly under Tommy Johnson.

14. Different singers emphasize different subjects in their lyrics, often building their nonthematic texts on the structural principles of contrast and association. Most of the stanzas used in "Big Road Blues" are ones that the singers associate with Tommy Johnson from his performances of this or other blues. Each performer creatively reshapes traditional elements, producing highly individual versions or performances.

15. Contextual factors often have an effect on versions of "Big Road Blues," causing such results as lengthening, shortening, garbling, and greater or lesser improvisation. The performer's personal stylistic idiosyncrasies and state of mind at the time of recording are also important factors governing performance.

Until more such comparative studies of single blues song types are made, it will be impossible to expand the above conclusions into generalizations about the folk blues tradition. Nevertheless, it is clear that our conclusions agree with all of those made by Paul Oliver in his comparative study of "The Forty-Fours." In that study he emphasized the importance of personal transmission, phonograph records, the singer's individual style, the influential performer, the creative reshaping of traditional material, and the fact that "The Forty-Fours" did not persist in tradition as a whole song but rather as a combination of elements to which each performer gave his own individual stamp. The study of "Big Road Blues" highlights these and other factors which are important for an understanding of the folk blues tradition.

FOLK BLUES
AND THE STUDY OF
FOLKLORE

T is hoped that the present study of the folk blues has provided not only some new information and insights on a single genre of folklore but that it has also made contributions to the field of folklore scholarship as a whole. In the following pages I shall discuss briefly the implications of this study's findings for various concerns, approaches, and theories of folklorists. This discussion is meant to be suggestive rather than conclusive or exhaustive. Throughout the preceding chapters I have tried to study a body of data directly concerned with the folk blues and draw conclusions from it, rather than apply to the blues theories and approaches derived from the study of other forms of folklore. Nevertheless, it would be ridiculous to deny my awareness of these theories and approaches or their possible influence on the findings of this study. And if they have had influence, then this study has the potential to contribute to their further use and development. Yet I hope that the findings presented here will be evaluated mainly for whatever contribution they make to the further understanding of the folk blues.

Perhaps the *comparative* approach has figured most prominently in this study. This has been the case not only in our look at the many versions of "Big Road Blues" in chapter 4, but also in the investigation of the local blues tradition of Drew, Mississippi, in chapter 3. Comparative scholarship has long played a prominent role in the field of folklore studies. Basically the comparative approach seeks to determine the origins and lines of development of items of folklore, and in doing so it often reveals processes of oral tradition and change. It is, then, the study of variation. In recent years this approach has been subjected to severe criticism from many quarters for its paucity of results, its aridity, and even for some of its basic assumptions. But most of all it has been subjected to neglect by many contemporary folklorists. I hope that this study of variation in the folk blues will help to restore the comparative approach to a place of prominence in the field of folklore by the new directions that it takes.

The present study differs from most other comparative studies in two important ways. First, it does not posit the existence of an *Urform* for an item. From our look at the processes of composition and learning, we have seen that with many folk blues only the individual textual, melodic, and instrumental elements have origins in time and space and that individual blues singers constantly combine and recombine these elements. Second, this study examines not only variations among performances by different blues singers but also variation by the same singer over time and under different conditions of performance.

These departures from the norm of comparative studies should open new forms of folklore to this approach as well as offer new possibilities for the treatment of genres and items that have already been studied comparatively. Certainly the kind of variation and improvisation that has been described here is not unique to the blues. Although it has not been treated in great detail, it would appear to be characteristic of such other forms of black American folksong as the spiritual and worksong.[1] Anyone dealing with these forms, however, would have to take into account the effect of group performance. A similar kind of variation and improvisation has been described for the folksongs of Afro-Americans in Jamaica,[2] and the roots of these practices would appear to lie in traditional African music.[3] Local musical traditions within single African societies have also been reported.[4]

In the Anglo-American folksong tradition most of these characteristics of variation and improvisation are absent or are not as strong.[5] Anglo-American folksongs do, of course, exhibit some variation, and they do so in some of the same ways as do Afro-American folksongs. Their singers forget, delete, and add verses, "patch up" damaged or nonsensical texts, invert stanzas, alter rhymes, modify tunes, combine parts of two or more songs, and even consciously recompose songs. Yet the kind of variation found in different singers' versions of "Big Road Blues," which is probably a typical case in the Afro-American folk blues tradition, would be extraordinary in Anglo-American tradition. Furthermore, the kind of extreme variation from one performance of a song to another by the same singer, which has been shown to be normal in the blues tradition, is almost unheard of in the Anglo-American tradition, as is original improvisation at the time of performance.[6] Abrahams and Foss have summarized the findings of many other researchers by stating that "improvisation of this sort is nearly totally absent from Anglo-American song traditions. Commonly here, the singer views himself as a voice for whatever piece he is performing; he places himself in the background, letting the piece speak for itself. He attempts to reproduce the song exactly as he has heard and learned it."[7] Many folk blues singers have been shown to have precisely the opposite attitude.

In assessing the nature and degree of improvisation and variation in Anglo-American tradition, we must keep in mind that almost all of the studies of these subjects have used as evidence the ballad tradition. Ballads, of course, are usually sung in the third person and have built-in story lines, which naturally tend to stabilize their texts. Nonnarrative folk songs are much less stable. For instance, Robert W. Gordon writes of Anglo-American fiddle songs, "They are not strictly narratives at all. Each verse is complete in itself, and may be sung in any order. A song made up of such verses is formless, without beginning or end, long or short as the occasion and the memory of those present may determine. It is never twice the same—or even approximately the same. Only the tune and one or two stock stanzas remain fixed."[8] Gordon fails to support his statement with sufficient evidence, but if he really is correct, then the fiddle song tradition would seem to work in much the same way as the folk blues tradition and would even seem to utilize something like the "blues core."

White camp meeting spirituals also appear to exhibit a similar pattern of variation and improvisation. Of them Samuel P. Bayard states, "The spiritual *words*, however, were textually incoherent, consisting of improvised lines and couplets freely used and recombined (in alternating solo-chorus patterns) with one another and with the debris of many formal hymns. Just so did the spiritual *melodies* often represent the rending asunder of phrases or halves of many familiar folktune versions and the random recombination of these *disjecta membra* into new melodies."[9]

Unfortunately, such terms as "formless," "incoherent," and "random" discourage comparative study as well as most other kinds of investigation of such songs. A refusal to posit an *Urform*, however, as was done in the study of "Big Road Blues," might make possible the comparative study of these Anglo-American traditional songs. It might also be possible to show that their nonthematic texts are built on structural principles like those of association and contrast. Other forms of white nonnarrative folksong too, such as play party songs, banjo songs, and the blues themselves, deserve more study directed at learning the processes of tradition that shape them. Indeed, it is remarkable how little attention has been paid by scholars to the folk blues in Anglo-American tradition, despite their popularity since the 1920s or earlier.

Some other concepts that have been developed in this study of the folk blues might have relevance to comparative research in Anglo-American traditions. It is known, for instance, that there are regional *stylistic* traditions in southern white fiddling.[10] It would be interesting to know whether regionalism or localism also plays an important role in other genres of folksong or folk music. In this regard Kenneth Thigpen's discussion of local tradition in Scottish balladry is highly suggestive for further research.[11] The concept of the folksong "core" may also be useful in the study of Anglo-American folksongs. Marina Bokelman has, in fact, used a "core" concept in her comparative study of the blues ballad "The Coon Can Game," a song known in both black and white tradition, although here the "core" consists of eight stanzas, enough to make up a whole song, along with three very similar tune types. Other stanzas are sometimes added to these or substituted.[12] The blues core, however, always has stanzas added to it. Tristram P. Coffin has developed the concept of the "emotional core" for the ballad.[13] This is the essentially lyric portion of the narrative ballad that has the greatest impact on the folk audience. It is the part of the song that often remains in folk tradition after the narrative details that frame it have been whittled down or abandoned. Obviously this is quite different from a blues core, but it does raise the question of why a blues core has the power to persist in an individual repertoire or in the larger folk blues tradition and whether this persistence is a consequence of the core's emotional appeal. Since I have suggested that each blues core contains striking imagery and/or musical features that set it apart from the more ordinary traditional elements, it would seem likely that the performers and their audiences do develop "emotional" attachments to these cores.

The findings of this study can also be considered a contribution to the study of *oral poetry* and in particular to the *oral formulaic theory*. This theory was developed by Milman Parry and Albert B. Lord to explain the composition or oral epic poetry.[14] They have shown that the basic units of composition in the epic are the traditional formula, the formulaic expression, and the theme. These units are woven together by the singers at the time of performance to produce lengthy epics. The formula is defined as "a group of words which is regularly employed under the same metrical conditions to express a given essential idea,"[15] while formulaic expressions are lines and half lines which "follow the basic patterns of rhythm and syntax and have at least one word in the same position in the line in common with other lines or half lines."[16] Themes are "groups of ideas regularly used in telling a tale in the formulaic style of traditional song."[17] By employing these basic elements in a creative manner, epic singers compose a new song with every performance, even though the story line might remain the same.

The findings of Parry and Lord have an obvious relevance for the study of folk blues. Certainly we have observed a great many stanzas, lines, and phrases which could be described as "formulaic" and which are added to the song at the time of performance. Yet we must be cautious about applying the oral formulaic theory to the folk blues in more than a general manner. Epics, after all, are lengthy, narrative, stichic, and rigidly metrical, whereas the blues are short, lyric, stanzaic, and have their meter carried mainly by the instrumental accompaniment.

We must also keep in mind that not all blues are composed of traditional formulaic elements, and some of those that do contain them are sung from memory.[18] We could note that there is also a "formulaic" quality to some melodic and instrumental elements of folk blues, yet we must keep in mind that these elements are chosen by the performer at the beginning of the song and usually display only minor variation thereafter.[19]

Attention to the use of traditional elements in the composition of oral poetry promises to provide many new insights to the field of folklore. Certain cautions must be observed, however, and the researcher should not assume automatically that all forms of oral poetry are "formulaic" or composed in the act of performance. In a recent survey of worldwide research on oral poetry, Ruth Finnegan found a great variety of approaches to composition and performance and was unwilling to develop a general theory to explain her subject matter.[20] Previous researchers often tended to borrow theories and concepts that had been developed for the study of one particular genre of oral poetry or the traditions of one particular culture and apply them to other genres or cross-culturally. Studies of folk ballads by Jones, Buchan, and McDowell, for example, have paid insufficient attention to the role of memorization,[21] and Rosenberg's study of oral sermons treats them as if they were rigidly metrical epics.[22] But these authors do at least point out the importance of traditional textual elements in composition within these genres. Perhaps an even more productive area for investigation of the creative use of traditional elements is the field of geometric and abstract folk art, where "formulaic" designs abound.[23] Creativity and variation have also been observed in the handling of traditional narrative elements in myths by American Indian storytellers, so that some of the approaches taken in the present study might profitably be adapted to such material.[24]

In recent years folklorists have devoted increasing attention to the *individual artist* and his repertoire, place in the tradition, and role in the community. Such an emphasis is certainly not lacking in the present study. Not only have the lives and repertoires of two blues singers, Mott Willis and Mager Johnson, been examined in some detail, but information about the life histories and personalities of a number of other singers has been used to explicate various examples. This sort of approach has been essential for our investigations. Most other studies that deal with individual folk performers focus on those with vast repertoires or those who are composers of original material.[25] The majority of the artists discussed in this study of the folk blues have only modest repertoires and have composed few, if any, truly original blues. Yet these artists are almost all fine performers. By featuring their productions here, I hope to emphasize the fact that creativity can consist of not only the invention of new expressions but also the artful selection, handling, and reworking of old ones.

Along with the interest in the individual artist, there has been much attention paid recently to the subject of *folk aesthetics*. This is a

topic that is fraught with many semantic difficulties, and any two writers on it are seldom discussing exactly the same thing.[26] Obviously folk
aesthetics must include the standards not only of the performers but of
their audiences as well. The present study has been concerned mainly
with the blues singers rather than their audiences. Yet it has been
noted that the performance of folk blues is usually a highly social activity. The singers, therefore, could hardly be unaware of the aesthetic
standards of their folk audiences, and, in fact, the general aesthetic
standards of the two groups are virtually identical. At this general level
it has been noted that originally the folk blues aesthetic placed a value
upon "truth" and sincerity, both in the song lyrics and in the overall
spirit of the musical performance. Later commercial trends introduced
values of thematic textual development and greater adherence to standardized musical patterns. Although these new values were often inconsistent with the older ones, the two aesthetics have generally been
able to coexist over the years among folk blues singers and their audiences.

I have not tried to go much beyond these general aesthetic principles to discuss the merits of individual performances and performers.
Obviously some are perceived as better than others by members of the
folk group, but here we encounter the differences of individual taste.
The factors that determine taste are so varied and the result of so many
other personal and contextual factors, that it is probably impossible to
come to any specific conclusions that would be applicable to the folk
group as a whole. We have seen that within the formal limitations of
the blues genre there is great variety in approach to lyric composition,
musical style, and meaning, and that many different kinds of people
perform and listen to the blues. This variety is really a tribute to the
flexibility of the blues genre and the many functions which it is able to
fulfill for people. All but a very few of the examples presented and
discussed in this study were performed by experienced and competent
blues singers, who presumably had continued to derive satisfaction
from their music and to find audiences for it, however large or small.
For these reasons the songs are important and worthy of our attention.

As for my own tastes, I have tried to keep them to myself, although in some cases I have not refrained from noting a particularly
outstanding performance, text, image, or musical figure. I have, however, tried above all to show the variety in the folk blues, and I hope
that this concern of mine will assure sufficient objectivity for this study.
The reader is, of course, welcome to ignore my occasional expressions
of enthusiasm or distaste and is, in fact, encouraged to listen to the
examples that have been issued on records and to an even broader selection of folk blues in order to make his own judgments on their
worth.

Because the topic has been so capably handled by other writers
like Odum and Oliver, I have paid little attention to the *sociological* significance of the folk blues. In doing so, I have not meant to ignore or
de-emphasize the relationship of the blues to black culture or their

usefulness for understanding important aspects of that culture. Instead, I have simply concentrated on some of the more neglected areas of blues scholarship. I have, however, attempted to shed some new light on the development of the blues genre within the context of American and Afro-American culture and history. I have also tried to emphasize aspects of the blues which are practically universal and which transcend the patterns of a single culture or historical period. I believe that the blues' universal meaning is just as important as their specific cultural meaning and that, in fact, the former enhances the latter.

Some of the findings of this study can be considered a contribution to the *psychological* approach to folklore. In the past most psychological studies have sought to find Freudian symbols or Jungian archetypes in various forms of folkloric expression.[27] Certainly the folk blues contain abundant material for these types of analysis, some of it expressed symbolically and some quite overtly. In the present study I have made use of such analysis only sparingly. I have, however, emphasized the role of personality in shaping blues composition and expression. I have also tried to point out the mental processes that shape composition, particularly in the case of nonthematic and improvised blues texts. The principles of association and contrast, which have been so frequently exemplified here, are undoubtedly related to the process of free association of ideas, which psychologists declare to be characteristic of the workings of the unconscious mind. This process can be brought into the open through psychoanalysis, the relating of dreams, hypnotism, and other experimental methods. Since the blues have been shown to have a strongly therapeutic function, it should be no great surprise that they manifest this process. Further studies of folk blues and their singers by psychologically oriented researchers, therefore, should prove rewarding.

Closely related to the psychological approach is the *structural* approach to folklore studies. On a number of occasions I have shown that folk blues texts of the sort other writers have labeled "incoherent" or "random" actually have an underlying structure. Often this structure contains symmetrical patterns of linked verses and thoughts. In this respect my analysis owes much to that of David Buchan, who has found somewhat similar structural patterns in Scottish ballad texts.[28] I have also noted two structural principles, association and contrast, by which some traditional blues texts are composed. The latter principle in particular deserves to be correlated with the principle of binary opposition, which Claude Lévi-Strauss and other structuralists find characteristic of human thought everywhere.[29] Lévi-Strauss and his followers have detected oppositional patterns, especially in mythic expression, from many human societies in both present and past times. They believe that the function of the myths is to mediate these oppositions which exist in the mind and in the mental construction of reality. If some folk blues use a similar form of expression, it might be worthwhile to examine in greater detail the ways in which their performance fulfills a religious or ritual function for their largely "secular" devotees and the ways in which the texts themselves serve as "myths" in such a context.[30]

In recent years a number of folklorists have stressed an approach to their discipline that treats singing, storytelling, artistic production, and so on, as *performance*. Instead of having a primary concern with the products of oral tradition, they are interested more in events, activities, processes, communication, interaction, and behavior, and instead of comparing individual items of folklore and searching for their origins and meaning, they are more concerned with distinguishing different types of folkloric performance and relating these to sociocultural factors. In taking this approach, they have been greatly aided by sociolinguistic and communication theory.[31] Certainly many of the findings of the present study give support to a performance-centered approach to folklore. In fact, I have often used the term performance instead of piece, song, text, version, or item, in order to highlight the variation and improvisation that are so characteristic of folk blues. I have also distinguished several different approaches to performance and composition on the basis of whether or not the songs are thematic and stable within the blues singer's repertoires, and I have examined the statements of performers themselves on how they think these processes operate.

Behavioral folklorists would probably consider an *item-centered* approach to folklore to be the antithesis of their own approach, yet I believe that this is essentially the approach that has been used in this study. Actually it is not a separate approach at all but one that incorporates what is useful from all of the other approaches. Its only distinguishing feature is that it places the item or items of folklore at the forefront of attention. In doing so it treats these items as artistic products, even though their artistic merit may vary greatly. It does not, however, preclude treatment of the items as literary texts, cultural documents, or performances, and, in fact, it encourages such treatment. It assumes, however, that once the performance has taken place, its cultural and behavioral context can never be fully recovered or reconstructed, even though we must strive as much as possible to do so. Also it recognizes that a single performance can have different meanings that we ourselves might later assign to it. Despite these difficulties, the basic concern in using this approach is with meaning. Attention to factors of oral transmission, formulaic composition, individual creativity, and personality, as well as the use of historical, aesthetic, sociological, functional, psychological, structural, and behavioral approaches can all help in this concern.

An item-centered approach to folklore is not really new. It has been used by folklorists for years in many specialized studies, often without any name that would call attention to it as a special approach. Others have called it "eclectic," "rational," "rationalistic," "pragmatic," and "humanistic." Perhaps its spirit has been captured best by D. K.

Wilgus, who stated in his 1972 Presidential Address to the American Folklore Society, "I have yet to find an approach to folklore from which I have learned nothing; I have yet to find one whose dominance is not dangerous."[32]

This approach, then, seeks to find meaning in and account for the existence of items of folklore, and it treats them as artistic products. They are also products of some permanence. When we record a manifestation of folklore in the field, we inevitably frame it in print or in a tape recording, phonograph record, photograph, or film. In doing so, we take it partially out of its context. In fact, we often make it into an "item" when it had been before considered only an example of human behavior. There is no way that we can avoid this process if we want to say anything about folklore. Yet, although we lose much, we also often gain much by recovering things of great beauty and intrinsic interest. In the case of folk blues there are thousands of examples available for appreciation and study, ranging from the poor to the excellent, but all of them containing something of interest. Eighty examples are printed here, and the reader is strongly urged to listen to those that have been issued on records and to the many other available records of folk blues. He is also urged to attend live performances if possible. These songs were created to be enjoyed by their audiences and performers and to give added flavor to their lives. Part of the enjoyment consists of remembering them after the performance, discussing them, learning them, modifying them, and passing them on to others. In discussing folk blues here, I am only trying to extend this process further.

NOTES

Introduction

1. See Maria Leach, ed., *Funk & Wagnalls Standard Dictionary of Folklore, Mythology, and Legend* (New York, 1949), pp. 398–403 (folklore), 1032–1050 (song: folk song and the music of folk songs); Alan Dundes, ed., *The Study of Folklore* (Englewood Cliffs, N.J., 1965), pp. 1–51 ("What Is Folklore?"); and Richard M. Dorson, ed., *Folklore and Folklife* (Chicago, 1972), pp. 1–50 ("Concepts of Folklore and Folklife Studies").

2. For another discussion of these subjects see David Evans, "Folk, Commercial, and Folkloristic Aesthetics in the Blues," *Jazzforschung*, 5 (1973), 11–32.

3. See, for example, Russell Ames, "Art in Negro Folksong," *Journal of American Folklore*, 56 (1943), 253; and "Implications of Negro Folk Song," *Science and Society*, 15 (1951), 170.

4. Robert Winslow Gordon, *Folk-Songs of America* (New York, 1938), p. 4.

5. An exception was Phillips Barry. See his "William Carter, the Bensontown Homer," *Journal of American Folklore*, 25 (1912), 156–168.

6. See, for example, Edward D. Ives, *Larry Gorman, the Man Who Made the Songs* (Bloomington, Ind., 1964); Ives, *Lawrence Doyle: Farmer-Poet of Prince Edward Island* (Orono, Maine, 1971); and Henry Glassie, Edward D. Ives, and John F. Szwed, eds., *Folksongs and Their Makers* (Bowling Green, Ohio, n.d.).

7. Richard A. Reuss, "Woody Guthrie and His Folk Tradition," *Journal of American Folklore*, 83 (1970), 273–303.

8. D. K. Wilgus, "The Rationalistic Approach," in *A Good Tale and a Bonnie Tune*, Publications of the Texas Folklore Society, no. 32, ed. Mody C. Boatright, Wilson M. Hudson, and Allen Maxwell (Dallas, 1964), pp. 229–232.

9. Roger D. Abrahams, ed., *A Singer and Her Songs: Almeda Riddle's Book of Ballads* (Baton Rouge, 1970), p. 117.

10. Some of these points are summarized briefly in David Evans, "Techniques of Blues Composition among Black Folksingers," *Journal of American Folklore*, 87 (1974), 240–249.

11. On this subject see Edward D. Ives, "A Man and His Song: Joe Scott

and 'The Plain Golden Band'," in *Folksongs and Their Makers*, ed. Henry Glassie, Edward D. Ives, and John F. Szwed (Bowling Green, Ohio, n.d.), pp. 71–74.

12. Some of the major studies on this subject have been Albert B. Lord, *The Singer of Tales* (Cambridge, Mass., 1964); Bruce A. Rosenberg, *The Art of the American Folk Preacher* (New York, 1970); and David Buchan, *The Ballad and the Folk* (London, 1972).

13. For a more detailed account of my blues research see David Evans, "Tradition and Creativity in the Folk Blues" (Ph.D. diss., University of California, Los Angeles, 1976), pp. 21–31. I have published preliminary findings on various aspects of the Drew tradition in "The Blues of Tommy Johnson: A Study of a Tradition" (M.A. thesis, University of California, Los Angeles, 1967); "Son House—Some Further Comments," *Blues Unlimited*, no. 43 (May 1967), pp. 8–10; "The Mississippi Blues," notes to *The Mississippi Blues, 1927–1940*, Origin Jazz Library 5, and *The Mississippi Blues No. 2: The Delta, 1929–1932*, Origin Jazz Library 11, 12" LPs (1968); "Blues on Dockery's Plantation: 1895 to 1967," in *Nothing But the Blues*, ed. Mike Leadbitter (London, 1971), pp. 129–132; and *Tommy Johnson* (London, 1971). Besides "Down the Big Road"/"Blues on My Mind" by Roosevelt Holts with Boogie Bill, Bluesman 100, 45 rpm record, I have produced the following documentary 12" LPs of my blues recordings: *Goin' up the Country*, British Decca LK 4931 (reissued on Rounder 2012); *Presenting the Country Blues: Roosevelt Holts*, Blue Horizon 7-63201; *It Must Have Been the Devil: Mississippi Country Blues by Jack Owens and Bud Spires*, Testament T-2222; *Roosevelt Holts and His Friends*, Arhoolie 1057; *South Mississippi Blues*, Rounder 2009; *The Legacy of Tommy Johnson*, Matchbox SDM-224; and *High Water Blues*, Flyright LP 512. A further album, *Big Road Blues*, Advent 2815, has been released concurrently with the publication of this book and contains many examples from my fieldwork in the Drew tradition discussed here. It is available from Advent Records, P.O. Box 772, El Cerrito, CA 94530.

14. The formulaic theory of oral epic composition was developed by Milman Parry and Albert B. Lord after years of field research in Yugoslavia. It is presented in Lord, *The Singer of Tales*.

15. This phase of blues research is discussed in Bob Groom, *The Blues Revival* (London, 1971), pp. 25–75.

16. Discographical details, dates, and places of all commercial blues recordings and field recordings for the Archive of Folk Song made by black performers between 1902 and 1942 will be found listed alphabetically by artist's name in John Godrich and Robert M. W. Dixon, *Blues & Gospel Records 1902–1942* (London, 1969). Commercially issued blues recordings made between 1943 and 1966 will be found similarly listed in Mike Leadbitter and Neil Slaven, *Blues Records: 1943–1966* (London, 1968). These details will not be given in this study except when directly pertinent to the discussion.

17. The fieldwork and methods of Lord and his colleagues are discussed in Milman Parry and Albert Bates Lord, *Serbocroatian Heroic Songs* (Cambridge, Mass., 1954), pp. 5–15.

18. Kenneth S. Goldstein, *A Guide for Field Workers in Folklore* (Hatboro, Pa., 1964), pp. 87–90; and "The Induced Natural Context: An Ethnographic Folklore Field Technique," in *Essays on the Verbal and Visual Arts*, ed. June Helm (Seattle, 1967), pp. 1–6. For a discussion of the problems that I encountered in my fieldwork see David Evans, "Fieldwork with Blues Singers: The Unintentionally Induced Natural Context," *Southern Folklore Quarterly*, 42 (1978), 9–16.

19. For a discussion of various descriptive notational systems and their uses see Mantle Hood, *The Ethnomusicologist* (New York, 1971), pp. 50–122.

20. John Fahey, *Charley Patton* (London, 1970), p. 35.

1: Folk and Popular Blues

1. Some of the most notable attempts have been Abbe Niles, "The Story of the Blues," in *Blues, An Anthology*, ed. W. C. Handy, revised by Jerry Silverman

(New York, 1972), pp. 12–20; Winthrop Sargeant, *Jazz: Hot and Hybrid* (New York, 1946), pp. 160–210; Otto Gombosi, "The Pedigree of the Blues," *Music Teachers National Association Proceedings*, 40 (1946), 382–389; Alfons M. Dauer, *Der Jazz, seine Ursprünge und seine Entwicklung* (Kassel, 1958), pp. 70–91, 157–166, 237–261; Alfons Michael Dauer, "Betrachtungen zur afro-amerikanischen Folklore, dargestellt an einem Blues von Lightnin' Hopkins," *Archiv für Völkerkunde*, 19 (1964–65), 11–30; Charles Keil, *Urban Blues* (Chicago, 1966), pp. 22–23; Harry Oster, *Living Country Blues* (Detroit, 1969), pp. 22–23; Harry Oster, "The Blues as a Genre," *Genre*, 2 (1969), 259–274; Richard Middleton, *Pop Music and the Blues* (London, 1972), pp. 31–54; and Jeff Titon, *Early Downhome Blues: A Musical and Cultural Analysis* (Urbana, Ill., 1977), pp. 138–177.

2. See, for example, Georgia White, "The Blues Ain't Nothin' But . . . ???," Decca 7562, reissued on *Out Came the Blues*, Decca DL 4434, 12" LP; and Robert Johnson, "Preachin' Blues," Vocalion 04630, reissued on *Robert Johnson/King of the Delta Blues Singers*, Columbia CL 1654, 12" LP.

3. Samuel Charters, *The Poetry of the Blues* (New York, 1963), pp. 12–14 (quoting Henry Townsend, Baby Tate, and Furry Lewis).

4. Paul Oliver, *Conversation with the Blues* (New York, 1965), pp. 1–2, 23.

5. Ibid., p. 23.

6. Ibid., p. 25.

7. Eric Mossel, "Every Day I Heard the Blues," *Blues World*, no. 8 (May 1966), p. 13.

8. Ibid., p. 15.

9. Ibid., p. 18.

10. David Evans, "Rubin Lacy," in *Nothing But the Blues*, ed. Mike Leadbitter (London, 1971), p. 244.

11. See, for example, Stephen Calt, "The Country Blues as Meaning," in *Country Blues Songbook*, by Stefan Grossman, Hal Grossman, and Stephen Calt (New York, 1973), pp. 16–19.

12. Oster, *Living Country Blues*, p. 81.

13. "Bird Nest Bound," Paramount 13070, reissued on *Charley Patton*, Yazoo L-1020, 12" double LP.

14. "Hard Times," recorded by David and Cheryl Evans, Bentonia, Mississippi, July 15, 1971.

15. For the views of several blues singers on this point see Robert Neff and Anthony Connor, *Blues* (Boston, 1975), pp. 3–9. Kimberly W. Benston has made a useful comparison of the blues singer to the tragic hero in "Tragic Aspects of the Blues," *Phylon*, 36 (1975), 164–176.

16. E. Franklin Frazier, *The Negro Church in America* (New York, 1964), pp. 44–46. Since the 1960s the black church has adopted a more worldly, activist, and progressive ideology, while in the secular world the blues have lost much of their popularity to songs with a more progressive orientation.

17. Oster, *Living Country Blues*, p. 23. Oster prints many examples passim.

18. Some of the more important discussions of the "blues scale" are Niles, pp. 27–28; Sargeant, pp. 160–172; Ernest Borneman, "Black Light and White Shadow: Notes for a History of American Negro Music," *Jazzforschung*, 2 (1970), 57–59; John Fahey, *Charley Patton* (London, 1970), pp. 38–50; Middleton, pp. 35–39; and Titon, pp. 154–156.

19. Fahey, pp. 38–50, claims not to hear "blue notes" in the blues of Charley Patton and Tommy Johnson, but only the major and minor. To my ear, however, "blue notes" are used by these and almost all other blues singers.

20. Cf. Marshall Stearns, *The Story of Jazz* (New York, 1958), pp. 197–198.

21. Paul Oliver, *Savannah Syncopators: African Retentions in the Blues* (New York, 1970), p. 84; David Evans, "Afro-American One-Stringed Instruments," *Western Folklore*, 29 (1970), 229–245.

22. For the probable origin of this technique see Evans, "Afro-American One-Stringed Instruments."

23. Tony Glover, *Blues Harp: An Instruction Method for Playing the Blues Harmonica* (New York, 1965), pp. 31–35.

24. Frederick E. Danker noted this function for the instrumental breaks in some blues ballads in "Towards an Intrinsic Study of the Blues Ballad: 'Casey Jones' and 'Louis Collins'," *Southern Folklore Quarterly*, 34 (1970), 94, 101.

25. On this point see Howard W. Odum and Guy B. Johnson, *The Negro and His Songs* (Chapel Hill, N.C., 1925), pp. 279–281; Rod Gruver, "A Closer Look at the Blues," *Blues World*, no. 26 (Jan. 1970), pp. 4–10; Rod Gruver, "The Blues As Dramatic Monologues," *John Edwards Memorial Foundation Quarterly*, 6 (1970), 28–31; Jeff Titon, "Autobiography and Blues Texts: A Reply to 'The Blues As Dramatic Monologues'," *John Edwards Memorial Foundation Quarterly*, 6 (1970), 79–82; Rod Gruver, "The Autobiographical Theory Re-Examined," *John Edwards Memorial Foundation Quarterly*, 6 (1970), 129–131; Calt, pp. 16–19; and Titon, *Early Downhome Blues*, pp. 43–45.

26. On this point see Paul Oliver, *The Meaning of the Blues* (New York, 1963), pp. 326–328.

27. See Odum and Johnson, pp. 159–166; Sterling A. Brown, "The Blues As Folk Poetry," in *Folk-Say, A Regional Miscellany: 1930*, ed. B. A. Botkin (Norman, Okla., 1930), pp. 324–339; Sterling A. Brown, "The Blues," *Phylon*, 13 (1952), 286–292; Oliver, *The Meaning of the Blues*; Paul Oliver, *Screening the Blues* (London, 1968); Charters, *The Poetry of the Blues*; Oster, *Living Country Blues*; Leonard Goines, "The Blues As Black Therapy: A Thematic Study," *Black World*, 23, No. 1 (Nov. 1973), 28–40; and Paul Garon, *Blues and the Poetic Spirit* (London, 1975), pp. 62–168.

28. On this subject see Oliver, *Screening the Blues*, pp. 44–89 ("Preaching the Blues").

29. See John Solomon Otto and Augustus M. Burns, "The Uses of Race and Hillbilly Recordings As Sources for Historical Research: The Problem of Color Hierarchy among Afro-Americans in the Early Twentieth Century," *Journal of American Folklore*, 85 (1972), 344–355.

30. Stanley Edgar Hyman, "The Folk Tradition," in *Mother Wit from the Laughing Barrel*, ed. Alan Dundes (Englewood Cliffs, N.J., 1973), pp. 50–53.

31. William Ferris, *Blues from the Delta* (Garden City, N.Y., 1978), pp. 109–111.

32. Cf. John A. Lomax, "Self-Pity in Negro Folk-Songs," *The Nation*, 105 (July–Dec. 1917), 141–145.

33. Cf. Mimi Clar Melnick, " 'I Can Peep through Muddy Water and Spy Dry Land': Boasts in the Blues," in *Folklore International: Essays in Traditional Literature, Belief, and Custom in Honor of Wayland Debs Hand*, ed. D. K. Wilgus and Carol Sommer (Hatboro, Pa., 1967), pp. 139–149.

34. Cf. Oliver, *Screening the Blues*, pp. 164–261 ("The Blue Blues").

35. For this point of view see Robert Springer, "The Regulatory Function of the Blues," *The Black Perspective in Music*, 4 (1976), 278–288.

36. See David Evans, "Bubba Brown: Folk Poet," *Mississippi Folklore Register*, 7 (1973), 15–31.

37. See, for example, Richard M. Dorson, *American Negro Folktales* (Greenwich, Conn., 1967), passim.

38. See *Negro Songs of Protest*, Rounder 4004, 12″ LP; Lawrence Gellert, *Negro Songs of Protest* (New York, 1936); Lawrence Gellert, *Me and My Captain* (New York, 1939); and John Greenway, *American Folksongs of Protest* (New York, 1971), pp. 67–120 ("Negro Songs of Protest").

39. For a fuller discussion of protest in the blues see Oliver, *The Meaning of the Blues*, pp. 320–324.

40. On this subject see Michael Haralambos, *Right On: From Blues to Soul in Black America* (London, 1974).

41. For surveys of this subject see Odum and Johnson, pp. 269–296; Sterling Brown, "The Blues As Folk Poetry" and "The Blues"; Charters, pp. 27–34; Oster, *Living Country Blues*, pp. 61–76; and Calt, pp. 8–35.

42. Calt, pp. 14–16, 23–24.

43. Ibid., pp. 24–27.

44. Paul Oliver, "Blues As an Art Form," *Blues World*, no. 21 (Oct. 1968), p. 4.

45. Borneman, p. 61; Garon, *Blues and the Poetic Spirit*.

46. William Harris, "Bull Frog Blues," Gennett 6661 (recorded 1928).

47. Howlin' Wolf (Chester Burnett), "Smoke Stack Lightning," Chess 1618 (recorded 1956).

48. Janheinz Jahn, *Neo-African Literature* (New York, 1968), p. 167.

49. For good discussions of this point see Borneman, pp. 59–68; and Oster, "The Blues As a Genre," pp. 262–273.

50. For surveys of preblues black folk music see Henry Edward Krehbiel, *Afro-American Folksongs* (New York, 1962); Eileen Southern, *The Music of Black Americans: A History* (New York, 1971), pp. 1–277; Eileen Southern, ed., *Readings in Black American Music* (New York, 1971), pp. 1–201; Robert C. Toll, *Blacking Up: The Minstrel Show in Nineteenth-Century America* (New York, 1974), pp. 195–269, 275–280; Kip Lornell, "Pre-Blues Banjo & Fiddle," *Living Blues*, no. 18 (Autumn 1974), pp. 25–27; and Dena J. Epstein, *Sinful Tunes and Spirituals: Black Folk Music to the Civil War* (Urbana, Ill., 1977).

51. Lafcadio Hearn, "Levee Life," in *The Selected Writings of Lafcadio Hearn*, ed. Henry Goodman (New York, 1949), pp. 215–233.

52. Krehbiel, *Afro-American Folksongs*.

53. Gates Thomas, "South Texas Negro Work-Songs: Collected and Uncollected," in *Rainbow in the Morning*, ed. J. Frank Dobie (Hatboro, Pa., 1965), p. 160.

54. Handy, ed., *Blues, An Anthology*, pp. 61, 206–207.

55. Elsewhere Handy has stated that he heard the song from a Phil Jones in Evansville in 1896. See W. C. Handy, *Father of the Blues* (New York, 1970), p. 148.

56. Ibid., pp. 147–148. In *Blues, An Anthology*, p. 206, Handy states that this song was "sung in Kentucky as early as, perhaps earlier than, the first decade of this century."

57. Handy, ed., *Blues, An Anthology*, p. 53.

58. See, for example, Blind Willie McTell, "East St. Louis," on *Blind Willie McTell—Memphis Minnie, 1949: Love Changin' Blues*, Biograph BLP-12035, 12″ LP; and Jimmy Rogers, "Out on the Road," Chess 1519.

59. Borneman, pp. 75–80.

60. Alan Lomax, *Mister Jelly Roll* (New York, 1950), pp. 20–21, 45, 48, 51–60, 120–121, 269–273, 276–277, 281.

61. Ibid., p. 51.

62. John J. Niles, "Shout, Coon, Shout!," *The Musical Quarterly*, 16 (1930), 519–521.

63. Charles Peabody, "Notes on Negro Music," *Journal of American Folklore*, 16 (1903), 148–152.

64. Ibid., p. 149.

65. See, for example, Texas Alexander, "Levee Camp Moan Blues," Okeh 8498, reissued on *The Country Blues, Volume Two*, RBF 9, 12″ LP.

66. John W. Work, *American Negro Songs and Spirituals* (New York, 1940), pp. 32–33.

67. Handy, *Father of the Blues*, p. 78.

68. Ibid., pp. 80–82. Handy prints several other arrangements of early blues in *Blues, An Anthology*, passim.

69. Thomas, pp. 172, 177–179.

70. Howard W. Odum, "Folk-Song and Folk-Poetry As Found in the Secular Songs of the Southern Negroes," *Journal of American Folklore*, 24 (1911), 255–294, 351–396.

71. Ibid., p. 263.

72. Ibid., p. 258.

73. E. C. Perrow, "Songs and Rhymes from the South," *Journal of American Folklore*, 28 (1915), 190 (No. 80).

74. Henry C. Davis, "Negro Folk-Lore in South Carolina," *Journal of American Folklore*, 27 (1914), 241–254.

75. John J. Niles, "Shout, Coon, Shout!," pp. 523–524.

76. Will H. Thomas, *Some Current Folk-Songs of the Negro* (Austin, 1912), pp. 9, 10, 12.

77. Anna Kranz Odum, "Some Negro Folk-Songs from Tennessee," *Journal of American Folklore*, 27 (1914), 265.

78. W. Prescott Webb, "Notes on Folk-Lore of Texas," *Journal of American Folklore*, 28 (1915), 291–296.

79. Ibid., p. 292.

80. John A. Lomax, "Self-Pity in Negro Folk-Songs," pp. 141–145.

81. Ibid., p. 141.

82. Ibid., p. 141.

83. Mary Wheeler, *Steamboatin' Days* (Baton Rouge, 1944) pp. 29–35, 46–51, 53–55, 80–83, 85–87, 97–98, 102–105, 113–118.

84. Ibid., p. 32.

85. Howard W. Odum, p. 258.

86. Webb, pp. 292, 296.

87. For further discussion of the social origins of the blues see Paul Fritz Laubenstein, "Race Values in Aframerican Music," *The Musical Quarterly*, 16 (1930), 395; Leroi Jones, *Blues People* (New York, 1963), pp. 60–80; and Arnold Shaw, *The World of Soul* (New York, 1971), pp. 63–64.

88. For a discussion of these musical and other artistic developments see Southern, *The Music of Black Americans: A History*, pp. 278–411.

89. See W. K. McNeil, "Syncopated Slander: The 'Coon Song,' 1890–1900," *Keystone Folklore Quarterly*, 17 (1972), 63–82.

90. Samuel Charters, *The Bluesmen* (New York, 1967), pp. 27–28; Paul Oliver, *The Story of the Blues* (London, 1969), pp. 17–25; Oster, *Living Country Blues*, pp. 11–13; Middleton, pp. 55–61; John A. and Alan Lomax, *Folk Song U.S.A.* (New York, 1966), p. 70; Alan Lomax, *The Folk Songs of North America* (Garden City, N.Y., 1960), p. 573. Bruce Cook unaccountably minimizes the obvious importance of field hollers in *Listen to the Blues* (New York, 1973), pp. 55–56.

91. Harold Courlander, *Negro Folk Music U.S.A.* (New York, 1963) pp. 80–88; Epstein pp. 161–183.

92. Frances Anne Kemble, *Journal of a Residence on a Georgian Plantation in 1838–1839* (New York, 1863), pp. 128–129.

93. Johann Tonsor, "Negro Music," *Music*, 3 (1892–93), 119–120.

94. Ibid., p. 120.

95. Ibid., pp. 120–121.

96. Ray B. Browne, "Some Notes on the Southern 'Holler'," *Journal of American Folklore*, 67 (1954), 73–77; Ray B. Browne, "The Alabama 'Holler' and Street Cries," *Journal of American Folklore*, 70 (1957), 363; Peter T. Bartis, "An Examination of the Holler in North Carolina White Tradition," *Southern Folklore Quarterly*, 39 (1975), 209–218; Mark Wilson, notes to *Hollerin'* Rounder 0071, 12″ LP.

97. Son House, "I Can Make My Own Songs," *Sing Out!*, 15, No. 3 (July 1965), 45. For a recording of one of House's own hollers with Fiddlin' Joe Martin see "Camp Hollers" on *Negro Blues and Hollers*, AFS L59, 12″ LP.

98. David Evans, "Booker White," in *Nothing But the Blues*, ed. Mike Leadbitter (London, 1971), p. 255.

99. Jack Owens, Bentonia, Miss., Sept. 1, 1970. Recorded by David Evans.

100. Othar Turner, "Black Woman." Senatobia, Miss., Mar. 22, 1969. Recorded by David Evans. Issued on *Afro-American Folk Music from Tate and Panola Counties, Mississippi*, AFS L67, 12″ LP.

101. Charters, *The Bluesmen*, pp. 27–28. See also Cook, pp. 56–58. For a detailed study of group and individual worksongs see Bruce Jackson, *Wake Up Dead Man: Afro-American Worksongs from Texas Prisons* (Cambridge, Mass., 1972).

102. Borneman, p. 55; Cook, p. 56.

103. Alan Lomax, *The Folk Songs of North America*, pp. 574–575.

104. Oliver, *The Story of the Blues*, pp. 22–25. See also Cook, pp. 58–60; and Abbe Niles in Handy, *Blues, An Anthology*, pp. 17–20.

105. Most of the best known blues ballads are indexed in G. Malcolm Laws, Jr., *Native American Balladry*, rev. ed. (Philadelphia, 1964), pp. 245–256, 275–276.

106. The guitar part is discussed and transcribed in tablature notation in Donald Garwood, *Masters of Instrumental Blues Guitar* (New York, 1968), pp. 47–49; and Stefan Grossman, *The Country Blues Guitar* (New York, 1968), pp. 44–47.

107. For more information on Hurt see Lawrence Cohn, "Mississippi John Hurt," *Sing Out!*, 14, No. 5 (Nov. 1964), 16–21; and George W. Kay, "Mississippi John Hurt," *Jazz Journal*, 17, No. 2 (Feb. 1964), 24–26.

108. Howard W. Odum, nos. 18, 20, 22, 23, 25, 39, 62, 69, 91, and 110.

109. Archie Green, *Only a Miner: Studies in Recorded Coal-Mining Songs* (Urbana, Ill., 1972), pp. 195–196. For versions of the song see Howard W. Odum, p. 351 (no. 54, AAA pattern); Handy, *Blues, An Anthology*, pp. 17–20, 210 (AAB pattern); William Broonzy, *Big Bill Blues*, rev. ed. (New York, 1964), pp. 53–59 (AAA pattern).

110. Handy, *Blues, An Anthology*, p. 19. See also Louis Ford and the Son Sims Four, "Joe Turner," on *Muddy Waters: Down on Stovall's Plantation*, Testament T-2210, 12″ LP.

111. Howard W. Odum, p. 282 (no. 32); Handy, *Blues, An Anthology*, p. 61; Wheeler, pp. 29, 49–51, 53, 81.

112. Lucius Smith, Sardis, Miss., Aug. 1, 1973. Recorded by David and Cheryl Evans. Abbe Niles in Handy, *Blues, An Anthology*, p. 210, suggested that "Joe Turner" might have been the prototype of all blues. Broonzy, pp. 53–54, set the date of its composition in 1890.

113. Lucius Smith, Sardis, Miss., June 27, 1971. Recorded by David and Cheryl Evans. For recordings by Smith and Sid Hemphill's band, including a blues ballad in an AB-refrain pattern, "The Carrier Line," see *Afro-American Folk Music from Tate and Panola Counties, Mississippi*, AFS L67, 12″ LP. For a similar view by another performer of Smith's generation that the blues began as a slow dance music, see Mack McCormick, "Mance Lipscomb, Texas Sharecropper and Songster," in *American Folk Music Occasional, No. 1*, ed. Chris Strachwitz (Berkeley, 1964), pp. 63–64.

114. John J. Niles, "Shout, Coon, Shout!," pp. 519–520.

115. Howard W. Odum, pp. 361–362 (No. 73).

116. Ibid., p. 274 (No. 14).

117. Ibid., p. 260.

118. Ibid., p. 268.

119. Brown performs three blues on *The Sound of the Delta*, Testament T-2209, 12″ LP. Quinn and Holmes perform one apiece on *South Mississippi Blues*, Rounder 2009, 12″ LP, and Quinn performs one on *Goin' up the Country*, British Decca LK 4931, 12″ LP (reissued on Rounder 2012).

120. Fahey, pp. 56–57.

121. Howard W. Odum, nos. 8, 10, and 13. Quinn's piece is issued on *Goin' up the Country*, British Decca LK 4931, 12″ LP (reissued on Rounder 2012).

122. Lacy's preaching and sermons have been the subject of a study by Bruce A. Rosenberg, *The Art of the American Folk Preacher* (New York, 1970).

123. Evans, "Rubin Lacy," p. 244.

124. See, for example, Rosalie Hill, "Bullyin' Well," on *The Blues Roll On*, Atlantic SD-1352, 12" LP.

125. Evans, "Rubin Lacy," p. 244.

126. For another analysis of this piece see Charters, *The Bluesmen*, pp. 120–121.

127. Evans, "Rubin Lacy," p. 244.

128. Townsend, Lewis, Short, and Borum are quoted in Charters, *The Poetry of the Blues* (New York, 1963), pp. 11–12.

129. Pete Welding, "Reverend Robert Wilkins," *Blues Unlimited*, no. 56 (Sept. 1968), p. 12.

130. Julius Lester, "Country Blues Comes to Town?: The View from the Other Side of the Tracks," *Sing Out!*, 14, No. 4 (Sept. 1964), 38.

131. George W. Kay, "William Christopher Handy, Father of the Blues—A History of Published Blues," *Jazz Journal*, 24, No. 3 (Mar. 1971), 10–12.

132. Handy's published blues are listed in *Father of the Blues*, pp. 317–321, and many by him and others are printed in his *Blues, An Anthology*. See also Perry Bradford, *Born with the Blues* (New York, 1965), for a discussion of his compositions and the work of other composers and performers.

133. Handy, *Father of the Blues*, p. 81.

134. Ibid., p. 148.

135. Handy, ed., *Blues, An Anthology*, pp. 86–89.

136. Handy, *Father of the Blues*, p. 149.

137. Handy, ed., *Blues, An Anthology*, pp. 100–103, 209–210.

138. Newman I. White, *American Negro Folk-Songs* (Cambridge, Mass., 1928), pp. 325–326, 339, 398.

139. Ibid., p. 391.

140. John J. Niles, *Singing Soldiers* (New York, 1927), passim.

141. Ibid., p. 93.

142. Jim Walsh, "The First Singer Who Made a 'Blues' Record: Morton Harvey," *Hobbies* (Dec. 1955), p. 30.

143. "Enigmatic Folksongs of the Southern Underworld," *Current Opinion*, 67 (July–Dec. 1919), 165–166.

144. Bradford, pp. 114–129.

145. "Quality in 'Blues'," *The Metronome*, 39, No. 9 (Sept. 1923), 140.

146. "Origin of 'Blues' Numbers," *Sheet Music News*, 2, No. 5 (Oct. 1923), 41.

147. Ibid., p. 9.

148. Max E. Vreede, *Paramount 12000/13000 Series* (London, 1971); Dan Mahony, *The Columbia 13/14000-D Series, A Numerical Listing*, rev. ed. (Stanhope, N.J., 1966).

149. Robert M. W. Dixon and John Godrich, *Recording the Blues* (New York, 1970), pp. 22–23.

150. For a year by year breakdown of these figures and those on the following pages see David Evans, "Tradition and Creativity in the Folk Blues," Ph.D. dissertation, University of California, Los Angeles, 1976, pp. 140–144, 159–162.

151. Her entire recorded output is now available for study on five 12" double LPs: *The World's Greatest Blues Singer*, Columbia GP 33; *Any Woman's Blues*, Columbia G 30126; *Empty Bed Blues*, Columbia G 30450; *The Empress*, Columbia G 30818; *Nobody's Blues But Mine*, Columbia G 31093.

152. Chris Albertson, *Bessie* (New York, 1972), p. 82.

153. Ibid.; Paul Oliver, *Bessie Smith* (London, 1959); Carman Moore, *Some-*

body's *Angel Child* (New York, 1969); and George Avakian, "Bessie Smith," in *The Art of Jazz*, ed. Martin T. Williams (New York, 1959), pp. 75–90.

154. "Origin of 'Blues' Numbers," p. 41.

155. Nat Shapiro and Nat Hentoff, eds., *Hear Me Talkin' to Ya* (New York, 1966), p. 240.

156. For further discussion of this piece see Albertson, pp. 69–73.

157. Ibid., pp. 149–50.

158. For a discussion of Jefferson's career see Samuel Charters, *The Country Blues* (New York, 1959), pp. 57–72; Charters, *The Bluesmen*, pp. 175–189; and Cook, pp. 104–106.

159. On white blues see Tony Russell, *Blacks, Whites and Blues* (New York, 1970); John S. Otto and Augustus M. Burns, "Black and White Cultural Interaction in the Early Twentieth Century South: Race and Hillbilly Music," *Phylon*, 35 (1974), 407–417; John Greenway, "Jimmie Rodgers—A Folksong Catalyst," *Journal of American Folklore*, 70 (1957), 231–234; David Evans, "Black Musicians Remember Jimmie Rodgers," *Old Time Music*, no. 7 (Winter 1972–73), pp. 12–14; and Mike Paris and Chris Comber, *Jimmie the Kid: The Life of Jimmie Rodgers* (London, 1977).

160. On these developments see Dixon and Godrich, *Recording the Blues*, pp. 33–63. Titon, *Early Downhome Blues*, pp. 225–269, views the new interest shown by the record companies in folk blues in 1926 as an attempt at avoiding or downplaying the threatening image of urban blacks and as part of a larger national turning toward an idealized image of the countryside.

161. Maurice Zolotow, "Hillbilly Boom," in *A History and Encyclopedia of Country, Western, and Gospel Music*, rev. ed., ed. Linnell Gentry (Nashville, 1969), p. 39.

162. Ibid., p. 39.

163. Ibid., p. 40.

164. Ibid., p. 36.

165. Mike Seeger, "Who Chose These Records? A Look into the Life, Tastes, and Procedures of Frank Walker," in *Anthology of American Folk Music*, ed. Josh Dunson and Ethel Raim (New York, 1973), pp. 12–13.

166. For further examples of talent scouts and recording directors suggesting songs to blues and hillbilly singers or modifying content or style see Kip Lornell, "Living Blues Interviews: J. B. Long," *Living Blues*, no. 29 (Sept.–Oct. 1976), pp. 15, 18, 20; and Charles Wolfe, "Toward a Contextual Approach to Old-Time Music," *The Journal of Country Music*, 5 (1974), 68–69.

167. Charles K. Wolfe, "Ralph Peer at Work: The Victor 1927 Bristol Sessions," *Old Time Music*, no. 5 (Summer 1972), p. 14.

168. On Speir's career see David Evans, "An Interview with H. C. Speir," *John Edwards Memorial Foundation Quarterly*, 8 (1972), 117–121; and Gayle Wardlow, "Legends of the Lost (The Story of Henry Speir)," in *Back Woods Blues*, ed. Simon Napier (Bexhill-on-Sea, England, 1968), pp. 25–28.

169. David Evans, *Tommy Johnson* (London, 1971), pp. 45–68.

170. On Patton see Fahey, *Charley Patton*, pp. 52–59.

171. Lester Melrose, "My Life in Recording," in *American Folk Music Occasional*, ed. Chris Strachwitz and Pete Welding (New York, 1970), p. 61.

172. Charters, *The Bluesmen*, pp. 177, 180.

173. Norman Cohen, " 'I'm a Record Man': Uncle Art Satherly Reminisces," *John Edwards Memorial Foundation Quarterly*, 8 (1972), 19; Donald Lee Nelson, "The West Virginia Snake Hunters: John and Emery McClung," *John Edwards Memorial Foundation Quarterly*, 10 (1974), 72.

174. All of Jefferson's lyrics have been transcribed by Bob Groom in *Blind Lemon Jefferson*, Blues World Booklet no. 3 (Knutsford, England, 1970); and "The Legacy of Blind Lemon," *Blues World*, no. 16 (Sept. 1967), p. 13; no. 18 (Jan.

1968), pp. 14–16; no. 20 (July 1968), pp. 33–37; no. 21 (Oct. 1968), pp. 30–32; no. 23 (Apr. 1969), pp. 5–7; no. 24 (July 1969), pp. 9–10; no. 25 (Oct. 1969), pp. 9–10; no. 27 (Feb. 1970), pp. 13–14; no. 28 (Mar. 1970), pp. 8–9; no. 29 (Apr. 1970), pp. 8–9; no. 30 (May 1970), pp. 13–14; no. 35 (Oct. 1970), pp. 19–20; no. 36 (Nov. 1970), p. 20; no. 40 (Autumn 1971), pp. 4–6; no. 50 (1974), p. 8. Some of Jefferson's songs have also been printed in *The Paramount Book of the Blues* (Port Washington, Wis., ca. 1927), pp. 3–8; and Stefan Grossman, *Ragtime Blues Guitarists* (New York, 1970), pp. 18–27, 76–90. Also useful has been Michael Taft, "Blind Lemon Jefferson Concordance," unpublished computer print-out. Most of Jefferson's blues have been reissued on the following 12″ LPs: *The Immortal Blind Lemon Jefferson*, Milestone 2004; *Blind Lemon Jefferson, Volume 2*, Milestone 2007; *Black Snake Moan*, Milestone 2013; *Blind Lemon Jefferson 1926–29*, Biograph 12000; *Master of the Blues, Blind Lemon Jefferson, Vol. 2, 1926–1929*, Biograph 12015; *Son House—Blind Lemon Jefferson*, Biograph 12040; *Blind Lemon Jefferson, Volume 2*, Roots RL-306.

175. These three versions are printed and discussed in Titon, *Early Downhome Blues*, pp. 38–42.

176. Selections of blues texts recorded since the 1940s are printed in A. X. Nicholas, *Woke Up This Mornin': Poetry of the Blues* (New York, 1973), pp. 81–91, 99–118; and Jeff Titon, "Downhome Blues Lyrics Since the Second World War: A Selection," *alcheringa/ethnopoetics*, n.s., 2, No. 1 (1976), 10–26. For an analysis of textual patterning in postwar blues see Jeff Titon, "Thematic Pattern in Downhome Blues Lyrics," *Journal of American Folklore*, 90 (1977), 316–330.

177. These and other trends are discussed in some detail in Oliver, *The Story of the Blues*; and Giles Oakley, *The Devil's Music: A History of the Blues* (London, 1976). For a critical guide to blues records see Albert McCarthy, Alun Morgan, Paul Oliver, and Max Harrison, *Jazz on Record* (London, 1968), passim. The activities of the record companies through 1942 are discussed in Dixon and Godrich, *Recording the Blues*, and after 1942 in Mike Leadbitter, *Crowley, Louisiana Blues* (Bexhill-on-Sea, England, 1968); Mike Leadbitter and Eddie Shuler, *From the Bayou* (Bexhill-on-Sea, England, 1969); and Leadbitter, ed., *Nothing But the Blues*, passim.

178. Oliver, *Screening the Blues*, p. 8.

179. Leadbitter and Shuler, *From the Bayou*, p. 52.

180. Ibid., p. 37.

181. Ibid., p. 35.

182. Oliver, *Conversation with the Blues* (New York, 1965), p. 118.

183. Don Lindenau, "Lowell Fulson," *Blues Unlimited*, no. 18 (Jan. 1965), p. 10.

184. Pete Welding, "John Lee Hooker: Me and the Blues," *Down Beat*, 35, No. 20 (Oct. 3, 1968), 15.

185. On B. B. King see Harvey Siders, "Talking with a King," *Down Beat*, 39, No. 6 (Mar. 30, 1972), 14–15; and Keil, pp. 96–113.

186. On this subject see Keil, pp. 76–95.

187. Jim O'Neal and Bill Greensmith, "Living Blues Interview: Jimmy Rogers," *Living Blues*, no. 14 (Autumn 1973), p. 15.

188. Ted Berkowitz, "Sittin' in with Shad," in *Nothing But the Blues*, ed. Mike Leadbitter (London, 1971), pp. 191–192.

189. Leadbitter, *Crowley, Louisiana Blues*, p. 9.

190. Leadbitter and Shuler, *From the Bayou*, p. 15.

191. Ibid., p. 14.

192. Ibid., p. 52.

193. Ibid., p. 37. See also Leadbitter, *Crowley, Louisiana Blues*, p. 10.

194. Oliver, *The Story of the Blues*, p. 168.

195. On this point see Christopher Lornell, "The Effects of Social and Eco-

nomic Changes on the Uses of Blues," *John Edwards Memorial Foundation Quarterly*, 11 (1975), 43–48.

196. On "soul" in black music see Keil, pp. 164–190. On the transition from blues to soul see Middleton, *Pop Music and the Blues*; Haralambos, *Right On*; and "Soul Music and Blues: Their Meaning and Relevance in Northern United States Black Ghettoes," in *Afro-American Anthropology: Contemporary Perspectives*, ed. Norman E. Whitten, Jr. and John F. Szwed (New York, 1970), pp. 367–384.

197. Many examples have been printed from the fieldwork of Harry Oster in *Living Country Blues*, passim. See also William R. Ferris, Jr., "Records and the Delta Blues Tradition," *Keystone Folklore Quarterly*, 14 (1969), 158–165.

198. See Oster, *Living Country Blues*, passim; and Evans, "Bubba Brown: Folk Poet," pp. 15–31.

199. "Enigmatic Folksongs of the Southern Underworld," pp. 165–166.

200. "Origin of 'Blues' Numbers," pp. 8–9, 41.

201. Carl Van Vechten, "The Black Blues," *Vanity Fair*, 24, No. 6 (Aug. 1925), 57, 86, 92.

202. Carl Van Vechten, "Prescription for the Negro Theatre," *Vanity Fair*, 25, No. 2 (Oct. 1925), 46, 92, 98.

203. Carl Van Vechten, "Negro 'Blues' Singers," *Vanity Fair*, 26, No. 1 (Mar. 1926), 67, 106, 108.

204. Carl Sandburg, *The American Songbag* (New York, 1927), pp. 225–247.

205. John J. Niles, *Singing Soldiers*, introduction (ii), p. 93.

206. Dorothy Scarborough, *On the Trail of Negro Folk-Songs* (Hatboro, Pa., 1963), p. 264.

207. Ibid., pp. 265–271.

208. Ibid., p. 272.

209. Ibid., p. 272.

210. Ibid., pp. 281–282.

211. Handy, ed., *Blues, An Anthology*, with a historical and critical text by Abbe Niles, revised by Jerry Silverman (New York, 1972). See also Abbe Niles, "Blue Notes," *The New Republic*, 45 (Nov. 25, 1925–Feb. 17, 1926), 292–293.

212. Handy, ed., *Blues, An Anthology*, p. 12.

213. Abbe Niles, "Ballads, Songs and Snatches," *Bookman*, 67 (Mar.–Aug. 1928), 422–424, 565–567, 687–689; 68 (Sept. 1928–Feb. 1929), 75–77, 213–215.

214. Henry O. Osgood, "The Blues," *Modern Music*, 4, No. 1 (Nov.–Dec. 1926), 27. See also Henry O. Osgood, *So This Is Jazz* (Boston, 1926), p. 63.

215. Odum and Johnson, pp. 151–156, 167.

216. Ibid., pp. 159–166, 269–296.

217. See also Howard W. Odum, "Down That Lonesome Road," *The Country Gentleman*, no. 91 (May 1926), pp. 18–19, 79.

218. Howard W. Odum and Guy B. Johnson, *Negro Workaday Songs* (Chapel Hill, N.C., 1926), pp. 17–34.

219. Ibid., p. 34.

220. Ibid., pp. 22–23.

221. Ibid., p. 17.

222. Ibid., pp. 33–34.

223. Howard W. Odum, *Rainbow Round My Shoulder* (Indianapolis, 1928); *Wings on My Feet* (Indianapolis, 1929); *Cold Blue Moon* (Indianapolis, 1931).

224. Guy B. Johnson, "Double Meaning in the Popular Negro Blues," *Journal of Abnormal and Social Psychology*, 22 (1927–28), 12–20.

225. Some of his material had been published earlier in Newman I. White, "Racial Traits in the Negro Song," *Sewanee Review*, 28 (1920), 396–404.

226. White, *American Negro Folk-Songs*, p. 389.

227. Johnson, p. 18.

228. White, *American Negro Folk-Songs*, p. 389.

229. Ibid., p. 390.

230. Ibid., p. 390.

231. Newman I. White, "The White Man in the Woodpile: Some Influences on Negro Secular Folk-Songs," *American Speech*, 4 (Oct. 1928–Aug. 1929), 214.

232. White, *American Negro Folk-Songs*, p. 388.

233. John A. and Alan Lomax, *American Ballads and Folk Songs* (New York, 1934), pp. 189–209; John A. and Alan Lomax, *Our Singing Country* (New York, 1941), pp. 347–376; Alan Lomax, *The Folk Songs of North America*, pp. 573–595.

234. John A. and Alan Lomax, *Negro Folk Songs as Sung by Lead Belly* (New York, 1936).

235. Alan Lomax, *Mister Jelly Roll*.

236. Alan Lomax, *List of American Folk Songs on Commercial Records* (Washington, 1940).

237. Alan Lomax, " 'Sinful' Songs of the Southern Negro," *Southwest Review*, 19 (1933–34), 105–131; Alan Lomax, "I Got the Blues," *Common Ground*, 8 (Summer 1948), 38–52; *Afro-American Blues and Game Songs*, AFS L4, 12" LP.

238. Gellert, *Negro Songs of Protest* and *Me and My Captain*.

239. Lyle Saxon, Robert Tallant, and Edward Dreyer, *Gumbo Ya-Ya* (New York, 1945), pp. 370–371, 454–464.

240. Carl Carmer, *Stars Fell on Alabama* (New York, 1934), pp. 18–24; Zora Neale Hurston, *Mules and Men* (Philadelphia, 1935), passim; David Cohn, *Where I Was Born and Raised* (1947; reprinted Notre Dame, Ind., 1967), pp. 357–365.

241. Work, *American Negro Songs and Spirituals*, pp. 28–36.

242. Muriel Davis Longini, "Folk Songs of Chicago Negroes," *Journal of American Folklore*, 52 (1939), 96–111.

243. John A. and Alan Lomax, *Our Singing Country*, pp. 364–366.

244. Russell Ames, "Art in Negro Folksong," *Journal of American Folklore*, 56 (1943), 241–254.

245. Russell Ames, "Implications of Negro Folk Song," *Science and Society*, 15 (1951), 163–173.

246. James Weldon Johnson, *Black Manhattan* (New York, 1930), p. 228.

247. Brown, "The Blues as Folk Poetry," pp. 324–339.

248. Ibid., pp. 325–326.

249. Brown, "The Blues," pp. 286–292.

250. Alain Locke, *The Negro and His Music* (New York, 1969), pp. 28–35.

251. Ibid., p. 80.

252. Ibid., pp. 86–89.

253. Handy, *Father of the Blues*.

254. Langston Hughes and Arna Bontemps, eds., *The Book of Negro Folklore* (New York, 1958), pp. 371–397.

255. E. Simms Campbell, "Blues," and William Russell, "Boogie Woogie," in *Jazzmen*, ed. Frederic Ramsey, Jr. and Charles Edward Smith (New York, 1939), pp. 101–118, 183–205.

256. Max Jones, "On Blues," in *The PL Yearbook of Jazz 1946*, ed. Albert McCarthy (London, 1946), pp. 72–107.

257. Ibid., p. 97.

258. Ibid., p. 82.

259. Rudi Blesh, *Shining Trumpets: A History of Jazz*, rev. ed. (New York, 1958), pp. 98–148, 292–321.

260. Titon, *Early Downhome Blues*, pp. xiii–xiv, expresses a preference for the term "downhome," but he makes it clear that it applies to the same material that other writers have called "country" blues.

261. *Horace Sprott, 1, 2, and 3*, Folkways FA 2651, 2652 and 2653; *Song, Play, and Dance*, Folkways FA 2654; *Cat-Iron*, Folkways FA 2389, 12" LPs. See also Frederic Ramsey, Jr., *Been Here and Gone* (New Brunswick, N.J., 1960).

262. Harold Courlander, *Negro Songs from Alabama*, rev. ed. (New York, 1963); Courlander, *Negro Folk Music U.S.A.*, pp. 123–145.

263. See especially *Roots of the Blues*, Atlantic SD 1348; *The Blues Roll On*, Atlantic SD 1352; and *Yazoo Delta Blues and Spirituals*, Prestige/International 25010, 12" LPs.

264. Cf. Bob Groom, *The Blues Revival* (London, 1971).

265. Charters, *The Poetry of the Blues*, passim; and *The Bluesmen*, pp. 73, 133, 134, 209.

266. Charters, *The Bluesmen*, p. 114.

267. Ibid., p. 13. For an even more extreme version of the same approach see Cook, pp. 6, 28–30, 43–44, 72, 108, 113, 243.

268. Paul Oliver, "Blues to Drive the Blues Away," in *Jazz*, ed. Nat Hentoff and Albert J. McCarthy (New York, 1959), pp. 83–103.

269. Oliver, *Screening the Blues*, pp. 2–11.

270. Ibid., pp. 90–91.

271. Oliver, *The Story of the Blues*, p. 30.

272. For a discussion of the scholarship concerned with African and European elements in the blues see Evans, "Tradition and Creativity in the Folk Blues," pp. 93–97; and David Evans, "African Elements in Twentieth-Century United States Black Folk Music," *Jazzforschung*, 10 (1978), 85–110.

273. See Pete Welding, "The Testament Story," *Blues World*, no. 42 (Spring 1972), pp. 3–4; no. 43 (Summer 1972), pp. 3–4; no. 44 (Autumn 1972), pp. 3–6; and the *Arhoolie Occasional*.

274. John Godrich and Robert M. W. Dixon, *Blues & Gospel Records 1902–1942* (London, 1969).

275. Dixon and Godrich, *Recording the Blues*.

276. Mike Leadbitter and Neil Slaven, *Blues Records: 1943–1966* (London, 1968).

277. Mahony, *The Columbia 13/14000-D Series*; Vreede, *Paramount 12000/13000 Series*; Brian Rust, *The Victor Master Book, Volume 2 (1925–1936)* (Stanhope, N.J., 1970).

278. Napier, ed., *Back Woods Blues*; Leadbitter, ed., *Nothing But the Blues*.

279. Russell, *Blacks, Whites and Blues*; Derrick Stewart-Baxter, *Ma Rainey and the Classic Blues Singers* (New York, 1970); Bengt Olsson, *Memphis Blues and Jug Bands* (London, 1970); Bruce Bastin, *Crying for the Carolines* (London, 1971).

280. Mike Leadbitter, *Delta Country Blues* (Bexhill-on-Sea, England, 1968); Mike Rowe, *Chicago Breakdown* (London, 1973); John Broven, *Walking to New Orleans* (Bexhill-on-Sea, England, 1974).

281. See also Peter Guralnick, *Feel Like Going Home* (New York, 1971); Samuel Charters, *The Legacy of the Blues* (New York, 1977); and *Guitar Player Magazine, Blues Guitarists* (Saratoga, Calif., 1975) for several portraits of folk and popular blues singers.

282. Broonzy, *Big Bill Blues*; Bradford, *Born with the Blues*.

283. Oliver, *Bessie Smith*; Moore, *Somebody's Angel Child*; Albertson, *Bessie*; Fahey, *Charley Patton*; Evans, *Tommy Johnson*; Karl Gert zur Heide, *Deep South Piano: The Story of Little Brother Montgomery* (London, 1970); James Rooney, *Bossmen: Bill Monroe & Muddy Waters* (New York, 1971), pp. 102–159; Paul Garon, *The Devil's Son-in-Law: The Story of Peetie Wheatstraw and His Songs* (London, 1971); Samuel Charters, *Robert Johnson* (New York, 1973).

284. This literature is summarized in Evans, "Tradition and Creativity in the Folk Blues," pp. 215–220. See also Garon, *Blues and the Poetic Spirit*; and Titon, *Early Downhome Blues*.

285. Oster, *Living Country Blues*, p. 24.

286. Ibid., pp. 94–95.

287. See Ed Kahn, "Hillbilly Music: Source and Resource," *Journal of Ameri-

can Folklore, 78 (1965), 257–266; and D. K. Wilgus, "An Introduction to the Study of Hillbilly Music," ibid., 195–203.

2: The Blues Singer

1. Three performances by Johnson and members of his family have been issued on *Sorrow Come Pass Me Around*, Advent 2805, 12" LP, and one piece by Johnson has been issued on *Big Road Blues*, Advent 2815, 12" LP. An interview with Johnson is printed in George Mitchell, *Blow My Blues Away* (Baton Rouge, 1971), pp. 130–151. "Robert Nighthawk" was also used as a pseudonym by another Mississippi blues singer, Robert McCollum.

2. David Evans, *Tommy Johnson* (London, 1971), p. 98.

3. David Evans, "Rubin Lacy," in *Nothing But the Blues*, ed. Mike Leadbitter (London, 1971), p. 242.

4. On the use of different repertoires for white and black audiences see William Ferris, *Blues from the Delta* (Garden City, N.Y., 1978), pp. 91–97; and William R. Ferris, Jr., "Racial Repertoires among Blues Performers," *Ethnomusicology*, 14 (1970), 439–449.

5. Howard W. Odum, "Folk-Song and Folk-Poetry as Found in the Secular Songs of the Southern Negroes," *Journal of American Folklore*, 24 (1911), 259.

6. Evans, *Tommy Johnson*, pp. 91–98.

7. David Evans, "The Johnny Temple Story," *Blues Unlimited*, no. 56 (Sept. 1968), pp. 7–8.

8. Lawrence Cohn, "Mississippi John Hurt," *Sing Out!*, 14, No. 5 (Nov. 1964), 16–21; George W. Kay, "Mississippi John Hurt," *Jazz Journal*, 17, No. 2 (Feb. 1964), 24–26.

9. Kip Lornell, "Sam Chatmon," *Jazz Journal*, 25, No. 6 (June 1972), 18.

10. Charles Keil, *Urban Blues* (Chicago, 1966), pp. 152–155.

11. For several good portraits of blues singers with an emphasis on personality see Peter Guralnick, *Feel Like Going Home* (New York, 1971). Phillips Barry showed an early awareness of these problems for folksong scholarship in "The Psychopathology of Ballad Singing," *Bulletin of the Folk-Song Society of the Northeast*, 11 (1936), 16–18.

12. Crystal Springs, Miss., Aug. 31, 1970. Recorded by David Evans.

13. David Evans, "Delta Reminiscences: Floyd Patterson Interviewed by David Evans (Crystal Springs, Mississippi—August 31 and September 2, 1970)," *Blues World*, no. 43 (Summer 1972), pp. 14–15.

14. For a discussion of repertoire, role, and audience as factors in the performance of folksongs, see Kenneth S. Goldstein, "On the Application of the Concepts of Active and Inactive Traditions in the Study of Repertory," *Journal of American Folklore*, 84 (1971), 62–67.

15. See, for example, Odum, p. 262; and Ferris, *Blues from the Delta*, pp. 57–58.

16. Jeff Titon, ed., *From Blues to Pop: The Autobiography of Leonard "Baby Doo" Caston* (Los Angeles, 1974), p. 23.

17. Evans, "Rubin Lacy," p. 244.

18. Paul Oliver, *Conversation with the Blues* (New York, 1965), p. 24.

19. Samuel Charters, *The Poetry of the Blues* (New York, 1963), p. 13.

20. Harry Oster and Richard Allen, notes to *Angola Prisoners' Blues*, Folk-Lyric LFS A-3, 12" LP.

21. Valerie Wilmer, "Blues People: Fred & Roosevelt," *Jazz Journal*, 19, No. 8 (Aug. 1966), 23.

22. Oliver, p. 24.

23. David Evans, "Booker White," in *Nothing But the Blues*, ed. Mike Leadbitter (London, 1971), p. 254.

24. Ibid., p. 255.

25. Evans, *Tommy Johnson*, pp. 91, 99.

26. Evans, "Booker White," pp. 253–254.

27. Wilmer, p. 24.

28. Al Wilson, "Robert Pete Williams, His Life and Music," *Little Sandy Review*, 2, No. 1 (July 1966), 21. See also Harry Oster, *Living Country Blues* (Detroit, 1969), p. 4.

29. Paul Oliver, *The Meaning of the Blues* (New York, 1963), pp. 332–338; Paul Oliver, *Screening the Blues* (London, 1968), pp. 48–49, 68–69.

30. *The Oxford English Dictionary*, 13 vol. ed. (1933), s.v. "blue devil."

31. Evans, *Tommy Johnson*, pp. 22–23. This account contains the following motifs listed in Stith Thompson, *Motif-Index of Folk-Literature*, rev. ed., 6 vols. (Bloomington, Ind., 1955–58): D1721.1 Magic power from devil; D1786 Magic power at cross-roads; G303.3.1.6 The devil as a black man; G303.6.1.1 Devil appears at midnight; and M211 Man sells soul to devil. The following related motifs are listed in Ernest W. Baughman, *Type and Motif-Index of the Folktales of England and North America* (The Hague, 1966): G303.25.23* The devil and music; and M211.10*(ca) Person sells soul for skill in fiddling.

32. See Newbell Niles Puckett, *Folk Beliefs of the Southern Negro* (Chapel Hill, N.C., 1926), pp. 553–554; Herbert Halpert, "The Devil and the Fiddle," *Hoosier Folklore Bulletin*, 2 (1943), 39–43; J. Mason Brewer, *American Negro Folklore* (New York, 1968), p. 281; Harry Middleton Hyatt, *Hoodoo—Conjuration—Witchcraft—Rootwork* (Washington, D.C., 1970), I, 108–111; and Bruce Bastin, "The Devil's Goin' to Get You," *North Carolina Folklore*, 21 (1973), 189–194.

33. David Evans, "Babe Stovall," in *Back Woods Blues*, ed. Simon A. Napier (Bexhill-on-Sea, England, 1968), p. 53; Jeff Todd Titon, *Early Downhome Blues: A Musical and Cultural Analysis* (Urbana, Ill., 1977), pp. 36–37.

34. Examples are "Love Hides All Faults" (Vocalion 1435) by Leroy Carr; "The First Shall Be Last and the Last Shall Be First" (Decca 7167) by Peetie Wheatstraw; and "It's a bad wind don't never change," used by Blind Lemon Jefferson in "See That My Grave's Kept Clean" (Paramount 12585) and "See That My Grave Is Kept Clean" (Paramount 12608). On the importance of blues records to singers and audiences see Ferris, *Blues from the Delta*, pp. 47–54; William R. Ferris, Jr., "Records and the Delta Blues Tradition," *Keystone Folklore Quarterly*, 14 (1969), 158–165; Howard W. Odum and Guy B. Johnson, *Negro Workaday Songs* (Chapel Hill, N.C., 1926), pp. 25–28; and Oliver, *Screening the Blues*, pp. 1–11.

35. David Evans, "A Talk with Boogie Bill," *Blues Unlimited*, no. 98 (Jan. 1973), p. 18.

36. Titon, *From Blues to Pop*, p. 4; Titon, *Early Downhome Blues*, pp. 271–276.

37. John Quincy Wolf, "Aunt Caroline Dye: The Gypsy in 'St. Louis Blues'," *Southern Folklore Quarterly*, 33 (1969), 330–346.

38. Hyatt, I, 745–746; II, 1417; Oliver, *The Meaning of the Blues*, p. 165.

39. On this point see Ferris, *Blues from the Delta*, pp. 53–54; and Ferris, "Records and the Delta Blues Tradition," pp. 163–165.

40. House made two recordings of this piece for the Library of Congress in 1941 and 1942, "Shetland Pony Blues" and "The Pony Blues." They have been issued on *Son House*, Folklyric 9002, 12″ LP.

41. "Talkin' 'bout You." Houston Stackhouse, vocal and harmonica; Carey "Ditty" Mason, guitar; Willis "Hill Bill" Kinebrew, guitar. Crystal Springs, Miss., Sept. 3, 1967. Recorded by David Evans and Marina Bokelman. Issued on *High Water Blues*, Flyright LP 512, 12″ LP.

42. On this process see Odum and Johnson, p. 27; Ferris, *Blues from the Delta*, pp. 58–59; and Ferris, "Records and the Delta Blues Tradition," p. 161.

43. A few instrumental passages were omitted on the LP issue.

44. Odum and Johnson, pp. 25–27.

45. On this subject see Odum and Johnson, pp. 27–28.

46. Stephen Calt, "The Country Blues as Meaning," in *Country Blues Song-book*, ed. Stefan Grossman, Hal Grossman, and Stephen Calt (New York, 1973), p. 22.

47. Oster, pp. 84–85.

48. Bruce Iglauer, Jim O'Neal, and Bea Van Geffen, "Living Blues Interview: Lowell Fulson," *Living Blues*, no. 6 (Autumn 1971), p. 18.

49. Barry Elmes, "Living Blues Interview: Sonny Terry & Brownie McGhee," *Living Blues*, no. 13 (Summer 1973), p. 20.

50. Charters, p. 20. See also Titon, *Early Downhome Blues*, p. 51.

51. Oliver, *Conversation with the Blues*, p. 105.

52. Evans, "Booker White," p. 252.

53. William Broonzy, *Big Bill Blues*, rev. ed. (New York, 1964), pp. 60–67, 70–73, 79–90, 99–103; Francis Smith, "Sleepy John Estes," in *Nothing But the Blues*, ed. Mike Leadbitter (London, 1971), pp. 237–239.

54. Evans, "A Talk with Boogie Bill," p. 18.

55. Stanzas 3 and 4 were deleted on the LP issue.

56. Evans, *Tommy Johnson*, pp. 48–49.

57. Pete Welding, "Reverend Robert Wilkins," *Blues Unlimited*, no. 56 (Sept. 1968), p. 13.

58. Smith, pp. 237–239.

59. Kip Lornell and Jim O'Neal, "Living Blues Interview: Hammie Nixon & Sleepy John Estes," *Living Blues*, no. 19 (Jan–Feb. 1975), p. 17.

60. David Evans, "Bubba Brown: Folk Poet," *Mississippi Folklore Register*, 7 (1973), 22–24, 30. Another version of the song by Boogie Bill Webb learned from Simmons and Brown has been issued on *Goin' up the Country*, British Decca LK 4931, 12" LP (reissued on Rounder 2012). A further version by Webb is printed in David Evans, "Tradition and Creativity in the Folk Blues," Ph.D. dissertation, University of California, Los Angeles, 1976, p. 275.

61. Oliver, *Conversation with the Blues*, p. 114; Evans, "Booker White," p. 252.

62. Welding, pp. 12–13.

63. Broonzy, pp. 74–78, 91–92.

64. Jim O'Neal and Bill Greensmith, "Living Blues Interview: Jimmy Rogers," *Living Blues*, no. 14 (Autumn 1973), p. 14.

65. See, for example, Oliver, *Conversation with the Blues*, p. 150; and Broonzy, pp. 97–98.

66. Pete Welding, "John Lee Hooker: Me and the Blues," *Down Beat*, 35, No. 20 (Oct. 3, 1968), 17.

67. Studs Terkel, "Big Bill's Last Session," *Jazz*, 1 (Oct. 1958), 12.

68. Titon, *From Blues to Pop*, pp. 23–24, 27; Oliver, *Conversation with the Blues*, pp. 101–102, 115; Jim O'Neal, "Living Blues Interview: Houston Stackhouse," *Living Blues*, no. 17 (Summer 1974), pp. 25, 36; Terkel, pp. 11–12.

69. For the story behind this blues see Son House, "I Can Make My Own Songs," *Sing Out!*, 15, No. 3 (July 1965), 46.

70. On this point see especially Oliver, *The Meaning of the Blues* and *Screening the Blues*.

71. Welding, "John Lee Hooker," p. 17.

72. Evans, "Booker White," pp. 253–254. See also Bukka White, *Sky Songs, Vols. 1 & 2*, Arhoolie F1019 and F1020, 12" LPs.

73. Evans, "Booker White," p. 253.

74. For more information on Williams see Guralnick, pp. 98–119; and Al Wilson, "Robert Pete Williams, His Life and Music," *Little Sandy Review*, 2, No. 1 (July 1966), 15–22; 2, No. 2 (Nov. 1966), 8–11.

75. On the role of speech impediments in the blues see David Evans, "The Singing Stammerer Motif in Black Tradition," *Western Folklore*, 35 (1976), 157–160.

76. On James see Barry Pearson, "The Late Great Elmore James," *Keystone Folklore Quarterly*, 17 (1972), 164.

77. Fahey, pp. 52–55; Titon, *Early Downhome Blues*, pp. 165–169.

78. Charles K. Wolfe, "Where the Blues Is At: A Survey of Recent Research," *Popular Music and Society*, 1 (1971–72), 159–160; Michael Taft, "Blind Lemon Jefferson Concordance," unpublished computer print-out.

79. Francis Lee Utley, "The Genesis and Revival of 'Dink's Song'," in *Studies in Language and Literature in Honor of Margaret Schlauch*, ed. Mieczysław Brahmer, Stanisław Helsztyński, and Julia Krzyżanowski (Warszawa, 1966), pp. 457–472.

80. Charters, pp. 23–26; Oster, pp. 76–95.

81. Samuel Charters, *The Bluesmen* (New York, 1967), p. 121.

82. For further examples of this kind of analysis see Evans, "Tradition and Creativity in the Folk Blues," pp. 291–295; and David Evans, "Structure and Meaning in the Folk Blues," in *The Study of American Folklore: An Introduction*, 2d ed., by Jan Harold Brunvand (New York, 1978), pp. 421–447.

83. Fahey, pp. 58–66.

84. W. C. Handy, ed., *Blues, An Anthology*, rev. ed. (New York, 1972), pp. 100–103.

85. Blind Boy Fuller, "Bye Bye Baby Blues" (Vocalion 04843), recorded in 1937. Other commercially recorded versions are Henry Thomas's 1927 "Red River Blues" (Vocalion 1137), Charley Patton's 1929 "Jim Lee Blues—Part 2" (Paramount 13133), and Joshua White's 1933 "Blood Red River" (Banner 32858, Melotone M12785, Oriole 8267, Perfect 0257, Romeo 5267, and Conqueror 8244).

86. Pete Welding, "Fred McDowell Talking," in *Nothing But the Blues*, ed. Mike Leadbitter (London, 1971), p. 146. See also Wilmer, p. 24.

87. For more information on Holts see David Evans, "Roosevelt Holts," *Blues World*, no. 15 (July 1967), pp. 3–6.

88. For more information on Stovall see Evans, "Babe Stovall," pp. 50–55.

89. Cf. Oster, pp. 2, 82.

90. On this point see William R. Ferris, Jr., "Creativity and the Blues," *Blues Unlimited*, no. 71 (Apr. 1970), pp. 13–14.

91. See Evans, *Tommy Johnson*, pp. 52–54.

92. John W. Work, *American Negro Songs and Spirituals* (New York, 1940), p. 36; Ferris, *Blues from the Delta*, pp. 67–70; William R. Ferris, Jr., "Gut Bucket Blues: Sacred and Profane," *Jazzforschung*, 5 (1973), 68–85.

93. This blues is derived from a 1935 recording by Buddy Moss, "Going to Your Funeral in a Vee-Eight Ford" (ARC 5-11-58, Conqueror 8578).

94. On this practice see Pearson, pp. 168–170.

95. See Eleanor Long, "Ballad Singers, Ballad Makers, and Ballad Etiology," *Western Folklore*, 32 (1973), 225–236. Long does recognize, however, that a single folk performer may "incorporate into his repertoire more than one of the *personae*" (pp. 231–232).

96. Rev. Rubin Lacy. Ridgecrest, Calif., Mar. 19, 1966. Recorded by David Evans, John Fahey, and Alan Wilson.

97. For discussions of such sessions of mostly popular blues see Ferris, *Blues from the Delta*, pp. 99–156; Ferris "Gut Bucket Blues," pp. 68–85; and Keil, pp. 114–142.

3: The Local Tradition

1. Alain Locke, *The Negro and His Music* (New York, 1969; originally published in 1936), pp. 30–31.

2. Samuel Charters, *The Bluesmen* (New York, 1967); Samuel Charters, *Sweet As the Showers of Rain* (New York, 1977); Paul Oliver, *The Story of the Blues* (London, 1969).

3. Mike Leadbitter, *Delta Country Blues* (Bexhill-on-Sea, England, 1968);

Karl Gert zur Heide, *Deep South Piano: The Story of Little Brother Montgomery* (London, 1970); Bruce Bastin, *Crying for the Carolines* (London, 1971).

4. Pete Welding, "Stringin' the Blues: The Art of Folk Blues Guitar," *Down Beat*, 32, No. 14 (July 1, 1965), 22-24, 56; Charles Keil, *Urban Blues* (Chicago, 1966), pp. 59-68, 217-224; Richard Middleton, *Pop Music and the Blues* (London, 1972), pp. 61-70.

5. For phonograph records that document local blues traditions see the following 12″ LPs: *Georgia Blues*, Rounder 2008 (Columbus, Georgia, region, collected by George Mitchell); *South Mississippi Blues*, Rounder 2009 (Tylertown, Miss., collected by David Evans); *Orange County Special*, Flyright LP 506 (Orange County, N.C., collected by Bruce Bastin); *Fort Valley Blues*, Matchbox SDM 250 (Peach County, Ga.). On this last tradition see Pete Lowry and Bruce Bastin, "Fort Valley Blues," *Blues Unlimited*, no. 111 (Dec.-Jan. 1974-75), pp. 11-13; no. 112 (Mar.-Apr. 1975), pp. 13-16; no. 114 (July-Aug. 1975), pp. 20-22.

6. See Oliver, pp. 30-35; and Bob Palmer, "What Is American Music?," *Down Beat*, 42, No. 4 (Feb. 27, 1975), 11, 29.

7. Bengt Olsson, *Memphis Blues and Jug Bands* (London, 1970); Charters, *Sweet As the Showers of Rain*; Mike Rowe, *Chicago Breakdown* (London, 1973); John Broven, *Walking to New Orleans* (Bexhill-on-Sea, England, 1974).

8. Karl Gert zur Heide, "Yancey Special," *Hot Jazz*, 5 (June 1969), 22-25.

9. John Fahey, *Charley Patton* (London, 1970); David Evans, *Tommy Johnson* (London, 1971); Al Wilson, *Son House* (Bexhill-on-Sea, England, 1966).

10. For discussions of life in the Delta before mechanization see Robert Brandfon, *Cotton Kingdom of the New South: A History of the Yazoo Mississippi Delta from Reconstruction to the Twentieth Century* (Cambridge, Mass., 1967); John Dollard, *Caste and Class in a Southern Town* (New Haven, 1937); Hortense Powdermaker, *After Freedom* (New York, 1968); and David Cohn, *Where I Was Born and Raised* (Notre Dame, Ind., 1967).

11. On this point see William Ferris, Jr., *Blues from the Delta* (Garden City, N.Y., 1978), pp. 96-97; and David Evans, "Delta Reminiscences: Floyd Patterson Interviewed by David Evans (Crystal Springs, Mississippi—August 31 and September 2, 1970)," *Blues World*, no. 43 (Summer 1972), pp. 14-15.

12. W. C. Handy, *Father of the Blues* (New York, 1970), pp. 78-82. In an unpublished untitled paper F. Jack Hurley tentatively identifies the trio in Cleveland as Willie Webb on guitar, Sherman on mandolin, and "Snow" on bass.

13. Viola Cannon, Patton's sister, gave me this date but has elsewhere given the date 1887. See Bernard Klatzko, notes to *The Immortal Charlie Patton*, Origin Jazz Library 7, 12″ LP. Patton's death certificate indicates that he was born in 1889 or 1890. See Gayle Wardlow and Jacques Roche, "Patton's Murder: Whitewash or Hogwash?," *78 Quarterly*, 1, No. 1 (Autumn 1967), 13.

14. Fahey, p. 18. This is denied, however, in Kip Lornell, "Sam Chatmon," *Jazz Journal*, 25, No. 6 (June 1972), 18.

15. Lornell, p. 18.

16. Mott Willis. Crystal Springs, Miss., Sept. 2, 1970, and July 14, 1971. Recorded by David and Cheryl Evans.

17. Tom Cannon, a nephew of Charley Patton, recalled a Bennie Starr, who may be the same man, living in Ruleville in 1967. He was very old and a former musician. I have been unable to locate this person.

18. Mott Willis. Crystal Springs, Miss., Sept. 2, 1970. Recorded by David Evans.

19. In *Tommy Johnson*, p. 22, I reported this date as 1912, but information provided by Steve LaVere on LeDell Johnson's marriage date, by which he dated his brother's move, indicates that 1915 is the correct date.

20. In *Tommy Johnson*, pp. 24-26, I reported the date of this move as 1916,

but a recently discovered newspaper account indicates that Sanders did not move to Drew until 1921.

21. Maybelle Johnson. Jackson, Miss., Sept. 8, 1966. Recorded by David Evans and Marina Bokelman.

22. Mott Willis. Crystal Springs, Miss., July 14, 1971. Recorded by David and Cheryl Evans.

23. Mager Johnson. Crystal Springs, Miss., Sept. 4, 1966. Recorded by David Evans and Marina Bokelman.

24. Mager Johnson. Crystal Springs, Miss., Sept. 4, 1966. Recorded by David Evans and Marina Bokelman.

25. For more information on the Johnson brothers, the other Crystal Springs musicians, and the men who were influenced by them, see Evans, *Tommy Johnson*, passim; Charters, pp. 132–135; and Gayle Wardlow, "LeDell Johnson Remembers His Brother Tommy," *78 Quarterly*, 1, No. 1 (Autumn 1967), 63–65.

26. Useful newspaper accounts for reconstructing this incident are printed in the *Los Angeles Times*, Dec. 15, 1923, p. 1; the *Jackson Daily Clarion-Ledger*, Dec. 16, 1923, p. 7; and the *Jackson Daily News*, Dec. 15, 1923, p. 1; Dec. 16, 1923, p. 1; and Dec. 17, 1923, p. 5. The names of those who provided oral accounts cannot be revealed. I collected accounts in Jackson in 1969 and Crystal Springs in 1970, and one was collected for me by Steve LaVere in Memphis in 1974. None of the three informants was living in Drew at the time of the incident.

27. Anonymous. Crystal Springs, Miss., 1970. Recorded by David Evans.

28. Paul Oliver, *Conversation with the Blues* (New York, 1965), p. 66.

29. John Godrich and Robert M. W. Dixon, *Blues & Gospel Records 1902–1942* (London, 1969), pp. 271, 458.

30. Mott Willis. Crystal Springs, Miss., Sept. 2, 1970, and July 14, 1971. Recorded by David and Cheryl Evans. Brown's commercial recordings were made in 1930.

31. Mott Willis. Crystal Springs, Miss., July 14, 1971. Recorded by David and Cheryl Evans.

32. For more information on Staples see Chris Strachwitz, "An Interview with the Staples Family," *American Folk Music Occasional*, 1 (1964), 13–17.

33. For more information on Patton see Fahey, *Charley Patton*; Klatzko, notes to *The Immortal Charlie Patton*, Origin Jazz Library 7, 12" LP; Charters, pp. 34–56; Wardlow and Roche, pp. 10–17; and David Evans, "Charlie Patton: His Life and Music," *Blues World*, no. 33 (Aug. 1970), pp. 11–15.

34. For more information on Brown see Charters, pp. 115–116. For more information on House see Son House, "I Can Make My Own Songs," *Sing Out!*, 15, No. 3 (July 1965), 38–47; Wilson, *Son House*; Gayle Wardlow, "Son House (Collectors Classics 14), Comments & Additions," *Blues Unlimited*, no. 42 (Mar.–Apr. 1967), pp. 7–8; David Evans, "Son House—Some Further Comments," *Blues Unlimited*, no. 43 (May 1967), pp. 8–10; Nick Perls, "Son House Interview," *78 Quarterly*, 1, No. 1 (Autumn 1967), 59–61; Bob Groom, "An Interview with Son House," *Blues World* no. 18 (Jan. 1968), pp. 5–8; Charters, pp. 57–70; and Jeff Titon, "Living Blues Interview: Son House," *Living Blues*, no. 31 (Mar.–Apr. 1977), pp. 14–22.

35. For more information on Howlin' Wolf see Paul Williams and Peter Guralnick, "Howling Wolf," *Crawdaddy*, no. 5 (Sept. 1966), pp. 11–13; Peter Guralnick, *Feel Like Going Home* (New York, 1971), pp. 120–136; Leadbitter, *Delta Country Blues*, pp. 8–11; Mike Leadbitter, "Still Worried All the Time," *Blues Unlimited*, no. 90 (Apr. 1972), pp. 12–14; Pete Welding, " 'I Sing for the People': An Interview with Bluesman Howling Wolf," *Down Beat*, 34, No. 25 (Dec. 14, 1967), 20–23; John Broven, "Howlin' Wolf," in *Nothing But the Blues*, ed. Mike Leadbit-

ter (London, 1971), pp. 39–44; and Charles Radcliffe, "Howlin' Wolf Revisited," in *Nothing But the Blues,* ed. Mike Leadbitter (London, 1971), pp. 44–45.

36. For more information on Johnson see Bob Groom, ed., *Robert Johnson* (Knutsford, England, 1967); Bob Groom, "Robert Johnson," *Blues World,* no. 50 (1974), pp. 6–7; Bob Groom, "Standing at the Crossroads: Robert Johnson's Recordings," *Blues Unlimited,* no. 118 (Mar.–Apr. 1976), pp. 17–20; no. 119 (May–June 1976), pp. 11–14; no. 120 (July–Aug. 1976), pp. 15–17; no. 121 (Sept.–Oct. 1976), pp. 20–21; John Earl, "A Lifetime in the Blues: Johnny Shines," *Blues World,* no. 46–49 (1973), pp. 12–13, 20–21; Charters, *The Bluesmen,* pp. 87–99; Samuel Charters, *Robert Johnson* (New York, 1973); and Stephen Calt, "Robert Johnson Recapitulated," *Blues Unlimited,* no. 86 (Nov. 1971), pp. 12–14.

37. For more information on Martin see David Evans, "The Fiddlin' Joe Martin Story," *Blues World,* no. 20 (July 1968), pp. 3–5.

38. For more information on Adams see David Evans, "The Woodrow Adams Story," in *Nothing But the Blues,* ed. Mike Leadbitter (London, 1971), pp. 142–144; and Leadbitter, *Delta Country Blues,* p. 42.

39. For more information on Johnson see George Mitchell, *Blow My Blues Away* (Baton Rouge, 1971), pp. 130–151.

40. Oliver, *Conversation with the Blues,* pp. 64–66, 71–72.

41. Mike Leadbitter, "Mike's Blues," *Blues Unlimited,* no. 111 (Dec.–Jan. 1974–75), p. 5.

42. The lyrics and melodies of almost all of Patton's blues are printed and discussed in Fahey, pp. 32–107. Tommy Johnson's blues lyrics are printed and discussed in Evans, *Tommy Johnson,* pp. 45–68. The lyrics and guitar parts of Willie Brown's "Future Blues" and "M & O Blues" are printed in Stefan Grossman, *Delta Blues Guitar* (New York, 1969), pp. 41–49. Discographies for Patton, Tommy Johnson, Brown, and Kid Bailey are printed under their names in alphabetical order in Godrich and Dixon, *Blues & Gospel Records 1902–1942.* Howlin' Wolf's discography through 1966 is printed in Mike Leadbitter and Neil Slaven, *Blues Records: 1943–1966* (London, 1968), pp. 149–152. Most of the relevant commercial recordings have been reissued on 12″ LPs. For Patton see especially *Charlie Patton No. 1,* Origin Jazz Library 1; *The Immortal Charlie Patton,* Origin Jazz Library 7; *Charley Patton,* Yazoo L-1020 (double LP); *Patton, Sims, & Bertha Lee,* Herwin 213; *Mississippi Blues 1927–1941,* Yazoo L-1001; and *Mississippi Moaners 1927–1942,* Yazoo L-1009. For Tommy Johnson see *Really! The Country Blues,* Origin Jazz Library 2; *Country Blues Encores,* Origin Jazz Library 8; *Blues Roots/Mississippi,* RBF 14; *Jackson Blues,* Yazoo L-1007; *Masters of the Blues 1928–1940,* Historical HLP-31; and *"Some Cold Rainy Day" 1927–1933,* Southern Preservation SPR 2. The commercial recordings of Kid Bailey and Willie Brown are reissued on *The Mississippi Blues No. 1,* Origin Jazz Library 5. Brown's recordings for the Library of Congress have been issued on *Walking Blues,* Flyright LP 541. The most important records by Howlin' Wolf have been reissued on the following 12″ LPs: *Howling Wolf Sings the Blues,* Crown 5240; *Moanin' in the Moonlight,* Chess LP 1434; and *Howlin' Wolf,* Chess LP 1469.

43. Jim O'Neal, "Living Blues Interview: Houston Stackhouse," *Living Blues,* no. 17 (Summer 1974), p. 26.

44. Willis's version of "It Ain't Gonna Rain No More" is issued on *Big Road Blues,* Advent 2815, 12″ LP.

45. For a discussion of the many recordings of the piano blues standard, "44 Blues," see Paul Oliver, *Screening the Blues* (London, 1968), pp. 90–127. The other pieces probably have the following sources, although there is the possibility of intermediate recorded sources for these popular blues: Joe Williams, "Baby Please Don't Go" (Bluebird B6200); Walter Davis, "Come Back Baby" (Bluebird B8510); Walter Davis, "M. & O. Blues" (Victor V38618); and Mississippi Sheiks, "Winter Time Blues" (Okeh 8773).

46. For other blues about Joe Louis see Oliver, *Screening the Blues*, pp. 148–163 ("Joe Louis and John Henry").

47. The text of this performance is printed in David Evans, "Tradition and Creativity in the Folk Blues," Ph.D. dissertation, University of California, Los Angeles, 1976, pp. 371–372.

48. See ibid., p. 384, for the text of this performance.

49. Willis recorded this part as a guitar solo in 1967.

50. Son House, however, claims that Charley Patton played a song called "Keep It Clean" with many "dirty" verses. This piece may have been similar to "Joking Blues." See Stefan Grossman, *The Country Blues Guitar* (New York, 1968), p. 71. The text of Willis's "Joking Blues" is printed in Evans, "Tradition and Creativity in the Folk Blues," p. 388.

51. Harry Middleton Hyatt, *Hoodoo—Conjuration—Witchcraft—Rootwork* (Washington, D.C., 1970), I, 620; II, 1458. For more information on Santa Claus symbolism in the blues see Oliver, *Screening the Blues*, pp. 26–43 ("The Santy Claus Crave").

52. For a version of "Sally, Take Your Time" learned from Mager Johnson's brother Tommy see Boogie Bill Webb, "Take Your Time," on *The Legacy of Tommy Johnson*, Matchbox SDM 224, 12" LP.

53. O'Neal, p. 23; Evans, *Tommy Johnson*, p. 31.

54. The two earliest versions were recorded by singers from Greenwood, Mississippi, in the Delta, thirty miles southeast of Drew. These are Robert Petway's 1941 "Catfish Blues" (Bluebird B8838) and Tommy McClennan's 1941 "Deep Blue Sea Blues" (Bluebird B9005). Mager Johnson's text is printed in Evans, "Tradition and Creativity in the Folk Blues," pp. 397–398. A version of "Catfish Blues" by Cary Lee Simmons learned from Mager Johnson's brother Tommy is issued on *Big Road Blues*, Advent 2815, 12" LP.

55. On Bankston, see Welding, " 'I Sing for the People'," p. 21.

56. Mager Johnson. Crystal Springs, Miss., Sept. 4, 1966. Recorded by David Evans and Marina Bokelman.

57. Crystal Springs, Miss., Sept. 4, 1966. Recorded by David Evans and Marina Bokelman.

58. Youngblood's piece is issued on *The Legacy of Tommy Johnson*, Matchbox SDM 224, 12" LP.

59. Evans, *Tommy Johnson*, pp. 56–58.

60. Two quite similar takes of Tommy Johnson's piece were recently issued for the first time as "Lonesome Blues" on *Masters of the Blues, 1928–1940*, Historical HLP-31, 12" LP.

61. David Evans, "An Interview with H. C. Speir," *John Edwards Memorial Foundation Quarterly*, 8 (1972), 120.

62. Evans, *Tommy Johnson*, pp. 45–68.

63. Ibid., p. 92.

64. For further discussion of these points see ibid., pp. 103–107; and *The Legacy of Tommy Johnson*, Matchbox SDM 224, 12" LP.

65. Texts of these versions are printed in Evans, "Tradition and Creativity in the Folk Blues," pp. 425–427. They have been issued on the following 12" LPs: *South Mississippi Blues*, Rounder 2009; *Robert Nighthawk—Houston Stackhouse*, Testament T-2215; and *The Legacy of Tommy Johnson*, Matchbox SDM 224.

66. Fahey, *Charley Patton*. See also Evans, "Charlie Patton: His Life and Music."

67. Fahey, p. 52, calls this group the "High Water Everywhere" family.

68. The variant guitar parts of "High Water Everywhere" and "Bird Nest Bound" are printed in Grossman, *Delta Blues Guitar*, pp. 23–32.

69. Fahey, pp. 53–54, divides this group into two families on the basis of minor variations. The guitar part of "Stone Pony Blues" is printed in Grossman, *Delta Blues Guitar*, pp. 15–18.

70. See Grossman, *Delta Blues Guitar*, pp. 11–14, for the guitar part of "Green River Blues."

71. See ibid., pp. 19–22, for the guitar part of Patton's "34 Blues."

72. John Barnie analyzes the "formulas" in these two blues by Patton in "Charley Patton's Jailhouse Blues," *Blues Unlimited*, no. 124 (Mar.–June 1977), pp. 22–23, but he fails to take into account their dependence on Ma Rainey's record.

73. Grossman, *Delta Blues Guitar*, p. 45. See also Perls, pp. 60–61.

74. Evans, *Tommy Johnson*, pp. 93–94, 105; David Evans, "Structure and Meaning in the Folk Blues," in *The Study of American Folklore*, 2d ed., by Jan Harold Brunvand (New York, 1978), pp. 439–442.

75. The text of Howlin' Wolf's "Saddle My Pony" is printed in Evans, "Tradition and Creativity in the Folk Blues," p. 439. Versions of "Pony Blues" by eight other performers, all learned from various Drew artists, are discussed ibid., pp. 439–441. To these versions one should add Floyd Jones's 1953 recording of "Early Morning" (Chess 1527; reissued on *Chicago Slickers, 1948–1953*, Nighthawk 102, 12″ LP).

76. Tommy Johnson's text and guitar part are printed in Grossman, *Delta Blues Guitar*, pp. 69–72. Versions of "Bye and Bye Blues" by four other performers, all learned from Tommy Johnson, are discussed in Evans, "Tradition and Creativity in the Folk Blues," p. 443.

77. Leadbitter and Slaven, *Blues Records: 1943–1966*, p. 150, claim that there are two guitarists, Willie Johnson and Otis ("Smokey") Smothers. Howlin' Wolf used this same guitar part and melody with a different text in "I'm the Wolf," issued on *Anthology of the Blues/Memphis Blues/Archive Series—Volume 2*, Kent KST 9002, 12″ LP.

78. Versions of "Cool Water Blues" by seven other performers, all learned from Tommy Johnson or from his record, are discussed in Evans, "Tradition and Creativity in the Folk Blues," p. 446.

79. Willie Brown's guitar part has been printed in Grossman, *Delta Blues Guitar*, pp. 41–44.

80. For other examples of folk blues guitar parts see Grossman, *The Country Blues Guitar*; Grossman, *Delta Blues Guitar*; Stefan Grossman, *Ragtime Blues Guitarists* (New York, 1970); Donald Garwood, *Masters of Instrumental Blues Guitar* (New York, 1968); Woody Mann, *Six Black Blues Guitarists* (New York, 1973); Happy Traum, *The Blues Bag* (New York, 1968); and Happy Traum, ed., *Guitar Styles of Brownie McGhee* (New York, 1971).

81. Grossman, *Delta Blues Guitar*, pp. 11–32, 41–49, 65–72.

82. On Patton, Tommy Johnson, and Howlin' Wolf see Fahey, pp. 21, 26, 31; Evans, *Tommy Johnson*, pp. 99–103; and Guralnick, pp. 127–132.

83. Fahey, pp. 39–41.

84. These two guitar parts are demonstrated by Roosevelt Holts in "Maggie Campbell Blues," issued on *Big Road Blues*, Advent 2815, 12″ LP.

85. Woodrow Adams, "Pony Blues." Robinsonville, Miss., Aug. 30, 1967. Recorded by David Evans.

86. For a further discussion of this point see Russell Ames, "Art in Negro Folksong," *Journal of American Folklore*, 56 (1943), 251–252.

87. Fahey, p. 27.

88. Evans, *Tommy Johnson*, pp. 69–70, 90.

89. Mott Willis. Crystal Springs, Miss., July 14, 1971. Recorded by David and Cheryl Evans.

90. A version of "Don't You Lie to Me," learned from Tommy Johnson, is performed by Boogie Bill Webb on *The Legacy of Tommy Johnson*, Matchbox SDM 224, 12″ LP.

91. Versions of "Prison Bound Blues," learned from Tommy Johnson, are

performed by Roosevelt Holts on *Presenting the Country Blues: Roosevelt Holts*, Blue Horizon 7-63201, and by Arzo Youngblood on *The Legacy of Tommy Johnson*, Matchbox SDM 224, 12″ LPs.

92. Maybelle and LeDell Johnson. Jackson, Miss., Sept. 8, 1966. Recorded by David Evans and Marina Bokelman.

93. Wilson, pp. 12–13; Grossman, *Delta Blues Guitar*, p. 41; Wardlow, "Son House (Collectors Classics 14), Comments & Additions," p. 7.

94. Fahey, pp. 72–107.

95. Several of Patton's disciples from outside the Drew tradition are discussed in Evans, "Tradition and Creativity in the Folk Blues," pp. 463–464.

96. House's "Dry Spell Blues—Parts 1 & 2" has been reissued on *The Mississippi Blues No. 2: The Delta, 1929–32*, Origin Jazz Library 11, 12″ LP. His "Empire State Express" and "Louise McGhee" are issued on *The Legendary Son House, Father of the Folk Blues*, Columbia CL 2417, 12″ LP. His other pieces are issued on *Son House*, Folklyric 9002, and *Walking Blues*, Flyright LP 541, 12″ LPs.

97. Robert Johnson's pieces have been reissued on *Robert Johnson, King of the Delta Blues Singers*, Columbia CL 1654, and *Robert Johnson, King of the Delta Blues Singers, Vol. II*, Columbia C 30034, 12″ LPs.

98. Evans, *Tommy Johnson*, p. 17; Calt, "Robert Johnson Recapitulated," pp. 12–14; Stephen Calt, notes to *Mr. Johnson's Blues*, Mamlish S-3807, 12″ LP.

99. Adams's "Pony Blues" is issued on *High Water Blues*, Flyright LP 512, 12″ LP.

100. See also Evans, *Tommy Johnson*, pp. 91–107; and *The Legacy of Tommy Johnson*, Matchbox SDM 224, 12″ LP.

101. This piece has been issued as "Packing Up Her Trunk to Leave" on *Roosevelt Holts and His Friends*, Arhoolie 1057, 12″ LP. An untitled blues by Isaac Youngblood that exhibits a similar process of combining elements learned from Tommy Johnson is printed and discussed in Evans, "Tradition and Creativity in the Folk Blues," p. 467. The piece is issued as "No Place to Go" on *Big Road Blues*, Advent 2815, 12″ LP.

102. Bob Groom, "Otto Virgial," *Blues World*, no. 27 (Feb. 1970), p. 16.

103. For an introduction to the Bentonia blues tradition see Bruce Jackson, "The Personal Blues of Skip James," *Sing Out!*, 15, No. 6 (Jan. 1966), 26–31; Guralnick, pp. 86–97; Skip James, "Skip James Talkin'," in *Nothing But the Blues*, ed. Mike Leadbitter (London, 1971), pp. 232–234; Jacques Roche, "Henry Stuckey: An Obituary," *78 Quarterly*, 1, No. 2 (1968), 11–14; the records by Skip James listed in Godrich and Dixon, p. 350, and Leadbitter and Slaven, pp. 161–162; and the pieces by Jack Owens and Cornelius Bright on *Goin' up the Country*, British Decca LK 4931 (reissued on Rounder 2012), and *It Must Have Been the Devil: Mississippi Country Blues by Jack Owens and Bud Spires*, Testament T-2222, 12″ LPs.

104. For an introduction to the Tylertown blues tradition see Evans, *Tommy Johnson*, pp. 74–80; David Evans, "Babe Stovall," in *Back Woods Blues*, ed. Simon A. Napier (Bexhill-on-Sea, England, 1968), pp. 50–55; David Evans, "Roosevelt Holts," *Blues World*, no. 15 (July 1967), pp. 3–6; *South Mississippi Blues*, Rounder 2009, 12″ LP; *Babe Stovall*, Verve VPM-1, 12″ LP; *The Babe Stovall Story*, Southern Sound SD 203, 12″ LP; *Presenting the Country Blues: Roosevelt Holts*, Blue Horizon 7-63201, 12″ LP; the pieces by Holts, Esau Weary, and Eli Owens on *Roosevelt Holts and His Friends*, Arhoolie 1057, 12″ LP; the pieces by Holts, Arzo Youngblood, Herb Quinn, and O. D. Jones on *Goin' up the Country*, British Decca LK 4931, 12″ LP (reissued on Rounder 2012); and the pieces by Isaac Youngblood, Arzo Youngblood, Stovall, and Holts on *The Legacy of Tommy Johnson*, Matchbox SDM 224, 12″ LP.

105. For an introduction to the black folk music tradition of Como and Senatobia see *Afro-American Folk Music from Tate and Panola Counties, Mississippi,*

AFS L67, 12″ LP (bibliography and discography in accompanying booklet); and *Traveling through the Jungle: Negro Fife and Drum Band Music from the Deep South*, Testament T-2223, 12″ LP.

106. For a survey of the regional blues tradition of the Carolinas see Bastin, *Crying for the Carolines*.

107. For an introduction to folk blues piano traditions see Zur Heide, *Deep South Piano*; Oliver, *The Story of the Blues*, pp. 73–94, 135–145; and Oliver, *Screening the Blues*, pp. 90–127.

108. For an introduction to some urban blues scenes see the references in footnote 7.

4: The Traditional Blues Song

1. W. Edson Richmond, "The Comparative Approach: Its Aims, Techniques, and Limitations," in *A Good Tale and a Bonnie Tune*, Publications of the Texas Folklore Society, no. 32, ed. Mody C. Boatright, Wilson M. Hudson, and Allen Maxwell (Dallas, 1964), pp. 219–220.

2. Ibid., p. 218.

3. Ibid., p. 219.

4. A discussion of the findings for the Anglo-American folk ballad tradition is presented in D. K. Wilgus, *Anglo-American Folksong Scholarship Since 1898* (New Brunswick, N.J., 1959), passim.

5. The comparative method is described in Kaarle Krohn, *Folklore Methodology Formulated by Julius Krohn and Expanded by Nordic Researchers*, trans. Roger L. Welsch (Austin, 1971).

6. Wilgus, pp. 317–326.

7. Paul Oliver, *Screening the Blues* (London, 1968), pp. 90–127.

8. Ibid., p. 126.

9. Ibid., pp. 219–246.

10. Paul Oliver, *The Story of the Blues* (London, 1969), pp. 27–29.

11. Bob Groom, "Kokomo Blues," *Blues World*, no. 24 (July 1969), pp. 10–13.

12. David Evans, "Tradition and Creativity in the Folk Blues," Ph.D. dissertation, University of California, Los Angeles, 1976, pp. 274–276, 423–427, 438–446.

13. Additional widespread blues types are listed in Oliver, *Screening the Blues*, pp. 16–17, 92–93, 247; and Oliver, *The Story of the Blues*, p. 29.

14. Wilgus, p. 326.

15. Simon A. Napier, " 'Cryin' Mama, Mama, Mama . . .' (A Look at Tommy Johnson, His Influence and Songs)," *Blues Unlimited*, no. 30 (Feb. 1966), pp. 14–15.

16. Oliver, *Screening the Blues*, pp. 92–93.

17. David Evans, *Tommy Johnson* (London, 1971), pp. 103–107. See also David Evans, "The Blues of Tommy Johnson: A Study of a Tradition," M.A. thesis, University of California, Los Angeles, 1967, passim.

18. Evans, *Tommy Johnson*, p. 90.

19. An inaccurate transcription of the guitar part is printed in Stefan Grossman, *Delta Blues Guitar* (New York, 1969), pp. 65–68.

20. Evans, *Tommy Johnson*, p. 50.

21. Howard W. Odum, "Folk-Song and Folk-Poetry as Found in the Secular Songs of the Southern Negoes," *Journal of American Folklore*, 24 (1911), 382.

22. William Broonzy, *Big Bill Blues*, rev. ed. (New York, 1964), pp. 53–59.

23. Mrs. Maebelle and Rev. LeDell Johnson. Jackson, Miss., Sept. 8, 1966. Recorded by David Evans and Marina Bokelman.

24. Pete Welding, " 'I Sing for the People': An Interview with Bluesman Howling Wolf," *Down Beat*, 34, No. 25 (Dec. 14, 1967), 21.

25. Evans, *Tommy Johnson*, p. 95.

26. Howlin' Wolf's records have been copied and adapted by a number of performers. For an outright copy of "Smoke Stack Lightning" see Clarence Edwards, "Smokes Like Lighting'," issued on *Country Negro Jam Sessions*, Folk-Lyric FL 111, 12" LP. Adaptations by "Muddy Waters" (McKinley Morganfield) and Eddie Taylor are discussed in Evans, "Tradition and Creativity in the Folk Blues," pp. 499–500.

27. Mike Rowe, "Floyd Jones," in *Nothing But the Blues*, ed. Mike Leadbitter (London, 1971), p. 64; Mike Rowe, *Chicago Breakdown* (London, 1973), p. 59.

28. J. D. Short, "Sliding Delta," issued on *The Blues*, Asch 101, 12" LP; and "Slidin' Delta," issued on *Legacy of the Blues Vol. 8*, Sonet SNTF 648, 12" LP. St. Louis, 1962. Recorded by Samuel Charters.

29. Samuel Charters, *The Bluesmen* (New York, 1967), p. 37.

30. Evans, *Tommy Johnson*, pp. 28–29.

31. Zora Neale Hurston, "Story in Harlem Slang," in *Mother Wit from the Laughing Barrel*, ed. Alan Dundes (Englewood Cliffs, N.J., 1973), p. 227.

32. Stetson Kennedy, *Palmetto Country* (New York, 1942), p. 154.

33. See Jim O'Neal, "Living Blues Interview: Houston Stackhouse," *Living Blues*, no. 17 (Summer 1974), p. 24; Evans, *Tommy Johnson*, p. 68; and John Cowley, "Some Thoughts on Tommy Johnson and Copyright," *Blues World*, no. 23 (Apr. 1969), pp. 29–30. On Vinson see Frank Proschan, "Walter Vinson, 1901–1975," *Living Blues*, no. 21 (May–June 1975), p. 55; and Evans, *Tommy Johnson*, pp. 37–44.

34. Fred McMullen, "Wait and Listen" (Banner 32690, Melotone M12616, Oriole 8209, Perfect 0233, Romeo 5209); Kokomo Arnold, "Stop Look and Listen" (Decca 7181); Jesse James, "Lonesome Day Blues" (Decca 7213); Lightnin' Hopkins, "Coolin' Board Blues," issued on *Lightning Hopkins, Early Recordings*, Arhoolie R2007, 12" LP; Lightnin' Hopkins, "Smokes Like Lightnin'," issued on *Smokes Like Lightnin'*, Bluesville BVLP 1070, 12" LP; Horace Sprott, "Smoked Like Lightning," issued on *Music from the South, Volume 2, Horace Sprott, 1*, Folkways FA 2651, 12" LP; Leon Strickland, "Smoke Like Lightnin'," in Harry Oster, *Living Country Blues* (Detroit, 1969), p. 180; Eddie Lee Jones, "Stop and Listen," issued on *Yonder Go That Old Black Dog*, Testament T-2224, 12" LP; Robert Pete Williams, "Somebody Help Poor Me," issued on *Robert Pete Williams, Louisiana Blues*, Takoma B 1011, 12" LP; Thomas Shaw, "Stop and Listen," issued on *Born in Texas: Thomas Shaw*, Advent 2801, 12" LP; Willie Morris, "New Stop and Listen Blues," issued on *The Memphis Blues Again, Vol. II*, Adelphi AD 1010, 12" LP. Sprott's text is printed in Frederic Ramsey, Jr., *Been Here and Gone* (New Brunswick, N.J., 1960), p. 38.

35. Evans, *Tommy Johnson*, p. 73.

36. Robert Pete Williams. Malibu, Calif., July 15, 1966. Recorded by David Evans, Alan Wilson, and Marina Bokelman.

37. "Stop and Listen Blues." Sam Chatmon, vocal and guitar in EBGDAD tuning, key of D. Hollandale, Miss., 1966. Recorded by Ken Swerilas.

38. Chatmon a few months earlier recorded another version of this blues containing stanzas 1, 2, 3, and 6 of Example 71, and one additional stanza. It has been issued as "Brownskin Women Blues" on *Sam Chatmon, The Mississippi Sheik*, Blue Goose 2006, 12" LP.

39. For more information on Chatmon see Galen Gart, "Sam Chatmon," *Blues Unlimited*, no. 83 (July 1971), pp. 9–10; and Kip Lornell, "Sam Chatmon," *Jazz Journal*, 25, No. 6 (June 1972), 18.

40. Evans, *Tommy Johnson*, p. 73.

41. Ibid., p. 72.

42. Roger Abrahams, *Deep Down in the Jungle*, rev. ed. (Chicago, 1970), pp. 79–81, 101–103, 120–129; Bruce Jackson, *"Get Your Ass in the Water and Swim Like Me": Narrative Poetry from Black Oral Tradition* (Cambridge, Mass., 1974), pp. 35–38, 180–196.

43. For more information on Gillum see Oliver, *The Story of the Blues*, p. 113.

44. For more information on Sims see Chris Strachwitz, "Frankie Lee Sims," *Blues Unlimited*, no. 122 (Nov.–Dec. 1976), pp. 20–22.

45. "Big Road Blues." Houston Stackhouse, vocal and guitar in EBGDAD tuning, key of D; Robert Nighthawk, guitar; James ("Peck") Curtis, drums. Dundee, Miss., Aug. 28, 1967. Recorded by George and Cathy Mitchell. Issued on *Robert Nighthawk/Houston Stackhouse*, Testament T-2215, 12″ LP.

46. "Big Road Blues." Houston Stackhouse, vocal and guitar in EBGDAD tuning, key of D; Carey "Ditty" Mason, guitar. Crystal Springs, Miss., Sept. 3, 1967. Recorded by David Evans and Marina Bokelman.

47. For more information on Stackhouse see Evans, *Tommy Johnson*, pp. 34–35; and O'Neal, pp. 20–36.

48. "Big Road Blues." Cary Lee Simmons, vocal and guitar in EBGDAD tuning, key of D. Jackson, Miss., Sept. 4, 1967. Recorded by David Evans and Marina Bokelman.

49. For more information on Simmons see Evans, *Tommy Johnson*, p. 72.

50. Arthur Rosenbaum, notes to *The Blues of Shirley Griffith: Saturday Blues*, Prestige/Bluesville 1087, 12″ LP.

51. The first version was issued on *The Blues of Shirley Griffith: Saturday Blues*, Prestige/Bluesville 1087, 12″ LP. A third version by Griffith, which I have been unable to hear, was issued on Flyright 523, 12″ LP.

52. For more information on Brown see Evans, *Tommy Johnson*, pp. 71–72, 93; David Evans, "The Bubba Brown Story," *Blues World*, no. 21 (Oct. 1968), pp. 7–9; and David Evans, "Bubba Brown: Folk Poet," *Mississippi Folklore Register*, 7 (1973), 15–31.

53. On Tommy Johnson and the Tylertown blues tradition see Evans, *Tommy Johnson*, pp. 74–80. For an anthology of blues by Tylertown musicians see *South Mississippi Blues*, Rounder 2009, 12″ LP.

54. These two versions have been issued respectively on *Presenting the Country Blues: Roosevelt Holts*, Blue Horizon 7-63201, 12″ LP, and on Bluesman 100, 45 rpm record (as "Down the Big Road").

55. For more information on Holts see David Evans, "Roosevelt Holts," *Blues World*, no. 15 (July 1967), pp. 3–6.

56. This version is issued on *Big Road Blues*, Advent 2815, 12″ LP.

57. "Big Road Blues." Herb Quinn, vocal and mandolin; David Evans, guitar in EBGDAD tuning, key of D. Clifton, La., Aug. 24, 1966. Recorded by David Evans and Marina Bokelman.

58. This performance was issued on *The Legacy of Tommy Johnson*, Matchbox SDM 224, 12″ LP.

59. This performance was issued as "Careless Love" on *Babe Stovall*, Verve VPM-1, 12″ LP.

60. For more information on Stovall see Simon A. Napier, "Gwine to New Orleans—Meet Babe Stovall," *Blues Unlimited*, no. 23 (June 1965), p. 10; David Evans, "Babe Stovall," in *Back Woods Blues*, ed. Simon A. Napier (Bexhill-on-Sea, England, 1968), pp. 50–55; Bruce Cook, *Listen to the Blues* (New York, 1973), pp. 93–94, 96–98; and Bryan Pickup and Chris Smith, "The Babe Stovall Story," *Talking Blues*, no. 4 (Jan.–Mar. 1977), pp. 2–5. A further performance of this song, entitled "Dirty Mistreater," has been issued on *Babe Stovall Story*, Southern Sound SD 203, 12″ LP.

61. Some of the most influential recordings of this blues were Arthur "Big Boy" Crudup's 1944 "Rock Me Mama" (Bluebird 34-0725); Lil' Son Jackson's 1950 "Rockin' and Rollin'" (Imperial 5113); and Muddy Waters's 1958 "Rock Me" (Chess 1652).

62. "Big Road Blues" (two takes). Eli Owens, vocal and guitar in standard

tuning, key of E; and EBGDAD tuning, key of D. Bogalusa, La., Aug. 24, 1970. Recorded by David Evans.

63. "Dark Road." Eli Owens, vocal and guitar in EBGDAD tuning, key of D. Bogalusa, La., Aug. 19, 1973. Recorded by David Evans.

64. Blind James Brewer, "Big Road Blues," issued on *Mississippi Blues*, Storyville SLP 180, 12" LP; "Big Road Blues." Blind James Brewer, vocal and guitar in EBGDAD tuning, key of D. Chicago, 1964. Recorded by Olle Hollander.

65. For more information on Brewer see Olle Hollander, "Blind James Brewer," *Blues World*, no. 7 (Apr. 1966), p. 7; and Clas Ahlstrand, "Blind Jimmie Brewer," in *Nothing But the Blues*, ed. Mike Leadbitter (London, 1971), pp. 55–56.

66. For more information on Douglas see David Evans, "K. C. Douglas," *Blues World*, no. 18 (Jan. 1968), pp. 4–5; Joe Garrett, "K. C. Douglas," *Blues Unlimited*, no. 81 (Apr. 1971), pp. 11, 13; and Tom Mazzolini, "Living Blues Interview: K. C. Douglas," *Living Blues*, no. 15 (Winter 1973–74), pp. 15–19.

67. These are issued on *K. C. Douglas, A Dead-Beat Guitar and the Mississippi Blues*, Cook 5002; *K. C. Douglas, Big Road Blues*, Bluesville 1050; and *I Have to Paint My Face*, Arhoolie F 1005, 12" LPs.

68. "Big Road Blues" (two takes). "Boogie" Bill Webb, vocal and guitar in EBGDAD tuning, key of D. New Orleans, La., Sept. 16, 1966. Recorded by David Evans and Marina Bokelman.

69. For more information on Webb see David Evans, "Boogie Bill Webb," *Blues Unlimited*, no. 57 (Nov. 1968), p. 14; and David Evans, "A Talk with Boogie Bill," *Blues Unlimited*, no. 97 (Dec. 1972), pp. 8–9; no. 98 (Jan. 1973), pp. 18–19.

70. J. B. Lenoir, "My Father's Style," issued on *Conversation with the Blues*, British Decca LK 4664, 12" LP.

71. Simon A. Napier, "Big Road by Myself," *Blues Unlimited*, no. 28 (Dec. 1965), p. 18.

72. For more information on Lenoir see John Broven, "J. B. Lenoir," in *Nothing But the Blues*, ed. Mike Leadbitter (London, 1971), pp. 35–39.

5: Folk Blues and the Study of Folklore

1. On the spiritual see Clifton Joseph Furness, "Communal Music among Arabians and Negroes," *The Musical Quarterly*, 16 (1930), 49–51; and Pete Seeger, "You Can't Write Down Freedom Songs," *Sing Out!*, 15, No. 3 (July 1965), 11. On the worksong see Robert Winslow Gordon, *Folk-Songs of America* (New York, 1938), pp. 13–14; and Bruce Jackson, *Wake Up Dead Man: Afro-American Worksongs from Texas Prisons* (Cambridge, Mass., 1972). The beginnings of a comparative study of a worksong, "Nine Pound Hammer," which has also entered Anglo-American tradition, have been made by Archie Green in *Only a Miner: Studies in Recorded Coal-Mining Songs* (Urbana, Ill., 1972), pp. 329–369.

2. Helen H. Roberts, "A Study of Folk Song Variants Based on Field Work in Jamaica," *Journal of American Folklore*, 38 (1925), 149–216.

3. For discussions of improvisation in African music see Furness, pp. 42–44; and J. H. Kwabena Nketia, *The Music of Africa* (New York, 1974), pp. 236–238. Processes somewhat similar to some of those used by blues composers are described in Paul Berliner, "The Poetic Song Texts Accompanying the *Mbira Dzavadzimu*," *Ethnomusicology*, 20 (1976), 451–482.

4. Alan P. Merriam, "The African Idiom in Music," *Journal of American Folklore*, 75 (1962), 121.

5. On this point see John A. Lomax, "Self-Pity in Negro Folk-Songs," *The Nation*, 105 (July–Dec. 1917), 141; Newman I. White, *American Negro Folk-Songs* (Cambridge, Mass., 1928), p. 26; Alan Lomax, "Folk Song Style," *American Anthropologist*, 61 (1959), 930–932; Howard Wright Marshall, " 'Keep on the Sunny Side of Life': Pattern and Religious Expression in Bluegrass Gospel Music," *New York Folklore Quarterly*, 30 (1974), 4–5; and David Evans, "Techniques of Blues

Composition among Black Folksingers," *Journal of American Folklore*, 87 (1974), 240–249.

6. On variation, change, and creativity in the Anglo-American tradition see D. K. Wilgus, *Anglo-American Folksong Scholarship Since 1898* (New Brunswick, N.J., 1959), pp. 276–284; Tristram P. Coffin, *The British Traditional Ballad in North America*, rev. ed. (Philadelphia, 1963), pp. 1–19; G. Malcolm Laws, Jr., *Native American Balladry*, rev. ed. (Philadelphia, 1964), pp. 68–82; G. Malcolm Laws, Jr., *American Balladry from British Broadsides* (Philadelphia, 1957), pp. 94–100, 104–122; Douglas J. McMillan, "A Survey of Theories concerning the Oral Transmission of the Traditional Ballad," *Southern Folklore Quarterly*, 28 (1964), 299–309; Phillips Barry, "Communal Re-creation," *Bulletin of the Folk-Song Society of the Northeast*, 5 (1933), 4–6; Roger D. Abrahams and George Foss, *Anglo-American Folksong Style* (Englewood Cliffs, N.J., 1968), pp. 12–36; John Quincy Wolf, "Folksingers and the Re-creation of Folksong," *Western Folklore*, 26 (1967), 101–111; Eleanor R. Long, "Ballad Singers, Ballad Makers, and Ballad Etiology," *Western Folklore*, 32 (1973), 225–236; Roger Abrahams, "Creativity, Individuality, and the Traditional Singer," *Studies in the Literary Imagination*, 3 (1970), 5–34; Foster B. Gresham, "The Jew's Daughter: An Example of Ballad Variation," *Journal of American Folklore*, 47 (1934), 358–361; Tristram P. Coffin, "The Problem of Ballad-Story Variation and Eugene Haun's 'The Drowsy Sleeper'," *Southern Folklore Quarterly*, 14 (1950), 87–96; Edward D. Ives, "A Man and His Song: Joe Scott and 'The Plain Golden Band'," in *Folksongs and Their Makers*, ed. Henry Glassie, Edward D. Ives, and John F. Szwed (Bowling Green, Ohio, n.d.), pp. 81–82, 120–121; and Roger D. Abrahams, ed., *A Singer and Her Songs: Almeda Riddle's Book of Ballads* (Baton Rouge, 1970), pp. 117–122. An admittedly exceptional case of variation from one performance to another by the same singer is presented in Henry Glassie, " 'Take That Night Train to Selma': An Excursion to the Outskirts of Scholarship," in *Folksongs and Their Makers*, ed. Henry Glassie, Edward D. Ives, and John F. Szwed (Bowling Green, Ohio, n.d.), pp. 1–68.

7. Abrahams and Foss, p. 12.

8. Gordon, p. 71.

9. Samuel P. Bayard, "American Folksongs and Their Music," *Southern Folklore Quarterly*, 17 (1953), 137.

10. Linda C. Burman-Hall, "Southern American Folk Fiddle Styles," *Ethnomusicology*, 19 (1975), 47–65.

11. Kenneth A. Thigpen, Jr., "A Reconsideration of the Commonplace Phrase and Commonplace Theme in the Child Ballads," *Southern Folklore Quarterly*, 37 (1973), 385–408.

12. Marina Bokelman, "The Coon Can Game: A Blues Ballad Tradition," M.A. thesis, University of California, Los Angeles, 1968, pp. 25–50, 93, 105–107.

13. Coffin, *The British Traditional Ballad in North America*, pp. 164–172.

14. An exposition of the oral formulaic theory is found in Albert B. Lord, *The Singer of Tales* (Cambridge, Mass., 1964). For related works see Edward R. Haymes, *A Bibliography of Studies Relating to Parry and Lord's Oral Theory*, Publications of the Milman Parry Collection, Documentation and Planning Series, no. 1 (Cambridge, Mass., 1973).

15. Lord, p. 30.

16. Ibid., p. 47.

17. Ibid., p. 68.

18. For attempts to use the oral formulaic theory for the analysis of blues texts see William R. Ferris, Jr., *Blues from the Delta* (Garden City, N.Y., 1978), pp. 57–89; Jeff Todd Titon, *Early Downhome Blues: A Musical and Cultural Analysis* (Urbana, Ill., 1977), pp. 178–182; and John Barnie, "Formulaic Lines and Stanzas in the Country Blues," *Ethnomusicology*, 22 (1978), 457–473.

19. Titon, pp. 154–177, analyzes a sampling of early blues vocal melodies and finds many of them to be members of "tune families" or constructed by

combining smaller traditional melodic elements. Thomas Adler applies the formulaic theory to an Anglo-American instrumental tradition in "Manual Formulaic Composition: Innovation in Bluegrass Banjo Styles," *The Journal of Country Music*, 5 (1974), 55–64.

20. Ruth Finnegan, *Oral Poetry: Its Nature, Significance and Social Context* (Cambridge, 1977).

21. James H. Jones, "Commonplace and Memorization in the Oral Tradition of the English and Scottish Popular Ballads," *Journal of American Folklore*, 74 (1961), 97–112; David Buchan, *The Ballad and the Folk* (London, 1972), pp. 145–167, 274–275; John H. McDowell, "The Mexican *Corrido*: Formula and Theme in a Ballad Tradition," *Journal of American Folklore*, 85 (1972), 205–220. For a criticism of Jones see Albert B. Friedman, "The Formulaic Improvisation Theory of Ballad Tradition—A Counterstatement," *Journal of American Folklore*, 74 (1961), 113–115; and Thigpen, pp. 407–408.

22. Bruce A. Rosenberg, *The Art of the American Folk Preacher* (New York, 1970), pp. 46–58. For a criticism of Rosenberg see Bennison Gray, "Repetition in Oral Literature," *Journal of American Folklore*, 84 (1971), 301–303.

23. For studies in this field that use the oral formulaic theory see James A. Notopoulos, "Homer and Geometric Art: A Comparative Study in the Formulaic Technique of Composition," *Athena*, 61 (1957), 65–93; and Cedric H. Whitman, *Homer and the Heroic Tradition* (Cambridge, Mass., 1958). Other suggestive studies are Ruth L. Bunzel, *The Pueblo Potter: A Study of Creative Imagination in Primitive Art* (New York, 1929); and Nancy D. Munn, *Walbiri Iconography: Graphic Representation and Cultural Symbolism in a Central Australian Society* (Ithaca, N.Y., 1973).

24. D. Demetracopoulou uses concepts of the *element, incident,* and *core* in showing how a myth can be synthesized out of intrinsically unrelated incidents in "The Loon Woman Myth: A Study in Synthesis," *Journal of American Folklore*, 46 (1933), 101–128. For extremes in flexibility and stability in the handling of myths by individual storytellers see Esther Goldfrank, "Isleta Variants: A Study in Flexibility," *Journal of American Folklore*, 39 (1926), 70–78; and May M. Edel, "Stability in Tillamook Folklore," *Journal of American Folklore*, 57 (1944), 116–127.

25. For examples of the former type see John A. and Alan Lomax, *Negro Folk Songs as Sung by Lead Belly* (New York, 1936): and Abrahams, ed., *A Singer and Her Songs*. For the latter see Henry Glassie, Edward D. Ives, and John F. Szwed, eds., *Folksongs and Their Makers* (Bowling Green, Ohio, n.d.).

26. For recent surveys of this subject see Jacques Maquet, *Introduction to Aesthetic Anthropology* (Reading, Mass., 1971); Michael Owen Jones, "The Concept of 'Aesthetic' in the Traditional Arts," *Western Folklore*, 30 (1971), 77–104; and Michael Owen Jones, " 'For Myself I Like a *Decent*, Plain-Made Chair': The Concept of Taste and the Traditional Arts in America," *Western Folklore*, 31 (1972), 27–52.

27. For discussions of these writings see Lily Weiser-Aall, *Volkskunde und Psychologie* (Berlin, 1937); Weston La Barre, "Folklore and Psychology," *Journal of American Folklore*, 61 (1948), 382–390; Paulo de Carvalho-Neto, *Folklore and Psychoanalysis*, trans. Jacques M. P. Wilson (Coral Gables, Fla., 1972); and Carlos C. Drake, "Jungian Psychology and Its Uses in Folklore," *Journal of American Folklore*, 82 (1969), 122–131. Phillips Barry used a Freudian approach to folksong scholarship in "The Psychopathology of Ballad-Singing," *Bulletin of the Folk-Song Society of the Northeast*, 11 (1936), 16–18.

28. Buchan, pp. 87–144.

29. For an introduction to the vast structuralist literature using this concept see Claude Lévi-Strauss, *Structural Anthropology*, trans. Claire Jacobson and Brooke Grundfest Schoepf (New York, 1963); E. Nelson Hayes and Tanya Hayes, eds., *Claude Lévi-Strauss: The Anthropologist as Hero* (Cambridge, Mass., 1970); and Michael Lane, ed., *Introduction to Structuralism* (New York, 1970).

30. On this subject see Rod Gruver, "The Blues as a Secular Religion," *Blues World*, no. 29 (Apr. 1970), pp. 3–6; no. 30 (May 1970), pp. 4–7; no. 31 (June 1970), pp. 5–7; no. 32 (July 1970), pp. 7–9; Stanley Edgar Hyman, "The Ritual View of Myth and the Mythic," in *Myth: A Symposium*, ed. Thomas A. Sebeok (Bloomington, Ind., 1965), pp. 149–150; Ralph Ellison, "Blues People," in *Shadow and Act* (New York, 1964), p. 256; Charles Keil, *Urban Blues* (Chicago, 1968), pp. 44–89; James H. Cone, *The Spirituals and the Blues: An Interpretation* (New York, 1972), pp. 108–142; and S. Margaret W. McCarthy, "The Afro-American Sermon and the Blues: Some Parallels," *The Black Perspective in Music*, 4 (1976), 269–277; and Ferris, pp. 77–89.

31. For a recent survey of the mushrooming literature using a behavioral approach to folklore see Richard Bauman, "Verbal Art as Performance," *American Anthropologist*, 77 (1975), 290–311.

32. D. K. Wilgus, " 'The Text Is the Thing'," *Journal of American Folklore*, 86 (1973), 252. For an earlier statement of this position see D. K. Wilgus, "The Rationalistic Approach," in *A Good Tale and a Bonnie Tune*, Publications of the Texas Folklore Society, no. 32, ed. Mody C. Boatright, Wilson M. Hudson, and Allen Maxwell (Dallas, 1964), pp. 227–237.

BIBLIOGRAPHY

Abrahams, Roger. "Creativity, Individuality, and the Traditional Singer." *Studies in the Literary Imagination*, 3 (1970), 5–34.

———. *Deep Down in the Jungle*. Rev. ed. Chicago: Aldine, 1970.

———, ed. *A Singer and Her Songs: Almeda Riddle's Book of Ballads*. Baton Rouge: Louisiana State University Press, 1970.

———, and George Foss. *Anglo-American Folksong Style*. Englewood Cliffs, N.J.: Prentice-Hall, 1968.

Adler, Thomas. "Manual Formulaic Composition: Innovation in Bluegrass Banjo Style." *The Journal of Country Music*, 5 (1974), 55–64.

Ahlstrand, Clas. "Blind Jimmie Brewer." *Nothing But the Blues*. Ed. Mike Leadbitter. London: Hanover Books, 1971, pp. 55–56.

Albertson, Chris. *Bessie*. New York: Stein and Day, 1972.

Ames, Russell. "Art in Negro Folksong." *Journal of American Folklore*, 56 (1943), 241–254.

———. "Implications of Negro Folk Song." *Science and Society*, 15 (1951), 163–173.

Avakian, George. "Bessie Smith." *The Art of Jazz*. Ed. Martin T. Williams. New York: Oxford University Press, 1959, pp. 75–90.

Barnie, John. "Charley Patton's Jailhouse Blues." *Blues Unlimited*, no. 124 (Mar.–June 1977), pp. 22–23.

———. "Formulaic Lines and Stanzas in the Country Blues." *Ethnomusicology*, 22 (1978), 457–473.

Barry, Phillips. "Communal Re-creation." *Bulletin of the Folk-Song Society of the Northeast*, 5 (1933), 4–6.

———. "The Psychopathology of Ballad-Singing." *Bulletin of the Folk-Song Society of the Northeast*, 11 (1936), 16–18.

———. "William Carter, the Bensontown Homer." *Journal of American Folklore*, 25 (1912), 156–168.

Bartis, Peter T. "An Examination of the Holler in North Carolina White Tradition." *Southern Folklore Quarterly*, 39 (1975), 209–218.

Bastin, Bruce. *Crying for the Carolines*. London: Studio Vista, 1971.

————. "The Devil's Goin' to Get You." *North Carolina Folklore*, 21 (1973), 189–194.

Baughman, Ernest W. *Type and Motif-Index of the Folktales of England and North America*. The Hague: Mouton, 1966.

Bauman, Richard. "Verbal Art as Performance." *American Anthropologist*, 77 (1975), 290–311.

Bayard, Samuel P. "American Folksongs and Their Music." *Southern Folklore Quarterly*, 17 (1953), 122–139.

Benston, Kimberly W. "Tragic Aspects of the Blues." *Phylon*, 36 (1975), 164–176.

Berkowitz, Ted. "Sittin' In with Shad." *Nothing But the Blues*. Ed. Mike Leadbitter. London: Hanover Books, 1971, pp. 191–192.

Berliner, Paul. "The Poetic Song Texts Accompanying the *Mbira Dzavadzimu*." *Ethnomusicology*, 20 (1976), 451–482.

Blesh, Rudi. *Shining Trumpets: A History of Jazz*. Rev. ed. New York: Alfred A. Knopf, 1958.

Bokelman, Marina. "The Coon Can Game: A Blues Ballad Tradition," master's thesis. Los Angeles: University of California, 1968.

Borneman, Ernest. "Black Light and White Shadow: Notes for a History of American Negro Music." *Jazzforschung*, 2 (1970), 24–93.

Bradford, Perry. *Born with the Blues*. New York: Oak Publications, 1965.

Brandfon, Robert. *Cotton Kingdom of the New South: A History of the Yazoo Mississippi Delta from Reconstruction to the Twentieth Century*. Cambridge, Mass.: Harvard University Press, 1967.

Brewer, J. Mason. *American Negro Folklore*. New York: Quadrangle, 1968.

Broonzy, William. *Big Bill Blues*. Rev. ed. New York: Oak Publications, 1964.

Broven, John. "Howlin' Wolf." *Nothing But the Blues*. Ed. Mike Leadbitter. London: Hanover Books, 1971, pp. 39–44.

————. "J. B. Lenoir." *Nothing But the Blues*. Ed. Mike Leadbitter. London: Hanover Books, 1971, pp. 35–39.

————. Walking to New Orleans. Bexhill-on-Sea, England: Blues Unlimited, 1974.

Brown, Sterling A. "The Blues." *Phylon*, 13 (1952), 286–292.

————. "The Blues as Folk Poetry." *Folk-Say, A Regional Miscellany: 1930*. Ed. B. A. Botkin. Norman: University of Oklahoma Press, 1930, pp. 324–339.

Browne, Ray B. "The Alabama 'Holler' and Street Cries." *Journal of American Folklore*, 70 (1957), 363.

————. "Some Notes on the Southern 'Holler'." *Journal of American Folklore*, 67 (1954), 73–77.

Buchan, David. *The Ballad and the Folk*. London: Routledge & Kegan Paul, 1972.

Bunzel, Ruth L. *The Pueblo Potter: A Study of Creative Imagination in Primitive Art*. New York: Columbia University Press, 1929.

Burman-Hall, Linda C. "Southern American Folk Fiddle Styles." *Ethnomusicology*, 19 (1975), 47–65.

Calt, Stephen. "The Country Blues as Meaning." *Country Blues Songbook*. Ed. Stefan Grossman, Hal Grossman, and Stephen Calt. New York: Oak Publications, 1973, pp. 8–35.

————. Notes to *Mr. Johnson's Blues*, Mamlish S-3807, 12″ LP, 1976.

————. "Robert Johnson Recapitulated." *Blues Unlimited*, no. 86 (Nov. 1971), pp. 12–14.

Campbell, E. Simms. "Blues." *Jazzmen*. Ed. Frederic Ramsey, Jr., and Charles Edward Smith. New York: Harcourt, Brace and Company, 1939, pp. 101–118.

Carmer, Carl. *Stars Fell on Alabama*. New York: Farrar & Rinehart, 1934.

Carvalho-Neto, Paulo de. *Folklore and Psychoanalysis*. Trans. Jacques M. P. Wilson. Coral Gables, Fla.: University of Miami Press, 1972.

Charters, Samuel. *The Bluesmen.* New York: Oak Publications, 1967.

———. *The Country Blues.* New York: Rinehart & Company, Inc., 1959.

———. *The Poetry of the Blues.* New York: Oak Publications, 1963.

———. *Robert Johnson.* New York: Oak Publications, 1973.

———. *Sweet As the Showers of Rain.* New York: Oak Publications, 1977.

Coffin, Tristram P. *The British Traditional Ballad in North America.* Rev. ed. Philadelphia: The American Folklore Society, 1963.

———. "The Problem of Ballad-Story Variation and Eugene Haun's 'The Drowsy Sleeper'." *Southern Folklore Quarterly,* 14 (1950), 87–96.

Cohen, Norman. " 'I'm a Record Man': Uncle Art Satherly Reminisces." *John Edwards Memorial Foundation Quarterly,* 8 (1972), 18–22.

Cohn, David. *Where I Was Born and Raised.* Notre Dame, Ind.: University of Notre Dame Press, 1967.

Cohn, Lawrence. "Mississippi John Hurt." *Sing Out!,* 14, No. 5 (Nov. 1964), 16–21.

Cone, James H. *The Spirituals and the Blues: An Interpretation.* New York: Seabury, 1972.

Cook, Bruce. *Listen to the Blues.* New York: Charles Scribner's Sons, 1973.

Courlander, Harold. *Negro Folk Music U.S.A.* New York: Columbia University Press, 1963.

———. *Negro Songs from Alabama.* Rev. ed. New York: Oak Publications, 1963.

Cowley, John. "Some Thoughts on Tommy Johnson and Copyright." *Blues World,* no. 23 (Apr. 1969), pp. 29–30.

Danker, Frederick E. "Towards an Intrinsic Study of the Blues Ballad: 'Casey Jones' and 'Louis Collins'." *Southern Folklore Quarterly,* 34 (1970), 90–103.

Dauer, Alfons M. "Betrachtungen zur afro-amerikanischen Folklore, dargestellt an einem Blues von Lightnin' Hopkins." *Archiv für Völkerkunde,* 19 (1964–65), 11–30.

———. *Der Jazz, seine Ursprünge und seine Entwicklung.* Kassel: Erich Röth, 1958.

Davis, Henry C. "Negro Folk-Lore in South Carolina." *Journal of American Folklore,* 27 (1914), 241–254.

Demetracopoulou, D. "The Loon Woman Myth: A Study in Synthesis." *Journal of American Folklore,* 46 (1933), 101–128.

Dixon, Robert M. W., and John Godrich. *Recording the Blues.* New York: Stein and Day, 1970.

Dollard, John. *Caste and Class in a Southern Town.* New Haven: Yale University Press, 1937.

Dorson, Richard M. *American Negro Folktales.* Greenwich, Conn.: Fawcett Publications, 1967.

———, ed. *Folklore and Folklife.* Chicago: University of Chicago Press, 1972.

Drake, Carlos C. "Jungian Psychology and Its Uses in Folklore." *Journal of American Folklore,* 82 (1969), 122–131.

Dundes, Alan, ed. *The Study of Folklore.* Englewood Cliffs, N.J.: Prentice-Hall, 1965.

Earl, John. "A Lifetime in the Blues: Johnny Shines." *Blues World,* no. 46–49 (1973), pp. 3–13, 20–22.

Edel, May M. "Stability in Tillamook Folklore." *Journal of American Folklore,* 57 (1944), 116–127.

Ellison, Ralph. "Blues People." *Shadow and Act.* New York: Random House, 1964, pp. 247–258.

Elmes, Barry. "Living Blues Interview: Sonny Terry & Brownie McGhee." *Living Blues,* no. 13 (Summer 1973), pp. 14–23.

"Enigmatic Folksongs of the Southern Underworld." *Current Opinion,* 67 (July–Dec. 1919), 165–166.

Epstein, Dena J. *Sinful Tunes and Spirituals*. Urbana: University of Illinois Press, 1977.

Evans, David. "African Elements in Twentieth-Century United States Black Folk Music." *Jazzforschung*, 10 (1978), 85–110.

———. "Afro-American One-Stringed Instruments." *Western Folklore*, 29 (1970), 229–245.

———. "Babe Stovall." *Back Woods Blues*. Ed. Simon A. Napier. Bexhill-on-Sea, England: Blues Unlimited, 1968, pp. 50–55.

———. "Black Musicians Remember Jimmie Rodgers." *Old Time Music*, no. 7 (Winter 1972/3), pp. 12–14.

———. "The Blues of Tommy Johnson: A Study of a Tradition," master's thesis. Los Angeles: University of California, 1967.

———. "Blues on Dockery's Plantation: 1895 to 1967." *Nothing But the Blues*. Ed. Mike Leadbitter. London: Hanover Books, 1971, pp. 129–132.

———. "Boogie Bill Webb." *Blues Unlimited*, no. 57 (Nov. 1968), p. 14.

———. "Booker White." *Nothing But the Blues*. Ed. Mike Leadbitter. London: Hanover Books, 1971, pp. 248–255.

———. "Bubba Brown: Folk Poet." *Mississippi Folklore Register*, 7 (1973), 15–31.

———. "The Bubba Brown Story." *Blues World*, no. 21 (Oct. 1968), pp. 7–9.

———. "Charlie Patton: His Life and Music." *Blues World*, no. 33 (Aug. 1970), pp. 11–15.

———. "Delta Reminiscences: Floyd Patterson Interviewed by David Evans (Crystal Springs, Mississippi—August 31 and September 2, 1970)." *Blues World*, no. 43 (Summer 1972), pp. 14–15.

———. "The Fiddlin' Joe Martin Story." *Blues World*, no. 20 (July 1968), pp. 3–5.

———. "Fieldwork with Blues Singers: The Unintentionally Induced Natural Context." *Southern Folklore Quarterly*, 42 (1978), 9–16.

———. "Folk, Commercial, and Folkloristic Aesthetics in the Blues." *Jazzforschung*, 5 (1973), 11–32.

———. "An Interview with H. C. Speir." *John Edwards Memorial Foundation Quarterly*, 8 (1972), 117–121.

———. "The Johnny Temple Story." *Blues Unlimited*, no. 56 (Sept. 1968), pp. 3–5.

———. "K. C. Douglas." *Blues World*, no. 18 (Jan. 1968), pp. 4–5.

———. "The Mississippi Blues." Notes to *The Mississippi Blues, 1927–1940*, Origin Jazz Library 5, and *The Mississippi Blues No. 2: The Delta, 1929–1932*, Origin Jazz Library 11, 12″ LPs, 1968.

———. "Roosevelt Holts." *Blues World*, no. 15 (July 1967), pp. 3–6.

———. "Rubin Lacy." *Nothing But the Blues*. Ed. Mike Leadbitter. London: Hanover Books, 1971, pp. 239–245.

———. "The Singing Stammerer Motif in Black Tradition." *Western Folklore*, 35 (1976), 157–160.

———. "Son House—Some Further Comments." *Blues Unlimited*, no. 43 (May 1967), pp. 8–10.

———. "Structure and Meaning in the Folk Blues." *The Study of American Folklore: An Introduction*. 2d ed. By Jan Harold Brunvand. New York: W. W. Norton, 1978, pp. 421–447.

———. "A Talk with Boogie Bill." *Blues Unlimited*, no. 97 (Dec. 1972), pp. 8–9; no. 98 (Jan. 1973), pp. 18–19.

———. "Techniques of Blues Composition among Black Folksingers." *Journal of American Folklore*, 87 (1974), 240–249.

———. *Tommy Johnson*. London: Studio Vista, 1971.

———. "Tradition and Creativity in the Folk Blues," Ph.D. dissertation. Los Angeles: University of California, 1976.

———. "The Woodrow Adams Story." *Nothing But the Blues*. Ed. Mike Leadbitter. London: Hanover Books, 1971, pp. 142–144.

Fahey, John. *Charley Patton*. London: Studio Vista, 1970.

Ferris, William R., Jr. *Blues from the Delta*. Garden City, N.Y.: Anchor, 1978.

———. "Creativity and the Blues." *Blues Unlimited*, no. 71 (Apr. 1970), pp. 13–14.

———. "Gut Bucket Blues: Sacred and Profane." *Jazzforschung*, 5 (1973), 68–85.

———. "Racial Repertoires among Black Performers." *Ethnomusicology*, 14 (1970), 439–449.

———. "Records and the Delta Blues Tradition." *Keystone Folklore Quarterly*, 14 (1969), 158–165.

Finnegan, Ruth. *Oral Poetry: Its Nature, Significance and Social Context*. Cambridge: Cambridge University Press, 1977.

Frazier, E. Franklin. *The Negro Church in America*. New York: Schocken, 1964.

Friedman, Albert B. "The Formulaic Improvisation Theory of Ballad Tradition— A Counterstatement." *Journal of American Folklore*, 74 (1961), 113–115.

Furness, Clifton Joseph. "Communal Music among Arabians and Negroes." *The Musical Quarterly*, 16 (1930), 38–51.

Garon, Paul. *Blues and the Poetic Spirit*. London: Eddison, 1975.

———. *The Devil's Son-in-Law: The Story of Peetie Wheatstraw and His Songs*. London: Studio Vista, 1971.

Garrett, Joe. "K. C. Douglas." *Blues Unlimited*, no. 81 (Apr. 1971), pp. 11, 13.

Gart, Galen. "Sam Chatmon." *Blues Unlimited*, no. 83 (July 1971), pp. 9–10.

Garwood, Donald. *Masters of Instrumental Blues Guitar*. New York: Oak Publications, 1968.

Gellert, Lawrence. *Me and My Captain*. New York: Hours Press, 1939.

———. *Negro Songs of Protest*. New York: Carl Fischer, Inc., 1936.

Glassie, Henry. " 'Take That Night Train to Selma': An Excursion to the Outskirts of Scholarship." *Folksongs and Their Makers*. Ed. Henry Glassie, Edward D. Ives, and John F. Szwed. Bowling Green, Ohio: Bowling Green University Popular Press, n.d., pp. 1–68.

———, Edward D. Ives, and John F. Szwed, eds. *Folksongs and Their Makers*. Bowling Green, Ohio: Bowling Green University Popular Press, n.d.

Glover, Tony. *Blues Harp: An Instruction Method for Playing the Blues Harmonica*. New York: Oak Publications, 1965.

Godrich, John, and Robert M. W. Dixon. *Blues & Gospel Records 1902–1942*. London: Storyville Publications, 1969.

Goines, Leonard. "The Blues as Black Therapy: A Thematic Study." *Black World*, 23, No. 1 (Nov. 1973), 28–40.

Goldfrank, Esther. "Isleta Variants: A Study in Flexibility." *Journal of American Folklore*, 39 (1926), 70–78.

Goldstein, Kenneth S. *A Guide for Field Workers in Folklore*. Hatboro, Pa.: Folklore Associates, Inc., 1964.

———. "The Induced Natural Context: An Ethnographic Folklore Field Technique." *Essays on the Verbal and Visual Arts*. Ed. June Helm. Seattle: University of Washington Press, 1967, pp. 1–6.

———. "On the Application of the Concepts of Active and Inactive Traditions to the Study of Repertory." *Journal of American Folklore*, 84 (1971), 62–67.

Gombosi, Otto. "The Pedigree of the Blues." *Music Teachers National Association Proceedings*, 40 (1946), 382–389.

Gordon, Robert Winslow. *Folk-Songs of America*. New York: National Service Bureau, 1938.

Gray, Bennison. "Repetition in Oral Literature." *Journal of American Folklore*, 84 (1971), 289–303.

Green, Archie. *Only a Miner: Studies in Recorded Coal-Mining Songs*. Urbana: University of Illinois Press, 1972.

Greenway, John. *American Folksongs of Protest*. New York: Octagon Books, 1971.

————. "Jimmie Rodgers—A Folksong Catalyst." *Journal of American Folklore*, 70 (1957), 231–234.

Gresham, Foster B. "The Jew's Daughter: An Example of Ballad Variation." *Journal of American Folklore*, 47 (1934), 358–361.

Groom, Bob. *Blind Lemon Jefferson*. Blues World Booklet No. 3. Knutsford, England: Blues World, 1970.

————. *The Blues Revival*. London: Studio Vista, 1971.

————. "An Interview with Son House." *Blues World*, no. 18 (Jan. 1968), pp. 5–8.

————. "Kokomo Blues." *Blues World*, no. 24 (July 1969), pp. 10–13.

————. "The Legacy of Blind Lemon." *Blues World*, no. 16 (Sept. 1967), p. 13; no. 18 (Jan. 1968), pp. 14–16; no. 20 (July 1968), pp. 33–37; no. 21 (Oct. 1968), pp. 30–32; no. 23 (Apr. 1969), pp. 5–7; no. 24 (July 1969), pp. 9–10; no. 25 (Oct. 1969), pp. 9–10; no. 27 (Feb. 1970), pp. 13–14; no. 28 (Mar. 1970), pp. 8–9; no. 29 (Apr. 1970), pp. 8–9; no. 30 (May 1970), pp. 13–14; no. 35 (Oct. 1970), pp. 19–20; no. 36 (Nov. 1970), p. 20; no. 40 (Autumn 1971), pp. 4–6; no. 50 (1974), p. 8.

————. "Otto Virgial." *Blues World*, no. 27 (Feb. 1970), pp. 16–18.

————. "Robert Johnson." *Blues World*, no. 50 (1974), pp. 6–7.

————, ed. *Robert Johnson*. Blues World Booklet No. 1. Knutsford, England: Blues World, 1967.

————. "Standing at the Crossroads: Robert Johnson's Recordings." *Blues Unlimited*, no. 118 (Mar.–Apr. 1976), pp. 17–20; no. 119 (May–June 1976), pp. 11–14; no. 120 (July–Aug. 1976), pp. 15–17; no. 121 (Sept.–Oct. 1976), pp. 20–21.

Grossman, Stefan. *The Country Blues Guitar*. New York: Oak Publications, 1968.

————. *Delta Blues Guitar*. New York: Oak Publications, 1969.

————. *Ragtime Blues Guitarists*. New York: Oak Publications, 1970.

Gruver, Rod. "The Autobiographical Theory Re-Examined." *John Edwards Memorial Foundation Quarterly*, 6 (1970), 129–131.

————. "The Blues as a Secular Religion." *Blues World*, no. 29 (Apr. 1970), pp. 3–6; no. 30 (May 1970), pp. 4–7; no. 31 (June 1970), pp. 5–7; no. 32 (July 1970), pp. 7–9.

————. "The Blues as Dramatic Monologues." *John Edwards Memorial Foundation Quarterly*, 6 (1970), 28–31.

————. "A Closer Look at the Blues." *Blues World*, no. 26 (Jan. 1970), pp. 4–10.

Guitar Player Magazine. Blues Guitarists. Saratoga, Calif.: Guitar Player Productions, 1975.

Guralnick, Peter. *Feel Like Going Home*. New York: Outerbridge & Dienstfrey, 1971.

Halpert, Herbert. "The Devil and the Fiddle." *Hoosier Folklore Bulletin*, 2 (1943), 39–43.

Handy, W. C. *Father of the Blues*. New York: Collier Books, 1970.

————, ed. *Blues, An Anthology*. With a Historical and Critical Text by Abbe Niles, revised by Jerry Silverman. New York: Macmillan, 1972.

Haralambos, Michael. *Right On: From Blues to Soul in Black America*. London: Eddison Press, 1974.

————. "Soul Music and Blues: Their Meaning and Relevance in Northern United States Black Ghettoes." *Afro-American Anthropology: Contemporary Perspectives*. Ed. Norman E. Whitten, Jr., and John F. Szwed. New York: The Free Press, 1970, pp. 367–384.

Hayes, E. Nelson and Tanya, eds. *Claude Lévi-Strauss: The Anthropologist as Hero*. Cambridge, Mass.: The M. I. T. Press, 1970.

Haymes, Edward R. *A Bibliography of Studies Relating to Parry's and Lord's Oral Theory*. Publications of the Milman Parry Collection, Documentation and Planning Series, No. 1. Cambridge, Mass., 1973.

Hearn, Lafcadio. "Levee Life." *The Selected Writings of Lafcadio Hearn*. Ed. Henry Goodman. New York: The Citadel Press, 1949, pp. 215–233.

Hollander, Olle. "Blind James Brewer." *Blues World*, no. 7 (Apr. 1966), p. 7.

Hood, Mantle. *The Ethnomusicologist*. New York: McGraw-Hill, 1971.

House, Son. "I Can Make My Own Songs." *Sing Out!*, 15, No. 3 (July 1965), 38–47.

Hughes, Langston, and Arna Bontemps, eds. *The Book of Negro Folklore*. New York: Dodd, Mead & Company, 1958.

Hurston, Zora Neale. *Mules and Men*. Philadelphia: J. B. Lippincott, 1935.

——. "Story in Harlem Slang." *Mother Wit from the Laughing Barrel*. Ed. Alan Dundes. Englewood Cliffs, N.J.: Prentice-Hall, Inc., 1973, pp. 222–229.

Hyatt, Harry Middleton. *Hoodoo—Conjuration—Witchcraft—Rootwork*. 4 vols. Washington, D.C.: American University Bookstore, 1970 (Vols. I–II). St. Louis: Western Publishing Co., 1973–74 (Vols. III–IV).

Hyman, Stanley Edgar. "The Folk Tradition." *Mother Wit from the Laughing Barrel*. Ed. Alan Dundes. Englewood Cliffs, N.J.: Prentice-Hall, 1973, pp. 46–56.

——. "The Ritual View of Myth and the Mythic." *Myth: A Symposium*. Ed. Thomas A. Sebeok. Bloomington: Indiana University Press, 1965, pp. 136–153.

Iglauer, Bruce, Jim O'Neal, and Bea Van Geffen. "Living Blues Interview: Lowell Fulson." *Living Blues*, no. 5 (Summer 1971), pp. 19–25; no. 6 (Autumn 1971), pp. 10–20.

Ives, Edward D. *Larry Gorman, the Man Who Made the Songs*. Bloomington: Indiana University Press, 1964.

——. *Lawrence Doyle: Farmer-Poet of Prince Edward Island*. Orono: University of Maine Press, 1971.

——. "A Man and His Song: Joe Scott and 'The Plain Golden Band'." *Folksongs and Their Makers*. Ed. Henry Glassie, Edward D. Ives, and John F. Szwed. Bowling Green, Ohio: Bowling Green University Popular Press, n.d., pp. 69–146.

Jackson, Bruce. *"Get Your Ass in the Water and Swim Like Me": Narrative Poetry from Black Oral Tradition*. Cambridge, Mass.: Harvard University Press, 1974.

——. "The Personal Blues of Skip James." *Sing Out!*, 15, No. 6 (Jan. 1966), 26–31.

——. *Wake Up Dead Man: Afro-American Worksongs from Texas Prisons*. Cambridge, Mass.: Harvard University Press, 1972.

Jahn, Janheinz. *Neo-African Literature*. New York: Grove Press, 1968.

James, Skip. "Skip James Talkin'." *Nothing But the Blues*. Ed. Mike Leadbitter. London: Hanover Books, 1971, pp. 232–234.

Johnson, Guy B. "Double Meaning in the Popular Negro Blues." *Journal of Abnormal and Social Psychology*, 22 (1927–28), 12–20.

Johnson, James Weldon. *Black Manhattan*. New York: Alfred A. Knopf, 1930.

Jones, James H. "Commonplace and Memorization in the Oral Tradition of the English and Scottish Popular Ballads." *Journal of American Folklore*, 74 (1961), 97–112.

Jones, LeRoi. *Blues People*. New York: William Morrow and Company, 1963.

Jones, Max. "On Blues." *The PL Yearbook of Jazz 1946*. Ed. Albert McCarthy. London: Editions Poetry, 1946, pp. 72–107.

Jones, Michael Owen. "The Concept of 'Aesthetic' in the Traditional Arts." *Western Folklore*, 31 (1972), 27–52.

——. " 'For Myself I Like a *Decent*, Plain-Made Chair': The Concept of Taste and the Traditional Arts in America." *Western Folklore*, 31 (1972), 27–52.

Kahn, Ed. "Hillbilly Music: Source and Resource." *Journal of American Folklore*, 78 (1965), 257–266.

Kay, George W. "Mississippi John Hurt." *Jazz Journal*, 17, No. 2 (Feb. 1964), 24–26.

——. "William Christopher Handy, Father of the Blues—A History of Published Blues." *Jazz Journal*, 24, No. 3 (Mar. 1971), 10–12.

Keil, Charles. *Urban Blues.* Chicago: University of Chicago Press, 1966.

Kemble, Frances Anne. *Journal of a Residence on a Georgian Plantation in 1838–1839.* New York: Harper & Brothers, 1863.

Kennedy, Stetson. *Palmetto Country.* New York: Duell, Sloan & Pearce, 1942.

Klatzko, Bernard. Notes to *The Immortal Charlie Patton,* Origin Jazz Library 7, 12" LP, 1964.

Krehbiel, Henry Edward. *Afro-American Folksongs.* New York: Frederick Ungar Publishing Co., 1962.

Krohn, Kaarle. *Folklore Methodology Formulated by Julius Krohn and Expanded by Nordic Researchers.* Publications of the American Folklore Society, Bibliographical and Special Series, No. 21. Trans. Roger L. Welsch. Austin: University of Texas Press, 1971.

La Barre, Weston. "Folklore and Psychology." *Journal of American Folklore,* 61 (1948), 382–390.

Lane, Michael, ed. *Introduction to Structuralism.* New York: Basic Books, 1970.

Laubenstein, Paul Fritz. "Race Values in Aframerican Music." *The Musical Quarterly,* 16 (1930), 378–403.

Laws, G. Malcolm, Jr. *American Balladry from British Broadsides.* Philadelphia: The American Folklore Society, 1957.

———. *Native American Balladry.* Rev. ed. Philadelphia: The American Folklore Society, 1964.

Leach, Maria, ed. *Funk & Wagnalls Standard Dictionary of Folklore, Mythology, and Legend.* New York: Funk & Wagnalls, 1949.

Leadbitter, Mike. *Crowley, Louisiana Blues.* Bexhill-on-Sea, England: Blues Unlimited, 1968.

———. *Delta Country Blues.* Bexhill-on-Sea, England: Blues Unlimited, 1968.

———. "Mike's Blues." *Blues Unlimited,* no. 111 (Dec.–Jan. 1974–75), p. 5.

———. "Still Worried All the Time." *Blues Unlimited,* no. 90 (Apr. 1972), pp. 12–14.

———, ed. *Nothing But the Blues.* London: Hanover Books, 1971.

———, and Eddie Shuler. *From the Bayou.* Bexhill-on-Sea, England: Blues Unlimited, 1969.

———, and Neil Slaven. *Blues Records: 1943–1966.* London: Hanover Books, 1968.

Lester, Julius. "Country Blues Comes to Town?: The View from the Other Side of the Tracks." *Sing Out!,* 14, No. 4 (Sept. 1964), 37–39.

Lévi-Strauss, Claude. *Structural Anthropology.* Trans. Claire Jacobson and Brooke Grundfest Schoepf. New York: Basic Books, 1963.

Lindenau, Don. "Lowell Fulson." *Blues Unlimited,* no. 18 (Jan. 1965), p. 10.

Locke, Alain. *The Negro and His Music.* New York: Arno Press, 1969.

Lomax, Alan. "Folk Song Style." *American Anthropologist,* 61 (1959), 927–954.

———. *The Folk Songs of North America.* Garden City, N.Y.: Doubleday & Company, Inc., 1960.

———. "I Got the Blues." *Common Ground,* 8 (Summer 1948), 38–52.

———. *List of American Folk Songs on Commercial Records.* Washington, D.C.: Department of State, 1940.

———. *Mister Jelly Roll.* New York: Grosset & Dunlap, 1950.

———. " 'Sinful' Songs of the Southern Negro." *Southwest Review,* 19 (1933–34), 105–131.

Lomax, John A. "Self-Pity in Negro Folk-Songs." *The Nation,* 105 (July–Dec. 1917), 141–145.

———, and Alan Lomax. *American Ballads and Folk Songs.* New York: Macmillan, 1934.

———, and Alan Lomax. *Negro Folk Songs as Sung by Lead Belly.* New York: Macmillan, 1936.

———, and Alan Lomax. *Our Singing Country.* New York: Macmillan, 1941.

Long, Eleanor R. "Ballad Singers, Ballad Makers, and Ballad Etiology." *Western Folklore*, 32 (1973), 225–236.

Longini, Muriel Davis. "Folk Songs of Chicago Negroes." *Journal of American Folklore*, 52 (1939), 96–111.

Lord, Albert B. *The Singer of Tales*. Cambridge, Mass.: Harvard University Press, 1964.

Lornell, Christopher. "The Effects of Social and Economic Changes on the Uses of Blues." *John Edwards Memorial Foundation Quarterly*, 11 (1975), 43–48.

———. "Pre-Blues Banjo & Fiddle." *Living Blues*, no. 18 (Autumn 1974), pp. 25–27.

———. "Sam Chatmon." *Jazz Journal*, 25, No. 6 (June 1972), 18.

———. "Living Blues Interview: J. B. Long." *Living Blues*, no. 29 (Sept.–Oct. 1976), pp. 13–22.

———, and Jim O'Neal. "Living Blues Interview: Hammie Nixon & Sleepy John Estes." *Living Blues*, no. 19 (Jan.–Feb. 1975), pp. 13–19.

Lowry, Pete, and Bruce Bastin. "Fort Valley Blues." *Blues Unlimited*, no. 111 (Dec.–Jan. 1974–75), pp. 11–13; no. 112 (Mar.–Apr. 1975), pp. 13–16; no. 114 (July–Aug. 1975), pp. 20–22.

McCarthy, Albert, Alun Morgan, Paul Oliver, and Max Harrison. *Jazz on Record*. London: Hanover Books, 1968.

McCarthy, S. Margaret W. "The Afro-American Sermon and the Blues: Some Parallels." *The Black Perspective in Music*, 4 (1976), 269–277.

McCormick, Mack. "Mance Lipscomb, Texas Sharecropper and Songster." *American Folk Music Occasional, No. 1*. Ed. Chris Strachwitz. Berkeley, Calif.: American Folk Music Occasional, 1964, pp. 61–73.

McDowell, John H. "The Mexican *Corrido*: Formula and Theme in a Ballad Tradition." *Journal of American Folklore*, 85 (1972), 205–220.

McMillan, Douglas J. "A Survey of Theories Concerning the Oral Transmission of the Traditional Ballad." *Southern Folklore Quarterly*, 28 (1964), 299–309.

McNeil, W. K. "Syncopated Slander: The 'Coon Song', 1890–1900." *Keystone Folklore Quarterly*, 17 (1972), 63–82.

Mahony, Dan. *The Columbia 13/14000-D Series, A Numerical Listing*. Rev. ed. Stanhope, N.J.: Walter C. Allen, 1966.

Mann, Woody. *Six Black Blues Guitarists*. New York: Oak Publications, 1973.

Maquet, Jacques. *Introduction to Aesthetic Anthropology*. Reading, Mass.: Addison-Wesley, 1971.

Marshall, Howard Wright. " 'Keep on the Sunny Side of Life': Pattern and Religious Expression in Bluegrass Gospel Music." *New York Folklore Quarterly*, 30 (1974), 3–43.

Mazzolini, Tom. "Living Blues Interview: K. C. Douglas." *Living Blues*, no. 15 (Winter 1973–74), pp. 15–19.

Melnick, Mimi Clar. " 'I Can Peep through Muddy Water and Spy Dry Land': Boasts in the Blues." *Folklore International: Essays in Traditional Literature, Belief, and Custom in Honor of Wayland Debs Hand*. Ed. D. K. Wilgus and Carol Sommer. Hatboro, Pa.: Folklore Associates, 1967, pp. 139–149.

Melrose, Lester. "My Life in Recording." *The American Folk Music Occasional*. Ed. Chris Strachwitz and Pete Welding. New York: Oak Publications, 1970, pp. 59–61.

Merriam, Alan P. "The African Idiom in Music." *Journal of American Folklore*, 75 (1962), 120–130.

Middleton, Richard. *Pop Music and the Blues*. London: Victor Gollancz, 1972.

Mitchell, George. *Blow My Blues Away*. Baton Rouge: Louisiana State University Press, 1971.

Moore, Carman. *Somebody's Angel Child*. New York: Thomas Y. Crowell Co., 1969.

Mossel, Eric. "Every Day I Heard the Blues." *Blues World*, no. 8 (May 1966), pp. 11–18.

Munn, Nancy D. *Walbiri Iconography: Graphic Representation and Cultural Symbolism in a Central Australian Society*. Ithaca, N.Y.: Cornell University Press, 1973.

Napier, Simon A. "Big Road by Myself." *Blues Unlimited*, no. 28 (Dec. 1965), p. 18.

———. " 'Cryin' Mama, Mama, Mama . . .' (A Look at Tommy Johnson, His Influence and Songs)." *Blues Unlimited*, no. 30 (Feb. 1966), pp. 14–15.

———. "Gwine to New Orleans—Meet Babe Stovall." *Blues Unlimited*, no. 23 (June 1965), p. 10.

———, ed. *Back Woods Blues*. Bexhill-on-Sea, England: Blues Unlimited, 1968.

Neff, Robert, and Anthony Connor. *Blues*. Boston: David R. Godine, 1975.

Nelson, Donald Lee. "The West Virginia Snake Hunters: John and Emery McClung." *John Edwards Memorial Foundation Quarterly*, 10 (1974), 68–73.

Nicholas, A. X. *Woke Up This Mornin': Poetry of the Blues*. New York: Bantam, 1973.

Niles, Abbe. "Ballads, Songs and Snatches." *Bookman*, 67 (Mar.–Aug. 1928), 422–424, 565–567, 687–689; 68 (Sept. 1928–Feb. 1929), 75–77, 213–215.

———. "Blue Notes." *The New Republic*, 45 (Nov. 25, 1925–Feb. 17, 1926), 292–293.

———. "The Story of the Blues." *Blues, An Anthology*. Ed. W. C. Handy, revised by Jerry Silverman. New York: Macmillan, 1972, pp. 12–45.

Niles, John J. "Shout, Coon, Shout!" *The Musical Quarterly*, 16 (1930), 516–530.

———. *Singing Soldiers*. New York: Charles Scribner's Sons, 1927.

Nketia, J. H. Kwabena. *The Music of Africa*. New York: W. W. Norton, 1974.

Notopoulos, James A. "Homer and Geometric Art: A Comparative Study in the Formulaic Technique of Composition." *Athena*, 61 (1957), 65–93.

Oakley, Giles. *The Devil's Music: A History of the Blues*. London: British Broadcasting Company, 1976.

Odum, Anna Kranz. "Some Negro Folk-Songs from Tennessee." *Journal of American Folklore*, 27 (1914), 255–265.

Odum, Howard W. *Cold Blue Moon*. Indianapolis: Bobbs-Merrill, 1931.

———. "Down That Lonesome Road." *The Country Gentleman*, no. 91 (May 1926), pp. 18–19, 79.

———. "Folk-Song and Folk-Poetry as Found in the Secular Songs of the Southern Negroes." *Journal of American Folklore*, 24 (1911), 255–294, 351–396.

———. *Rainbow Round My Shoulder*. Indianapolis: Bobbs-Merrill, 1928.

———. *Wings on My Feet*. Indianapolis: Bobbs-Merrill, 1929.

———, and Guy B. Johnson. *The Negro and His Songs*. Chapel Hill: University of North Carolina Press, 1925.

———, and Guy B. Johnson. *Negro Workaday Songs*. Chapel Hill: University of North Carolina Press, 1926.

Oliver, Paul. *Bessie Smith*. London: Cassell, 1959.

———. "Blues as an Art Form." *Blues World*, no. 21 (Oct. 1968), pp. 1–7.

———. "Blues to Drive the Blues Away." *Jazz*. Ed. Nat Hentoff and Albert J. McCarthy. New York: Holt, Rinehart and Winston, Inc., 1959, pp. 83–103.

———. *Conversation with the Blues*. New York: Horizon Press, 1965.

———. *The Meaning of the Blues*. New York: Collier Books, 1963.

———. *Savannah Syncopators: African Retentions in the Blues*. New York: Stein and Day, 1970.

———. *Screening the Blues*. London: Cassell, 1968.

———. *The Story of the Blues*. London: Barrie & Rockliff, 1969.

Olsson, Bengt. *Memphis Blues and Jug Bands*. London: Studio Vista, 1970.

O'Neal, Jim. "Living Blues Interview: Houston Stackhouse." *Living Blues*, no. 17 (Summer 1974), pp. 20–36.

——, and Bill Greensmith. "Living Blues Interview: Jimmy Rogers." *Living Blues,* no. 14 (Autumn 1973), pp. 11–20.

"Origin of 'Blues' Numbers." *Sheet Music News,* 2, No. 5 (Oct. 1923), 8–9, 41.

Osgood, Henry O. "The Blues." *Modern Music,* 4, No. 1 (Nov.–Dec. 1926), 25–28.

——. *So This Is Jazz.* Boston: Little, Brown, and Company, 1926.

Oster, Harry. "The Blues as a Genre." *Genre,* 2 (1969), 259–274.

——. *Living Country Blues.* Detroit: Folklore Associates, 1969.

——, and Richard Allen. Notes to *Angola Prisoners' Blues,* Folk-Lyric LFS A-3, 12" LP, ca. 1961.

Otto, John Solomon, and Augustus M. Burns. "Black and White Cultural Interaction in the Early Twentieth Century South: Race and Hillbilly Music." *Phylon,* 35 (1974), 407–417.

——. "The Use of Race and Hillbilly Recordings as Sources for Historical Research: The Problem of Color Hierarchy among Afro-Americans in the Early Twentieth Century." *Journal of American Folklore,* 85 (1972), 344–355.

The Oxford English Dictionary. 13 vols. Oxford: At the Clarendon Press, 1933.

Palmer, Bob. "What Is American Music?" *Down Beat,* 42, No. 4 (Feb. 27, 1975), 11, 29–32.

The Paramount Book of the Blues. Port Washington, Wis.: The New York Recording Laboratories, ca. 1927.

Paris, Mike, and Chris Comber. *Jimmie the Kid: The Life of Jimmie Rodgers.* London: Eddison, 1977.

Parry, Milman, and Albert Bates Lord. *Serbocroatian Heroic Songs.* Cambridge, Mass.: Harvard University Press, 1954.

Peabody, Charles. "Notes on Negro Music." *Journal of American Folklore,* 16 (1903), 148–152.

Pearson, Barry. "The Late Great Elmore James." *Keystone Folklore Quarterly,* 17 (1972), 162–172.

Perls, Nick. "Son House Interview." *78 Quarterly,* 1, No. 1 (Autumn 1967), 59–61.

Perrow, E. C. "Songs and Rhymes from the South." *Journal of American Folklore,* 25 (1912), 137–155; 26 (1913), 123–173; 28 (1915), 129–190.

Pickup, Bryan, and Chris Smith. "The Babe Stovall Story." *Talking Blues,* no. 4 (Jan.–Mar. 1977), pp. 2–5.

Proschan, Frank. "Walter Vinson, 1901–1975." *Living Blues,* no. 21 (May–June 1975), p. 55.

Powdermaker, Hortense. *After Freedom.* New York: Russell & Russell, 1968.

Puckett, Newbell Niles. *Folk Beliefs of the Southern Negro.* Chapel Hill: University of North Carolina Press, 1926.

"Quality in 'Blues'." *The Metronome,* 39, No. 9 (Sept. 1923), 140.

Radcliffe, Charles. "Howlin' Wolf Revisited." *Nothing But the Blues.* Ed. Mike Leadbitter. London: Hanover Books, 1971, pp. 44–45.

Ramsey, Frederic, Jr. *Been Here and Gone.* New Brunswick, N.J.: Rutgers University Press, 1960.

Reuss, Richard A. "Woody Guthrie and His Folk Tradition." *Journal of American Folklore,* 83 (1970), 273–303.

Richmond, W. Edson. "The Comparative Approach: Its Aims, Techniques, and Limitations." *A Good Tale and a Bonnie Tune.* Publications of the Texas Folklore Society, No. 32. Ed. Mody C. Boatright, Wilson M. Hudson, and Allen Maxwell. Dallas: Southern Methodist University Press, 1964, pp. 217–227.

Roberts, Helen H. "A Study of Folk Song Variants Based on Field Work in Jamaica." *Journal of American Folklore,* 38 (1925), 149–216.

Roche, Jacques. "Henry Stuckey: An Obituary." *78 Quarterly,* 1, No. 2 (1968), 11–14.

Rooney, James. *Bossmen: Bill Monroe & Muddy Waters.* New York: The Dial Press, 1971.

Rosenbaum, Arthur. Notes to *The Blues of Shirley Griffith: Saturday Blues*, Prestige/ Bluesville 1087, 12″ LP, 1961.

Rosenberg, Bruce A. *The Art of the American Folk Preacher*. New York: Oxford University Press, 1970.

Rowe, Mike. *Chicago Breakdown*. London: Eddison Press, 1973.

———. "Floyd Jones." *Nothing But the Blues*. Ed. Mike Leadbitter. London: Hanover Books, 1971, p. 64.

Russell, Tony. *Blacks, Whites and Blues*. New York: Stein and Day. 1970.

Russell, William. "Boogie Woogie." *Jazzmen*. Ed. Frederic Ramsey, Jr., and Charles Edward Smith. New York: Harcourt, Brace and Company. 1939, pp. 183–205.

Rust, Brian. *The Victor Master Book, Volume 2 (1925–1936)*. Stanhope, N.J.: Walter C. Allen, 1970.

Sandburg, Carl. *The American Songbag*. New York: Harcourt, Brace and Company, 1927.

Sargeant, Winthrop. *Jazz: Hot and Hybrid*. New York: E. P. Dutton & Company, Inc., 1946.

Saxon, Lyle, Robert Tallant, and Edward Dreyer. *Gumbo Ya-Ya*. New York: Bonanza Books, 1945.

Scarborough, Dorothy. *On the Trail of Negro Folk-Songs*. Hatboro, Pa.: Folklore Associates, 1963.

Seeger, Mike. "Who Chose These Records? A Look into the Life, Tastes, and Procedures of Frank Walker." *Anthology of American Folk Music*. Ed. Josh Dunson and Ethel Raim. New York: Oak Publications, 1973, pp. 8–17.

Seeger, Pete. "You Can't Write Down Freedom Songs." *Sing Out!*, 15, No. 3 (July 1965), 11.

Shapiro, Nat, and Nat Hentoff, eds. *Hear Me Talkin' to Ya*. New York: Dover Publications, Inc., 1966.

Shaw, Arnold. *The World of Soul*. New York: Paperback Library, 1971.

Siders, Harvey. "Talking with a King." *Down Beat*, 39, No. 6 (Mar. 30, 1972), 14–15.

Smith, Francis. "Sleepy John Estes." *Nothing But the Blues*. Ed. Mike Leadbitter. London: Hanover Books, 1971, pp. 237–239.

Southern, Eileen. *The Music of Black Americans: A History*. New York: W. W. Norton, 1971.

———, ed. *Readings in Black American Music*. New York: W. W. Norton, 1971.

Springer, Robert. "The Regulatory Function of the Blues." *The Black Perspective in Music*, 4 (1976), 278–288.

Stearns, Marshall. *The Story of Jazz*. New York: Oxford University Press, 1958.

Stewart-Baxter, Derrick. *Ma Rainey and the Classic Blues Singers*. New York: Stein and Day, 1970.

Strachwitz, Chris. "Frankie Lee Sims." *Blues Unlimited*, no. 122 (Nov.–Dec. 1976), pp. 20–22.

———. "An Interview with the Staples Family." *American Folk Music Occasional, No. 1*. Ed. Chris Strachwitz. Berkeley, Ca.: American Folk Music Occasional, 1964, pp. 13–17.

Taft, Michael. "Blind Lemon Jefferson Concordance." Unpublished computer print-out.

Terkel, Studs. "Big Bill's Last Session." *Jazz*, no. 1 (Oct. 1958), pp. 9–18.

Thigpen, Kenneth A., Jr. "A Reconsideration of the Commonplace Phrase and Commonplace Theme in the Child Ballads." *Southern Folklore Quarterly*, 37 (1973), 385–408.

Thomas, Gates. "South Texas Negro Work-Songs: Collected and Uncollected." *Rainbow in the Morning*. Publications of the Texas Folklore Society, no. 5. Ed. J. Frank Dobie. Hatboro, Pa.: Folklore Associates, 1965, pp. 154–180.

Thomas, Will H. *Some Current Folk-Songs of the Negro*. Austin: Folk-Lore Society of Texas, 1912.

Thompson, Stith. *Motif-Index of Folk-Literature*. Rev. ed. 6 vols. Bloomington: Indiana University Press, 1955–58.

Titon, Jeff. "Autobiography and Blues Texts: A Reply to 'The Blues as Dramatic Monologues'." *John Edwards Memorial Foundation Quarterly*, 6 (1970), 79–82.

———. "Downhome Blues Lyrics Since the Second World War: A Selection." *alcheringa: ethnopoetics*, n.s., 2, No. 1 (1976), 10–26.

———. *Early Downhome Blues: A Musical and Cultural Analysis*. Urbana: University of Illinois Press, 1977.

———. "Living Blues Interview: Son House." *Living Blues*, no. 31 (Mar.–Apr. 1977), pp. 14–22.

———. "Thematic Pattern in Downhome Blues Lyrics." *Journal of American Folklore*, 90 (1977), 316–330.

———, ed. *From Blues to Pop: The Autobiography of Leonard "Baby Doo" Caston*. Los Angeles: John Edwards Memorial Foundation, 1974.

Toll, Robert C. *Blacking Up: The Minstrel Show in Nineteenth-Century America*. New York: Oxford University Press, 1974.

Tonsor, Johann. "Negro Music." *Music*, 3 (1892–93), 119–122.

Traum, Happy. *The Blues Bag*. New York: Consolidated Music Publishers, 1968.

———, ed. *Guitar Styles of Brownie McGhee*. New York: Oak Publications, 1971.

Utley, Francis Lee. "The Genesis and Revival of 'Dink's Song'." *Studies in Language and Literature in Honor of Margaret Schlauch*. Ed. Mieczysław Brahmer, Stanisław Helsztyński, and Julian Krzyżanowski. Warszawa: Polish Scientific Publishers, 1966, pp. 457–472.

Vechten, Carl Van. "The Black Blues." *Vanity Fair*, 24, No. 6 (Aug. 1925), 57, 86, 92.

———. "Negro 'Blues' Singers." *Vanity Fair*, 26, No. 1 (Mar. 1926), 67, 106, 108.

———. "Prescription for the Negro Theatre." *Vanity Fair*, 25, No. 2 (Oct. 1925), 46, 92, 98.

Vreede, Max E. *Paramount 12000/13000 Series*. London: Storyville Publications and Co., 1971.

Walsh, Jim. "The First Singer Who Made a 'Blues' Record: Morton Harvey." *Hobbies* (Nov. 1955), pp. 36–38, 41; (Dec. 1955), pp. 30–32.

Wardlow, Gayle. "LeDell Johnson Remembers His Brother Tommy." *78 Quarterly*, 1, No. 1 (Autumn 1967), 63–65.

———. "Legends of the Lost (The Story of Henry Speir)." *Back Woods Blues*. Ed. Simon A. Napier. Bexhill-on-Sea, England: Blues Unlimited, 1968, pp. 25–28.

———. "Son House (Collectors Classics 14), Comments & Additions." *Blues Unlimited*, no. 42 (Mar.–Apr. 1967), pp. 7–8.

———, and Jacques Roche. "Patton's Murder: Whitewash or Hogwash?" *78 Quarterly*, 1, No. 1 (Autumn 1967), 10–17.

Webb, W. Prescott. "Notes to Folk-Lore of Texas." *Journal of American Folklore*, 28 (1915), 290–299.

Weiser-Aall, Lily. *Volkskunde und Psychologie*. Berlin: W. de Gruyter, 1937.

Welding, Pete. "Fred McDowell Talking." *Nothing But the Blues*. Ed. Mike Leadbitter. London: Hanover Books, 1971, pp. 145–146.

———. "'I Sing for the People': An Interview with Bluesman Howling Wolf." *Down Beat*, 34, No. 25 (Dec. 14, 1967), 20–23.

———. "John Lee Hooker: Me and the Blues." *Down Beat*, 35, No. 20 (Oct. 3, 1968), 15–17, 38.

———. "Reverend Robert Wilkins." *Blues Unlimited*, no. 51 (Mar. 1968), pp. 14–15; no. 52 (Apr. 1968), pp. 3–4; no. 53 (May 1968), pp. 5–7; no. 54 (June 1968), p. 14; no. 55 (July 1968), pp. 11–12; no. 56 (Sept. 1968), pp. 12–13.

————. "Stringin' the Blues: The Art of Folk Blues Guitar." *Down Beat*, 32, No. 14 (July 1, 1965), 22–24, 56.

————. "The Testament Story." *Blues World*, no. 42 (Spring 1972), pp. 3–4; no. 43 (Summer 1972), pp. 3–4; no. 44 (Autumn 1972), pp. 3–6.

Wheeler, Mary. *Steamboatin' Days.* Baton Rouge: Louisiana State University Press, 1944.

White, Newman I. *American Negro Folk-Songs.* Cambridge, Mass.: Harvard University Press, 1928.

————. "Racial Traits in Negro Song." *Sewanee Review*, 28 (1920), 396–404.

————. "The White Man in the Woodpile: Some Influences on Negro Secular Folk-Songs." *American Speech*, 4 (Oct. 1928–Aug. 1929), 207–215.

Whitman, Cedric H. *Homer and the Heroic Tradition.* Cambridge, Mass.: Harvard University Press, 1958.

Wilgus, D. K. *Anglo-American Folksong Scholarship Since 1898.* New Brunswick, N.J.: Rutgers University Press, 1959.

————. "An Introduction to the Study of Hillbilly Music." *Journal of American Folklore*, 78 (1965), 195–203.

————. "The Rationalistic Approach." *A Good Tale and a Bonnie Tune.* Publications of the Texas Folklore Society, no. 32. Ed. Mody C. Boatright, Wilson M. Hudson, and Allen Maxwell. Dallas: Southern Methodist University Press, 1964, pp. 227–237.

————. "'The Text Is the Thing'." *Journal of American Folklore*, 86 (1973), 241–252.

Williams, Paul, and Peter Guralnick. "Howling Wolf." *Crawdaddy*, no. 5 (Sept. 1966), pp. 11–13.

Wilmer, Valerie. "Blues People: Fred & Roosevelt." *Jazz Journal*, 19, No. 8 (Aug. 1966), 22–24.

Wilson, Al. "Robert Pete Williams, His Life and Music." *Little Sandy Review*, 2, No. 1 (July 1966), 15–22; 2, No. 2 (Nov. 1966), 8–11.

————. *Son House.* Bexhill-on-Sea, England: Blues Unlimited, 1966.

Wilson, Mark. Notes to *Hollerin'*, Rounder 0071, 12" LP, 1976.

Wolf, John Quincy. "Aunt Caroline Dye: The Gypsy in the 'St. Louis Blues'." *Southern Folklore Quarterly*, 33 (1969), 339–346.

————. "Folksingers and the Re-creation of Folksong." *Western Folklore*, 26 (1967), 101–111.

Wolfe, Charles K. "Ralph Peer at Work: The Victor 1927 Bristol Sessions." *Old Time Music*, no. 5 (Summer 1972), pp. 10–15.

————. "Toward a Contextual Approach to Old-Time Music." *The Journal of Country Music*, 5 (1974), 65–75.

————. "Where the Blues Is At: A Survey of Recent Research." *Popular Music and Society*, 1 (1971–72), 152–166.

Work, John W. *American Negro Songs and Spirituals.* New York: Bonanza Books, 1940.

Zolotow, Maurice. "Hillbilly Boom." *A History and Encyclopedia of Country, Western, and Gospel Music.* Rev. ed. Ed. Linnell Gentry. Nashville: Clairmont Corp., 1969, pp. 36–42.

Zur Heide, Karl Gert. *Deep South Piano: The Story of Little Brother Montgomery.* London: Studio Vista, 1970.

————. "Yancey Special." *Hot Jazz*, 5 (June 1969), 22–25.

INDEX

18, 22, 28, 58; tension in, 18, 19, 28, 31–32; contrast in, 18, 31–32, 58, 146; contradiction and inconsistency in, 19, 28; universality of, 19; and social conditions of black Americans, 19–22; and progress, 22, 29; singing, 23–26, 31; duets, 23, 155–61; vocal quartets, 23, 25, 26, 33, 39, 272; meter of texts, 23–24, 46; instrumental accompaniments, 25–27, 31; instrumental pieces, 26; instrumental choruses, 26–27; relationship to field hollers, 27; as lyric songs, 27; censorship in, 30; call and response in, 31; ambiguity in, 31–32; compactness of, 31; improvisational variation in, 31, 39; early reports of, 32–40; as a term for a type of music, 33; as folksongs, 39, 87; social origins of, 40–41, 87–88; African traits in, 42, 101; dancing to, 47–48; and individualism, 48; and truth, 53–54, 58–59, 61; in sheet music, 59–62; in World War I, 61–62; by white artists, 85; "underworld" origins of, 87–88, 91; artistic qualities of, 94–95; stream of consciousness in, 102, 141–44; and worry, 112–13; and sadness, 112–13; and happiness, 113; as a spiritual force, 114–15; and the devil, 115; and God, 115; and inheritance, 115; stability in, 138–39; spontaneous improvisation in, 139–44; surrealism in, 139–44; therapeutic function of, 144, 318; tune families in, 145; concatenation of, 303–304; sociological study of, 317–18; mentioned, 3. *See also* City blues; Country blues; Folk blues; Popular blues; Talking blues
Blues aesthetic, 86–87
Blues ballads, 32, 41, 44–47, 239
Blues form: twelve-bar AAB pattern, 22–23, 23–24, 26, 30–31, 33, 35, 37, 44–47, 48, 53; AAA pattern, 22, 35, 46; AAAB pattern, 22, 35, 44; AB pattern, 22, 35, 37; AB with refrain pattern, 22, 35, 46; irregular patterns, 22–23, 53; and blues imagery, 30; and blues ideology, 31–32; ABB pattern, 35, 37; ABA pattern, 35; AAAA pattern, 35, 44; AA pattern, 35; AABC pattern, 35; ABCA pattern, 35; one-verse songs, 35–36, 42; origins of, 41–48; mentioned, 15, 18, 22–23
Blues ideology: and blues form, 31–32; mentioned, 19–22, 28, 29
Blues logic, 30–31, 146–54
Blues lyrics: relationship to social factors, 9; relationship to singer's life, 27–28, 53–58; exaggeration in, 27, 30; imagination in, 27; subject matter of, 28–30, 38; secular outlook of, 28; major themes of, 28–29, 31, 165; imagery in, 28, 29, 30; sources of, 30; metaphor and simile in, 30, 32; irony in, 30, 32; likened to proverbs, 30; as clichés, 30; surrealism in, 30, 139–44; logic in, 30, 146–54; personalization of, 30; enjambment in, 30; double meaning in, 32; lack of thematic coherence in, 49–52, 162–66; contrast in, 58, 146, 219, 318; association in, 58, 153, 219, 318; thematic texts in, 131–44, 161–62; celebration of character in, 135–36; celebration of place in, 136–37; stability in, 138–39, 161–62; traditional elements in, 139; unrhymed lines in, 139; mentioned, 17, 32, 48
Bluesman, 108–109
Blues revival, 99, 101, 104–105, 167
Blues scales, 24
Blues singers: life histories of, 9, 12; life-styles of, 9; rediscovery of early recording artists, 9; repertoires of, 12; women as, 62–70, 88, 96, 97–98, 102; whites as, 62–71, 85, 95, 102; personality of, 109; speech impediments among, 144; alcoholism among, 144; prison experiences among, 144; mentioned, 2
Blues songwriters, 62–64
Blues Unlimited, 101
Blues World, 101
Bo Diddley (Ellas McDaniel), 280
Bogalusa, Louisiana, 127
Bokelman, Marina, 10–12, 315
"The Boll Weevil," 45
Bolton, Mississippi, 108, 175, 176, 179–80, 274, 285, 286–87
Bonner, Juke Boy, 82–83
Bontemps, Arna, 95
"Boogie" (by Mager Johnson), 234
Boogie-woogie: piano style, 33, 96, 97; mentioned, 82
Boogie Woogie Red, 112
"Boom Boom" (by John Lee Hooker), 137–38
"Booze and Blues" (by Ma Rainey), 240
Borneman, Ernest, 33
Borum, Memphis Willie, 58
Bottleneck guitar. *See* Guitar, slide technique
Boyle, Mississippi, 174, 176, 180, 194, 199
Bracey, Rev. Ishmon, 10, 11, 44, 220, 237, 271, 286, 289, 293
Bradford, Perry, 59, 62, 102
Bragg, Ardell, 129, 241
Brewer, Blind James, 308
Brookhaven, Mississippi, 308
Broonzy, Big Bill, 82, 102, 132, 137, 138, 273
Br'er Rabbit, 59
Broven, John, 102
Brown, Elijah, 52
Brown, Gabriel, 93
Brown, John Henry "Bubba," 11, 29, 116, 136, 274, 296–97, 296 (photo)
Brown, Josie. *See* Bush, Josie
Brown, Uncle Rich, 93 (photo)

Designer: Randall Goodall

Compositor: Computer Typesetting Services, Inc.

Text: APS-5 Palatino

Display: Solotype Wood Type

Printer: Malloy Lithographing, Inc.

Binder: Malloy Lithographing, Inc.